EIGHTH EDITION

Discovering the American Past

A Look at the Evidence

VOLUME II: SINCE 1865

William Bruce Wheeler
University of Tennessee

Lorri Glover
Saint Louis University

CENGAGE
Learning®

Australia • Brazil • Mexico • Singapore • United Kingdom • United States

CENGAGE
Learning®

Discovering the American Past: A Look at the Evidence, Volume II: Since 1865, **Eighth Edition**
William Bruce Wheeler and Lorri Glover

Product Director: Paul Banks

Product Manager: Clint Attebery

Content Developer: Anàis Wheeler

Product Assistant: Andrew Newton

Marketing Manager: Kyle Zimmerman

IP Analyst: Alexandra Ricciardi

IP Project Manager: Farah J Fard

Manufacturing Planner: Fola Orekoya

Art and Design Direction, Production Management, and Composition: Lumina Datamatics, Inc.

Cover Image: © Library of Congress, LC-USZ62-134607 (O'Shaughnessy Dam)

© Kim Steele / Getty Images (Hetch Hetchy Dam)

© Encyclopaedia Britannica / Getty Images (Map of Yosemite Valley)

For product information and technology assistance, contact us at **Cengage Learning Customer & Sales Support, 1-800-354-9706**

For permission to use material from this text or product, submit all requests online at **www.cengage.com/permissions**. Further permissions questions can be emailed to **permissionrequest@cengage.com**.

Library of Congress Control Number: 2015948805

Student Edition: ISBN: 978-1-305-63043-7

Cengage Learning
20 Channel Center Street
Boston, MA 02210
USA

Cengage Learning is a leading provider of customized learning solutions with employees residing in nearly 40 different countries and sales in more than 125 countries around the world. Find your local representative at **www.cengage.com**.

Cengage Learning products are represented in Canada by Nelson Education, Ltd.

To learn more about Cengage Learning Solutions, visit **www.cengage.com**.

Purchase any of our products at your local college store or at our preferred online store **www.cengagebrain.com**.

Printed in the United States of America
Print Number: 01 Print Year: 2015

Contents

Preface   viii

CHAPTER **1**

The Road to True Freedom: African American
Alternatives in the New South   1

The Problem   1
Background   4
The Method   11
The Evidence   14

  Excerpt from Ida B. Wells' United States Atrocities (1892)
  Booker T. Washington's Atlanta Exposition Address (1895)
  Excerpt from Henry McNeal Turner's "The American Negro
      and His Fatherland" (1895)
  Excerpt from W. E. B. DuBois Niagara Address (1906)
  Excerpt from E. W. Harper's "Enlightened Motherhood" (1892)
  Table showing migration of Negro population by U.S. regions, 1870–1920

Questions to Consider   28
Epilogue   30

 CHAPTER **2**

Rose Cohen Comes to America: Living and
Remembering the Immigrant Experience   34

The Problem   34
Background   35
The Method   38
The Evidence   40

  Excerpts from the published memoirs of a young Jewish
      immigrant from Russia

Questions to Consider   51
Epilogue   52

CHAPTER **3**

Who Controls America's Natural Resources? Water Rights, Public Lands, and the Contest over the Hetch Hetchy Valley 54

The Problem 54
Background 56
The Method 60
The Evidence 62
  Excerpts from Gifford Pinchot and John Muir
  Congressional testimony
  Excerpts from the Raker Act
  Photographs
Questions to Consider 87
Epilogue 88

CHAPTER **4**

Homogenizing a Pluralistic Nation: Propaganda During World War I 90

The Problem 90
Background 93
The Method 97
The Evidence 99
  War songs and poetry
  Advertisements and posters
  Editorial cartoons
  Speeches
  Motion picture stills and ads
Questions to Consider 120
Epilogue 122

CHAPTER **5**

A "Revolution in Manners and Morals": Women's Changing Roles in the 1920s 127

The Problem 127
Background 129

The Method   134
The Evidence   137
    College regulations regarding women
    Advice on women's roles
    Photographs
    Margaret Sanger on birth control
Questions to Consider   157
Epilogue   159

CHAPTER **6**

Understanding Rural Poverty During the Great Depression   162

The Problem   162
Background   164
The Method   168
The Evidence   170
    Children's letters to Eleanor Roosevelt
    Documentary photographs from the Farm Security
       Administration
Questions to Consider   188
Epilogue   189

CHAPTER **7**

The American Judicial System and Japanese Internment During World War II: *Korematsu v. United States* (323 U.S. 214)   192

The Problem   192
Background   194
The Method   203
The Evidence   205
    Excerpts from prosecution and defense attorneys
    U.S. Supreme Court opinions and dissenting opinions
      in Korematsu v. U.S. *(323 U.S. 214)*
Questions to Consider   214
Epilogue   215

CHAPTER **8**

The 1960 Student Campaign for Civil Rights   220

The Problem   220
Background   223
The Method   228
The Evidence   230
    Jim Crow laws
    Sample literacy test
    Excerpts from interviews with student sit-in leaders
    Sit-in literature and songs
    National news coverage of the students sit-ins
    Photographs of sit-in participants
Questions to Consider   260
Epilogue   261

CHAPTER **9**

A Generation in War and Turmoil: The Agony of Vietnam   265

The Problem   265
Background   266
The Method   273
The Evidence   277
    Interviews and photographs with a sampling
      of the Vietnam Generation
Questions to Consider   297
Epilogue   298

CHAPTER **10**

The Religious Revolution in Post–World War II America: The Pivotal Role of Southern California   306

The Problem   306
Background   307
The Method   314
The Evidence   316
    Charts and statistics on church membership
    Interviews with individuals at the 1949 Los Angeles revival

Sermons and writings by Billy Graham
Excerpt from the book Come Help Change the World *by Bill Bright*
Remarks by Jerry Falwell
Two speeches and one remark by Ronald Reagan

Questions to Consider   335
Epilogue   335

CHAPTER **11**

The War on Drugs and the Rise of the Prison State   338
The Problem   338
Background   340
The Method   345
The Evidence   347
   Speech by Nancy and Ronald Reagan
   Congressional legislation
   New York Times *reportage*
   California's "three-strikes" legislation
   Statistics on incarceration rates
   Speech by Attorney General Eric Holder
Questions to Consider   381
Epilogue   382

CHAPTER **12**

History Skills in Action: Designing Your Own History Project   383
The Problem   383
Background: Choosing a Topic   384
The Method: Formulating Your Questions   385
The Evidence   386
   Defining the problem, planning the method, finding evidence for an
     individual project
   Suggestions of possible topics
Questions to Consider   387
Epilogue   388

Preface

In his 1990 State of the Union Address, President George Herbert Walker Bush set forth a set of National Education Goals, one of which was the objective that by the year 2000 "American students will leave grades four, eight, and twelve having demonstrated competency in . . . English, mathematics, science, history, and geography."[1]

Almost immediately large committees were established in each of the above disciplines, including the National Council for History Standards, composed of history professors, pre-college teachers, members of numerous organizations, educators, and parents. For two years the Council worked to draft a voluntary set of National History Standards that would provide teachers, parents, and American history textbook publishers with guidelines regarding what students ought to know about the U.S. past.

Yet even before the Standards were released to the general public, a storm of controversy arose, in which the Council was accused of a "great hatred of traditional history," of giving in to "political correctness," and of jettisoning the Founding Fathers, the Constitution, and people and events that have made the nation great in favor of individuals and events that portrayed the United States in a less complimentary light. Finally, in January 1995, the U.S. Senate, by a vote of 99–1, approved a "sense-of-the-Senate" resolution condemning the standards developed by the National Council for History Standards and urging that any future guidelines for history should not be based on them.[2]

This was not the first time that American history standards and textbooks had been the sources of bitter controversy. In the late nineteenth century, northern and southern whites had radically different ideas about the Civil War and Reconstruction and demanded that public school textbooks reflect those notions. As a result, publishers created separate chapters on these periods for northern and southern schools. At the same time, Roman Catholic leaders in the United States complained about Protestant control of public education and of history textbooks, resulting in Catholics writing their own textbooks for their parochial schools.[3]

Then, in the 1940s, the popular American history textbooks of Professor Harold Rugg of Columbia University were assaulted as being too radical, mainly because Rugg had discussed subjects such as economic classes, inequality, and what he called the apparent failure of laissez-faire economics. By 1944, sales of his public school

---

1. Transcript, State of the Union Address, January 31, 1990, in C-SPAN.org/Transcripts /SOTU-1990.aspx. See also U.S. Department of Education, *National Goals for Education* (Washington: Dept. of Education, 1990), p. 1.
2. The Senate proceedings are summarized in Gary B. Nash, Charlotte Crabtree, and Ross E. Dunn, *History on Trial: Culture Wars and the Teaching of the Past* (New York: Alfred A. Knopf, 1997), pp. 231–235. The lone senator who voted against the resolution was Bennett Johnston of Louisiana.
3. Joseph Moreau, *Schoolbook Nation: Conflicts over American History Textbooks from the Civil War to the Present* (Ann Arbor: University of Michigan Press, 2003), pp. 15–20.

textbooks had dropped 90 percent, and by 1951 they had totally disappeared from American classrooms. The Cold War and the fear of communism extended this controversy and led to the removal from most textbooks of the sensitive subjects that had gotten Rugg into so much trouble.[4]

By the 1960s, scholars in many American colleges and universities had begun to view the nation's past in decidedly different ways, due in part to the gradual inclusion of African Americans, women, Native Americans, laborers, immigrants, and the "common folk" in the story of America's past. As these individuals took their places alongside the nation's founders, presidents, generals, corporate leaders, and intellectuals (almost all male and white), the texture and shape of American history began to change. At the same time, the Vietnam War prompted some scholars to look at the U.S. overseas record in new, less laudable ways.[5]

Some parents, school officials, and politicians, however, objected to what was being called the "new history." In the mid-1960s, distinguished historians John W. Caughey, John Hope Franklin, and Ernest R. May collaborated on a new eighth-grade American history textbook that raised a storm of protest in California and other states. Critics attacked the textbook as "very distasteful, slanted, and objectionable [and] stressed one-world government, quoted accused communists, portrayed the United States as a bully, [and] distorted history by putting American forefathers in a bad light." The authors made revisions, but "citizen groups" increased their attacks, pointing out that a speech by Patrick Henry was labeled "a tirade," that the military exploits of Generals George Patton and Omar Bradley were eliminated, and that Nathan Hale and Davy Crockett were not mentioned. Several school districts in California refused to adopt the book and some parents refused to allow their children to read it. In 1968, *Time* magazine reported that the textbook showed up on a list of 335 books that some groups demanded be banned. It seems as if both sides agreed with George Orwell when he wrote (in *1984*), "He who controls the past controls the future." Conflicts continue, over textbooks, Common Core, and what America's young men and women ought to know about their past upon their graduation.[6]

How can students hope to come to *their own* understanding of America's past? One way to do this is to go directly to the sources themselves, the "raw material" of history. In *Discovering the American Past,* we have included an engaging and at the same time challenging mixture of types of evidence, ranging from more traditional sources such as letters, newspapers, public documents, speeches, and oral reminiscences to more innovative evidence such as photographs, art, statistics, cartoons, and interviews. In each chapter students will use this varied evidence to solve the problem or answer the central question that each chapter poses.

---

4. *Ibid.*, pp. 219–221. Frances Fitzgerald, *America Revised: History Schoolbooks in the Twentieth Century* (Boston: Atlantic Monthly Press, 1979), pp. 36–37. For one attack on textbooks, see E. Merrill Root, *Brainwashing in the High Schools: An Examination of Eleven American History Textbooks* (New York: The Devin-Adair Co., 1958).
5. On the inclusion movements of the 1960s and 1970s, see Joyce Appleby, Lynn Hunt, and Margaret Jacob, *Telling the Truth About History* (New York: W.W. Norton, 1994), pp. 147–198.
6. John Hope Franklin, *Mirror to America: The Autobiography of John Hope Franklin* (New York: Farrar, Straus, and Giroux, 2005), pp. 227–231; Nicholas J. Karolides, *Banned Books: Literature Suppressed on Political Grounds* (New York: Facts on File, rev. ed. 2006), pp. 300–302. On Common Core see *Huffington Post*, January 30, 2014.

Soon they will understand that the historian operates in much the same way as a detective in novels, films, or television programs does when solving a crime.[7]

As much as possible, we have tried to "let the evidence speak for itself" and have avoided (we hope) leading students toward one particular interpretation or another. *Discovering the American Past,* then, is a sort of historical sampler that we believe will help students learn the methods and skills all educated people must be able to master, as well as help them learn the historical content. In the words of an old West African saying, "However far the stream flows, it never forgets its source." Nor, we trust, will you.[8]

Format of the Book

Each chapter is divided into six parts: The Problem, Background, The Method, The Evidence, Questions to Consider, and Epilogue. Each part builds upon the others, creating a uniquely integrated chapter structure that helps guide the reader through the analytical process. The Problem section begins with a brief discussion of the central issues of the chapter and then states the questions students will explore. A Background section follows, designed to help students understand the historical context of the problem. The Method section gives students suggestions for studying and analyzing the evidence. The Evidence section is the heart of the chapter, providing a variety of primary source material on the particular historical event or issue described in the chapter's Problem section. Questions to Consider, the section that follows, focuses students' attention on specific evidence and on linkages among different evidence material. The Epilogue section gives the aftermath or the historical outcome of the evidence—what happened to the people involved, who won an election, how a debate ended, and so on.

Changes in the Eighth Edition

Each chapter in this edition has had to pass three important screening groups: (1) the authors (and some of our graduate students) who used the chapters to teach our students, (2) student evaluators who used *Discovering the American Past* in class, and (3) instructors who either used the book or read and assessed the new and revised chapters. With advice from our screeners, we have made the following alterations that we believe will make this edition of *Discovering the American Past* even more useful and contemporary.

Volume I contains four entirely new chapters. Chapter 1, "The Beginning of the World," concentrates on Native American and Judeo-Christian accounts of creation and what they tell us about the people who embraced them; Chapter 3, "From English Servants to African Slaves," allows students to explore the evolution of racial slavery in late seventeenth- and early eighteenth-century Virginia; Chapter 10, on Civil War nurses of the Union and Confederacy, uses women's letters, diaries, and memoirs to understand the conflict through their eyes; and Chapter 12, which makes

7. See the exciting Robin W. Winks, ed., *The Historian as Detective: Essays on Evidence* (New York: Harper & Row, 1968), esp. pp. xiii–xxiv.
8. For the saying, see Nash, *History on Trial*, p. 8.

a new turn in the volume by closing with a chapter that guides students toward designing their own research projects. In addition, the evidence in Chapters 5, 6, 7, and 8 has been streamlined, and in Chapter 9 (on the "Peculiar Institution") we replaced the excerpt from Frederick Douglass with some of the writings of Solomon Northup (students perhaps will know about Northup's ordeals from the Academy Award–winning film *Twelve Years a Slave*). The chapter retains many of the materials from the WPA ex-slave interviews, but it also has been further revised to include freedom suits from antebellum St. Louis. These depositions allow students to see another way in which slaves told their own stories.

Volume II contains five entirely new chapters: Chapter 2 brings to life the transformative experience of immigration in the late nineteenth and early twentieth centuries by using the autobiography of a Russian Jewish girl who came of age in New York City working in the garment industry. Chapter 3 introduces students to environmental history by having them enter early twentieth-century debates about the damming of the Tuolumne River and the flooding of the Hetch Hetchy Valley in Yosemite National Park to provide safe and reliable water to the city of San Francisco. Chapter 10 surveys the rise of religious conservatism in the 1950s and 1960s and its role in American politics. A new Chapter 11 turns to the War on Drugs in the 1980s and the consequent rise of the prison state to try to untangle why the United States has the highest rate of incarceration in the world. Chapter 12, "History Skills in Action," offers students the opportunity to undertake their own individual research projects. In addition, all of the other chapters have been revised, Chapters 5 and 9 in a major way.

In all, we have paid close attention to students, fellow instructors, and reviewers in our efforts to keep *Discovering the American Past* fresh, challenging, and relevant. Earlier editions have shown clearly students' positive responses to the challenge of being, as Robin Winks put it, "historical detectives" who use historical evidence to reach their own conclusions.

Instructor's Resource Manual

Because we value the teaching of American history and yet fully understand how difficult it is to do well, we have written our own Instructor's Resource Manual to accompany *Discovering the American Past*. In this manual, we explain our specific content and skills objectives for each chapter. In addition, we include an expanded discussion of the Method and Evidence sections. We also answer some of our students' frequently asked questions about the material in each problem. Our suggestions for teaching and evaluating student learning draw not only upon our own experiences but also upon the experiences of those of you who have shared your classroom ideas with us. Finally, we wrote updated bibliographic essays for each problem.

Acknowledgments

We would like to thank all the students and instructors who have helped us in developing and refining our ideas for this edition. In addition, we extend deep thanks to those reviewers who offered us candid and enormously helpful advice and saved us from more than a few errors.

At Saint Louis University, Ivy McIntyre and Joshua Mather provided invaluable research assistance, and Torrie Hester, Stefan Bradley, and Flannery Burke generously shared their expertise and advice. Mike Everman showed us the rich potential of the St. Louis, Missouri, freedom suits. In Richmond, Virginia, Livia Marrs offered invaluable help in locating Civil War nurses and their memoirs. In Tennessee, Laura Vaught helped us through the maze of court records regarding Japanese internment suits, and SFC Darrell Rowe, Dr. Ed Caudill, and Joe and Justin Distretti helped us to understand the complicated legacy of Vietnam. Linda Claire Wheeler read almost every word and offered enlightened suggestions and gentle flogging. Dan Smith discussed, read, and encouraged, always with good cheer. Will Fontanez of the University of Tennessee Cartography Department created important maps for three chapters.

Finally, we owe a great deal to the members of the publishing team who worked together to make our ideas and words into a well-organized and attractive book. And to Jean Woy, who was present at the creation of the first edition of *Discovering the American Past* and who offered her steady and helpful guidance, we owe intellectual debts that can never be repaid. Also at Cengage, Clint Attebery represented this edition as the current U.S. History product manager. Prashanth Kamavarapu at Lumina Datamatics, guided the project through the production process. Lastly, we'd like to especially thank Anais Wheeler at Cengage, who kindly shared her wisdom on more matters than we can list.

And last, this edition is dedicated to Linda Claire Wheeler and Dan Smith, who kept the ship afloat when the waters all around us were considerably less than calm.

Any errors that do appear in any of the chapters are ours, not theirs.

The Road to True Freedom: African American Alternatives in the New South

The Problem

On January 21, 1875, Ohio congressman James Garfield wrote to his friend and political ally Julius Converse to relate his troubles and fears regarding the collapse of Reconstruction and the erosion of the rights of freedmen and women:

> I have for some time had the impression that there is a general apathy among the people concerning the War and the Negro. The public seems to have tired of the subject and all appeals to do justice to the Negro seem to be set down to the credit of partisan prejudice.[1]

There is little doubt that, even before emancipation and Radical Reconstruction, African Americans had made some significant accomplishments in establishing churches and schools, organizing political and social clubs, choosing leaders, petitioning state and federal governments for expanded civil rights, and negotiating with their former masters or new employers for wages and working conditions. Then, during the Radical Reconstruction period, freedmen gained the right to vote, and received assistance from the Freedmen's Bureau (technically the Bureau of Refugees, Freedmen, and Abandoned Lands) in medical services, establishing branches of the Freedmen's Bank, issuing food to the temporarily needy, and protecting freedmen

1. Garfield to Converse, January 21, 1875, quoted in Vincent P. De Santis, *Republicans Face the Southern Question: The New Departure Years, 1877–1897* (New York: Greenwood Press, 1969), p. 131. In 1880 Republicans nominated Garfield for president and he won in a razor-thin contest. Just a few months after his inauguration (on July 2, 1881), he was shot by a disappointed office seeker and died on September 19, 1881.

◆ CHAPTER 1

The Road to
True Freedom:
African American
Alternatives in the
New South

and women against violence as best it could with limited resources.[2]

Yet in many ways the situation of the freedmen had barely improved from that of servitude, and in some ways it had actually deteriorated and many hopes had been dashed. Economically, very few had been able to acquire land of their own (along with voting, a major goal), and the vast majority who remained in rural areas continued to work for white landowners under various forms of labor arrangements and sometimes even under outright peonage.[3] Political and civil rights supposedly had been guaranteed under the Fourteenth and Fifteenth Amendments to the Constitution and enforced by a small number of U.S. Army soldiers. But those rights often were violated. Federal courts offered little assistance, and as the states of the former Confederacy gradually returned to the control of Southern Democrats, protection of the freedmen and women evaporated.

Finally, as Garfield had feared, the North grew tired of Reconstruction, coming to the conclusion that former slaves could never achieve equality or ever *earn* equality. Many white northerners agreed with Editor E. L. Godkin, who denounced Radical Republicans for "the insane task of making newly emancipated field hands, led by barbers and barkeepers, fancy they knew as much about government and were as capable of administering it, as the whites. . . . It was a silly attempt, doubly silly when made through the use of troops."[4] Even as the nation prepared to celebrate its centennial in 1876, whites in both the North and the South called for an end to sectional animosity and an embrace of national unity—even if it was only on the surface and would require the betrayal of democracy and of the freedmen and women. At that point African Americans understood all too well what lay ahead.[5]

Gradually the South came to appreciate the fact that it could move with impunity against African Americans and that there would not be a repeat of Radical Reconstruction—even though southern leaders threatened white voters with that possibility. The Supreme Court's decision in the 1883 Civil Rights Cases made it clear that the federal

2. See John Hope Franklin and Alfred A. Moss, Jr., *From Slavery to Freedom: A History of African Americans* (New York: Alfred a. Knopf, 8th ed. 2000), pp. 250–275 passim. On leaders see Steven Hahn, *A Nation Under Our Feet: Black Political Struggles in the Rural South from Slavery to the Great Migration* (Cambridge, MA: Harvard University Press, 2003), parts 1 and 2; Eric Foner, *Freedom's Lawmakers: A Directory of Black Officeholders During Reconstruction* (Baton Rouge: Louisiana State University Press, rev. ed. 1996).

3. Whatever names were given to these labor arrangements (tenancy, sharecropping, and so on), in most of the arrangements a white landowner or merchant furnished farm workers with foodstuffs and fertilizers on credit, taking a percentage of the crops grown in return. For a fascinating description of how the system worked, see Theodore Rosengarten, *All God's Dangers: The Life of Nate Shaw* (New York: Alfred A. Knopf, 1974). On peonage see Pete Daniel, *The Shadow of Slavery: Peonage in the South, 1901–1969* (Urbana: University of Illinois Press, 1972), esp. p. 22.

4. *The Nation*, August 24, October 16, 1876, quoted in De Santis, *Republicans Face the Southern Question*, p. 44.

5. In 1876 *Scribner's Monthly* hoped that "the 'Spirit of '76' was one that would heal all the old wounds, reconcile all the old differences." For national reunification and the *Scribner's Monthly* quote, see Edward J. Blum, *Reforging the White Republic: Race, Religion, and American Nationalism, 1865–1898* (Baton Rouge: Louisiana State University Press, 2005), pp. 3, 137.

government would offer the South a free hand in dealing with the freedmen and women, even if that meant segregation laws and an irregular "army" of volunteer armed civilians to enforce second-class citizenship for African Americans.[6]

Beginning in the early 1890s, southern states began a successful campaign to disfranchise black voters and to institute legal segregation through legislation that collectively became known as Jim Crow laws.[7] In some ways far more dangerous, violence against African Americans was increasing and in most cases was going unpunished. Between 1889 and 1900, 1,357 lynchings of African Americans were recorded in the United States, the vast majority in the states of the former Confederacy. In 1898, in New Bern, North Carolina, one white orator proposed "choking the Cape Fear River with the bodies of Negroes." In truth, by the 1890s it had become evident for all who cared to see that Lincoln's emancipation of southern slaves had been considerably less than complete.

Economic semiservitude, disfranchisement, assaults on black women, and widespread lynchings combined to undercut the African American male's sense of his own manhood. Alternately portrayed by whites as childlike creatures or as brutish sexual predators, black males tried desperately, though not always successfully, to assert their manhood. At the beginning of the Spanish American War in 1898, many African American men rushed to enlist in the armed services, and one unit actually rescued Theodore Roosevelt's Rough Riders from a difficult situation in their soon-to-be-famous "charge up San Juan Hill."

Many whites, however, refused to allow African American men to express their masculinity. Indeed, more than a few white men actually believed that *they themselves* displayed their own masculinity by keeping blacks in their "place." During the racially charged North Carolina state elections in 1898, one newspaper published a poem that specifically expressed that sentiment:

> Rise, ye sons of Carolina!
> Proud Caucasians, one and all;
> Be not deaf to Love's appealing—
> Hear your wives and daughters call,
> See their blanched and anxious faces,
> Note their frail, but lovely forms
> Rise, defend their spotless virtue
> With your strong and manly arms.[8]

Thus, in the eyes of many African Americans their lot appeared not to be rising but rather descending. A number of spokespersons offered significantly

6. In the 1883 Civil Rights Cases (109 U.S. 3), the Supreme Court ruled in an 8–1 decision that the Civil Rights Act of 1875 was unconstitutional because it attempted to regulate private conduct of individuals with regard to racial discrimination, an action that was beyond the scope of the Fourteenth Amendment, which applied only to the states. John J. Patrick, *The Supreme Court of the United States: A Student Companion* (New York: Oxford University Press, 3rd ed. 2006), pp. 81–82.

7. The term *Jim Crow*, generally used to refer to issues relating to African Americans, originated in the late 1820s with white minstrel singer Thomas "Daddy" Rice, who performed the song "Jump Jim Crow" in blackface makeup. By the 1840s, the term was used to refer to racially segregated facilities in the North.

8. *Wilmington (NC) Messenger*, November 8, 1898, quoted in Glenda Elizabeth Gilmore, *Gender and Jim Crow: Women and the Politics of White Supremacy in North Carolina, 1896–1920* (Chapel Hill: University of North Carolina Press, 1996), p. 91. Gilmore's study is highly recommended for anyone who wishes to delve more deeply into this topic.

✦ CHAPTER 1

The Road to
True Freedom:
African American
Alternatives in the
New South

different strategies for improving the situation of African Americans in the South. For this chapter's Evidence section, we have chosen five such spokespersons, all of them well known to blacks in the New South. Ida B. Wells (1862–1931) was a journalist, lecturer, and crusader who was highly regarded in both the United States and Europe. Booker T. Washington (1856–1915) was a celebrated educator, author, and political figure who many believed should have inherited the mantle of Frederick Douglass as the principal spokesperson for African Americans. Henry McNeal Turner (1834–1915) was a bishop of the African Methodist Episcopal (AME) Church and a controversial speaker and writer. W. E. B. DuBois (pronounced *Du Boys'*, 1868–1963) was an academician and editor and one of the founders of the National Association for the Advancement of Colored People (NAACP). Finally, Frances Ellen Watkins Harper (1825–1911) was a popular poet and writer who gave numerous speeches in support of both African American and women's rights. Each of these spokespersons offered a contrasting alternative for African Americans in the New South.

In this chapter, you will be analyzing the situation that southern blacks faced in the years after Reconstruction and identifying and evaluating the principal alternatives offered by these five important African American spokespersons to deal with their deteriorating conditions. **What different strategies did Wells, Washington, Turner, DuBois, and Harper call for to improve the collective lot of African Americans? Were there other options that they did *not* address?** Based on your examination of southern blacks' deteriorating position in the post-Reconstruction South *and* the five recommended alternatives, what do you think were the strengths and weaknesses of each approach as well as any other approaches you may have uncovered? Finally, keep in mind that while the five spokespersons did not always get along or agree with one another, all of them advocated taking different paths to the *same* ultimate goal: full equality for African Americans.

✦

Background

Unbeknownst to almost all southern whites, black slaves had surprising and fairly sophisticated ways of passing information, what historian Eric Foner referred to as a "grapevine telegraph," some of which included songs, quilts with secret messages in the patterns, whispers from plantation to plantation, overhearing white conversations, and so on. Thus as early as the outbreak of the war in 1861, slaves were well aware of the war's progress as well as what that conflict meant for them. On November 7, 1861, a U.S. naval squadron sailed into Port Royal Sound in South Carolina and reduced the two Confederate batteries to rubble. And when one black child mistook the ships' guns for thunder, his mother comforted him by saying, "Son, dat ain't no t'under, dat Yankees come to gib you freedom." As far away as California, one African American predicted, "Old things are passing away. . . . The revolution has begun."[9]

Unquestionably, the new Confederate nation (if it ever had in fact become a nation) had begun to unravel not long after the beginning of hostilities. The Confederate government, such as it was, was unable to exert its authority over large sections of the South. As for the vaunted Confederate armies, they could fight fiercely, but they also could desert when they felt like it or believed they had done their duty. General Robert E. Lee complained to President Jefferson Davis that "Our ranks are very much diminished— I fear from a third to one-half of our original numbers." And on the home front, in spite of increased patrols to capture or kill runaway slaves or deserters, as early as the fall of 1861, slaves began to "walk away" from their plantations and, with the "home guard" eventually diminished, many whites were afraid of violence by the former slaves. One Alabama physician confided to a nurse at a Confederate hospital that he "had left his young wife on his plantation, with more than a hundred Negroes upon it, and no white man but an overseer. He had told the Negroes, before he left, if they desired to leave, they could do so when they pleased." And they often did leave, many to Union army

lines. In March 1862 Congress passed an act forbidding the army from returning slaves to their masters. Indeed, before Lincoln's Emancipation Proclamation, slavery had virtually collapsed in large areas of the South, and for the so-called Confederate nation it was only a matter of time.[10]

As the war staggered to its bloody conclusion, African Americans celebrated their freedom, went to search for family members who had been either traded or sold, began to establish their own churches and schools, performed legal marriages, attempted to set up work agreements with their former masters or other potential employers, and formed clubs and political societies, which held meetings to select leaders who could petition the federal government to assist them in winning their rights (especially the right to vote). As one African American observed, "They tell me before Mr. Lincoln made them free they had nothing to work for, to look up to, now they have everything, and will, by God's help, make their best of it."[11]

9. See Eric Foner, *Reconstruction: America's Unfinished Revolution, 1863–1877* (New York: Harper & Row, 1988), p. 3. One southern white warned that "the black waiters are all ears now." Hahn, *A Nation Under Their Feet*, p. 36. For Port Royal see Willie Lee Rose, *Rehearsal for Reconstruction: The Port Royal Experiment* (Indianapolis: Bobbs-Merrill, 1964), p. 12. For a report on the bombardment, see Frank Moore, ed., *The Rebellion Record* (New York: G.P. Putnam, 1864), supplement to vol. 1, pp. 192–197. For the Californian, see Foner, *Reconstruction*, p. 27.

10. For the Confederate government and army desertions, see David Donald, "Died of Democracy," in David Donald, ed., *Why the North Won the Civil War* (Baton Rouge: Louisiana State University Press, 1969), pp. 77–90, esp. 79. For the Alabama physician, see Richard Barksdale Harwell, ed., *Kate: The Journal of a Confederate Nurse* (Baton Rouge: Louisiana State University Press, 1959), p. 17. On the 1862 Act of Congress, see Foner, *Reconstruction*, p. 6. For patrols and "walking off," see Franklin and Moss, *From Slavery to Freedom*, pp. 233–234.

11. For one such celebration see Hahn, *A Nation Under Their Feet*, p. 113. For one African American's observation see Foner, *Reconstruction*, p. 95. For one such petition having to do with achieving the right to vote, see Ira Berlin, ed., *Free at Last: A Documentary History of Slavery, Freedom, and the Civil War* (New York: New Press, 1992), pp. 497–505.

◆ CHAPTER 1

The Road to
True Freedom:
African American
Alternatives in the
New South

This is not to say that these gains came easily, for they did not. With the war ending in the spring, it was essential for crops to be planted immediately. Landowners desperately needed black labor and often either refused to free their slaves or forced freedmen and women to work without pay. In some states, blacks could be jailed as vagrants and were hired out to anyone able to pay their fines (former masters had the right of "first hire"). In the former Confederate states, laws were passed in an attempt to set up a system somewhere between slavery and freedom. In some states African Americans could not own firearms or alcoholic beverages; had to obey city curfews; and suffer punishment for insulting gestures to whites, "bad behavior," and so forth.

Violence against freedmen and women was widespread. In Texas between 1865 and 1868, over one thousand blacks were murdered for a number of reasons. In Pine Bluff, Arkansas, in 1866 whites set fire to a black community; shot those who tried to escape the flames; and hanged twenty-four men, women, and children. And in Memphis, Tennessee, a three-day riot resulted in forty African Americans being killed; dozens wounded; several raped; and black churches, schools, and homes destroyed. Finally, throughout the South, informal organizations such as the Ku Klux Klan and other groups engaged in wholesale drownings, whippings, shootings, and lynchings of freedmen and women who attempted to exercise their rights. As *Richmond Examiner* editor Edward A. Pollard put it, "[t]he war did not decide negro equality; it did not decide negro suffrage; it did not decide State Rights. . . . And these things, which the war did not decide, the southern people will still cling to."[12]

Angered by President Andrew Johnson's unwillingness to take action against white southerners who refused to accept defeat or to recognize slaves' emancipation, Congress passed and overrode Johnson's veto of a series of acts that created a harsher reconstruction of the South. These acts included sending U.S. Army troops to assist the Freedmen's Bureau (created in 1865) in negotiating labor contracts, providing food and medical supplies, establishing schools, and registering freedmen to vote. In addition, southern states were required to elect delegates (with African American males enfranchised and disloyal whites disfranchised) to conventions that would write new state constitutions to be approved by Congress. When the constitution was approved *and* when the state had ratified the Fourteenth Amendment (by 1868 seven southern states had yet to do so), that state could be readmitted to the Union and could send senators and representatives to Congress.

And yet, despite the efforts of some federal officeholders, officials of the Freedmen's Bureau, a minority of U.S. Army soldiers, and the African Americans themselves, Reconstruction, according to historian William Gillette, "was virtually over almost as soon as it had begun." To begin with,

12. For "black codes," see Foner, *Reconstruction*, pp. 199–209. For violence see *ibid*, pp. 119–123; Stephen V. Ash, *A Massacre in Memphis: The Race Riot That Shook the Nation One Year After the Civil War* (New York: Hill & Wang, 2013). For Pollard's remark, see David Goldfield, *America Aflame: How the Civil War Created a Nation* (New York: Bloomsbury Press, 2011), quoted p. 406.

the scope and power of America's mid-nineteenth-century government were only fractions of what they would become a half century later. The Freedmen's Bureau had only about nine hundred officials in the entire South (only one in the entire state of Mississippi); the U.S. Army troops were small in number and scattered about the former Confederacy; and not a few of the federal officials were inefficient—some were corrupt, and a goodly number were racists. At last, as popular support in the North for Reconstruction evaporated, Republican candidates for office ceased to "wave the bloody shirt" and drum up sympathy for the freedmen and women. The feelings evoked by Harriet Beecher Stowe's *Uncle Tom's Cabin* (1852) were virtually gone.[13]

The gradual end of Reconstruction by the federal government left the South in the hands of political and economic leaders who chose to call themselves "Redeemers." Many of these men came from the same planter elite that had led the South prior to the Civil War, thus giving the post-Reconstruction South a high degree of continuity with earlier eras. Also important, however, was a comparatively new group of southerners, men who called for a "New South" that would be highlighted by increased industrialization, urbanization, and diversified agriculture.

In many ways, the New South Movement was an undisguised attempt to imitate the industrialization that was sweeping through the North in the mid to late nineteenth century. Indeed, the North's industrial prowess had been one reason for its ultimate military victory. As Reconstruction collapsed in the southern states, many southern bankers, business leaders, and newspaper editors became convinced that the South should not return to its previous, narrow economic base of plantations and one-crop agriculture, but instead should follow the North's lead toward modernization through industry. Prior to the Civil War, many of these people had called for economic diversification, but they had been overwhelmed by the plantation aristocracy that dominated southern state politics and had used that control to further its own interests. By the end of Reconstruction, however, the planter elite had lost a good deal of its authority, thus creating a power vacuum into which advocates of a New South could move.

Nearly every city, town, and hamlet of the former Confederacy had its New South boosters. Getting together in industrial societies or chambers of commerce, the boosters called for the erection of mills and factories. Why, they asked, should southerners export their valuable raw materials elsewhere, only to see them return from northern and European factories as costly finished products? Why couldn't southerners set up their own manufacturing establishments and become prosperous within a self-contained economy? And if the southerners were short of capital, why not encourage rich northern investors to put up money in return for promises of great profits? In fact, the South had all the ingredients required of an industrial system: raw materials, a rebuilt

13. For William Gillette's opinion, see his *Retreat from Reconstruction, 1869–1879* (Baton Rouge: Louisiana State University Press, 1979), pp. 363, 380. For the Republicans' shift in strategy from relying on freedmen to build a Republican party in the South to an embrace of pro-business southern whites, see De Santis, *Republicans Face the Southern Question*, p. 11.

✦ CHAPTER 1

The Road to
True Freedom:
African American
Alternatives in the
New South

transportation system, labor, potential consumers, and the possibility of obtaining capital. As they fed each other's dreams, the New South advocates pictured a resurgent South, a prosperous South, a triumphant South, and a South of steam and power rather than plantations and cotton.

Undoubtedly, the leading spokesman of the New South Movement was Henry Grady, editor of the *Atlanta Constitution* and one of the most influential figures in the southern states. Born in Athens, Georgia, in 1850, Grady was orphaned in his early teens when his father was killed in the Civil War. Graduating from his hometown college, the University of Georgia, Grady began a long and not particularly profitable career as a journalist. In 1879, aided by northern industrialist Cyrus Field, he purchased a quarter interest in the *Atlanta Constitution* and became that newspaper's editor. From that position, he became the chief advocate of the New South Movement.

Whether speaking to southern or northern audiences, Grady had no peer. Addressing a group of potential investors in New South industries in New York in 1886, he delighted his audience by saying that he was glad the Confederacy had lost the Civil War, for that defeat had broken the power of the plantation aristocracy and provided the opportunity for the South to move into the modern industrial age. Northerners, Grady continued, were welcome: "We have sown towns and cities in the place of theories, and put business above politics . . . and have . . . wiped out the place where Mason and Dixon's line used to be."[14]

14. Grady's speech is in Richard N. Current and John A. Garraty, eds., *Words That Made American History* (Boston: Little, Brown, 1962), Vol. II, pp. 23–31.

To those southerners who envisioned a New South, the central goal was a harmonious, interdependent society in which each person and thing had a clearly defined place. Most New South boosters stressed industry and the growth of cities because the South had few factories and mills and almost no cities of substantial size. But agriculture also would have its place, although it would not be the same as the cash-crop agriculture of the pre-Civil War years. Instead, New South spokespersons advocated a diversified agriculture that would still produce cash crops for export or for home manufacturing but would also make the South more self-sufficient by cultivating food crops and raw materials for the anticipated factories. Small towns would be used for collection and distribution, a rebuilt railroad network would transport goods, and northern capital would finance the entire process. Hence, each part of the economy and, indeed, each person would have a clearly defined place in the New South, and that would ensure everyone a piece of the New South's prosperity.

But even as Grady and his counterparts were fashioning their dreams of a New South and selling that vision to both northerners and southerners, a less beneficial, and less prosperous side of the New South was taking shape. In spite of the New South advocates' successes in establishing factories and mills (for example, Knoxville, Tennessee, witnessed the founding of more than ninety such enterprises in the 1880s alone), the post-Reconstruction South remained primarily agricultural. Furthermore, many of the farms were worked by sharecroppers or tenant farmers who eked out a bare subsistence while the profits went to the landowners or to the banks. This situation was especially prevalent in the lower South, where by 1910 a great proportion of farms were worked by tenants: South Carolina (63.0 percent), Georgia (65.6 percent), Alabama (60.2 percent), Mississippi (66.1 percent), and Louisiana (55.3 percent).[15] Even as factory smokestacks were rising on portions of the southern horizon, the majority of southerners remained in agriculture and in poverty.

Undeniably, African Americans suffered the most. More than four million African American men, women, and children had been freed by the Civil War. During Reconstruction, some advances were made, especially in the areas of public education and voter registration. Yet even these gains were either impermanent or incomplete. By 1880 in Georgia, only 33.7 percent of the black school-age population was enrolled in school, and by 1890 (twenty-five years after emancipation), almost half of all blacks aged ten to fourteen in the Deep South were still illiterate.[16] As for voting rights, the vast majority of African American men chose not to exercise them, fearing intimidation and violence.

Many blacks and whites at the time recognized that African Americans would never be able to improve their situation economically, socially, or politically without owning land. Yet even many Radical Republicans were reluctant to give land to the former slaves.

Such a move would mean seizing land from the white planters, a proposal that clashed with the notion of the sanctity of private property. As a result, most African Americans were forced to take menial, low-paying jobs in southern cities or to work as farmers on land they did not own. By 1880, only 1.6 percent of the landowners in Georgia were African Americans, although blacks constituted 47 percent of the state's population.

As poor urban laborers or tenant farmers, African Americans were dependent on their employers, landowners, or bankers and prey to vagrancy laws, the convict lease system, peonage, and outright racial discrimination. Moreover, the end of Reconstruction in the southern states eventually was followed by a reimposition of rigid racial segregation, at first through a return to traditional practices and later (in the 1890s) by state laws governing nearly every aspect of southern life. For example, voting by African Americans was discouraged, initially by intimidation and then by more formal means such as poll taxes and literacy tests. African Americans who protested or strayed from their "place" were dealt with harshly. Between 1880 and 1918, more than 2,400 African Americans were lynched by southern white mobs, each action being a grim reminder to African Americans of what could happen to those who challenged the status quo. For their part, the few southern whites who spoke against such outrages were themselves subjects of intimidation and even violence. Indeed, although most African American men and women undoubtedly would have disagreed, African Americans' relative position in some ways had deteriorated since the end of the Civil War.

15. Bureau of the Census, *Farm Tenancy in the United States* (Washington: Government Printing Office, 1924), pp. 207–208.
16. Roger L. Ransom and Richard Sutch, *One Kind of Freedom: The Economic Consequences of Emancipation* (Cambridge: Cambridge University Press, 1977), pp. 28, 30.

◆ CHAPTER 1

The Road to
True Freedom:
African American
Alternatives in the
New South

To be sure, a black middle class did exist and was growing in the South, principally in cities such as New Orleans, Richmond, Durham, and Atlanta. Most were men and women who served the African American community (editors, teachers, clergy, undertakers, retailers, restauranteurs, realtors, and so forth), people who owned their own homes, saw to it that their sons and daughters received good educations, and maintained a standard of living superior to the majority of whites and blacks in the South.[17] Although some of them spoke out in the interests of fellow African Americans, more preferred to live out of the spotlight and challenged the region's status quo quietly—when they did so at all.

Many New South advocates openly worried about how potential northern investors and politicians might react to the disturbing erosion of African Americans' position or to the calls of some middle-class blacks for racial justice. Although the dream of the New South rested on the concept of a harmonious, interdependent society in which each component (industry or agriculture, for example) and each person (white or black) had a clearly defined place, it appeared that African Americans were being kept in their "place" largely by laws, intimidation, and violence. Who would want to invest in a region where the status quo of mutual deference and "place" often was maintained by force? To calm northern fears, Grady and his cohorts assured northerners that African Americans' position was improving and that southern society was

one of mutual respect between the races. "We have found," Grady stated, "that in summing up, the free Negro counts for more than he did as a slave."[18] Most northerners believed Grady because they wanted to, because they had no taste for another bitter Reconstruction, and in many cases because they shared white southerners' prejudice against African Americans. Grady was able to reassure them because they wanted to be reassured.

Thus, for southern African Americans, the New South Movement had done little to better their collective lot. Indeed, in some ways their position actually had deteriorated. Tied economically either to land they did not own or to the lowest-paying jobs in towns and cities, subjects of an increasingly rigid code of racial segregation and loss of political rights, and victims of an upswing in racially directed violence, African Americans in the New South had every reason to question the oratory of Henry Grady and other New South boosters. Jobs in the New South's mills and factories generally were reserved for whites, so the opportunities that European immigrants in the North had to work their way gradually up the economic ladder were closed to southern blacks.

How did African Americans respond to this deteriorating situation? In the 1890s, numerous African American farmers joined the Colored Alliance, part of the Farmers' Alliance Movement that swept the South and Midwest in the 1880s and 1890s. This movement attempted to reverse the farmers' eroding position through the establishment of

17. On home ownership, in North Carolina in 1870, only 5.6 percent of African Americans owned their own homes. By 1910, that figure had risen to 26 percent. Gilmore, *Gender and Jim Crow*, p. 15.

18. *The New South: Writings and Speeches of Henry Grady* (Savannah: The Beehive Press, 1971), p. 8.

farmers' cooperatives, to sell their crops together for higher prices and to purchase manufactured goods wholesale, and by entering politics to elect candidates sympathetic to farmers, who would draft legislation favorable to farmers. Many feared, however, that this increased militancy of farmers—white and black—would produce a political backlash that would leave them even worse off. Such a backlash occurred in the South in the 1890s with the defeat of the Populist revolt.

Wells, Washington, Turner, DuBois, and Harper offered southern African Americans alternative means of confronting the economic, social, and political difficulties they faced. And, as African American men and women soon discovered, there were other options as well.

Your task in this chapter is to analyze the Evidence section in order to answer the following central questions:

1. What were the different alternatives offered by Wells, Washington, Turner, DuBois, and Harper?
2. Were there other options those five spokespersons did not mention?
3. What were the strengths and weaknesses of each alternative? Note: Remember that you are evaluating the five alternatives *not* from a present-day perspective but in the context and time in which they were advocated (1892–1906).
4. How would you support your assessment of the strengths and weaknesses of each alternative?

The Method

In this chapter, the Evidence section is from speeches delivered by five well-known African Americans or from their writings that were also given as speeches. Although all five spokespersons were known to southern African Americans, they were not equally prominent. It is almost impossible to tell which of the five was the best known (or least known) in her or his time, although fragmentary evidence suggests that Washington and Harper were the most famous figures among African Americans in various socioeconomic groups.

The piece by Ida B. Wells (Source 1) is excerpted from a pamphlet published simultaneously in the United States and England in 1892, but it is almost certain that parts of it were

delivered as a speech by Wells in that same year. The selections by Booker T. Washington (Source 2), Henry McNeal Turner (Source 3), W. E. B. DuBois (Source 4), and Frances E. W. Harper (Source 5) are transcriptions, or printed versions, of speeches delivered between 1895 and 1906.

Ida B. Wells was born a slave in Holly Springs, Mississippi, in 1862. After emancipation, her father and mother, as a carpenter and a cook, respectively, earned enough money to send her to freedmen's school. In 1876, her parents died in a yellow fever epidemic. Only fourteen years old, Wells lied about her age and got a job teaching in a rural school for blacks, eventually moving to Memphis, Tennessee, to teach in the city's school

◆ CHAPTER 1

The Road to
True Freedom:
African American
Alternatives in the
New South

for African Americans. In September 1883, she was forcibly removed from a railroad passenger car for refusing to move to the car reserved for "colored" passengers (she bit the conductor's hand in the scuffle). She won a lawsuit against the Chesapeake and Ohio Railroad, but that lawsuit was overturned by the Tennessee Supreme Court in 1887.[19] About this time Wells began writing articles for many black-owned newspapers (one of which, *Free Speech,* she co-owned), mostly on the subject of unequal educational opportunities for whites and blacks in Memphis. As a result, the Memphis school board discharged her, and she became a full-time journalist and lecturer. Then, in March 1892, three black men, one of them a friend of Wells, were lynched in Memphis. Her angry editorial in *Free Speech* resulted in the newspaper's destruction. The other co-owner was threatened with hanging and castration, the paper's former owner was pistol-whipped, and Wells herself was threatened with lynching if she returned to Memphis (she was in New York when her editorial was published). Relocating to Chicago, in 1895 she married black lawyer-editor Ferdinand Lee Barnett and from that time went by the name Ida Wells-Barnett, a somewhat radical practice in 1895.

Like Wells, Booker T. Washington was born a slave, in Franklin County, Virginia. Largely self-taught before entering Hampton Institute, a school for African Americans, at age seventeen he worked his way through school

mostly as a janitor. While a student at Hampton Institute, he came to the attention of Gen. Samuel C. Armstrong (1839–1893), one of the school's founders, who recommended Washington for the post as principal of the newly chartered normal school for blacks in Tuskegee, Alabama. Washington spent thirty-four years as the guiding force at Tuskegee Institute, shaping the school into his vision of how African Americans could better their lot. In great demand as a speaker to white and black audiences alike, Washington received an honorary degree from Harvard College in 1891. Four years later, he was chosen as the principal speaker at the opening of the Negro section of the Cotton States and International Exposition in Atlanta, after which he became the most well-known African American in the United States, courted by corporate leaders, philanthropists, and U.S. presidents. His invitation by President Theodore Roosevelt to have dinner at the White House outraged southern white leaders, including one senator from South Carolina who charged that it was an act so obnoxious that it would require "lynching a thousand niggers in the South before they will learn their place again."[20]

Henry McNeal Turner was born a free black near Abbeville, South Carolina. Mostly self-taught, he joined the Methodist Episcopal Church, South, in 1848 and was licensed to preach in 1853. In 1858, he abandoned that denomination to become a minister in the AME Church, and by 1862 he was the pastor of the large Israel Church in Washington, D.C. During the Civil War he served as chaplain in the Union Army,

19. Wells was not the first African American woman to challenge Tennessee's racial segregation of railroad passenger cars. See Paula J. Giddings, *Ida, A Sword Among Lions: Ida B. Wells and the Campaign Against Lynching* (New York: Amistad, 2008), pp. 52–59.

20. Robert J. Norrell, *Up from History: The Life of Booker T. Washington* (Cambridge: Harvard University Press, 2009), p. 4.

assigned to the First U.S. Colored Regiment. After the war, he became an official of the Freedmen's Bureau in Georgia and afterward held a succession of political appointments. One of the founders of the Republican Party in Georgia, Turner was made a bishop of the AME Church in Georgia in 1880. In that position, he met and befriended Ida B. Wells, who also was a member of the AME Church.

William Edward Burghardt DuBois was born in Great Barrington, Massachusetts, one of approximately fifty blacks in a town of five thousand people. He was educated with the white children in the town's public school and, in 1885, was enrolled at Fisk University, a college for African Americans in Nashville, Tennessee. It was there, according to his autobiography, that he first encountered overt racial prejudice. Graduated from Fisk in 1888, he entered Harvard as a junior. He received his bachelor's degree in 1890 and his Ph.D. in 1895. His book *The Philadelphia Negro* was published in 1899. In this book DuBois asserted that the problems African Americans faced were the results of their history (slavery and racism) and environment, not of some imagined genetic inferiority. By the early twentieth century, he had emerged as Washington's principal rival as the leader of and spokesman for African Americans. In 1909, he was one of the founders of the NAACP, a biracial group of white liberals and northern blacks who sought to overthrow Booker T. Washington, whom they generally considered too accommodating to powerful whites and too conservative in his strategies for African American progress.[21]

Frances Ellen Watkins Harper was born in Maryland in 1825, the only child of free parents. Orphaned at an early age, she was raised by an aunt, who enrolled her in a school for free blacks run by an uncle, who headed the Academy for Negro Youth and was a celebrated African American abolitionist (he was friends with both William Lloyd Garrison and Benjamin Lundy). Ending her formal education at the age of thirteen, Harper worked as a seamstress and needlework teacher. But she yearned to write and, in 1845, published her first book of poetry. It was later followed by ten more volumes of poetry (all commercially successful), a short story—the first to be published by a black woman—in 1859, and an immensely popular novel in 1892. She was a founder of the National Association of Colored Women, along with Ida B. Wells, and served as the organization's vice president. In 1860, she married Fenton Harper, who died in 1864. The couple had one child, a daughter, who was in continuous poor health and died in 1909.

This is not the first time that you have had to analyze speeches. Our society is virtually bombarded by speeches delivered by politicians, business figures, educators and others, most of whom are trying to convince us to adopt a set of ideas or actions. As we listen to such speeches, we invariably weigh the options presented to us, often using other available evidence to help us make our decisions. One purpose of this exercise is to help you think more critically and use evidence more thoroughly when assessing different options.

---

21. For the first decade or so of the NAACP's history, the majority of offices and power were held by whites, principally Mary White Ovington, William English Walling, and Oswald Garrison Villard. Other prominent white members included Jane Addams, John Dewey, Lincoln Steffens, William Dean Howells, Ray Stannard Baker, Stephen Wise, Clarence Darrow, and Franz Boaz.

◆ CHAPTER 1

The Road to
True Freedom:
African American
Alternatives in the
New South

In analyzing the speeches in the Evidence, it would be very helpful to know the backgrounds of the respective speakers, as those backgrounds clearly may have influenced the speakers' ideas and proposals. For example, how would the fact that Washington lived and worked in Alabama and was dependent on white philanthropists and politicians help to shape his thinking? Or that DuBois was born and grew up in a town in western Massachusetts in which African Americans comprised only one percent of the population? Or that Wells and Harper were women? Before you begin analyzing the speeches in the Evidence section, study the backgrounds of the speakers.

It is logical to begin by analyzing each of the speeches in turn. As you read each selection, make a rough chart like the one that follows to help you remember the main points.

Once you have carefully defined the alternatives presented by Wells, Washington, Turner, DuBois, and Harper, return to the Background section of the chapter. As you reread that section, determine the strengths and weaknesses of each alternative offered for African Americans living in the New South in the late nineteenth and early twentieth centuries. What evidence would you use to determine each alternative's strengths and weaknesses?

African American Alternatives

Speaker	Suggested Alternatives	How Does Speaker Develop Her/His Arguments?	Strengths and Weaknesses (Fill in Later)
Wells			
Washington			
Turner			
DuBois			
Harper			

◆

The Evidence

Source 1 from Ida B. Wells, *United States Atrocities* (London: Lux Newspaper and Publishing Co., 1892), pp. 13–18; in the United States, published as *Southern Horrors*. See Jacqueline Jones Royster, ed., *Southern Horrors and Other Writings: The Anti-Lynching Campaign of Ida B. Wells, 1892–1900* (Boston: Bedford Books, 1997), pp. 49–72.

1. Ida B. Wells's *United States Atrocities*, 1892 (excerpt).

Mr. Henry W. Grady, in his well-remembered speeches in New England and New York, pictured the Afro-American as incapable of self-government. Through him and other leading men the cry of the South to the country has been "Hands off! Leave us to solve our problem." To the Afro-American the South says, "The white man must and will rule." There is little difference between the Ante-bellum South and the New South. Her white citizens are wedded to any method however revolting, any measure however extreme, for the subjugation of the young manhood of the dark race. They have cheated him out of his ballot, deprived him of civil rights or redress in the Civil Courts thereof, robbed him of the fruits of his labour, and are still murdering, burning and lynching him.

The result is a growing disregard of human life. Lynch Law has spread its [insidious] influence till men in New York State, Pennsylvania and on the free Western plains feel they can take the law in their own hands with impunity, especially where an Afro-American is concerned. The South is brutalized to a degree not realized by its own inhabitants, and the very foundation of government, law, and order are imperilled.

Public sentiment has had a slight "reaction," though not sufficient to stop the crusade of lawlessness and lynching. The spirit of Christianity of the great M.E. Church[22] was sufficiently aroused by the frequent and revolting crimes against a powerless people, to pass strong condemnatory resolutions at its General Conference in Omaha last May. The spirit of justice of the grand old party[23] asserted itself sufficiently to secure a denunciation of the wrongs, and a feeble declaration of the belief in human rights in the Republican platform at Minneapolis, June 7th. A few of the great "dailies" and "weeklies" have swung into line declaring the Lynch Law must go. The President of the United States issued a proclamation that it be not tolerated in the territories over which he has jurisdiction. . . .

These efforts brought forth apologies and a short halt, but the lynching mania has raged again through the past twelve months with unabated fury. The strong arm of the law must be brought to bear upon lynchers in severe punishment, but this cannot and will not be done unless a healthy public sentiment demands and sustains such action. The men and women in the South who disapprove of lynchings and remain silent on the perpetration of such outrages are *particeps criminis*[24] accomplices, accessories before and after the fact, equally guilty with the actual law-breakers, who would not persist if they did not know that neither the law nor militia would be deployed against them.

In the creation of this healthier public sentiment, the Afro-American can do for himself what no one else can do for him. The world looks on with wonder that we have conceded so much, and remain law-abiding under such great outrage and provocation.

To Northern capital and Afro-American labour the South owes its rehabilitation. If labour is withdrawn capital will not remain. The

22. M.E. Church: The Methodist Episcopal Church, North. The Methodist Church split in 1844 over the issue of whether a bishop in that church could own slaves. The two churches did not reunite until 1939.
23. *Grand old party* refers to the Republican Party, the GOP.
24. A *particeps criminis* is one who has a share in a crime, an accomplice.

◆ CHAPTER 1

The Road to
True Freedom:
African American
Alternatives in the
New South

Afro-American is thus the backbone of the South. A thorough knowledge and judicious exercise of this power in lynching localities could many times affect a bloodless revolution. The white man's dollar is his god, and to stop this will be to stop outrages in many localities.

The Afro-Americans of Memphis denounced the lynching of three of their best citizens, and urged and waited for the authorities to act in the matter, and bring the lynchers to justice. No attempt was made to do so, and the black men left the city by thousands, bringing about great stagnation in every branch of business. Those who remained so injured the business of the streetcar company by staying off the cars, that the superintendent, manager, and treasurer called personally on the editors of the *Free Speech*, and asked them to urge our people to give them their patronage again. Other businessmen became alarmed over the situation, and the *Free Speech* was suppressed that the coloured people might be more easily controlled. A meeting of white citizens in June, three months after the lynching, passed resolutions for the first time condemning it. *But they did not punish the lynchers.* Every one of them was known by name because they had been selected to do the dirty work by some of the very citizens who passed these resolutions! Memphis is fast losing her black population, who proclaim as they go that there is no protection for the life and property of any Afro-American citizen in Memphis who will not be a slave. . . .

[*Wells then urged African Americans in Kentucky to boycott railroads in the state, since the legislature had passed a law segregating passenger cars. She claimed that such a boycott would mean a loss to the railroads of $1 million per year.*]

The appeal to the white man's pocket has ever been more effectual than all the appeals ever made to his conscience. Nothing, absolutely nothing, is to be gained by a further sacrifice of manhood and self-respect. By the right exercise of his power as the industrial factor of the South, the Afro-American can demand and secure his rights, the punishment of lynchers, and a fair trial for members of his race accused of outrage.

Of the many inhuman outrages of this present year, the only case where the proposed lynching did *not* occur, was where the men armed themselves in Jacksonville, Florida, and Paducah, Kentucky, and prevented it. The only times an Afro-American who was assaulted got away has been when he had a gun, and used it in self-defence. The lesson this teaches, and which every Afro-American should ponder well, is that a Winchester rifle should have a place of honour in every black home, and it should be used for that protection which the law refuses to give. When the white man, who is always the aggressor, knows he runs a great risk of biting the dust every time his Afro-American victim does, he will have greater respect for Afro-American life. The more the Afro-American yields and cringes and begs, the more he has to do so, the more he is insulted, outraged, and lynched.

Source 2 from Louis R. Harlan, ed., *The Booker T. Washington Papers,* (Urbana: University of Illinois Press, 1974), Vol. III, pp. 583–587.

2. Booker T. Washington's Atlanta Exposition Address (standard printed version), September 1895.

[Atlanta, Ga., Sept. 18, 1895]

Mr. President and Gentlemen of the Board of Directors and Citizens:

One-third of the population of the South is of a Negro race. No enterprise seeking the material, civil, or moral welfare of this section can disregard this element of our population and reach the highest success. I but convey to you, Mr. President and Directors, the sentiment of the masses of my race when I say that in no way have the value and manhood of the American Negro been more fittingly and generously recognized than by the managers of this magnificent Exposition at every stage of its progress. It is a recognition that will do more to cement the friendship of the two races than any occurrence since the dawn of our freedom.

Not only this, but the opportunity here afforded will awaken among us a new era of industrial progress. Ignorant and inexperienced, it is not strange that in the first years of our new life we began at the top instead of at the bottom; that a seat in Congress or the state legislature was more sought than real estate or industrial skill; that the political convention or stump speaking had more attractions than starting a dairy farm or truck garden.

A ship lost at sea for many days suddenly sighted a friendly vessel. From the mast of the unfortunate vessel was seen a signal, "Water, water; we die of thirst!" The answer from the friendly vessel at once came back, "Cast down your bucket where you are." A second time the signal, "Water, water; send us water!" ran up from the distressed vessel, and was answered, "Cast down your bucket where you are." And a third and fourth signal for water was answered, "Cast down your bucket where you are." The captain of the distressed vessel, at last heeding the injunction, cast down his bucket, and it came up full of fresh, sparkling water from the mouth of the Amazon River. To those of my race who depend on bettering their condition in a foreign land or who underestimate the importance of cultivating friendly relations with the Southern white man, who is their next-door neighbour, I would say: "Cast down your bucket where you are"—cast it down in making friends in every manly way of the people of all races by whom we are surrounded.

Cast it down in agriculture, mechanics, in commerce, in domestic service, and in the professions. And in this connection it is well to bear in mind that whatever other sins the South may be called to bear, when it comes to business, pure and simple, it is in the South that the Negro is given a man's chance in the commercial world, and in nothing is this Exposition more eloquent than in emphasizing this chance. Our greatest danger is that in the great leap from slavery to freedom we may overlook the fact that the masses of us are to live by the productions

[17]

✦ CHAPTER 1

The Road to
True Freedom:
African American
Alternatives in the
New South

of our hands, and fail to keep in mind that we shall prosper in proportion as we learn to dignify and glorify common labour, and put brains and skill into the common occupations of life; shall prosper in proportion as we learn to draw the line between the superficial and the substantial, the ornamental gewgaws of life and the useful. No race can prosper till it learns that there is as much dignity in tilling a field as in writing a poem. It is at the bottom of life we must begin, and not at the top. Nor should we permit our grievances to overshadow our opportunities.

To those of the white race who look to the incoming of those of foreign birth and strange tongue and habits for the prosperity of the South, were I permitted I would repeat what I say to my own race, "Cast down your bucket where you are." Cast it down among the eight millions of Negroes whose habits you know, whose fidelity and love you have tested in days when to have proved treacherous meant the ruin of your firesides. Cast down your bucket among these people who have, without strikes and labour wars, tilled your fields, cleared your forests, builded your railroads and cities, and brought forth treasures from the bowels of the earth, and helped make possible this magnificent representation of the progress of the South. Casting down your bucket among my people, helping and encouraging them as you are doing on these grounds, and to education of head, hand, and heart, you will find that they will buy your surplus land, make blossom the waste places in your fields, and run your factories. While doing this, you can be sure in the future, as in the past, that you and your families will be surrounded by the most patient, faithful, law-abiding, and unresentful people that the world has seen. As we have proved our loyalty to you in the past, in nursing your children, watching by the sick-bed of your mothers and fathers, and often following them with tear-dimmed eyes to their graves, so in the future, in our humble way, we shall stand by you with a devotion that no foreigner can approach, ready to lay down our lives, if need be, in defense of yours, interlacing our industrial, commercial, civil, and religious life with yours in a way that shall make the interests of both races one. In all things that are purely social we can be as separate as the fingers, yet one as the hand in all things essential to mutual progress.

There is no defense or security for any of us except in the highest intelligence and development of all. If anywhere there are efforts tending to curtail the fullest growth of the Negro, let these efforts be turned into stimulating, encouraging, and making him the most useful and intelligent citizen. Effort or means so invested will pay a thousand per cent interest. These efforts will be twice blessed—"blessing him that gives and him that takes."

There is no escape through law of man or God from the inevitable:

"The laws of changeless justice bind
  Oppressor with oppressed;
And close as sin and suffering joined
  We march to fate abreast."

Nearly sixteen millions of hands will aid you in pulling the load upward, or they will pull against you the load downward. We shall constitute one-third and more of the ignorance and crime of the South, or one-third [of] its intelligence and progress; we shall contribute one-third to the business and industrial prosperity of the South, or we shall prove a veritable body of death, stagnating, depressing, retarding every effort to advance the body politic.

Gentlemen of the Exposition, as we present to you our humble effort at an exhibition of our progress, you must not expect overmuch. Starting thirty years ago with ownership here and there in a few quilts and pumpkins and chickens (gathered from miscellaneous sources), remember the path that has led from these to the inventions and production of agricultural implements, buggies, steam-engines, newspapers, books, statuary, carving, paintings, the management of drug stores and banks, has not been trodden without contact with thorns and thistles. While we take pride in what we exhibit as a result of our independent efforts, we do not for a moment forget that our part in this exhibition would fall far short of your expectations but for the constant help that has come to our education life, not only from the Southern states, but especially from Northern Philanthropists, who have made their gifts a constant stream of blessing and encouragement.

The wisest among my race understand that the agitation of questions of social equality is the extremest folly, and that progress in the enjoyment of all the privileges that will come to us must be the result of severe and constant struggle rather than of artificial forcing. No race that has anything to contribute to the markets of the world is long in any degree ostracized. It is important and right that all privileges of the law be ours, but it is vastly more important that we be prepared for the exercise of these privileges. The opportunity to earn a dollar in a factory just now is worth infinitely more than the opportunity to spend a dollar in an opera-house.

In conclusion, may I repeat that nothing in thirty years has given us more hope and encouragement, and drawn us so near to you of the white race, as this opportunity offered by the Exposition; and here bending, as it were over the altar that represents the results of the struggles of your race and mine, both starting practically empty-handed three decades ago, I pledge that in your effort to work out the great and intricate problem which God has laid at the doors of the South, you shall have at all times the patient, sympathetic help of my race; only let this be constantly in mind, that, while from representations in these buildings of the product of field, of forest, of mine, of factory, letters, and art, much good will come, yet far above and beyond material benefits will be that higher good, that, let us pray God, will come, in a blotting out of sectional differences and racial animosities and suspicions in a determination to administer absolute justice, in a willing obedience among all classes to the mandates of law. This, coupled with our material prosperity, will bring into our beloved South a new heaven and a new earth.

♦ CHAPTER 1

The Road to
True Freedom:
African American
Alternatives in the
New South

Source 3 from Edwin S. Redkey, ed., *Respect Black: The Writings and Speeches of Henry McNeal Turner* (New York: Arno Press, 1971).

3. Henry McNeal Turner's "The American Negro and His Fatherland," December 1895 (excerpt).

It would be a waste of time to expend much labor, the few moments I have to devote to this subject, upon the present status of the Negroid race in the United States. It is too well-known already. However, I believe that the Negro was brought to this country in the providence of God to a heaven-permitted if not a divine-sanctioned manual laboring school, that he might have direct contact with the mightiest race that ever trod the face of the globe.

The heathen Africans, to my certain knowledge, I care not what others may say, eagerly yearn for that civilization which they believe will elevate them and make them potential for good. The African was not sent and brought to this country by chance, or by the avarice of the white man, single and alone. The white slave-purchaser went to the shores of that continent and bought our ancestors from their African masters. The bulk who were brought to this country were the children of parents who had been in slavery a thousand years. Yet hereditary slavery is not universal among the African slaveholders. So that the argument often advanced, that the white man went to Africa and stole us, is not true. They bought us out of a slavery that still exists over a large portion of that continent. For there are millions and millions of slaves in Africa today. Thus the superior African sent us, and the white man brought us, and we remained in slavery as long as it was necessary to learn that a God, who is a spirit, made the world and controls it, and that that Supreme Being could be sought and found by the exercise of faith in His only begotten Son. Slavery then went down, and the colored man was thrown upon his own responsibility, and here he is today, in the providence of God, cultivating self-reliance and imbibing a knowledge of civil law in contradistinction to the dictum of one man, which was the law of the black man until slavery was overthrown. I believe that the Negroid race has been free long enough now to begin to think for himself and plan for better conditions [than] he can lay claim to in this country or ever will. *There is no manhood future in the United States for the Negro.* He may eke out an existence for generations to come, but he can never be a *man*—full, symmetrical and undwarfed. . . .

[*Here Turner asserted that a "great chasm" continued to exist between the races, that whites would have no social contact with blacks, and (without using Booker T. Washington's name) that any black who claimed that African Americans did not want social equality immediately "is either an ignoramus, or is an advocate of the perpetual servility and degradation of his race. . . ."*]

. . . And as such, I believe that two or three millions of us should return to the land of our ancestors, and establish our own nation, civilization, laws, customs, style of manufacture, and not only give the world, like other race varieties, the benefit of our individuality, but build up social conditions peculiarly our own, and cease to be grumblers, chronic complainers and a menace to the white man's country, or the country he claims and is bound to dominate.

The civil status of the Negro is simply what the white man grants of his own free will and accord. The black man can demand nothing. He is deposed from the jury and tried, convicted and sentenced by men who do not claim to be his peers. On the railroads, where the colored race is found in the largest numbers, he is the victim of proscription, and he must ride in the Jim Crow car or walk. The Supreme Court of the United States decided, October 15th, 1883, that the colored man had no civil rights under the general government,[25] and the several States, from then until now, have been enacting laws which limit, curtail and deprive him of his civil rights, immunities and privileges, until he is now being disfranchised, and where it will end no one can divine. . . .

The discriminating laws, all will concede, are degrading to those against which they operate, and the degrader will be degraded also. "For all acts are reactionary, and will return in curses upon those who curse," said Stephen A. Douglass [sic], the great competitor of President Lincoln. Neither does it require a philosopher to inform you that degradation begets degradation. Any people oppressed, proscribed, belied, slandered, burned, flayed and lynched will not only become cowardly and servile, but will transmit that same servility to their posterity, and continue to do so *ad infinitum*, and as such will never make a bold and courageous people. The condition of the Negro in the United States is so repugnant to the instincts of respected manhood that thousands, yea hundreds of thousands, of miscegenated will pass for white, and snub the people with whom they are identified at every opportunity, thus destroying themselves, or at least *unracing* themselves. They do not want to be black because of its ignoble condition, and they cannot be white, thus they become monstrosities. Thousands of young men who are even educated by white teachers never have any respect for people of their own color and spend their days as devotees of white gods. Hundreds, if not thousands, of the terms employed by the white race in the English language are also degrading to the black man. Everything that is satanic, corrupt, base and infamous is denominated *black*, and all that constitutes virtue, purity, innocence, religion, and that which is divine and heavenly, is represented as *white*. Our Sabbath-school children, by the time they reach proper consciousness, are taught to sing to the laudation of white and to the contempt of black. Can any one with an ounce of common sense expect that these children, when they reach maturity, will ever have any respect for their black or colored faces, or the faces of their associates? But, without multiplying words, the terms used in our religious experience, and the hymns we sing in many instances, are degrading, and will

25. See the Civil Rights Cases, fn 6.

◆ CHAPTER 1

The Road to
True Freedom:
African American
Alternatives in the
New South

be as long as the black man is surrounded by the idea that *white* represents God and *black* represents the devil. The Negro should, therefore, build up a nation of his own, and create a language in keeping with his color, as the whites have done. Nor will he ever respect himself until he does it.

What the black man needs is a country and surroundings in harmony with his color and with respect for his manhood. Upon this point I would delight to dwell longer if I had time. Thousands of white people in this country are ever and anon advising the colored people to keep out of politics, but they do not advise themselves. If the Negro is a man in keeping with other men, why should he be less concerned about politics than any one else? Strange, too, that a number of would-be colored leaders are ignorant and debased enough to proclaim the same foolish jargon. For the Negro to stay out of politics is to level himself with a horse or a cow, which is no politician, and the Negro who does it proclaims his inability to take part in political affairs. If the Negro is to be a man, full and complete, he must take part in everything that belongs to manhood. If he omits a single duty, responsibility or privilege, to that extent he is limited and incomplete.

Time, however, forbids my continuing the discussion of this subject, roughly and hastily as these thoughts have been thrown together. Not being able to present a dozen or two more phases, which I would cheerfully and gladly do if opportunity permitted, I conclude by saying the argument that it would be impossible to transport the colored people of the United States back to Africa is an advertisement of folly. Two hundred millions of dollars would rid this country of the last member of the Negroid race, if such a thing was desirable, and two hundred and fifty millions would give every man, woman and child excellent fare, and the general government could furnish that amount and never miss it, and that would only be the pitiful sum of a million dollars a year for the time we labored for nothing, and for which somebody or some power is responsible. The emigrant agents at New York, Boston, Philadelphia, St. John, N. B., and Halifax, N. S., with whom I have talked, establish beyond contradiction, that over a million, and from that to twelve hundred thousand persons, come to this country every year, and yet there is no public stir about it. But in the case of African emigration, two or three millions only of self-reliant men and women would be necessary to establish the conditions we are advocating in Africa.

Source 4 from Herbert Atheker, ed., *Pamphlets and Leaflets by W. E. B. Du Bois* (White Plains, NY: Kraus-Thomson Organization Ltd., 1986).

4. DuBois's Niagara Address, 1906 (excerpt).

In detail our demands are clear and unequivocal. First, we would vote; with the right to vote goes everything: Freedom, manhood, the honor of your wives, the chastity of your daughters, the right to work, and the chance to rise, and let no man listen to those who deny this.

We want full manhood suffrage, and we want it now, henceforth and forever.

Second. We want discrimination in public accommodation to cease. Separation in railway and street cars, based simply on race and color, is un-American, undemocratic, and silly. We protest against all such discrimination.

Third. We claim the right of freemen to walk, talk, and be with them that wish to be with us. No man has a right to choose another man's friends, and to attempt to do so is an impudent interference with the most fundamental human privilege.

Fourth. We want the laws enforced against rich as well as poor; against Capitalist as well as Laborer; against white as well as black. We are not more lawless than the white race, we are more often arrested, convicted and mobbed. We want justice even for criminals and outlaws. We want the Constitution of the country enforced. We want Congress to take charge of Congressional elections. We want the Fourteenth Amendment carried out to the letter and every State disfranchised in Congress which attempts to disfranchise its rightful voters. We want the Fifteenth Amendment enforced and no State allowed to base its franchise simply on color.

The failure of the Republican Party in Congress at the session just closed to redeem its pledge of 1904 with reference to suffrage conditions [in] the South seems a plain, deliberate, and premeditated breach of promise, and stamps that party as guilty of obtaining votes under false pretense.

Fifth. We want our children educated. The school system in the country districts of the South is a disgrace and in few towns and cities are the Negro schools what they ought to be. We want the national government to step in and wipe out illiteracy in the South. Either the United States will destroy ignorance or ignorance will destroy the United States.

And when we call for education we mean real education. We believe in work. We ourselves are workers, but work is not necessarily education. Education is the development of power and ideal. We want our children trained as intelligent human beings should be, and we will fight for all time against any proposal to educate black boys and girls simply as servants and underlings, or simply for the use of other people. They have a right to know, to think, to aspire.

These are some of the chief things which we want. How shall we get them? By voting where we may vote, by persistent, unceasing agitation, by hammering at the truth, by sacrifice and work.

We do not believe in violence, neither in the despised violence of the raid nor the lauded violence of the soldier, nor the barbarous violence of the mob, but we do believe in John Brown, in that incarnate spirit of justice, that hatred of a lie, that willingness to sacrifice money, reputation, and life itself on the altar of right. And here on the scene of John Brown's martyrdom we

◆ CHAPTER 1

The Road to
True Freedom:
African American
Alternatives in the
New South

reconsecrate ourselves, our honor, our property to the final emancipation of the race which John Brown died to make free.

Our enemies, triumphant for the present, are fighting the stars in their courses. Justice and humanity must prevail. We live to tell these dark brothers of ours—scattered in counsel, wavering and weak—that no bribe of money or notoriety, no promise of wealth or fame, is worth the surrender of a people's manhood or the loss of a man's self-respect. We refuse to surrender the leadership of this race to cowards and trucklers. We are men; we will be treated as men. On this rock we have planted our banners. We will never give up, though the trump of doom find us still fighting.

And we shall win. The past promised it, the present foretells it. Thank God for John Brown! Thank God for Garrison and Douglass! Sumner and Phillips, Nat Turner and Robert Gould Shaw,[26] and all the hallowed dead who died for freedom! Thank God for all those today, few though their voices be, who have not forgotten the divine brotherhood of all men, white and black, rich and poor, fortunate and unfortunate.

We appeal to the young men and women of this nation, to those whose nostrils are not yet befouled by greed and snobbery and racial narrowness: Stand up for the right, prove yourselves worthy of your heritage and whether born north or south dare to treat men as men. Cannot the nation that has absorbed ten million foreigners into its political life without catastrophe absorb ten million Negro Americans into that same political life at less cost than their unjust and illegal exclusion will involve?

Courage, brothers! The battle for humanity is not lost or losing. All across the skies sit signs of promise. The Slav is rising in his might, the yellow millions are tasting liberty, the black Africans are writhing toward the light, and everywhere the laborer, with ballot in his hand, is voting open the gates of Opportunity and Peace. The morning breaks over blood-stained hills. We must not falter, we may not shrink. Above are the everlasting stars.

26. William Lloyd Garrison (1805–1879): editor of *The Liberator*, major figure in the abolition movement.
Frederick Douglass (1817–1895): escaped slave; noted African American abolitionist, journalist, orator; his autobiography (1845) is still in print.
Charles Sumner (1811–1874): U.S. senator from Massachusetts; leading antislavery person in the Senate; on May 22, 1856, he was assaulted and seriously injured in the Senate chamber by South Carolina representative Preston Brooks.
Wendell Phillips (1811–1884): attorney, orator, and important abolitionist.
Nat Turner (1800–1831): African American preacher and leader of a slave rebellion in Virginia in 1831.
Robert Gould Shaw (1831–1863): white Civil War officer who commanded the Fifty-fourth Massachusetts Infantry Regiment; he was killed leading an assault on Fort Wagner in South Carolina.

Source 5 from Frances Smith Foster, ed., *A Brighter Coming Day: A Frances Ellen Watkins Harper Reader* (New York: Feminist Press, 1990), pp. 285–292.

5. Frances E. W. Harper's "Enlightened Motherhood," an Address to the Brooklyn Literary Society, November 15, 1892 (excerpt).

It is nearly thirty years since an emancipated people stood on the threshold of a new era, facing an uncertain future—a legally unmarried race, to be taught the sacredness of the marriage relation; an ignorant people, to be taught to read the book of the Christian law and to learn to comprehend more fully the claims of the gospel of the Christ of Calvary. A homeless race, to be gathered into homes of peaceful security and to be instructed how to plant around their firesides the strongest batteries against the sins that degrade and the race vices that demoralize. A race unversed in the science of government and unskilled in the just administration of law, to be translated from the old oligarchy of slavery into the new commonwealth of freedom, and to whose men came the right to exchange the fetters on their wrists for the ballots in their right hands—a ballot which, if not vitiated by fraud or restrained by intimidation, counts just as much as that of the most talented and influential man in the land.

While politicians may stumble on the barren mountain of fretful controversy, and men, lacking faith in God and the invisible forces which make for righteousness, may shrink from the unsolved problems of the hour, into the hands of Christian women comes the opportunity of serving the ever blessed Christ, by ministering to His little ones and striving to make their homes the brightest spots on earth and the fairest types of heaven. The school may instruct and the church may teach, but the home is an institution older than the church and antedates school, and that is the place where children should be trained for useful citizenship on earth and a hope of holy companionship in heaven. . . .

The home may be a humble spot, where there are no velvet carpets to hush your tread, no magnificence to surround your way, nor costly creations of painter's art or sculptor's skill to please your conceptions or gratify your tastes; but what are the costliest gifts of fortune when placed in the balance with the confiding love of dear children or the true devotion of a noble and manly husband whose heart can safely trust in his wife? You may place upon the brow of a true wife and mother the greenest laurels; you may crowd her hands with civic honors; but, after all, to her there will be no place like home, and the crown of her motherhood will be more precious than the diadem of a queen. . . .

Marriage between two youthful and loving hearts means the laying [of] the foundation stones of a new home, and the woman who helps erect that

◆ CHAPTER 1

The Road to
True Freedom:
African American
Alternatives in the
New South

home should be careful not to build it above the reeling brain of a drunkard or the weakened fibre of a debauchee. If it be folly for a merchant to send an argosy, laden with the richest treasure, at midnight on a moonless sea, without a rudder, compass, or guide, is it not madness for a woman to trust her future happiness, and the welfare of the dear children who may yet nestle in her arms and make music and sunshine around her fireside, in the unsteady hands of a characterless man, too lacking in self-respect and self-control to hold the helm and rudder of his own life; who drifts where he ought to steer, and only lasts when he ought to live?

The moment the crown of motherhood falls on the brow of a young wife, God gives her a new interest in the welfare of the home and the good of society. If hitherto she had been content to trip through life a lighthearted girl, or to tread amid the halls of wealth and fashion the gayest of the gay, life holds for her now a high and noble service. She must be more than the child of pleasure or the devotee of fashion. Her work is grandly constructive. A helpless and ignorant babe lies smiling in her arms. God has trusted her with a child, and it is her privilege to help that child develop the most precious thing a man or woman can possess on earth, and that is a good character. Moth may devour our finest garments, fire may consume and floods destroy our fairest homes, rust may gather on our silver and tarnish our gold, but there is an asbestos that no fire can destroy, a treasure which shall be richer for its service and better for its use, and that is a good character. . . .

Are there not women, respectable women, who feel that it would wring their hearts with untold anguish, and bring their gray hairs in sorrow to the grave, if their daughters should trail the robes of their womanhood in the dust, yet who would say of their sons, if they were trampling their manhood down and fettering their souls with cords of vice, "O, well, boys will be boys, and young men will sow their wild oats."

I hold that no woman loves social purity as it deserves to be loved and valued, if she cares for the purity of her daughters and not her sons; who would gather her dainty robes from contact with the fallen woman and yet greet with smiling lips and clasp with warm and welcoming hands the author of her wrong and ruin. How many mothers to-day shrink from a double standard for society which can ostracise the woman and condone the offense of the man? How many mothers say within their hearts, "I intend to teach my boy to be as pure in his life, as chaste in his conversation, as the young girl who sits at my side encircled in the warm clasp of loving arms?" How many mothers strive to have their boys shun the gilded saloon as they would the den of a deadly serpent? Not the mother who thoughtlessly sends her child to the saloon for a beverage to make merry with her friends. How many mothers teach their boys to shrink in horror from the fascinations of women, not as God made them, but as sin has degraded them? . . .

I would ask, in conclusion, is there a branch of the human race in the Western Hemisphere which has greater need of the inspiring and uplifting influences that can flow out of the lives and examples of the truly enlightened than ourselves? Mothers who can teach their sons not to love pleasure or fear death; mothers who can teach their children to embrace every opportunity, employ every power, and use every means to build up a future to contrast with the old sad past. Men may boast of the aristocracy of blood; they may glory in the aristocracy of talent, and be proud of the aristocracy of wealth, but there is an aristocracy which must ever outrank them all, and that is the aristocracy of character.

Source 6 from U.S. Bureau of the Census, *Historical Statistics of the United States, Colonial Times to 1970* (Washington, D.C.: U.S. Government Printing Office, 1975).

6. Estimated Net Intercensal Migration* of Negro Population by Region, 1870–1920 (in thousands).

Region	1870–1880	1880–1890	1890–1900	1900–1910	1910–1920
New England[1]	4.5	6.6	14.2	8.0	12.0
Middle Atlantic[2]	19.2	39.1	90.7	87.2	170.1
East North Central[3]	20.8	16.4	39.4	45.6	200.4
West North Central[4]	15.7	7.9	23.5	10.2	43.7
South Atlantic[5]	−47.9	−72.5	−181.6	−111.9	−158.0
East South Central[6]	−56.2	−60.1	−43.3	−109.6	−246.3
West South Central[7]	45.1	62.9	56.9	51.0	−46.2

*A net intercensal migration represents the amount of migration that took place between U.S. censuses, which are taken every ten years. The net figure is computed by comparing in-migration to with out-migration from a particular state. A minus figure means that out-migration from a state was greater than in-migration to it.
1. Maine, New Hampshire, Vermont, Massachusetts, Rhode Island, and Connecticut.
2. New York, New Jersey, and Pennsylvania.
3. Ohio, Indiana, Illinois, Michigan, and Wisconsin.
4. Minnesota, Iowa, Missouri, North Dakota, South Dakota, Nebraska, and Kansas.
5. Delaware, Maryland, District of Columbia, Virginia, West Virginia, North Carolina, South Carolina, Georgia, and Florida.
6. Kentucky, Tennessee, Alabama, and Mississippi.
7. Arkansas, Louisiana, Oklahoma, and Texas.

◆ CHAPTER 1

The Road to
True Freedom:
African American
Alternatives in the
New South

◆

Questions to Consider

The Background section of this chapter strongly suggests that the prospects for African Americans in the post-Reconstruction South were bleak. Although blacks certainly preferred sharecropping or tenancy to working in gangs as in the days of slavery, neither system offered African Americans much chance to own their own land. Furthermore, the industrial opportunities available to European immigrants, which allowed many of them gradually to climb the economic ladder, were generally closed to southern blacks, in part because the South was never able to match the North in the creation of industrial jobs and in part because what jobs the New South industrialization did create often were closed to blacks. As we have seen, educational opportunities for African Americans in the South were severely limited—so much so that by 1890, more than 75 percent of the adult black population in the Deep South remained illiterate (as opposed to 17.1 percent of the adult white population). In addition, rigid segregation laws and racial violence had increased dramatically. Indeed, the prospects for southern blacks were far from promising.

Begin by analyzing Ida B. Wells's response (Source 1) to the deteriorating condition of African Americans in the South. In her view, how did blacks in Memphis and Kentucky provide a model for others? What was that model? In addition to that model, Wells tells us how blacks in Jacksonville, Florida, and Paducah, Kentucky,

were able to prevent lynchings in those towns. What alternative did those blacks present? Was Wells advocating it? Finally, what role did Wells see the African American press playing in preventing lynchings?

The alternative presented by Booker T. Washington (Source 2) differs markedly from those offered by Wells. In his view, what process should African Americans follow to enjoy their full rights? How did he support his argument? What did Washington conceive the role of southern whites in African Americans' progress to be? Remember that his *goals* were roughly similar to those of Wells. Also use some inference to imagine how Washington's audiences would have reacted to his speech. How would southern whites have greeted his speech? Southern blacks? What about northern whites? Northern blacks? To whom was Washington speaking?

Now move on to Henry McNeal Turner's alternative (Source 3). At first Bishop Turner seems to be insulting blacks. What was he really trying to say? Why did he think that God ordained blacks to be brought to America in chains? In Turner's view, once blacks were freed, what was their best alternative? Why? Turner's view of whites is at serious odds with that of Washington. How do the two views differ on this point? Why do you think this was so? How did Turner use his view of whites to support his alternative for blacks?

The speech by W. E. B. DuBois at the Niagara Falls meeting in 1906 (Source 4) was intended to lead African

American professional men away from the philosophy of Booker T. Washington. How did DuBois's philosophy differ from that of Washington? How does his suggested *process* differ from that of Washington? Furthermore, how did DuBois's view differ with respect to timing? Tactics? Tone? Remember, however, that the long-term goals of both men were similar.[27]

Perhaps you have been struck by the fact that both Turner and DuBois pinned their hopes for progress on African American *men*. Turner refers frequently to "manhood" and DuBois to "exceptional men." Why do you think this was so? Why do you think the concept of African American manhood was important to these two thinkers?

For Frances E. W. Harper (Source 5), the hopes of African Americans lay not with black men but with black *women*. Why did she believe this was so? As opposed to education, work, or the political arena, in Harper's view what was the importance of the African American home? Would Harper have agreed or disagreed with Wells? Washington? Turner? DuBois? How might African American men such as Washington, Turner, and DuBois have reacted to her arguments?

The ideas of Wells and Harper differed significantly from those of Washington, Turner, and DuBois. What role do you think gender played in the formation of Wells's and Harper's ideas? Of Washington's? Turner's? DuBois's?

After you have examined each of the alternatives, move on to your assessment of the strengths and weaknesses of each argument. As noted earlier, you will need to review the Background section of this chapter in order to establish the historical context in which the five arguments were made. Then, keeping in mind that context, try to imagine the reactions that these alternatives might have elicited in the following situations:

1. What would have happened if southern African Americans had adopted Wells's alternatives? Where might the process outlined by Wells have led? Were there any risks for African Americans? If so, what were they?

2. What would have happened if southern African Americans had adopted Washington's alternative? How long would it have taken them to realize Washington's goals? Were there any risks involved? If so, what were they?

3. What would have happened if southern African Americans had adopted Turner's alternative? Were there any risks involved? How realistic was Turner's option?

4. What would have happened if southern African Americans had adopted DuBois's alternative? How long would DuBois's process have taken? Were there any risks involved?

5. Was white assistance necessary according to Wells? To Washington? To Turner? To DuBois? How did each spokesperson perceive the roles of the federal government

27. In 1903 DuBois wrote an essay titled "The Talented Tenth," in which he called for leading African Americans to graduate from college, secure good business and academic positions, and then labor to "lift up" the race. "The Negro race, like all other races, is going to be saved by its exceptional men." See Nathan Huggins, comp., *W. E. B. DuBois Writings* (New York: Library of America, 1986), pp. 842–861. On the Niagara meeting, see Norrell, *Up from History*, pp. 321–322. The meeting was attended by twenty-nine men.

◆ CHAPTER 1

The Road to
True Freedom:
African American
Alternatives in the
New South

and the federal courts? How did the government and courts stand on this issue at the time [*Clue:* What was the Supreme Court decision in *Plessy v. Ferguson* (1896)?]

6. How might blacks and whites have reacted to Harper's arguments? Black women? Black men? As with the ideas of Washington, how long would it have taken for African Americans who embraced Harper's ideas to reach the goals of social, economic, and political equality?

To be sure, it is very nearly impossible for us to put ourselves completely in the shoes of these men and women. Although racism still is a strong force in American life still, the intellectual and cultural environment was dramatically different in the time these five spokespersons were offering their ideas to African Americans. Even so, by placing each spokesperson in a historical context, we should be able to evaluate the strengths and weaknesses of each argument.

Epilogue

For advocates of the New South, the realization of their dream seemed to be right over the horizon, always just beyond their grasp. Many factories did make a good deal of money, but profits often flowed out of the South to northern investors. And factory owners usually maintained profits by paying workers pitifully low wages, which led to the rise of a poor white urban class that lived in slums and faced enormous problems of malnutrition, poor health, family instability, and crime. To most of those who had left their meager farms to find opportunities in the burgeoning southern cities, life there appeared even worse than it had been in the rural areas. Many whites returned to their rural homesteads disappointed and dispirited by urban life. For African Americans, their collective lot was even worse.

At the same time that the New South philosophy was gaining advocates and power, parallel to those ideas was the glorification of the Old South and of those who fought a war to retain it. Interestingly, many white southerners embraced both intellectual strains, not unlike what historian David Goldfield described as the ideology of Bismarckian Germany that "marched forward to modernity, while looking to the past for its inspiration and guidance."

In the years after Reconstruction, white southerners created a Confederate nationalism for the nation that never really was, constructed statues and memorials, proudly flew the stars and bars of the Confederate battle flag, held veterans' reunions, founded the Union of Confederate Veterans (1888) and the Daughters of the Confederacy (1894), and rewrote the South's history to absolve the section for the coming of the War Between the States and to give countless speeches on the myth of the Lost Cause.[28]

In sum, the Lost Cause was a powerful myth that many white southerners stubbornly clung to. French-American novelist and diarist Julian Green (1901–1998), child of an expatriate Savannah family that exiled itself to France after the war, wrote of his mother,

> She made of her sons and daughters the children of a nation which no longer existed but lived on in her heart. She cast over us the shadow of a tragedy which darkened for her even the clearest days. We were the eternally conquered but unreconciled—rebels, to employ a word dear to her. [The banner of the Confederacy was framed in gold on the wall of the salon of their apartment on the Rue de Passy in Paris. Regularly she pointed to the flag and said to her children] ". . . your flag. . . . Remember it. That and no other."

Indeed, in some ways the post-Reconstruction white South was moving in the opposite direction from much of the rest of the Western world. It is not difficult to imagine where African Americans "fit"—or did not fit—into a New South that sought to chart for itself a new future while lauding its created past.[29]

For roughly twenty years after his 1895 Atlanta address, Booker T. Washington remained the nominal leader and spokesman for African Americans. On the surface an accommodationist and a gradualist, beneath the surface Washington worked to secure government jobs for blacks; protested discrimination on railroads, in voting, in education, and regarding lynching; and organized and funded court challenges to disfranchisement, all-white juries, and peonage. By 1913, he had openly criticized southern white leaders, stating that "the best white citizenship must take charge of the mob and not have the mob take charge of civilization."[30]

Yet Washington's style, as well as his jealous guarding of his own power, caused serious divisions among black leaders. African American editor William Monroe Trotter accused Washington of being "a miserable toady" and "the Benedict Arnold of the Negro race." The NAACP was founded by Washington's critics in 1909 with the main objective of wresting power from Washington and being considerably more assertive in demanding equal rights for the nation's black people.

Yet at the May 1909 organizational meeting of the NAACP, Washington's opponents were themselves sharply divided. DuBois purposely removed Wells-Barnett's name from the Committee of Forty (later the "Founding Forty"), causing her to walk out of the

28. For Goldfield's comparison see his *Still Fighting the Civil War: The American South and Southern History* (Baton Rouge: Louisiana State University Press, 2002), p. 17. For an excellent discussion of the two strains see James C. Cobb, *Away Down South: A History of Southern Identity* (New York: Oxford University Press, 2005), esp. ch. 3.
29. For Green see William Pfaff, *The Wrath of Nations: Civilization and the Furies of*

Nationalism (New York: Simon and Schuster, 1993), p. 174. For Green's obituary see *Time Magazine*, August 31, 1998, p. 22. Green once described himself as "a Southerner lost in Europe, no matter what I do."
30. Norrell, *Up from History*, pp. 392–393, 408–410.

◆ CHAPTER 1

The Road to
True Freedom:
African American
Alternatives in the
New South

meeting (she later returned), perhaps because he feared that she was too strident, or because she opposed so many of the organization's offices being given to whites, or because he feared her popularity and power. It took years for the chasm and the power struggle within the organization to be mended.[31]

Meanwhile, for an increasing number of African Americans, the solution seemed to be to abandon the South entirely. Beginning around the time of World War I (1917–1918), a growing number of African Americans migrated to the industrial cities of the Northeast, Midwest, and West Coast (Source 6). But there, too, they met racial hostility and racially inspired riots.

In the North, African Americans could vote and thereby influence public policy. By the late 1940s, it had become clear that northern urban African American voters, by their very number, could force politicians to deal with racial discrimination. By the 1950s, it seemed equally evident that the South would have to change

its racial policies, if not willingly then by force. It took federal courts, federal marshals, and occasionally federal troops, but the crust of discrimination in the South began to be broken in the 1960s. Attitudes changed slowly, but the white southern politician draped in the Confederate flag, and calling for resistance to change became a figure of the past. Although much work still needed to be done, the Civil Rights Movement brought profound change to the South, laying the groundwork for more changes ahead. Indeed, by the 1960s, the industrialization and prosperity (largely through in-migration) of the Sunbelt seemed to show that Grady's dream of a New South might become a reality.

Yet, for all the hopeful indications (black voting and office holding in the South, for instance), in many ways the picture still was a somber one. By the 1970s, several concerned observers, both black and white, feared that the poorest 30 percent of all black families, instead of climbing slowly up the economic ladder, were in the process of forming a permanent underclass, complete with a social pathology that included crime, drugs, violence, and grinding poverty. Equally disturbing in the 1980s was a new wave of racial intolerance among whites, a phenomenon that even invaded many American colleges and universities. In short, although much progress had been made since the turn of the nineteenth century, in many ways, as in the New South, the dream of equality and tolerance remained over the horizon.[32]

31. For Trotter see David L. Lewis, *W. E. B. DuBois: A Biography* (New York: Henry Holt & Co., 2009), pp. 78–79 passim; Norrell, *Up from History*, pp. 6–7. Trotter graduated from Harvard in 1895, the first man of color to be awarded a Phi Beta Kappa key. The story of the DuBois-Wells conflict at the May 1909 meeting has been often told. See Lewis, *W. E. B. DuBois*, p. 259; Patricia A. Schechter, *Ida B. Wells-Barnett and American Reform, 1880–1930* (Chapel Hill: University of North Carolina Press, 2001), pp. 136–137; Linda O. McMurry, *To Keep the Waters Troubled: The Life of Ida B. Wells* (New York: Oxford University Press, 1998), pp. 280–282; and Giddings, *Ida*, pp. 474–479. Mary White Ovington, a white leader in the NAACP, later wrote that Wells-Barnett was "perhaps not fitted to accept the restraint of organization." See Ovington's *The Walls Came Tumbling Down* (New York: Schocken Books, 1947), p 106.

32. For an excellent account, see Isabel Wilkerson, *The Warmth of Other Suns: The Epic*

By this time, of course, Wells, Washington, Turner, DuBois, and Harper were dead. Wells continued to write militant articles for the African American press, became deeply involved in the women's suffrage movement, and carried on a successful crusade to prevent the racial segregation of the Chicago city schools. She died in Chicago in 1931. For his part, Washington publicly clung to his notion of self-help while secretly supporting more aggressive efforts to gain political rights for African Americans. He died in Tuskegee, Alabama, in 1915.

Turner's dream of thousands of blacks moving to Africa never materialized. In response, he grew more strident and critical of African Americans who opposed his ideas. In 1898, Turner raised a storm of protest when his essay "God Is a Negro" was published. The essay began, "We have as much right . . . to believe that God is a Negro, as you buckra, or white, people have to believe that God is a fine looking, symmetrical and ornamented white man."[33] He died while on a speaking trip to Canada in 1915. As for DuBois, he eventually turned away from his championship of a "Talented Tenth" in favor of more mass protests. As a harbinger of many African Americans of the 1960s and 1970s, he embraced pan-Africanism, combining it with his long-held Marxist ideas. He died in Ghana on the midnight before the historic March on Washington of August 28, 1963. DuBois's death was announced to the 250,000 who attended the event just a few minutes before the Rev. Martin Luther King, Jr., began his "I Have a Dream" speech. To many people, the two events taking place on the same day represented a symbolic passing of the torch of African American leadership from DuBois to King.[34]

Harper was one of the most popular poets of her time. After her husband's death, she became increasingly vocal on feminist issues; was a friend and ally of Susan B. Anthony; and, in 1866, delivered a moving address before the National Women's Rights Convention. She died in Philadelphia, Pennsylvania, from heart disease in 1911. Her home has been preserved as a national historic landmark.

In their time, Wells, Washington, Turner, DuBois, and Harper were important and respected figures. Although often publicly at odds with one another, they shared the same dream of African Americans living with pride and dignity in a world that recognized them as equal men and women. In an era in which few people championed the causes of African Americans in the New South, these five spokespersons stood out as courageous individuals.

Story of America's Great Migration (New York: Random House, 2010).

33. Redkey, *Respect Black*, pp. 176–177.

34. Lewis, *W. E. B. DuBois*, pp. 1–4.

CHAPTER

2

Rose Cohen Comes to America: Living and Remembering the Immigrant Experience

♦

The Problem

In 1892, twelve-year-old Rahel Gollup made a harrowing journey, leaving behind her mother and siblings and all she knew in Czarist Russia to travel over four thousand miles to America. Though sorrowful and frightened, she was not alone and not without purpose. Her father, Avrom Gollup, who had fled Russia a year and a half before, awaited her in New York City. He had worked tirelessly and saved every possible penny to pay the passage for Rahel and her aunt Masha. The two females traveled together, escaping Russian authorities, fending off criminals, and enduring deprivation and seasickness during their long Atlantic crossing. At times, Rahel and Masha feared they might not survive their effort to reach the United States. But at last they did. Rahel was reunited with her father, and soon she set to work alongside him in New York City's booming garment industry. Their work was hard, long, poorly compensated, and sometimes dangerous. They continued to save their money and

a year later managed to bring Rahel's mother and siblings to America, too.

Rahel Gollup grew up in the Lower East Side of New York City, during a time of profound change. Her immigrant odyssey—making a perilous passage to America, laboring in the sweatshops of New York City, struggling to maintain her Jewish faith, and finding a place in her new country—left deep impressions that time did not erase. In 1918, at the age of thirty-eight, she could still recall with remarkable clarity the sights and sounds and the events and emotions of her coming-of-age experience. Married then, and with a new, more American-sounding name—Rose Cohen—she published an autobiography, called *Out of the Shadow*.[1]

1. As you will discover later in the chapter, soon after her arrival in America, Rahel Gollup took a different first name: Ruth. This was common among immigrants. Her father, Avrom, became known as Abraham, and her mother, whose Russian name was never given in the book, was called Annie after she emigrated. The autobiography ends before Rahel/

The evidence in this chapter consists of excerpts from that autobiography, still touching and relatable a century later. Reading this firsthand account of one girl's life in late nineteenth- and early twentieth-century America will provide the foundation for investi-gating the chapter's central question: **What can Rose Cohen's autobiography reveal about immigrant experiences in America?** But, as you will discover, this question is not so simple and clear-cut as it might seem.

Background

The decades between the 1880s and the 1910s were marked by unprecedented industrialization, both in the United States and in countries around the world. This global move toward mechanization of labor and mass production of goods changed not only how people worked but also how—and where—they lived.

The United States experienced the highest rate of economic development in the world during these decades. After the Civil War, America was better poised to ex-ploit a greater supply of natural resourc-es than virtually any other country: coal, timber, oil, land for commercial farming, and raising livestock. By the early twen-tieth century, the United States ranked first in world markets in steel, timber, oil, textiles, wheat, and meat.

Immigrants made possible America's move to the forefront of industrializa-tion.[2] No period in world history saw greater movement of people across the globe, and no country attracted more immigrants than the United States. In the eyes of many potential emigrants, the United States offered more jobs and greater safety than their home countries. In America, they saw the promise of being part of the nation's flourishing industrial economy, of en-joying political and religious freedom, and of building a brighter future.

In the decades after the Civil War, im-migrants came from southern and east-ern Europe, from Asia, and indeed from around the globe to fill jobs in America's booming industrial cities. Around fif-teen million newcomers migrated to the United States between 1865 and 1900, and that pattern increased in the first decades of the twentieth century. To be sure, American citizens left the country-side to move to industrializing cities, too. This domestic farm-to-factory migration played a crucial role in the growth of these cities' populations and industries, but the majority of new city dwellers moved from other countries.

Northeastern and midwestern cit-ies saw the greatest expansion. Boston,

Ruth married, and throughout the text she re-fers to herself as Ruth. However, she published the book under her married surname with yet another first name: Rose Cohen. *Out of the Shadow* is available as a Google book as well as in a modern print edition, with an excellent introduction by historian Thomas Dublin, pub-lished by Cornell University Press in 1995.
2. The Library of Congress maintains an excel-lent website on the history of immigration in America: http://www.loc.gov/teachers/classroom-materials/presentationsandactivities/presenta-tions/immigration/index.html. Also at the Library of Congress website, you can view films made of early twentieth-century life in New York City.

◆ CHAPTER 2

Rose Cohen
Comes to
America: Living
and Remembering
the Immigrant
Experience

Philadelphia, Chicago, St. Louis, and Milwaukee all had unprecedented population growth in the last decades of the nineteenth century. New York City alone attracted over one million immigrants between 1880 and 1910. The city's foreign-born population grew from 567,812 in 1870 to 902,643 in 1890 to nearly two million in 1910. By 1910, immigrants and their American-born children comprised 75 percent of the population of New York City as well as of Chicago, Detroit, and Boston.[3]

The work that immigrants found in their new country was often disappointing and exploitative. Immigrants struggling to learn English and unfamiliar with U.S. employment practices were especially vulnerable to the corrupt tactics of employers and hiring agents. Factory work could be very dangerous, and workers—especially immigrants—enjoyed few protections. In the late nineteenth century, the United States had the highest rate of workplace injuries and deaths of any industrial country. Housing conditions were also bleak. Most immigrants to American cities could afford to live only in dangerously overcrowded tenements, with little natural light and few places for children to play. (In 1900, the neighborhood that Rahel Gollup's family lived in, the Lower East Side, contained seven hundred people per acre, making it the most crowded neighborhood in the world.) Despite reform efforts to clean up water supplies and develop sewage systems and

garbage collection, epidemics of diseases routinely swept through working-class and immigrant neighborhoods.

But as difficult as life could be in the United States, many immigrants found it a better place to make a future than the country they left. In addition to the "pulls" of jobs and an imagined new start in America, factors in their country of origin often provided powerful "pushes" for immigrants. Political instability, joblessness, poverty, crop failures and famine, violence, and religious and ethnic persecution could all influence the decision to emigrate. The pushes and pulls varied by country of origin, by class and religion and ethnicity, and even by individual.

In the case of Russian Jewish families like Rahel Gollup's, we can make some general conclusions about why they moved to New York City in the early 1890s by looking at life in Russia.[4] Rahel and her family lived, as did most Jews in Czarist Russia, in the Pale of Settlement, a region between the Black Sea and the Baltic Sea, along the borders of Prussia and Austria-Hungary. The Pale was created in the late eighteenth century, after the partition of Poland meant that large numbers of Jews now lived in Russian-controlled territory. From the 1770s and the expansion into Poland until the 1880s, imperial authorities struggled with defining the place of Jews in

---

3. Those curious about immigration history and immigrants' experiences may want to start with an excellent and wide-ranging reader, which blends interpretive essays by scholars with primary sources: David A. Gerber and Alan M. Kraut, eds., *American Immigration and Ethnicity* (New York: Palgrave Macmillan, 2005).

4. For more firsthand accounts of Jews in Russia during this era, see Chaeran Y. Freeze and Jay M. Harris, eds., *Everyday Jewish Life in Imperial Russia: Select Documents, 1772–1914* (Lebanon, NH: University Press of New England, 2013). For Jewish immigrant women, see Susan A. Glenn, *Daughters of the Shtetl: Life and Labor in the Immigrant Generation* (Ithaca: Cornell University Press, 1990). And for the Lower East Side, see Hasia R. Diner, *Lower East Side Memories: A Jewish Place in America* (Princeton: Princeton University Press, 2000).

Russia. At times, they sought to better integrate Jews—who had long been persecuted across Europe—in order to promote their allegiance to Russia and therefore foster stability on Russia's western borders. These attempts at integration were highly selective, however. Government policies distinguished between skilled and unskilled Jewish men and women; only the former could usually move out of the Pale of Settlement. At other times, Russian authorities enforced rigid codes defining which jobs Jews could hold and where they could live. The only way to escape exclusion and persecution was to abandon Judaism and convert to Orthodox Christianity. But their faith was central to the lives of Jewish men and women living in Czarist Russian: the foundation not only of their religion but also their cultural identity and family life.

Imperial Russian treatment of Jews took a sharp and dangerous turn in the decade before Rahel's family emigrated. In 1882, the "May Laws"—a supposedly temporary set of laws that actually lasted for decades—even more strictly circumscribed Jewish residency outside the Pale and forbade Jews from acquiring mortgages or property deeds. A few years later, more restrictions followed, including quotas for Jewish involvement in government and many professions and attendance at universities. The year Rahel's father left, twenty thousand Jews living in Moscow were expelled and forced to move to the Pale. Violent pogroms grew out of these policies, with Jewish businesses and homes attacked and individuals being beaten, raped, and murdered. In addition to this state-sanctioned anti-Semitism, industrial changes pushed many Russian Jewish artisans into unskilled work and poverty. And then, a famine swept Russia in 1891–1892, and four hundred thousand people died.

Between 1880 and 1914, over two million Jews fled Russia. This was nearly one-third of the Jewish population of Russia. Leaving was not easy, however. Despite widespread discrimination against Jews, the Russian government closely monitored emigration. Because of these emigration controls, Jews could not obtain passports and emigration papers without proper documentation, which included certification from local police that the emigrant had no criminal record and no outstanding civil suits. Jews hoping to leave Russia also had to submit high fees with their paperwork and sometimes pay drummed-up and exorbitant fines. Or, they could try to flee in secrecy, which is how Rahel and Masha were able to leave the Pale of Settlement. Avrom Gollup left secretly, too, but he endured an even greater ordeal than Rahel and Masha. Unable to acquire a passport, he resolved to make the trip covertly. But he was arrested and returned to his village for prosecution. He managed to escape authorities and, on his second attempt, board a ship for America.

Like tens of thousands of other Jewish emigrants, Rahel's father set his sights on New York City, and the Lower East Side in particular. It was a Jewish neighborhood by 1890, the largest and most well known in the United States. The Lower East Side was terribly overcrowded and poor, but it was safer than the Pale of Settlement and home to a thriving community. Synagogues and mutual aid societies welcomed newcomers, and schools stood ready to educate their children. Established members of the community ran businesses, banks, and social clubs—all Jewish owned and operated. During the industrial era, New York and other major U.S. cities became

◆ CHAPTER 2

Rose Cohen
Comes to
America: Living
and Remembering
the Immigrant
Experience

home to countless such ethnic and immigrant neighborhoods: everything from Chinatown to Little Italy. Although life in these neighborhoods was difficult and dangerous and sometimes deadly, immigrants could start to fulfill the promise of a new life in the United States.

Appreciating the world that Rahel Gollup left behind as a twelve-year-old girl is the first crucial step to understanding her autobiography. Alongside her vivid accounts of life in the Lower East Side and her work in New York's garment industry, her religious faith and her memories of Russia will enable you to begin to see what her autobiography reveals about immigrant experiences in America.

◆

The Method

In this chapter you will be using a firsthand, individual account—one woman's story about her life—to gain insight into a larger pattern in U.S. history: the unprecedented migration into America's industrializing cities in the late nineteenth and early twentieth centuries. But before you read Rose Cohen's work, you need to think about the medium as well as the message.

Autobiographies and memoirs along with diaries can connect readers to the past in rare and compelling ways.[5] Firsthand accounts often have an immediacy and a relatability that many other kinds of historical sources cannot match. Autobiographers, memoirists, and diarists can transport readers into the historical moment, bringing to life episodes that might otherwise seem flat or abstract. The very best firsthand writing humanizes and personalizes the past, forging a connection between the present-day reader and the historical writer. Think, for example, about the transcendent power of Anne Frank's diary to enable readers to understand what it was like to try and survive in Nazi Germany. Other individual accounts seem to perfectly exemplify an era. Benjamin Franklin's autobiography is a classic example; historians often think of him as the "first American" because of the riveting story he told of his self-determination, practicality, and achievement. Likewise, Anne Moody's autobiography, *Coming of Age in Mississippi*, movingly captured the desire for young African Americans in the mid-twentieth-century South to end racial segregation and the barrage of violence they withstood as a consequence.[6]

On the other hand, individual accounts of the past such as Rose Cohen's cannot, by their very nature, convey aggregate historical changes or societal patterns. Historians must consult census records to chart the numbers

---

5. The line between autobiography and memoir, both written for publication, can be blurry. Autobiographies typically cover the span of a life—from birth or first memories to near the time of the book's publication. Memoirs, also self-authored, generally focus on a discrete episode or experience in a writer's life. Memoirs also tend to be more personal and less linear than autobiographies. Diaries, though sometimes published, often after the writer has died, are personal writings not expressly intended for publication.

6. Anne Frank's diary, usually published as *The Diary of a Young Girl*; *The Autobiography of Benjamin Franklin*; and Anne Moody's *Coming of Age in Mississippi* are all widely available in varied editions.

of immigrants who moved to America, governmental debates and legislation to understand immigration policy, and statistics to explain wealth distribution and population density.

It will also be important for you to consider the differences and the links between history and biography: the story of the past versus the experiences of an individual. Single-subject accounts, whether written by individuals about their own past (autobiography and memoir) or by historians and journalists studying individual historical figures (biography), can be stirring and compelling. But they can also lack distance and perspective, seeing the world writ small in the life of one person.

Insights gained from firsthand accounts of the past can vary according to the gender, age, religion, and ethnicity of the writer. For example, Rose Cohen's autobiography tells us a great deal about the experiences of Russian Jews in turn-of-the-century New York City. We can see, too, in her coming-of-age conflicts with her parents and her new ideas about acceptable women's roles, some patterns commonplace with young female immigrants.[7] There are larger issues she raises, too: the economic hardships that immigrants often faced when they arrived in America; the discrimination and even violent assaults they sometimes endured from native-born citizens; and their struggles to balance Old World traditions, including religion, against the pressure to become "Americanized." Most immigrants coming to

America in the late nineteenth and early twentieth centuries dealt with such issues irrespective of ethnicity or place of settlement. (Many of these patterns remain common in immigrant experiences in the early twenty-first century.)

On the other hand, there were important differences in immigrant experiences that you should keep in mind as you read the following excerpts. For example, in the industrializing era Jewish immigration was mostly a family affair, as was the case with the Gollup family. Men usually migrated first, but children and wives and extended family soon followed. Conversely, many Italian men emigrated in this era without plans to bring their families; they wanted to earn money and eventually return home.

Do not forget that Rose Cohen's autobiography was written for publication. Attention to a public audience invariably shapes what stories get told in any autobiography, how the person tells them, and what she or he leaves out. As Winston Churchill famously said about his place in accounts of World War II politics and diplomacy, "History will be kind to me, for I intend to write it myself."

The fact that Cohen published her autobiography makes it different from other firsthand, individually based sources such as personal letters or a diary. Those primary sources also have an audience, of course. Letters were meant to be shared, often with an individual but sometimes more broadly. Some diarists write to create a legacy. But even if a diary is meant for the writer's eyes only, not everything is put to the page; the stories we tell ourselves about our lives are always selective. Writing for a public audience, however, can shape that selectivity, even in ways the author may not intend or even realize. So, when historians use

7. For the experiences of Chinese women enduring especially virulent racism while exercising greater rights, see Judy Yung, *Unbound Feet: A Social History of Chinese Women in San Francisco* (Berkeley: University of California Press, 1995).

◆ CHAPTER 2

Rose Cohen
Comes to
America: Living
and Remembering
the Immigrant
Experience

an autobiography written for publication as a primary source, they must be careful to consider how the form of writing influences the information in the writing.

Cohen wrote her book in her thirties, so she was working from memory, as do all autobiographers. This adds yet another layer to the puzzle of how to use her writing as an historical source.

So, as you consider the central question in this chapter, remember that it contains three interrelated issues: Rose Cohen, the immigrant experience, and autobiography. Thinking about these three matters makes the question more complicated but also more interesting and more revealing of the historian's craft. As you read the Evidence section, think about:

1. The nature of the source: What are the benefits and limits of a firsthand, self-reported life story, recreated from memory and for publication?

2. The pros and cons of individual experiences to understanding history: How much can one person tell historians about an era? What is the difference between history and biography?

3. Rose Cohen's life: While weighing the source and the individual case study, analyze the contents of Cohen's life story. What can we learn from her about immigrant experiences in America in the late nineteenth and early twentieth centuries?

◆

The Evidence

Source from Rose Cohen, *Out of the Shadow* (New York: George H. Doran Company, 1918), pp. 35, 48–49, 69–70, 73–74, 81–82, 84, 104–105, 112–113, 115, 142–143, 156–157, 175, 246–248.

Rahel begins her autobiography with her earliest memories of childhood in Russia. She was the eldest of five siblings, and her family lived with her paternal grandparents in a small village in the Pale of Settlement. Her father, Avrom, was a tailor by trade. She and her siblings were taught to sew, Rahel wrote, "as soon as we were able to hold a needle." She also remembered herself as an especially pious child. Her father's departure for America was a signal event in her life. His first letter from America brought word that he was boarding with a Jewish family and earning $10 per week. Avrom soon made plans for Rahel and his unmarried sister Masha, who was in her twenties, to come to America. Rahel, he predicted, could earn $3 per week and speed the effort to make enough money to pay passage for the other members of the family. The story picks up next, when the family receives the tickets and instructions for Rahel and Masha to come to America.

I do not know whether I considered myself fortunate in going to America or not. But I do remember that when I convinced myself, by looking at the tickets often, that it was not a dream like many others I had had, that I would really start for America in a month or six weeks, I felt a great joy. Of course I was a little ashamed of this joy. I saw that mother was unhappy. And grandmother's sorrow, very awful, in its calmness, was double now. . . .

[When the time to depart came, Rahel and Masha grieved at leaving their relatives and feared the dangerous passage to America. Rahel's mother accompanied the two on part of the journey.]

As we jogged off I heard uncle calling after us, "Don't forget God." And it seemed to me that the frogs from the neighbouring swamps took up the words and croaked, "Don't forget God! Don't forget God!"

The road was very uneven, and every time the wheels passed over a stone I heard Aunt Masha's head bump against the wagon. Mother gave her some more straw to put there, but she refused.

"What," she said, peevishly, "is this pain or any other pain that I have ever had, compared with what my mother suffers to-night." And so she let her head bump as if that would give her mother relief. For a long time I felt Aunt Masha's body shaking with sobs. But by degrees it grew quieter, the breathing became regular, and she slept. Then I saw mother, who I thought was also asleep, sit up. She took some straw from her side of the wagon and bending over me towards Aunt Masha she raised her head gently and spread the straw under it. . . .

[Masha and Rahel eventually made their way to Hamburg, Germany, for their ocean crossing. They had to stay a week in a fetid building run by the steamer company and sleep on bug-infested cots. After a perilous voyage, Rahel and Masha arrived in New York City. At first Rahel did not recognize her father, but then they all enjoyed a joyous and tearful reunion. As Rahel recalled, "the three of us stood clinging to one another."]

From Castle Garden[8] we drove to our new home in a market wagon filled with immigrants' bedding. Father tucked us in among the bundles, climbed up beside the driver himself and we rattled off over the cobbled stone pavement, with the noon sun beating down on our heads.

As we drove along I looked about in bewilderment. My thoughts were chasing each other. I felt a thrill: "Am I really in America at last?" But the next moment it would be checked and I felt a little disappointed, a little homesick. Father was so changed. I hardly expected to find him in his black long tailed coat in which he left home. But of course yet with his same full grown beard and earlocks. Now instead I saw a young man with a closely cut beard and no sign of earlocks. As I looked at him I could scarcely believe my eyes. Father had been the most pious Jew in our neighbourhood. I wondered was it true then as Mindle said that "in America one at once became a libertine"?

Father's face was radiantly happy. Every now and then he would look over his shoulder and smile. But he soon guessed what troubled me for after a while he began to talk in a quiet, reassuring manner. He told me he would take me to

---

8. Castle Garden was an immigration center that preceded Ellis Island. After 1892 Ellis Island replaced Castle Garden as the primary site for immigration to New York City and, more generally, the entire United States.

◆ CHAPTER 2

Rose Cohen
Comes to
America: Living
and Remembering
the Immigrant
Experience

his own shop and teach me part of his own trade. He was a men's coat finisher. He made me understand that if we worked steadily and lived economically we should soon have money to send for those at home. "Next year at this time," he smiled, "you yourself may be on the way to Castle Garden to fetch mother and the children." So I too smiled at the happy prospect, wiped some tears away and resolved to work hard. . . .

[Rahel, her father, and her aunt boarded with the Felesberg family. Mr. Felesberg, like Avrom Gollup, worked in a factory in the garment industry. As was commonplace among Jewish immigrant families, Mrs. Felesberg took in sewing work.]

From Mrs. Felesberg we learned at once the more serious side of life in America. Mrs. Felesberg was the woman with whom we were rooming. A door from our room opened into her tiny bedroom and then led into the only other room where she sat a great part of the day finishing pants which she brought in big bundles from a shop, and rocking the cradle with one foot. She always made us draw our chairs quite close to her and she spoke in a whisper scarcely ever lifting her weak peering eyes from her work. When she asked us how we liked America, and we spoke of it with praise, she smiled a queer smile. "Life here is not all that it appears to the 'green horn,'" she said. She told us that her husband was a presser on coats and earned twelve dollars when he worked a full week. Aunt Masha thought twelve dollars was a good deal. Again Mrs. Felesberg smiled. "No doubt it would be," she said, "where you used to live. You had your own house, and most of the food came from the garden. Here you will have to pay for everything; the rent!" she sighed, "for the light, for every potato, every grain of barley.". . .

Perhaps it was due to these talks that I soon noticed how late my father worked. When he went away in the morning it was still dark, and when he came home at night the lights in the halls were out. It was after ten o'clock. I thought that if mother and the children were here they would scarcely see him.

One night when he came home and as he sat at the table eating his rice soup, which he and Aunt Masha had taught me to cook, I sat down on the cot and asked timidly, knowing that he was impatient of questions, "Father, does everybody in America live like this? Go to work early, come home late, eat and go to sleep? And the next day again work, eat, and sleep? Will I have to do that too? Always?"

Father looked thoughtful and ate two or three mouthfuls before he answered. "No," he said smiling. "You will get married.". . .

[Soon, Masha was offered a job caring for young children, which required living with the family that hired her. When Rahel and Avrom went to visit Masha, they were surprised to hear the woman who employed Masha call her a new, American name: Jennie. This was, as Rahel would soon learn firsthand, a common occurrence.]

On the following day father came home at noon and took me along to the shop where he worked. We climbed the dark, narrow stairs of a tenement house on

Monroe Street and came into a bright room filled with noise. I saw about five or six men and a girl. The men turned and looked at us when we passed. I felt scared and stumbled. One man asked in surprise:

"Avrom, is this your daughter? Why, she is only a little girl!"

My father smiled. "Yes," he said, "but wait till you see her sew."

He placed me on a high stool opposite the girl, laid a pile of pocket flaps on the little narrow table between us, and showed me how to baste.

All afternoon I sat on my high stool, a little away from the table, my knees crossed tailor fashion, basting flaps. As I worked I watched the things which I could see by just raising my eyes a little. I saw that the girl, who was called Atta, was very pretty.

A big man stood at a big table, examining, brushing and folding coats. There was a window over his table through which the sun came streaming in, showing millions of specks of dust dancing over the table and circling over his head. He often puffed out his cheeks and blew the dust from him with a great gust so that I could feel his breath at our table.

The machines going at full speed drowned everything in their noise. But when they stopped for a moment I caught the clink of a scissors laid hastily on a table, a short question and answer exchanged, and the pounding of a heavy iron from the back of the room. Sometimes the machines stopped for a whole minute. Then the men looked about and talked. I was always glad when the machines started off again. I felt safer in their noise.

Late in the afternoon a woman came into the shop. She sat down next to Atta and began to sew on buttons. Father, who sat next to me, whispered, "This is Mrs. Nelson, the wife of the big man, our boss. She is a real American."

She, too, was pretty. Her complexion was fair and delicate like a child's. Her upper lip was always covered with shining drops of perspiration. I could not help looking at it all the time.

When she had worked a few minutes she asked father in very imperfect Yiddish: "Well, Mr. -----, have you given your daughter an American name?"

"Not yet," father answered. "What would you call her? Her Yiddish name is Rahel."

"Rahel, Rahel," Mrs. Nelson repeated to herself, thoughtfully, winding the thread around a button; "let me see." The machines were going slowly and the men looked interested.

The presser called out from the back room: "What is there to think about? Rahel is Rachel."

I was surprised at the interest every one showed. Later I understood the reason. The slightest cause for interruption was welcome, it broke the monotony of the long day.

◆ CHAPTER 2

Rose Cohen
Comes to
America: Living
and Remembering
the Immigrant
Experience

Mrs. Nelson turned to me: "Don't let them call you Rachel. Every loafer who sees a Jewish girl shouts 'Rachel' after her. And on Cherry Street where you live there are many saloons and many loafers. How would you like Ruth[9] for a name?"

I said I should like to be called Ruth. . . .

. . . I liked my work and learned it easily, and father was pleased with me. As soon as I knew how to baste pocket-flaps he began to teach me how to baste the coat edges. This was hard work. The double ply of overcoat cloth stitched in with canvas and tape made a very stiff edge. My fingers often stiffened with pain as I rolled and basted the edges. Sometimes a needle or two would break before I could do one coat. Then father would offer to finish the edge for me. But if he gave me my choice I never let him. At these moments I wanted so to master the thing myself that I felt my whole body trembling with the desire. And with my habit of personifying things, I used to bend over the coat on my lap, force the obstinate and squeaking needle, wet with perspiration, in and out of the cloth and whisper with determination: "No, you shall not get the best of me!" When I succeeded I was so happy that father, who often watched me with a smile, would say, "Rahel, your face is shining. Now rest a while." He always told me to rest after I did well. I loved these moments. I would push my stool closer to the wall near which I sat, lean my back against it, and look about the shop. . . .

[The 1892 presidential election pitted Grover Cleveland, a Democrat from New York and former president, against Benjamin Harrison, a Republican from Indiana and the sitting president. In the nineteenth century, elections sometimes gave rise to anti-immigrant violence, and this was the case on election day in 1892 in New York City. As night fell, "Gentile boys" set fire to mattresses and barrels they piled up outside tenements housing Jewish families. They harassed and assaulted Jewish men making their way home from work. From a window in the tenement, Ruth watched with growing anxiety for her father to come home. She saw the son of a neighbor beaten by a mob. The same mob chased her father, but he made it safely home. Ruth did not linger over what exactly happened to her father, but the event clearly made a deep impression.]

I had seen from the first that Jews were treated roughly on Cherry Street. I had seen the men and boys that stood about the saloons at every corner make ugly grimaces at the passing Jews and throw after them stones and shoes pulled out of the ash cans. I had often seen these "loafers," as we called them, attack a Jewish pedlar, dump his push cart of apples into the gutter, fill their pockets and walk away laughing and eating. I had run for the apples in the gutter, rolling in every direction, and helped to pick them up. I myself had often walked two blocks out of my way to reach home through Montgomery Street where there were three saloons. And yet as soon as I was safe in the house I scarcely gave the matter a second thought. Perhaps it was because to see a Jew maltreated was nothing new

9. Ruth was a very important figure in the Hebrew Bible, a paragon of faith. It is unclear when Ruth changed her name to Rose, or if she just adopted Ruth instead of Rose for the autobiography.

for me. Here where there were so many new and strange things for me to see and understand this was the one familiar thing. I had grown used to seeing strange Jews mistreated whenever they happened to come to our village in Russia.

But after election night I felt differently. I was haunted by the picture of the little old woman's son struggling with the young Irish-Americans near the bonfire, and of my father coming up the stairs, pale and hatless. I was never easy in my mind now except when I was with father. I always sat up at night until he came home; and if he happened to be a few minutes late I was beside myself with fear. I pictured him murdered and burned alive. I listened to every tale about Cherry and Water Streets. I heard that a policeman had been found in a dark hallway with his head stuck into a barrel, smothered to death. And for a time I could think about nothing else.

One Friday afternoon, soon after election, I finished my washing and cleaning early and I went out into the street. I was returning about five o'clock through Clinton Street when I saw a Jewish pedlar with a push cart standing on the corner of Monroe Street and looking about helplessly. I saw him watching me as I came up. When I was near he asked, "Are you Jewish?" I nodded my head and stopped. I saw that his push cart held fish, mixed with chunks of ice. "You can do me a favour," he said in a pleading tone. "You see this handful of fish? This is all my profit. If I could get over to that group of Jewish houses on Cherry Street," he pointed to our tenements, "I could still sell it though it is late. But I dare not pass those loafers hanging around the saloons." "But, what can I do?" I asked. "You can do much," he said with a smile. "They have great respect for a lady in America."

"But—" I began. "That is all right," he said with a wave of the hand. "You look like a lady. And if you will just walk beside me while I am passing the loafers, they won't touch me." I remembered now often having seen Jewish men escorted past dangerous places. And the women would as often be Irish.

I stepped into the gutter, and for greater safety laid my hand on the push cart and walked along beside him. When we were passing the saloon the "loafers" made grimaces and shouted after him, but did not touch him. . . .

[Over the next year, Ruth changes jobs several times. One boss seemed kind at the outset, but then fired her when she refused his sexual advances. Another, who was overtly cruel, suddenly closed his shop without paying the laborers for their work for the week. The excerpt below recounts yet another form of exploitation she endured. She was not yet fifteen years old when all this happened.]

The next morning when I came into the shop at seven o'clock, I saw at once that all the people were there and working as steadily as if they had been at work a long while. I had just time to put away my coat and go over to the table, when the boss shouted gruffly, "Look here, girl, if you want to work here you better come in early. No office hours in my shop." It seemed very still in the room, even the machines stopped. And his voice sounded dreadfully distinct. I

◆ CHAPTER 2

Rose Cohen
Comes to
America: Living
and Remembering
the Immigrant
Experience

hastened into the bit of space between the two men and sat down. He brought me two coats and snapped, "Hurry with these!"

From this hour a hard life began for me. He refused to employ me except by the week. He paid me three dollars and for this he hurried me from early until late. He gave me only two coats at a time to do. When I took them over and as he handed me the new work he would say quickly and sharply, "Hurry!" And when he did not say it in words he looked at me and I seemed to hear even more plainly, "Hurry!" I hurried but he was never satisfied. By looks and manner he made me feel that I was not doing enough. Late at night when the people would stand up and begin to fold their work away and I too would rise feeling stiff in every limb and thinking with dread of our cold empty little room and the uncooked rice, he would come over with still another coat.

"I need it the first thing in the morning," he would give as an excuse. I understood that he was taking advantage of me because I was a child. And now that it was dark in the shop except for the low single gas jet over my table and the one over his at the other end of the room, and there was no one to see, more tears fell on the sleeve lining as I bent over it than there were stitches in it.

I did not soon complain to father. I had given him an idea of the people and the work during the first days. But when I had been in the shop a few weeks I told him, "The boss is hurrying the life out of me." I know now that if I had put it less strongly he would have paid more attention to it. Father hated to hear things put strongly. Besides he himself worked very hard. He never came home before eleven and he left at five in the morning.

He said to me now, "Work a little longer until you have more experience; then you can be independent."

"But if I did piece work, father, I would not have to hurry so. And I could go home earlier when the other people go."

Father explained further, "It pays him better to employ you by the week. Don't you see if you did piece work he would have to pay you as much as he pays a woman piece worker? But this way he gets almost as much work out of you for half the amount a woman is paid."

I myself did not want to leave the shop for fear of losing a day or even more perhaps in finding other work. To lose half a dollar meant that it would take so much longer before mother and the children would come. And now I wanted them more than ever before. . . .

. . . In proportion as life in the shop became harder, it also became harder at home. I had to do the washing and cleaning at night now. One night a week I cleaned and one I washed. I used to hang my dress on a string over Mrs. Felesberg's stove to dry over night. In the morning I pulled it straight and put it right on. The rest of the night I slept. During these days I could not seem to get enough sleep. Sometimes when I remembered how a few months before mother had to chase me to bed with cries and with scoldings it hardly seemed true. That time seemed so far away, so vague, like a dream.

Now on coming into the room I would light the lamp and the kerosene oil stove and put on the soup to cook. Then I would sit down with my knees close to the soap box on which the stove stood, to keep myself warm. But before long my body relaxed, my head grew heavy with the odour of the burning oil and I longed to lie down. I knew that it was bad to go to sleep without supper. Two or three times father woke me. But it was no use, I could not eat then. And so I tried hard to keep awake. But finally I could not resist it. The cot was so near, just a step away. I could touch it with my hand. I would rise a little from the chair and all bent over as I was, I would tumble right in and roll myself in the red comforter, clothes and all. It was on these nights that I began to forget to pray. . . .

[Ruth and her father continued to scrupulously save their earnings to bring her mother and siblings to the United States. At last they had enough money and sent word and tickets to Russia.]

As the days passed and the time drew near for their coming, I became more and more impatient and nervous and found it more difficult than ever to sit in one place in the shop and think about the work. However, I did not always think about it. Often as I sat sewing on buttons or felling a sleeve lining I pictured them on the steamer and went over their whole journey in my mind, sure that it was very much as my own had been. First I saw them jogging along in Makar's straw-lined wagon from our village to Minsk, then travelling by railroad and finally packed into a wagon of mouldy hay and driven through swampy meadows in the dead of night, stealing across the boundary. Though a year had passed I could still feel the Russian soldier's heavy hand on my back, and hear his thick voice demanding, "What have you here?" The answer a jingle of silver coins and the thick voice call, "Drive on!" I pictured them sleeping in the bare, dirty little cots in Hamburg. I saw mother with the four children standing in the large hall all day for a week and waiting for their names to be called. Then I saw them in the midst of a hundred others bent over to one side or stooping under their bundles, passing through a sort of tunnel. Meekly, and looking neither to right nor to left, they followed a uniformed person. "Tramp, tramp, tramp," I heard the dull sound of many feet and two onlookers calling to each other, "The Emigrants!" and the echo calling back, "The Emigrants!"

"But now," I thought joyfully, "they are on the steamer, very near America. How will mother like America? Will she be much shocked at father's and my impiety?" For I too was not so pious now. I still performed some of the little religious rites assigned to a girl, but mechanically, not with the ever-present consciousness of God. There were moments of deep devotion, but they were rare.

Sometimes when I thought of it I felt sad, I felt as if I had lost something precious. . . .

◆ CHAPTER 2

Rose Cohen
Comes to
America: Living
and Remembering
the Immigrant
Experience

[The joy of her mother and siblings' arrival was tempered by two setbacks. Ruth developed the first of several, mostly undefined illnesses. And the United States entered a depression in 1893. Soon, the Gollup's neighborhood was experiencing widespread joblessness. Ruth and her father did not escape the lay-offs.]

Every day now all over the city shops were being closed. Nevertheless father went out every morning, always looking bright, and hopeful of finding at least a few hours' work. He would return at noon looking not quite so bright. He was not discouraged, but as week after week passed, his face grew thinner and the smile that had always lit up his whole face became rare. But still he spoke cheerfully. "This can't last much longer," he would say. "There must be an end to it. It is almost two months now."

All this weighed more heavily on mother. Her face was paler, her features stood out sharply and her eyes seemed to have gone deeper into her head. She was always serious and now she looked as if a dreadful calamity were hanging over us. "Among strangers in a strange country." She began counting the potatoes she put into the pot and would ask the children over and over again when they wanted more bread, "Are you sure you want it?"

Two months passed and a great change seemed to have come over the people. The closed shops turned the workers out into the streets and they walked about idly, looking haggard and shabby. Often as I sauntered along through Cherry or Monroe Street I would meet some one with whom I had worked. We avoided each other. We felt ashamed of being seen idle. We felt ashamed of our shabby clothes. We avoided each other's eyes to save each other pain and humiliation. The greeting of those who could not possibly avoid one another was something like this, "What! A holiday in your shop, too?" Nor would they remain talking long. Both would stand looking away gloomily for a few minutes and finally with a short nod they would walk apart dejectedly. . . .

[With the economic crisis worsening and Ruth and Abraham unemployed, the Gollup family took in boarders to pay their rent, and Ruth's younger sister Leah made some money running errands. Ruth's parents hated the idea of her becoming a servant, but they ultimately had no other choice. After she and her father had been three months without work, Ruth accepted an offer to live with and work as a maid for the Corlove family.]

Living with the Corloves was a great change for me. At home I had been spared all the hard work for my health had continued to be poor.[10] But now I was suddenly treated not only as if my strength were normal but unlimited. I rose when the men rose to go to work, and as they had to come into the kitchen to wash at the sink, I would creep into the niche behind the stove to dress. On

10. It was quite common for child laborers to suffer from chronic, job-related illnesses. Ruth was often sick from this point forward in her autobiography. The nature of her illnesses was rarely defined, though at one point she was diagnosed with anemia. During several illnesses, doctors prescribed rest, a better diet, and fresh air—things in short supply for immigrant child laborers.

Monday morning, as I crouched there, I listened for Mrs. Corlove's footsteps and the thud of the big bundle of clothes on the floor. When I heard it I crept out quickly, whether completely dressed or not, and my work began. I carried up the coal from the cellar and made the fire, I lifted the boiler half filled with clothes, I washed and scrubbed all day long. When night came I crept gladly in between the two soiled quilts on my chairs.[11] And though the house was full of life, for the gas lights flared, the people talked and the children ran races from room to room, I slept. Tuesday and Wednesday I ironed. On Thursday I scaled the fish and plucked and cleaned the fowl. Soon my hands grew red and coarse and I was no longer repelled at touching soiled or mushy things. I would run out to the store with my hands covered with flour or black with the scrubbing water, for Mrs. Corlove could never wait for me to wash them. . . .

[Ruth much preferred factory work to being a household servant. Even if working in the garment industry was grueling, she could be with her own family in the evenings. During the daytime, she worked alongside others who respected her, she wrote, "as an equal and a companion." As a servant, she continued, "I had to be constantly in the presence of people who looked down upon me as an inferior." Ruth quit the Corloves as soon as the economy rebounded and went back to industrial work.

When Ruth was sixteen, her parents started to search out for her a suitable mate. She consented to the match they made but then broke the engagement, much to her father's disappointment. She also fell terribly ill and was treated for a time at the Henry Street Settlement, founded and run by Lillian D. Wald, a nurse and progressive reformer who pioneered public health nursing.[12] Ruth was eventually sent to Presbyterian Hospital for three months. That experience, along with the connection she formed with Lillian Wald at Henry Street, changed her life, as she explains in this part of her autobiography.]

Although almost five years had passed since I had started for America it was only now that I caught a glimpse of it. For though I was in America I had lived in practically the same environment which we brought from home. Of course there was a difference in our joys, in our sorrows, in our hardships, for after all this was a different country; but on the whole we were still in our village in Russia. A child that came to this country and began to go to school had taken the first step into the New World. But the child that was put into the shop remained in the old environment with the old people, held back by the old traditions, held back by illiteracy. Often it was years before he could stir away from it, sometimes it would take a lifetime. Sometimes, too, it happened as in fairy tales, that a hand was held out to you and you were helped out.

In my own case it was through the illness which had seemed such a misfortune that I had stirred out of Cherry Street. But now that I had had a glimpse of the New World, a revolution took place in my whole being. I was filled with a desire

11. The entire time she worked for the Corlove family, she slept on two chairs pushed together.
12. To learn more about Wald's life and work, see Doris Groshen Daniels, *Always a Sister: The Feminism of Lillian D. Wald* (New York: The Feminist Press of the City University of New York, 1989).

◆ CHAPTER 2

Rose Cohen
Comes to
America: Living
and Remembering
the Immigrant
Experience

to get away from the whole old order of things. And I went groping about blindly, stumbling, suffering and making others suffer. And then through the experience, intelligence and understanding of other beings a little light came to me and I was able to see that the Old World was not all dull and the new not all glittering. And then I was able to stand between the two, with a hand in each.

The first thing that I can recall after I came from the hospital, is a feeling of despondency. The rooms seemed smaller and dingier than they had been. In the evening the lamp burned more dimly. And there was a general look of hopelessness over everything. It was in every face, it was in every corner of our dull home as well as in all the other homes that I saw. It was in every sound that came in from the street, in every sigh that I heard in the house. I saw the years stretching ahead of me, always the same, and I wept bitterly. I had never been so aware of it all.

In the shop where I found work now it was as at home. As I looked at the men I could not help comparing them with those other men. To the little insinuating jokes and stories I listened now, not with resignation as before but with anger. "Why should this be? Why should they talk like that?" And I was filled with a blinding dislike for the whole class of tailors.

But I did not give my entire thought to what I saw about me. As the days passed I became aware that I was waiting for something, for what I could scarcely say. Away in the back of my head there was this thought, "Surely this would not end here. Would this be all I would see of that other world outside of Cherry Street?" And I waited from day to day.

In the meantime I filled up the days at work with dreaming of that other life I had seen. I thought a good deal about that fine old man the minister. His words and his voice had remained fresh in my mind. Of course I must not breathe a word at home about him, about the New Testament.[13] This necessity for secrecy soon led to other little secret thoughts and actions. It soon occurred to me, "Why should I not read the New Testament if I want to? Why should I not do anything I like? If four months ago father thought me old enough to get married, then I am certainly old enough now to decide things for myself." So I stopped consulting mother and began to do little things independently. It was not hard to do this for during the three months I had grown away from home a good deal and now with the thought of my experience in which they had no part, every day I was slipping away little by little. . . .

13. Christian missionaries were deeply interested in converting Jewish immigrants. They worked in hospitals, neighborhoods, and schools. At the school Ruth's younger siblings Leah and Ezekiel attended, missionaries gave bread and honey to hungry children who agreed to join in Christian prayers.

Questions to Consider

We hope you found the excerpts from Rose Cohen's published autobiography edifying and engaging. Historians typically see this book as a valuable primary source that offers rich insight into Cohen's life and, more generally, the experiences of Jewish immigrants to America during this era.

It is easy when reading autobiography and memoir to identify with the writer. Readers carry in their hearts books such as *I Know Why the Caged Bird Sings*, by Maya Angelo; *Walden* by Henry David Thoreau; and *North Toward Home*, by Willie Morris.[14] No matter how long it's been, many readers vividly recall when they first encountered Anne Frank's diary and will find these words hauntingly familiar since we know her ultimate fate: "It's a wonder I haven't abandoned all my ideals, they seem so absurd and impractical. Yet I cling to them because I still believe, in spite of everything, that people are truly good at heart. It's utterly impossible for me to build my life on a foundation of chaos, suffering and death. I see the world being slowly transformed into a wilderness, I hear the approaching thunder that, one day, will destroy us, too. I feel the suffering of millions. And yet, when I look up at the sky, I somehow feel that everything will change for the better, that this cruelty too shall end, that peace and tranquility will return once more."

14. Maya Angelou, *I Know Why the Caged Bird Sings* (New York: Random House, 1969); Henry David Thoreau, *Walden; or, Life in the Woods* (Boston: Ticknor and Fields, 1854); and Willie Morris, *North Toward Home* (Boston: Houghton Mifflin, 1967).

But your job as historian is to critically evaluate Rose Cohen's autobiography in particular and first-person accounts of the past more generally. Remember, *critical* does not mean *criticizing*. Your analysis may turn out to be very positive in terms of the usefulness of Cohen's work. But you should develop that opinion based on an analytical and not an emotional reaction.

Before you turn to the specific insight offered in this autobiography, weigh with your classmates the strengths and weaknesses of autobiography and memoir as historical sources. You will want to discuss memory and how reliable memory is when recalling childhood experiences and signal moments in life, including both celebrations and traumas. Also consider how the fact that Cohen wrote for publication affects your perspective on using her autobiography as historical evidence. Would publication make her more careful about confirming that her memory of people, places, and events is accurate? Or would it cause her to erase some and emphasize other parts of her family's past?

Closely related to these matters of memory and audience is the issue of the proper place of individual life stories in the study of history—and the line between biography and history. What are the main differences between historical biography and history? All historians, of course, tell stories about people, individually and collectively. But what can one person's life illuminate or obscure about an historical period, particularly regarding immigration in late nineteenth- and early twentieth-century America?

✦ CHAPTER 2

Rose Cohen
Comes to
America: Living
and Remembering
the Immigrant
Experience

Consider this, too: Do you think long after you have forgotten the statistics about immigration patterns you will remember this personal story? If so, why?

Finally, concentrate your conversation on what precisely you see in this autobiography. What are the most significant events in Rose Cohen's life? How did she and her family work and live? What was different in America than in Russia? What struggles did they confront as they tried to remain part of a traditional Jewish culture while living in a foreign country? What did you learn about ethnic neighborhoods, city life, industrial labor, the treatment of immigrants, and the importance of family and faith to immigrants? How much of what you learned do you think transcends the Lower East Side of New York City, Jewish immigrant communities, and the Gollup family? And, finally, what are the most important ways in which you and your classmates have complicated what started out as a seemingly simple question: What can Rose Cohen's autobiography reveal about immigrant experiences in America?

✦

Epilogue

Through the Henry Street Settlement, Ruth Gollup met a supportive network of female friends, got help with her work problems, her English language skills, and her health, and found a new sense of her place in America—which was exactly what the settlement movement was all about. Settlement houses were begun in England in the 1880s to respond to growing industrial poverty. By 1890 there were over four hundred settlement houses in the United States, nearly half in the industrial centers of New York, Boston, and Chicago. As Henry Street did in New York City, settlement houses throughout the United States provided social services to immigrant families while also trying to teach middle-class values to working-class newcomers. The most famous of these settlement houses was in Chicago: Hull House, run by Jane Addams. As Addams and Wald reflected, most settlement houses were run by women, and they were particularly committed to working with immigrant women within their shared communities.

As the rest of her story unfolded, Ruth took advantage of the opportunities afforded her at Henry Street Settlement to better her education and to spend summers working in Connecticut at a camp for immigrant children, far from the dangers and dreariness of the Lower East Side factories. She was a voracious reader, and her love of books and writing made a great difference in the course of her life.

Ruth struggled, though, with her health, and she was in and out of work as a consequence. To her father's dismay and then outrage, she also became intrigued by Christianity. Ruth even had a romance with a young man who converted to Christianity. He had, his relatives shamefully admitted, spent too much time with the missionaries. Ruth's parents were appalled. In their eyes, a converted Jew was a disgrace and outcast.

The young couple's relationship ended when he went to seminary, much to her family's relief, and she never converted herself. We do not meet her husband, Joseph Cohen, in the autobiography.

Ruth's story closes not with her marriage, which was the source of much emphasis in the last quarter of her book, or even with the start of her writing career, but rather with her family's successes. By 1902, Abraham Gollup had saved enough money to open a small grocery story. His daughter Leah proved a brilliant manager: she was "the most competent and modern" of the siblings, well educated in English and math, and she shepherded the business into quick success. Ruth's brother was educated, too. To his parents' great pride, he studied at Columbia University. As she became a young woman with her own mind and priorities, Ruth often clashed with her father: over religion, romance, and work. But she gave him the last word in her book, as he reflected on his children's lives: "Ah! After all this is America."

When Rose Cohen published her autobiography in 1918, Lillian Wald wrote a glowing review. She predicted *Out of the Shadow* would "interest deeply a good many different kinds of readers" and that it would "be accepted as a social document transcending in value many volumes that have been brought forth by academically trained searchers for data on the conditions that the writer has experienced."[15] Do you think she is right?

Cohen published several short stories between 1918 and 1922, but nothing

thereafter. She died at age forty-five in 1925, perhaps by her own hand. There is some evidence she committed suicide, but the end of her life remains a mystery.

From other kinds of historical evidence, however, we can know a good deal about immigration policy and the treatment of new immigrants in early twentieth-century America. In 1924, the U.S. government passed the Johnson-Reed Act (also known as the Immigration Act of 1924). This legislation set strict quotas on immigration based on the country of origin. In addition to completely excluding Asians, the law privileged western Europeans and made it difficult for eastern European and Jewish families to follow the path taken by the Gollups in the late nineteenth century. Along with the Chinese Exclusion Act of 1882, this 1924 law marked a crucial turning point in U.S. immigration policy. It was slightly altered over the next few decades, but the basic quota system remained in place until 1965. During those same decades, Jews, like African Americans, were also systematically—and legally—excluded from neighborhoods and civic organizations and clubs.

Today, U.S. immigration patterns and policy often center on Latin America rather than eastern Europe. The motivations and experiences of men and women leaving Latin American nations for the United States are distinctive in many important ways. Still, many of the issues raised nearly a century ago in Rose Cohen's autobiography persist today. In particular, generational conflicts and changing gender roles continue to reshape many immigrant families while labor, ethnicity, and class still inform policy debates.

15. Wald quoted in Thomas Dublin, "Introduction" to *Out of the Shadow: A Russian Jewish Girlhood on the Lower East Side* (Ithaca: Cornell University Press, 1995), p. xiv.

3

Who Controls America's Natural Resources? Water Rights, Public Lands, and the Contest over the Hetch Hetchy Valley

◆

The Problem

Until the discovery of gold in California in 1848, San Francisco was just a small trading outpost, with no more than a few hundred residents. But the 1849 Gold Rush attracted thousands upon thousands of ambitious, daring, and desperate newcomers—mostly men. Migrants came overland and by sea, from across the United States, Europe, Central America, and Asia, turning San Francisco into a boomtown nearly overnight. Within two years, the city's population hit twenty-five thousand.

Surrounded on three sides by saltwater, San Francisco struggled in the wake of this population explosion with water demands that taxed the abilities of municipal authorities and private companies alike. There were tremendous profits to be earned by serving San Franciscans' water needs, and public officials and business entrepreneurs experimented with various innovations: they carted barreled water into the city, shipped it on boats, and built flumes and dams. But neither city leaders nor privately held corporations could keep pace with residents' ever-growing water needs. The problem only got bigger every year.

By 1900, San Francisco was home to more than 340,000 people—larger than any city west of the Mississippi except for St. Louis, Missouri, and nearly three and a half times larger than Los Angeles. The mayor of San Francisco at that time was James Phelan. (He was first elected in 1897 and held the office until 1902.) Phelan was determined to modernize the city's infrastructure. He advanced initiatives to improve sewer systems, public parks, and schools. He also tried—unsuccessfully—to solve the city's chronic water problem.[1] In 1900, city engineers, at Phelan's initiative, undertook a broad-based study of over a dozen potential water sources. That same year, the U.S. Geological Survey launched its own report. Both studies reached the same, highly controversial conclusion: the best solution to San Francisco's water needs lay with the Tuolumne River, over a hundred miles east and in the middle of Yosemite National Park. Damming the Tuolumne could, the experts calculated, provide clean water to San Francisco for at least a hundred years and bring inexpensive and reliable hydroelectric power to tens of thousands—turning San Francisco into a world-class city. But damming the river would radically transform the natural wonder that many Americans treasured in the country's most famous national park.

The idea of turning to Yosemite for a long-term water supply for San Francisco languished, until the early morning of April 18, 1906, when a violent earthquake struck the bay area at 5:13 a.m. It lasted less than a minute, but the aftermath devastated the city. The 1906 San Francisco earthquake remains one of the worst natural disasters in American history.

A good part of the catastrophe was man-made, however. Without reliable water sources to fight fires resulting from the quake, flames engulfed whole neighborhoods. The fires were far more catastrophic than the deadly quake: the city burned uncontrollably for three days.[2] The earthquake and fires killed three thousand people, destroyed twenty-eight thousand buildings and five hundred entire city blocks, and left nearly half the population (some 200,000 people) homeless. As San Franciscans struggled to rebuild their city, water was at the forefront of their concerns.

The pressure to find a safe and reliable source of water for the city of San Francisco eventually turned into a fierce national debate about the purpose of America's natural resources. John Muir, the widely admired founder of the Sierra Club and leading figure behind the creation of both the Sequoia and Yosemite National Parks in the 1890s, held one view. Gifford Pinchot, chief of the U.S. Forestry Service and the most powerful political voice in the nation for the utilitarian use of natural resources, held another. These men— once friends—and their respective political allies and supporters fought in the court of public opinion and the halls of Congress over how to balance the water needs of residents in San Francisco against the protection of America's public lands. In this chapter, you will be entering the early

1. Phelan was also deeply committed to Asian Exclusion.

2. The National Archives maintains an impressive digital repository of accounts and photographs from the disaster. To learn more, visit www.archives.gov/legislative/features/sf/.

✦ CHAPTER 3

Who Controls
America's Natural
Resources? Water
Rights, Public
Lands, and the
Contest over the
Hetch Hetchy
Valley

twentieth-century debates about damming the Tuolumne River and flooding the Hetch Hetchy Valley in Yosemite National Park. **Why did John Muir and Gifford Pinchot strongly disagree over the use of land and water? What were the consequences of these struggles?**

✦

Background

In the thirty years after the Civil War, U.S. corporate, scientific, and political leaders shepherded the reunited country into an unprecedented, transformative industrial age. During those decades, the United States experienced the highest rate of economic development in the world. This remarkable growth was driven by the nation's bountiful natural resources—no country in the world was able to truly compete with the vast and resource-rich United States. By the turn of the twentieth century, the U.S. dominated world markets in steel, timber, oil, and textiles. Corporate innovators also applied the industrial approaches of mass production and global distribution to America's farmlands and livestock, turning the United States into the number-one producer of wheat, cotton, and meat.

American industrialization depended on immigration, urbanization, and technological innovations, too. As you learned in the previous chapter, fifteen million immigrants arrived in the United States between 1865 and 1900. The population of the country doubled during those approximate years. According to the 1870 census, just over 38 million people lived in the United States. By 1900, that number had risen to 76 million. Most of the population growth occurred in cities, where immigrants sought factory employment: meatpacking in Chicago, steel in Pittsburgh, and textiles in New York City.

At these factories, technological innovations made mass production possible even as they transformed industrial capabilities and workers' lives. Electrical power reshaped every part of the industrial model, from the city streetcars and subways that carried workers to factories to the motors powering machinery to the light bulbs that redefined the workday. The greatest inventor of the age, Thomas Alva Edison, ran what he called a "science village"—the first American research laboratory—in Menlo Park, New Jersey, where he invented the phonograph, the light bulb, and the motion picture camera.[3] Another brilliant inventor from that era, Alexander Graham Bell, invented the telephone in 1876. Within twenty years, there were over 300,000 telephones in use, revolutionizing communications. The automobile, mass-produced by the design of Henry Ford, soon followed.

3. For a fascinating look at the influence of Edison's life and work, see Ernest Freeberg, *The Age of Edison: Electric Light and the Invention of Modern America* (New York: Penguin, 2013).

By the first decade of the twentieth century, America was so radically transformed in so many ways as to be nearly unrecognizable from just a few decades before.

There was a high price to be paid for this speed of production, innovation, and population growth, and it fell disproportionately on working-class Americans. Financiers and industrialists grew extraordinarily wealthy not only from their own investments and innovations but also by creating monopolies and aggressively driving their competitors out of business. Few legal or political impediments to predatory corporate practices existed, and political corruption advantaged these "captains of industry." Mark Twain called these decades the "Gilded Age," because the incredible wealth accumulated by a very small percentage of the richest Americans disguised widespread poverty and deprivation.

The factory work, mining, and commercial agriculture that drove America's industrial expansion could be extraordinarily dangerous. Industries in the United States had the highest rate of workplace injuries and deaths in the world. Workers enjoyed virtually no protections through government regulation and no guaranteed rights. None of the social services available for present-day Americans existed then: no unemployment insurance, no Social Security for the elderly and disabled, and no federally funded housing or food programs. Since much of the labor in the era of mass industrialization was unskilled, workers could be easily replaced and wages could be kept low. As a result, families often had to put their children to work in order to survive. By 1880, one in six American children under the age of fourteen worked full time—which meant laboring ten or twelve hours a day, six days a week. Their jobs were as dangerous as their parents; children as young as nine years old worked alongside adults in coal mines, steel mills, canneries, and stockyards.

The natural resources that underlay America's mass industrialization were ruthlessly exploited, too. Industrialization led to clear-cutting forests, unregulated mining operations (especially coal), overgrazing, and unchecked pollution of waterways.

Between the 1890s and the 1920s, American reformers began to confront these and other such troubling consequences of rapid industrialization. Led at first by journalists such as Jacob Riis and social activists like Jane Addams, supporters of progressive reforms believed that a well-functioning democratic government should and could solve the problems deriving from industrialization: poverty, corruption, class and racial conflicts, greed, and waste. Solutions to the ills besetting industrial society, they believed, lay in practical, government-centered changes. The belief in the necessity and benefit of governmental authority was new and a hallmark of progressivism. To these reformers, the problems wrought by unchecked and rapid industrial development were too large for civic and volunteer groups to overcome and beyond the scope of moral suasion—the preferred tactic of early nineteenth-century social reformers.

What started as a series of social and economic reforms therefore soon became a political movement.

[57]

◆ CHAPTER 3

Who Controls
America's Natural
Resources? Water
Rights, Public
Lands, and the
Contest over the
Hetch Hetchy
Valley

Progressive-minded voters and politicians pushed state legislatures and the federal government toward a number of formal policy changes that reined in the previously unchecked actions of big business: child labor and workplace safety laws, regulations aimed at keeping America's food supply safe, stronger oversight over corporations and industries, and scientifically based management of natural resources.

In 1901, Progressives gained perhaps their most meaningful political influence when Theodore Roosevelt became president of the United States. (Vice President Roosevelt rose to the presidency after William McKinley was assassinated.) Roosevelt was determined to pursue federal regulation of business and industry, and he had a special commitment to conservation. In 1908, President Roosevelt hosted a conference on conserving natural resources at the White House. His speech during the event revealed the dire straits of the country's natural resources and the pressing need for his policy changes. "We have become great," he said, "because of the lavish use of our resources. But the time has come to inquire seriously what will happen when our forests are gone, when the coal, the iron, the oil, and the gas are exhausted, when the soils have still further impoverished and washed into the streams, polluting the rivers, denuding the fields and obstructing navigation."

President Roosevelt championed government-led conservation of America's waterways and public lands. During his administration he created the Inland Waterways Commission in 1907, charged with improving and managing America's waterways. President Roosevelt insisted that rivers should be "considered and conserved as great natural resources." He certainly recognized the tremendous value of waterway navigation to industrial prosperity: for producing power, trafficking goods, and irrigation. But he also believed that scientific study and governmental management could ensure that all these needs could be met while using waterways for the good of all of the American population.[4]

The National Conservation Commission, which Roosevelt established in 1909, broadened this kind of federal oversight to include not only waterways but also forests, lands, and minerals. President Roosevelt also ensured the creation of the U.S. Forest Service. During Roosevelt's presidency and because of his strong advocacy, the U.S. government designated 150 new national forests and five additional national parks, created over fifty bird preserves and four game preserves, and protected 230 million acres of land.[5]

As President Roosevelt pursued these policies, he relied on Gifford Pinchot as his most trusted advisor. The two men shared a zeal for scientifically based governmental

4. President Roosevelt delivered this charge for the Inland Waterways Commission in March 1907.
5. Though often informally used as interchangeable terms, *national parks* and *national forests* have quite different meanings. Commercial activities such as mining, grazing, and logging are allowed in national forests but forbidden in national parks. Ken Burn's PBS documentary series "The National Parks: America's Best Ideas" offers a visually moving introduction to national park projects.

management of natural resources, and Pinchot rose to national prominence because of his connections to Roosevelt. Pinchot chaired the president's National Conservation Commission and became the first head of the U.S. Forest Service. Pinchot thought of forestry as a form of agriculture. If used wisely, forests could supply the United States with valuable resources, namely, timber, in perpetuity. "Conservation," he maintained, "means the greatest good to the greatest number for the longest time."[6]

John Muir, the most formidable and eloquent defender of America's natural wonders, did not share this utilitarian approach. Muir was (and remains) widely admired for his stalwart leadership in preserving some of the most beautiful and significant forests in the United States. He led the late nineteenth-century efforts to stop overgrazing, clear-cutting, and overuse of nature, especially on public lands. To that end, he founded in 1892 the Sierra Club: an organization of scientists, intellectuals, naturalists, and politicians committed to protecting public lands specifically and the natural environment generally. Muir's advocacy led to the creation of the Yosemite National Park and the Sequoia National Forest and the protection of the Grand Canyon and Petrified Forest. He is

widely hailed as the "father of the national parks."[7]

In the 1890s, John Muir often worked with Gifford Pinchot, and the two became friends. Muir was also friends with Theodore Roosevelt. In 1903, Muir and Roosevelt camped in the Yosemite Valley: the trip convinced Roosevelt that Yosemite deserved greater federal protection. All three men shared a lifelong admiration of the natural world.

But Muir and Pinchot differed on specific tactics as well as general philosophy, and those disagreements grew deeper and more vocal in the early twentieth century. Muir advocated the preservation of America's forests, particularly in the West. Land and waterways should be protected for aesthetic, ecological, and moral reasons. Individuals should be able to visit sites of great natural beauty, and government should ensure they lasted forever by careful preservation measures. Forests and streams and grasslands should not be harvested or otherwise exploited for financial gain. Pinchot came to believe this approach was impractical, detrimental to national economic interests, and elitist. He derided John Muir for seemingly having "nothing else to consider but the delight of the few men and women who would yearly" visit national forests. Muir, conversely, charged Pinchot with sacrificing irreplaceable natural environments for short-term and

6. Gifford Pinchot laid out his convictions about conservation and the use of natural resources in *The Fight for Conservation* (New York: Doubleday, Page & Company, 1910), an excerpt of which is included in this chapter's evidence. For the best introduction to Pinchot, see Char Miller, *Gifford Pinchot and the Making of Modern Environmentalism* (Washington, D.C.: Island Press, 2001).

7. Environmental historians are often drawn to Muir's life and work. To learn more, start with the excellent biography by Donald Worster, *A Passion for Nature: The Life of John Muir* (New York: Oxford University Press, 2008).

♦ CHAPTER 3

Who Controls
America's Natural
Resources? Water
Rights, Public
Lands, and the
Contest over the
Hetch Hetchy
Valley

counterproductive industrial gains. He disparaged Pinchot as a "devotee to raging consumerism."

The two camps clashed over a number of policy issues in the Progressive Era, but none created as much controversy as the proposal out of California to flood the Hetch Hetchy Valley in Yosemite National Park to build a reservoir to provide water for San Francisco.[8] Not only did John Muir and Gifford Pinchot, the two leading figures in conservationism, natural resources policy, and the creation of national parks, have a bitter falling-out over the proposed damming of the Tuolumne River, but the U.S. Congress deliberated over the matter, too. Indeed the question of whether to flood the Hetch Hetchy Valley sparked a long and fierce national debate. Pinchot and his allies thought that federally owned lands

should be put to use for the public good, in this particular case to provide reliable clean water to San Francisco. Muir's camp strongly disagreed, condemning the plan to intentionally destroy the Hetch Hetchy Valley for the benefit of a city 160 miles away as unethical and even illegal.

The evidence in this chapter reveals the philosophical and political disagreements over this specific proposal and, more generally, Progressive Era debates about the purpose and proper use of nature. Carefully reading the primary sources will allow you to understand why John Muir and Gifford Pinchot so strongly disagreed over the use of land and water. You will see, too, the consequences of this struggle, which were deeply meaningful in the early twentieth century and echo still, a hundred years later.

The Method

The following primary source evidence begins with Gifford Pinchot's and John Muir's differing perspectives on water and land. The excerpts from their respective books (Sources 1 and 2)

8. For a full accounting of this controversy, see Robert W. Righter, *The Battle over Hetch Hetchy: America's Most Controversial Dam and the Birth of Modern Environmentalism* (New York: Oxford University Press, 2005). For a fascinating global perspective on dams, see Jacques Leslie, *Deep Water: The Epic Struggle over Dams, Displaced People, and the Environment* (New York: Farrar, Straus, and Giroux, 2005).

reflect these two men's larger philosophical convictions about nature, natural resources, and public lands and waterways. In working through the evidence in this chapter, you should develop a clear understanding of these views: where Pinchot's and Muir's ideas intersected and where and why they diverged. The fundamental disagreement they had about utilitarian conservation versus aesthetic preservation persists in present-day debates about environmentalism. Should the guiding principle of natural resource use be, as Pinchot argued, "an equal opportunity for every American citizen to get his fair share of benefit from those resources, both now and hereafter"? Or, is Muir right that "everybody needs beauty as well as bread, places to play in and pray in, where Nature may heal and cheer and give strength to body and soul alike"?

While each man held a principled position, neither Pinchot nor Muir undertook their writing as intellectual exercises or abstract theories. Rather, both wanted to see their convictions enacted as official government policy. That required moving citizens and politicians, so you should also read their writings as advocacy pieces, lobbying for a specific policy decision.

Their books thus connect directly to the campaign for public support (Sources 3 and 4) and to the debates in the U.S. Congress (Sources 5–7). Be attentive to the different tactics in these diverse sources.

In the end, Gifford Pinchot's camp won the debate over Hetch Hetchy. The excerpt from the 1913 Raker Act (Source 8), the photographs of the Hetch Hetchy Valley before and after the construction of the O'Shaughnessy Dam (Sources 9–11), and the diagram of the present-day water system (Source 12) all reveal the consequences of that political victory.

As you read these materials, keep in mind some of the larger debates in the Progressive Era that the Hetch Hetchy controversy laid bare: about governmental power, ideas about nature, and economic development.

Progressive Era Americans, not unlike citizens today, disagreed about how to balance local, state, and federal powers. When the federal government gave the city of San Francisco sweeping rights in Yosemite National Park—to build everything from aqueducts to power plants to railroads—many Americans who did not share John Muir's convictions about the sanctity of nature bristled. It was a familiar pattern. When, for example, the federal government tried to regulate forestry by granting exclusive timber rights on public lands to particular corporations, it necessarily outlawed some common local practices. Residents could find themselves barred from grazing animals or cutting trees for firewood or to repair their homes. Federal and state water rights and gaming laws—designed to scientifically manage rivers and wildlife—meant that local fishers and hunters, trying to feed their families, could be guilty of poaching. The consequences of such policies provoked strong debates and frequent complaints about corporations setting conservation policy. Who should determine the best use of fields, streams, forests, and rivers: the U.S. government, individual states, or municipalities? Corporations? Communities? What guiding principles should they follow?

It will be tempting to think of those supporting the Hetch Hetchy project as singularly driven by economic ambitions and to assume that the opponents treasured only natural beauty. The truth is more complicated, on both sides. Marsden Manson, the city engineer of San Francisco who promoted the Hetch Hetchy proposal, was a long-standing member of the Sierra Club. And defenders of the Hetch Hetchy Valley argued forcefully

◆ CHAPTER 3

Who Controls
America's Natural
Resources? Water
Rights, Public
Lands, and the
Contest over the
Hetch Hetchy
Valley

for the economic benefits of nature tourism. Yosemite attracted vacationers with disposable income, they knew, which benefited nearby businesses and boosted the national economy. Some conservation-minded Americans thus debated which would pay the highest financial dividend: ensuring safe water for the burgeoning city of San Francisco or leaving unaltered the magnificent Hetch Hetchy Valley?

At the same time, John Muir clearly championed the intrinsic moral and aesthetic value of forests and waterways. Gifford Pinchot may have won the battle over Hetch Hetchy, but in many ways John Muir won the war. Muir is widely celebrated as a prescient advocate for and founder of the modern environmental movement. His ideas endure, even as the Hetch Hetchy Valley sits under 300 feet of water.

Many issues raised during the Hetch Hetchy contest echo today, in current environmental policy debates. As with the sources you read, these matters are at once practical and philosophical. How much does fracking endanger our water supply? How should we balance

nature and economic growth? Should ranchers be allowed to let their livestock graze on public lands? What are the purposes of national parks? Does nature have value beyond human use? What limits does nature place on humans? Is it possible to preserve nature?

Finally, as you weigh the following evidence, keep in mind that historians must seek to understand the past on its own terms, in its proper historical context. At the same time, the past often speaks to the present. As William Faulkner famously said, "The past is never dead. It's not even past." So, one challenge in this chapter—and in many of the chapters focusing on the recent past—will be to consider the evidence in the context of the Progressive Era and not to pass judgments based on your present-day personal convictions about environmentalism or economic development. At the same time, you will see reflections of the present in this historical controversy, and what you know from your twenty-first-century perspective may offer important, revealing insight into the contest over Hetch Hetchy.

◆

The Evidence

Source 1 from Gifford Pinchot, *The Fight for Conservation* (New York: Doubleday, Page and Company, 1910), pp. 53–54, 59–61, 64–66, 79–84.

1. Excerpt from Gifford Pinchot, *The Fight for Conservation.*

The conquest of our rivers is one of the largest commercial questions now before us.

The commercial consequences of river development are incalculable. Its results cannot be measured by the yard-stick of present commercial needs. River improvement means better conditions of transportation than we have now, but it means development too. We cannot see this problem clearly and see it whole in the light of the past alone.

The actual problems of river development are not less worthy of our best attention than their commercial results. Every river is a unit from its source to its mouth. If it is to be given its highest usefulness to all the people, and serve them for all the uses they can make of it, it must be developed with that idea clearly in mind. To develop a river for navigation alone, or power alone, or irrigation alone, is often like using a sheep for mutton, or a steer for beef, and throwing away the leather and the wool. A river is a unit, but its uses are many, and with our present knowledge there can be no excuse for sacrificing one use to another if both can be subserved. . . .

Every public officer responsible for any part of the conservation of natural resources is a trustee of the public property. If conservation is vital to the welfare of this Nation now and hereafter, as President Roosevelt so wisely declared, then few positions of public trust are so important, and few opportunities for constructive work so large. Such officers are concerned with the greatest issues which have come before this Nation since the Civil War. They may hope to serve the Nation as few men ever can. Their care for our forests, waters, lands, and minerals is often the only thing that stands between the public good and the something-for-nothing men, who, like the daughters of the horse-leech, are forever crying, "Give, Give." The intelligence, initiative, and steadfastness that can withstand the unrelenting pressure of the special interests are worth having, and the Forest Service has given proof of all three. But the counter-pressure from the people in their own interest is needed far more often than it is supplied.

The public welfare cannot be subserved merely by walking blindly in the old ruts. Times change, and the public needs change with them. The man who would serve the public to the level of its needs must look ahead, and one of his most difficult problems will be to make old tools answer new uses— uses some of which, at least, were never imagined when the tools were made. That is one reason why constructive foresight is one of the great constant needs of every growing nation. . . .

After the transfer of the National Forests from the Interior Department to the Forest Service in 1905, some things were done that had never been done before, such as initiating Government control over water-power monopoly in the National Forest, giving preference to the public over commercial corporations in the use of the Forests, and trying to help the small man make a living rather than the big man make a profit (but always with the

◆ CHAPTER 3

Who Controls
America's Natural
Resources? Water
Rights, Public
Lands, and the
Contest over the
Hetch Hetchy
Valley

effort to be just to both). Always and everywhere we have set the public welfare above the advantage of the special interests.

Because it did these things the Forest Service has made enemies, of some of whom it is justly proud. It has been easy for these enemies to raise the cry of illegality, novelty, and excess of zeal. But in every instance the Service has been fortified either by express statutes, or by decisions of the Supreme Court and other courts, of the Secretary of the Interior, of the Comptroller, or the Attorney-General, or by general principles of law which are beyond dispute. If there is novelty, it consists simply in the way these statutes, decisions, and principles have been used to protect the public. The law officers of the Forest Service have had the Nation for their client, and they are proud to work as zealously for the public as they would in private practice for a fee.

So I think the ghost of illegality in the Forest Service may fairly be laid at rest. But it is not the only one which is clouding the issues of conservation in the public mind. Another misconception is that the friends of conservation are trying to prevent the development of water power by private capital. Nothing could be father from the truth. The friends of conservation were the first to call public attention to the enormous saving to the Nation which follows the substitution of the power of falling water, which is constantly renewed, for our coal, which can never be renewed. They favor development by private capital and not by the Government, but they also favor attaching such reasonable conditions to the right to develop as will protect the public and control water-power monopoly in the public interest, while at the same time giving to enterprising capital its just and full reward. They believe that to grant rights to water power in perpetuity is a wrongful mortgage of the welfare of our descendants, and to grant them without insisting on some return for value received is to rob ourselves. . . .

The central thing for which Conservation stands is to make this country the best possible place to live in, both for us and for our descendants. It stands against the waste of the natural resources which cannot be renewed, such as coal and iron; it stands for the perpetuation of the resources which can be renewed, such as the food-producing soils and the forests; and most of all it stands for an equal opportunity for every American citizen to get his fair share of benefit from these resources, both now and hereafter.

Conservation stands for the same kind of practical common-sense management of this country by the people that every business man stands for in the handling of his own business. It believes in prudence and foresight instead of reckless blindness; it holds that resources now public property should not become the basis for oppressive private monopoly; and it demands the complete and orderly development of all our resources for the benefit of all the people, instead of the partial exploitation of them for the benefit of a few. It recognizes fully the right of the present generation to use what it needs and all it needs of the natural resources now available, but it recognizes equally our obligation so to use what we need that our descendants shall not be deprived of what they need.

Conservation has much to do with the welfare of the average man of to-day. It proposes to secure a continuous and abundant supply of the necessaries of life, which means a reasonable cost of living and business stability. It advocates fairness in the distribution of the benefits which flow from the natural resources. It will matter very little to the average citizen, when scarcity comes and prices rise, whether he can not get what he needs because there is none left or because he can not afford to pay for it. In both cases the essential fact is that he can not get what he needs. Conservation holds that it is about as important to see that the people in general get the benefit of our natural resources as to see that there shall be natural resources left.

Conservation is the most democratic movement this country has known for a generation. It holds that the people have not only the right, but the duty to control the use of the natural resources, which are the great sources of prosperity. And it regards the absorption of these resources by the special interests, unless their operations are under effective public control, as a moral wrong. Conservation is the application of common-sense to the common problems for the common good, and I believe it stands nearer to the desires, aspirations, and purposes of the average man than any other policy now before the American people.

The danger to the Conservation policies is that the privileges of the few may continue to obstruct the rights of the many, especially in the matter of water power and coal. Congress must decide immediately whether the great coal fields still in public ownership shall remain so, in order that their use may be controlled with due regard to the interest of the consumer, or whether they shall pass into private ownership and be controlled in the monopolistic interest of a few.

Congress must decide also whether immensely valuable rights to the use of water power shall be given away to special interests in perpetuity and without compensation instead of being held and controlled by the public. In most cases actual development of water power can best be done by private interests acting under public control, but it is neither good sense nor good morals to let these valuable privileges pass from the public ownership for nothing and forever. Other conservation matters doubtless require action, but these two, the conservation of water power and of coal, the chief sources of power of the present and the future, are clearly the most pressing.

◆ CHAPTER 3

Who Controls
America's Natural
Resources? Water
Rights, Public
Lands, and the
Contest over the
Hetch Hetchy
Valley

It is of the first importance to prevent our water powers from passing into private ownership as they have been doing, because the greatest source of power we know is falling water. Furthermore, it is the only great unfailing source of power. Our coal, the experts say, is likely to be exhausted during the next century, our natural gas and oil in this. Our rivers, if the forests on the watersheds are properly handled, will never cease to deliver power. Under our form of civilization, if a few men ever succeed in controlling the sources of power, they will eventually control all industry as well. If they succeed in controlling all industry, they will necessarily control the country. This country has achieved political freedom; what our people are fighting for now is industrial freedom. And unless we win our industrial liberty, we can not keep our political liberty. I see no reason why we should deliberately keep on helping to fasten the handcuffs of corporate control upon ourselves for all time merely because the few men who would profit by it most have heretofore had the power to compel it. . . .

Source 2 from John Muir, *The Yosemite* (New York: The Century Company, 1920), pp. 251–252, 254–256, 257, 259–262.

2. Excerpt from John Muir, *The Yosemite*.

Imagine yourself in Hetch Hetchy on a sunny day in June, standing waist-deep in grass and flowers (as I have often stood), while the great pines sway dreamily with scarcely perceptible motion. Looking northward across the Valley you see a plain, gray granite cliff rising abruptly out of the gardens and groves to a height of 1800 feet, and in front of it Tueeulala's silvery scarf burning with irised sun-fire. In the first white outburst at the head there is abundance of visible energy, but it is speedily hushed and concealed in divine repose, and its tranquil progress to the base of the cliff is like that of a downy feather in a still room. Now observe the fineness and marvelous distinctness of the various sun-illumined fabrics into which the water is woven; they sift and float from form to form down the face of that grand gray rock in so leisurely and unconfused a manner that you can examine their texture, and patterns and tones of color as you would a piece of embroidery held in the hand. Toward the top of the fall you see groups of booming, comet-like masses, their solid, white heads separate, their tails like combed silk interlacing among delicate gray and purple shadows, ever forming and dissolving, worn out by friction in their rush through the air. Most of these vanish a few hundred feet below the summit, changing to varied forms of cloud-like drapery. Near the bottom the width of the fall has increased from about twenty-five feet to a hundred feet. Here it is composed of yet finer tissues, and is still without a trace of disorder—air, water and sunlight woven into stuff that spirits might wear. . . .

The floor of the Valley is about three and a half miles long, and from a fourth to half a mile wide. The lower portion is mostly a level meadow about a mile long, with the trees restricted to the sides and the river banks, and partially separated from the main, upper, forested portion by a low bar of glacier-polished granite across which the river breaks in rapids.

The principal trees are the yellow and sugar pines, digger pine, incense cedar, Douglas spruce, silver fir, the California and golden-cup oaks, balsam cottonwood, Nuttall's flowering dogwood, alder, maple, laurel, tumion, etc. The most abundant and influential are the great yellow or silver pines like those of Yosemite, the tallest over two hundred feet in height, and the oaks assembled in magnificent groves with massive rugged trunks four to six feet in diameter, and broad, shady, wide-spreading heads. The shrubs forming conspicuous flowery clumps and tangles are manzanita, azalea, spiraea, brier-rose, several species of ceanothus, calycanthus, philadelphus, wild cherry, etc.; with abundance of showy and fragrant herbaceous plants growing about them or out in the open in beds by themselves— lilies, Mariposa tulips, brodiaeas, orchids, iris, spraguea, draperia, collomia, collinsia, castilleja, nemophila, larkspur, columbine, goldenrods, sunflowers, mints of many species, honeysuckle, etc. Many fine ferns dwell here also, especially the beautiful and interesting rockferns—pellaea, and cheilanthes of several species—fringing and rosetting dry rock-piles and ledges; woodwardia and asplenium on damp spots with fronds six or seven feet high; the delicate maiden-hair in mossy nooks by the falls, and the sturdy, broad-shouldered pteris covering nearly all the dry ground beneath the oaks and pines.

It appears, therefore, that Hetch Hetchy Valley, far from being a plain, common, rock-bound meadow, as many who have not seen it seem to suppose, is a grand landscape garden, one of Nature's rarest and most precious mountain temples. As in Yosemite, the sublime rocks of its walls seem to glow with life, whether leaning back in repose or standing erect in thoughtful attitudes, giving welcome to storms and calms alike, their brows in the sky, their feet set in the groves and gay flowery meadows, while birds, bees, and butterflies help the river and waterfalls to stir all the air into music—things frail and fleeting and types of permanence meeting here and blending, just as they do in Yosemite, to draw her lovers into close and confiding communion with her.

◆ CHAPTER 3

Who Controls
America's Natural
Resources? Water
Rights, Public
Lands, and the
Contest over the
Hetch Hetchy
Valley

Sad to say, this most precious and sublime feature of the Yosemite National Park, one of the greatest of all our natural resources for the uplifting joy and peace and health of the people, is in danger of being dammed and made into a reservoir to help supply San Francisco with water and light, thus flooding it from wall to wall and burying its gardens and groves one or two hundred feet deep. This grossly destructive commercial scheme has long been planned and urged (though water as pure and abundant can be got from sources outside of the people's park, in a dozen different places), because of the comparative cheapness of the dam and of the territory which it is sought to divert from the great uses to which it was dedicated in the Act of 1890 establishing the Yosemite National Park.

The making of gardens and parks goes on with civilization all over the world, and they increase both in size and number as their value is recognized. Everybody needs beauty as well as bread, placed to play in and pray in, where Nature may heal and cheer and give strength to body and soul alike. . . .

Nevertheless, like anything else worth while, from the very beginning, however well guarded, they have always been subject to attack by despoiling gain-seekers and mischief-makers of every degree from Satan to Senators, eagerly trying to make everything immediately and selfishly commercial, with schemes disguised in smug-smiling philanthropy, industriously, shampiously crying, "Conservation, conservation, panutilization," that man and beast may be fed and the dear Nation made great. Thus long ago a few enterprising merchants utilized the Jerusalem temple as a place of business instead of a place of prayer, changing money, buying and selling cattle and sheep and doves; and earlier still, the first forest reservation, including only one tree, was likewise despoiled. Ever since the establishment of the Yosemite National Park, strife has been going on around its borders and I suppose this will go on as part of the universal battle between right and wrong, however much its boundaries may be shorn, or its wild beauty destroyed. . . .

Should Hetch Hetchy be submerged for a reservoir, as proposed, not only would it be utterly destroyed, but the sublime cañon way to the heart of the High Sierra would be hopelessly blocked and the great camping ground, as the watershed of a city drinking system, virtually would be closed to the public. So far as I have learned, few of all the thousands who have seen the park and seek rest and peace in it are in favor of this outrageous scheme.

One of my later visits to the Valley was made in the autumn of 1907 with the late William Keith, the artist. The leaf-colors were then ripe, and the great godlike rocks in repose seemed to glow with life. The artist, under their spell, wandered day after day along the river and through the groves and gardens, studying the wonderful scenery; and, after making about forty sketches, declared with enthusiasm that although its walls were less sublime in height, in picturesque beauty and charm Hetch Hetchy surpassed even Yosemite.

That any one would try to destroy such a place seems incredible; but sad experience shows that there are people good enough and bad enough for anything. The proponents of the dam scheme bring forward a lot of bad arguments to prove that the only righteous thing to do with the people's parks is to destroy them bit by bit as they are able. Their arguments are curiously like those of the devil, devised for the destruction of the first garden—so much of the very best Eden fruit going to waste; so much of the best Tuolumne water and Tuolumne scenery going to waste. Few of their statements are even partly true, and all are misleading.

Thus, Hetch Hetchy, they say, is a "low-lying meadow." On the contrary, it is a high-lying natural landscape garden, as the photographic illustrations show.

"It is a common minor feature, like thousands of others." On the contrary it is a very uncommon feature; after Yosemite, the rarest and in many ways the most important in the National Park.

"Damming and submerging it 175 feet deep would enhance its beauty by forming a crystal-clear lake." Landscape gardens, places of recreation and worship, are never made beautiful by destroying and burying them. The beautiful sham lake, forsooth, would be only an eyesore, a dismal blot on the landscape, like many others to be seen in the Sierra. For, instead of keeping it at the same level all the year, allowing Nature centuries of time to make new shores, it would, of course, be full only a month or two in the spring, when the snow is melting fast; then it would be gradually drained, exposing the slimy sides of the basin and shallower parts of the bottom, with the gathered drift and waste, death and decay of the upper basins, caught here instead of being swept on to decent natural burial along the banks of the river or in the sea. Thus the Hetch Hetchy dam-lake would be only a rough imitation of a natural lake for a few of the spring months, an open sepulcher for the others.

"Hetch Hetchy water is the purest of all to be found in the Sierra, unpolluted, and forever unpollutable." On the contrary, excepting that of the Merced below Yosemite, it is less pure than that of most of the other Sierra streams, because of the sewerage of camp grounds draining into it, especially of the Big Tuolumne Meadows camp ground, occupied by hundreds of tourists and mountaineers, with their animals, for months every summer, soon to be followed by thousands from all the world.

These temple destroyers, devotees of ravaging commercialism, seem to have a perfect contempt for Nature, and, instead of lifting their eyes to the God of the mountains, lift them to the Almighty Dollar.

◆ CHAPTER 3

Who Controls
America's Natural
Resources? Water
Rights, Public
Lands, and the
Contest over the
Hetch Hetchy
Valley

Dam Hetch Hetchy! As well dam for water-tanks the people's cathedrals and churches, for no holier temple has ever been consecrated by the heart of man. . . .

Sources 3 and 4 are part of John Muir's campaign in 1909 to save the Hetch Hetchy Valley, available through the Library of Congress American Memory digital collection (memory.loc.gov).

3. "Let Everyone Help to Save the Famous Hetch Hetchy Valley."

LET EVERYONE HELP TO SAVE THE FAMOUS HETCH HETCHY VALLEY AND STOP THE COMMERCIAL DESTRUCTION WHICH THREATENS OUR NATIONAL PARKS

To the American Public:

The famous Hetch Hetchy Valley, next to Yosemite the most wonderful and important feature of our Yosemite National Park, is again in danger of being destroyed. Year after year attacks have been made on this Park under the guise of development of natural resources. At the last regular session of Congress the most determined attack of all was made by the City of San Francisco to get possession of the Hetch Hetchy Valley as a reservoir site, thus defrauding ninety millions of people for the sake of saving San Francisco dollars.

As soon as this scheme became manifest, public-spirited citizens all over the country poured a storm of protest on Congress. Before the session was over, the Park invaders saw that they were defeated and permitted the bill to die without bringing it to a vote, so as to be able to try again.

The bill has been re-introduced and will be urged at the coming session of Congress, which convenes in December. Let all those who believe that our great national wonderlands should be preserved unmarred as places of rest and recreation for the use of all the people, now enter their protests. Ask Congress to reject this destructive bill, and also urge that the present Park laws be so amended as to put an end to all such assaults on our system of National Parks.

Faithfully yours,
John Muir
November, 1909.

4. "A Brief Statement of the Hetch Hetchy Case to Date."

A BRIEF STATEMENT OF THE HETCH HETCHY CASE TO DATE.

The Yosemite National Park is not only the greatest and most wonderful national playground in California, but in many of its features it is without a rival in the whole world. It belongs to the American people and is among their most priceless possessions. In world wide interest it ranks with the Yellowstone and the Grand Canyon of the Colorado. The Yosemite Park embraces the headwaters of two rivers—the Merced and the Tuolomne. The Yosemite Valley is in the Merced basin, and the Hetch Hetchy Valley, the Grand Canyon of the Tuolomne, and the Tuolumne Meadows are in the Tuolomne basin is the finer and larger half of the Park. Practically the entire Tuolumne basin drains directly into Hetch Hetchy Valley, which is a wonderfully exact counterpart of the great Yosemite, not only in its crystal river, sublime cliffs and waterfalls, but in the gardens, groves, and meadows of its flowery park-like floor. This park-like floor is especially adapted for pleasure camping, and is the focus of all the trails from both the north and the south which lead into and through this magnificent camp ground.

The Yosemite National Park was created in 1890 by Congress in order that this great natural wonderland should be preserved in pure wilderness for all time for the benefit of the entire nation. The Yosemite Valley was already preserved in a State Park, and the National Park was created primarily to protect the Hetch Hetchy Valley and Tuolumne Meadows from invasion.

In spite of the fact that this is a national property dedicated as a public park for all time in which every citizen of the United States has a direct interest, certain individuals in San Francisco conceived the idea that here would be an opportunity to acquire a water supply for the city at the expense of the nation. They made application to the late Hon. E. A. Hitchcock, then Secretary of the Interior, for the privilege of using Hetch Hetchy Valley and Lake Eleanor as reservoir sites from which to draw a municipal supply of water. After giving the question careful consideration, he denied these rights on January 20, 1903, and on a rehearing again emphatically denied them December 22, 1903. Thereupon a bill designed to override Secretary Hitchcock's decision was introduced in Congress but the Committee on Public Lands refused to give it standing. The matter was again taken up with the President, who referred it to Hon. Victor H. Metcalf, then Secretary of Commerce and Labor. He upheld Secretary

[71]

♦ CHAPTER 3

Who Controls
America's Natural
Resources? Water
Rights, Public
Lands, and the
Contest over the
Hetch Hetchy
Valley

Hitchcock's opinion and again denied the right of the city to enter a national park. When Hon. James R. Garfield became Secretary of the Interior, the city advocates renewed their efforts to have these rights granted which had been so many times refused, and at last prevailed. Secretary Garfield on May 11, 1908, rendered an opinion so prejudicial to the interests of the American public in their National Parks, as to practically nullify the whole national park policy and throw those great public playgrounds open to all kinds of destructive invasion from local and comparatively private interests. Fortunately the rights granted by Secretary Garfield, if they possess any legality at all are revocable at the discretion of any Secretary of the Interior. Armed with this Garfield permit to flood the Hetch Hetchy Valley and destroy its use as a public playground, the Park invaders again applied to Congress in December, 1908, to confirm Garfield's action and render it irrevocable by securing title to the floor of Hetch Hetchy in fee simple. The matter was referred to the Public Lands Committees of the House and Senate for recommendation. While a majority vote of eight in the House Committee favored the abandonment of this priceless national property, there were seven who voted against it, and one other member later joined the minority, making the vote a tie. Many friends of the National Park system were ready to champion the people's cause if the bill had reached the floor of the House, but the closing days of the session made it impossible to have the bill brought up. Before the Senate Committee the bill did not fare as well and it became known that, if brought to a vote, the result would have been unfavorable to San Francisco and this would have been fatal to future attempts to pass the bill. Therefore, the bill died with the Sixtieth Congress.

The same bill has been re-introduced in the present Congress, and a last desperate attempt to force it through will be made.

If San Francisco could not obtain pure water elsewhere, this great national sacrifice might be justified, but hydraulic engineers of unquestioned standing have reported on many other adequate and available sources. In this respect, probably, no large city in the world is more favorably situated. . . .

HOW TO HELP TO PRESERVE THE HETCH HETCHY VALLEY AND THE YOSEMITE PARK.

1. Write at once to Hon. Richard A. Ballinger, Secretary of the Interior, Washington, D.C., requesting him to revoke the Garfield permit to flood the Hetch Hetchy Valley.

2. Send a copy of the letter to President William H. Taft.

3. See personally if possible, or write to, the Senators and Congressmen from your State, and as many others as you can reach, requesting them to vigorously oppose any bill having for its object the confirmation of the Garfield permit to flood Hetch Hetchy Valley, and request them to favor legislation designed to protect our parks from invasion, and particularly to favor improving the Yosemite Park. After December 1, 1909, address them either "Senate Chamber" or "House of Representatives," Washington, D.C.

4. After December 1st write to each member of the Public Lands Committees of both the Senate and the House, Washington, D.C., requesting them to oppose any and all legislation having for its object the destruction of the Hetch Hetchy Valley and to favor any legislation designed to protect the parks. Write to all if you can, but if you cannot, at least write to the Chairman of each committee. (The names of the members of the committees will be found on the opposite page.)

5. Get as many of your friends as possible to write. Remember! Every letter and every protest counts.

6. Interest your newspapers and get them to publish editorials and news items and send copies to your Senators and Representatives.

7. Send the names and addresses of any persons who would be interested in receiving this pamphlet to "Society for the Preservation of National Parks, 302 Mills Building, San Francisco, Cal."

EDITORS are respectfully requested to write brief editorials and news items informing the public and calling on them to write to their Congressmen and Senators and protest.

CLUBS should send copies of resolutions they may adopt to President Taft, Secretary Ballinger, and each member of the Public Lands Committees, and the Senators and Representatives from their State.

FUNDS ARE NEEDED to carry on this fight. A few have generously carried the burden of expense connected with the issuance of this literature, but more money is required to spread information. Those who would like to render pecuniary assistance may send their contributions to JOHN MUIR, President of Society for the Preservation of National Parks, 302 MILLS BUILDING, SAN FRANCISCO, CAL. . . .

◆ CHAPTER 3

Who Controls
America's Natural
Resources? Water
Rights, Public
Lands, and the
Contest over the
Hetch Hetchy
Valley

Sources 5–7 are excerpted from the U.S. Congressional debates about Hetch Hetchy in 1913. Source 5 is from Washington, D.C.: U.S. Government Printing Office, 1913. Source 6 is from Congressional Record, U.S. House of Representatives, 1913. Source 7 is from Congressional Record, United States Senate, 1913.[9]

5. Gifford Pinchot, June 24, 1913.

STATEMENT OF HON. GIFFORD PINCHOT.

THE CHAIRMAN. In deference to Mr. Pinchot's wishes, as he desires to leave the city, he will be permitted to address the committee at this time if there is no objection.

MR. PINCHOT. Mr. Chairman and gentlemen of the committee, my testimony will be very short. I presume that you very seldom have the opportunity of passing upon any measure before the Committee on the Public Lands which has been so thoroughly thrashed out as this one. This question has been up now, I should say, more than 10 years, and the reasons for and against the proposition have not only been discussed over and over again, but a great deal of the objections which could be composed have been composed, until finally there remains simply the one question of the objection of the Spring Valley Water Co. I understand that the much more important objection of the Tuolumne irrigation districts have been overcome. There is, I understand, objection on the part of other irrigators, but that does not go to the question of using the water, but merely to the distribution of the water. So we come now face to face with the perfectly clean question of what is the best use to which this water that flows out of the Sierras can be put. As we all know, there is no use of water that is higher than the domestic use. Then, if there is, as the engineers tell us, no other source of supply that is anything like so reasonably available as this one; if this is the best, and, within reasonable limits of cost, the only means of supplying San Francisco with water, we come straight to the question of whether the advantage of leaving this valley in a state of nature is greater than the advantage of using it for the benefit of the city of San Francisco.

Now, the fundamental principle of the whole conservation policy is that of use, to take every part of the land and its resources and put it to that use in which it will best serve the most people, and I think there can be no question at all but that in this case we have an instance in which all weighty considerations demand the passage of the bill. There are, of course, a very large number of incidental changes that will arise

9. Transcripts of other parts of the extensive Congressional debates over Hetch Hetchy are available through the Library of Congress: memory.loc.gov/ammem/amrvhtml/conshome.html.

after the passage of the bill. The construction of roads, trails, and telephone systems which will follow the passage of this bill will be a very important help in the park and forest reserves. The national forest telephone system and the roads and trails to which this bill will lead will form an important additional help in fighting fire in the forest reserves. As has already been set forth by the two Secretaries, the presence of these additional means of communication will mean that the national forest and the national park will be visited by very large numbers of people who can not visit them now. I think that the men who assert that it is better to leave a piece of natural scenery in its natural condition have rather the better of the argument, and I believe if we had nothing else to consider than the delight of the few men and women who would yearly go into the Hetch Hetchy Valley, then it should be left in its natural condition. But the considerations on the other side of the question to my mind are simply overwhelming, and so much so that I have never been able to see that there was any reasonable argument against the use of this water supply by the city of San Francisco, provided the bill was a reasonable bill. Now, there are two or three small changes in the bill which I would like to suggest.

THE CHAIRMAN. Inasmuch as you will not be here when we go through this bill section by section, I would be glad, Mr. Pinchot, if you would indicate the pages, sections, and lines in which you suggest changes.

MR. PINCHOT. On page 7, line 4, after the words "Secretary of Agriculture," I would suggest inserting:

Provided, That no timber shall be cut in the Yosemite National Park, except from lands to be overflowed, or such timber as may be constituted an action obstruction upon a right of way.

In other words, I do not believe that a national park should be used as a source of timber supply, and I understand the representatives from San Francisco are entirely willing that that should be added.

MR. RAKER. There is already an act which permits them to dispose of it. If there is down or dead timber you would not want them to go 5 or 6 miles? There is an act permitting that in the Yosemite National Park.

MR. PINCHOT. Then I am wrong about that.

MR. RAKER. There was a special bill passed two years ago permitting the Secretary of the Interior to dispose of ripe, down, or dead timber in the Yosemite National Park. You would not object to using that sort of timber?

MR. PINCHOT. Not in a national park.

MR. RAKER. Dead and dying?

MR. PINCHOT. A place like a national park should be protected against that. I think we can have a little timber fall down and die for the sake of

◆ CHAPTER 3

Who Controls
America's Natural
Resources? Water
Rights, Public
Lands, and the
Contest over the
Hetch Hetchy
Valley

having the place look like no human foot had ever been in it. I do not think that the national parks should be used as a source of lumber supply.

MR. RAKER. Suppose the timber is ripe and ready to be disposed of, that there is a tree which could be used, you would not want to leave that there and go to the expense of going to some other place, if it does not affect the scenic beauty of the park?

MR. PINCHOT. That does not apply to the national parks, but here is a different situation, here is one of the great wonders of the world, and I would leave it just as it is so far as possible in the Yosemite National Park.

MR. RAKER. For instance, a tree falls down, one of the largest in the park, that should not be left there to destroy the balance?

MR. PINCHOT. It will not destroy the balance.

MR. RAKER. I am just taking the statement of the others.

MR. PINCHOT. I will mention that among the greatest of the beauties are some of the fallen trees. I would not touch one of them.

MR. RAKER. They would not want one of those great trees for building purposes?

MR. PINCHOT. No, sir. That does not apply to the national parks. The parks are set aside for seeding purposes in this particular manner. I would leave the trees alone. Outside of the parks I think the point of view of use is the dominant matter which should control. . . .

MR. RAKER. Taking the scenic beauty of the park as it now stands, and the fact that the valley is sometimes swamped along in June and July, is it not a fact that if a beautiful dam is put there, as is contemplated, and as the picture is given by the engineers, with the roads contemplated around the reservoir and with other trails, it will be more beautiful than it is now, and give more opportunity for the use of the park?

MR. PINCHOT. Whether it will be more beautiful, I doubt, but the use of the park will be enormously increased. I think there is no doubt about that.

MR. RAKER. In other words, to put it a different way, there will be more beauty accessible than there is now?

MR. PINCHOT. Much more beauty will be accessible than now.

MR. RAKER. And by putting in roads and trails the Government, as well as the citizens of the Government, will get more pleasure out of it than at the present time?

MR. PINCHOT. You might say from the standpoint of enjoyment of beauty and the greatest good to the greatest number, they will be conserved by the passage of this bill, and there will be a great deal more use of the beauty of the park than there is now.

MR. RAKER. Have you seen Mr. John Muir's criticism of the bill? You know him?

MR. PINCHOT. Yes, sir; I know him very well. He is an old and a very good friend of mine. I have never been able to agree with him in his attitude toward the Sierras for the reason that my point of view has never appealed to him at all. When I became Forester and denied the right to exclude sheep and cows from the Sierras, Mr. Muir thought I had made a great mistake, because I allowed the use by an acquired right of a large number of people to interfere with what would have been the utmost beauty of the forest. In this case I think he has unduly given away to beauty as against use.

6. Scott Ferris, June 30, 1913.

Hon. SCOTT FERRIS,
Chairman Committee on the Public Lands, House of Representatives.

MY DEAR MR. FERRIS: I wish to acknowledge receipt of your request for a report upon the bill (H.R. 4319) granting to the city and county of San Francisco certain rights of way through the public lands and reservations of the United States. On June 24 the Secretary of Agriculture addressed a letter to you giving the views of this department. The Forest Service participated in the preparation of the Secretary's report, which was designed to represent the agreed policy of the department, including the Forest Service.

Very sincerely, yours,
H.S. GRAVES, *Forester.*

I telegraphed to Mr. Pinchot, and some of the other members did likewise, urging him to appear before the committee. Mr. Pinchot is well known to this House and well known to the country. He has given much patriotic attention to conservation questions. Mr. Pinchot came down from Pennsylvania, where he was temporarily, and before our committee in the strongest sort of terms, as the printed hearings show, and as his letter shows, he indorsed this as true conservation. I here present his testimony at the committee hearing:

PINCHOT INDORSES BILL.

(Extracts from statement of Hon. Gifford Pinchot, former Chief Forester, before Public Lands Committee, House of Representatives, June 25, 1913.)

✦ CHAPTER 3

Who Controls
America's Natural
Resources? Water
Rights, Public
Lands, and the
Contest over the
Hetch Hetchy
Valley

We come now face to face with the perfectly clean question of what is the best use to which this water that flows out of the Sierras can be put. As we all know, there is no use of water that is higher than the domestic use. Then, if there is, as the engineers tell us, no other source of supply that is anything like so reasonably available as this one; if this is the best, and, within reasonable limits of cost, the only means of supplying San Francisco with water, we come straight to the question of whether the advantage of leaving this valley in a state of nature is greater than the advantage of using it for the benefit of the city of San Francisco.

Now, the fundamental principle of the whole conservation policy is that of use, to take every part of the land and its resources and put it to that use in which it will best serve the most people, and I think there can be no question at all but that in this case we have an instance in which all weighty considerations demand the passage of the bill.

The construction of roads, trails, and telephone systems which will follow the passage of this bill will be a very important help in the park and forest reserves. The national forest telephone system and the roads and trails to which this bill will lead will form an important additional help in fighting fire in the forest reserves. As has already been set forth by the two Secretaries, the presence of these additional means of communication will mean that the national forest and the national park will be visited by very large numbers of people who cannot visit them now. I think that the men who assert that it is better to leave a piece of natural scenery in its natural condition have rather the better of the argument, and I believe if we had nothing else to consider than the delight of the few men and women who would yearly go into the Hetch Hetchy Valley, then it should be left in its natural condition. But the considerations on the other side of the question to my mind are simply overwhelming, and so much so that I have never been able to see that there was any reasonable argument against the use of this water supply by the city of San Francisco, provided the bill was a reasonable bill.

The (sanitary) regulations which are required are substantially what ought to be followed by any well-intentioned camper.

Now, some people have had an unusual and extraordinary idea of what conservation is. At times in my life I have had the same feeling about it; but when Mr. Pinchot came on the stand and told the committee that the conservation people believed in the use of our natural resources, I was glad to enlist with him. I have never believed in the form of conservation which purposes to bottle things up, but I do believe in that form of conservation which uses things and puts them to the highest and most beneficial and economic use. I am in favor of making war on graft, monopoly, and waste, but I am in favor of use, progress, and development.

Water in California is almost like gold dust. Every drop of it will have to be used for some purpose sooner or later. I call the attention of the committee to the fact that no higher purpose, no higher use, no higher conservation can ever be practised than furnishing a municipality with clear, pure water to drink and to bathe in. This bill accomplishes this for a heroic people who only ask an opportunity to do for themselves at their own expense what many others would not undertake.

Some gentleman may want to know what are the complications. This valley is just a rough craggy gorge between two mountains, which constitutes a good natural dam site. Below the gorge is the San Joaquin Valley. Some one may ask, "Are you going to do justice to the San Joaquin Valley." The answer is "Yes." The irrigationists were present by two able and patriotic attorneys who knew and preserved their every right.

The city and county of San Francisco are doing justice to the San Joaquin Valley by giving them the entire flow of the river and a part of the flood water with which to irrigate the land. San Francisco and the San Joaquin Valley people came together honorably as men and have aided the committee materially.

The fact is that San Francisco purposes to go out and spend $77,000,000 of her own money to corral the flood water that comes out of the snows and flood waters of the higher Sierra, to impound it in her waterworks system for herself, the irrigationists, and the other cities about her. I contend, and I believe this committee will conclude that there can be no higher form of conservation than to use flood waters for drinking, bathing, and other domestic purposes rather than to let them flow idly, unsubdued, and unattended into the sea.

I do not think there is or will be much opposition to this bill. There is a little up in New England. I think one gentleman from Boston came down and appeared before the committee, and he was of the opinion that it was wrong to construct this dam, because he thought that this gorge ought to be left in its original condition. Well, now, I think that practical, thoughtful men, who really want water put to its highest use, can not agree with him. That gentleman from Boston has visited this park two or three times, at great expense and great inconvenience to himself, and while I do not attack his patriotism or his earnestness, his judgment will not squire with any principle of economics known to man. The 11 Members of the California delegation approve this bill, all holding commissions from their people won on the battle field of politics. The Secretary of the Interior approves this bill,

◆ CHAPTER 3

Who Controls
America's Natural
Resources? Water
Rights, Public
Lands, and the
Contest over the
Hetch Hetchy
Valley

and he knows conditions there in California, as he has long been a resident of that State. Gifford Pinchot approves this bill, and he is always careful to safeguard the interests of the Government and those concerned. Mr. Graves, the Chief Forester, approves this bill, and he knows what is safe and unsafe in forestry and park matters. The Army engineers approve this bill, and they are not swayed by politics or partisanship at any time. The irrigation people below the dam approve this bill; they know when their rights are secure. The city of Oakland and the other cities surrounding San Francisco approve this bill, and it will be a blessing and a godsend to them. The only opposition that the committee have been able to find, in two or three months' painstaking investigation, has been that of a few people who believe it is wrong to dam up a gorge and collect the mountain waters that come down from the melting snows and use them for the highest economic purposes. These patriotic, earnest men believe that it is a crime to clip a twig, turn over a rock, or in any way interfere with Nature's task. I should be grieved if I thought practicability should completely drive out of me my love of nature in its crude form, but when it comes to weighing the highest conservation, on one hand, of water for domestic use against the preservation of a rocky, craggy canyon, allowing 200,000,000 gallons of water daily to run idly to the sea, doing no one any good, there is nothing that will appeal to a thoughtful brain of a common-sense, practical man.

I have never feared the judgment of this House when Members can understand what is going on. I do not speak with any disrespect of these people who think that a rugged, jagged gorge is of more importance than a beautiful lake of fresh bathing and drinking water for the people, but I respectfully differ with them. What is more beautiful than a beautiful lake supplying a great and growing city with water to drink and with water to bathe in, and who is there of us that can long contend that a rugged, jagged gorge between two mountains in the Sierras is of more importance, and that it is a crime to convert it into a beautiful lake?

7. William Borah, November 6, 1913.

327 Lexington Avenue.
New York, November 6, 1913.

Hon. William E. Borah,
United States Senate, Washington.

My Dear Senator: I have just seen the letter of September 18, 1913, addressed to Dr. Noble, of Spokane, from Mr. Gifford Pinchot, stating his attitude regarding the Hetch Hetchy bill. As this is a matter of public interest and Mr. Pinchot's letter has been published in the CONGRESSIONAL RECORD, I beg to reply to it point by point. Mr. Pinchot says:

"First. I am fully persuaded that there is no other comparable source of supply available at anything like a reasonable cost to the cities around San Francisco Bay."

Answer. The advisory board of Army engineers reports that there are several other sources of supply, any one of which would be available at a cost which, in the absence of any adequate and impartial investigation, the board estimates at $13,000,000 in favor of the Hetch Hetchy scheme. (Report, p. 50.) The board distinctly states that no thorough or complete investigation has been made of any other source except the Sacramento River. It is claimed that half a dozen other sources are available. Mr. Pinchot is here considering the "reasonable cost" to San Francisco, but that is only one side of the question. Of course San Francisco wishes to get its water as cheaply as possible and wishes the Nation to help foot the bills, but the question of reasonable cost is one that must be considered from the point of view of the Nation as well as of the city. It is being demonstrated that an overwhelming proportion of the people, including a host of conservationists, differ with Mr. Pinchot's view of what constitutes a reasonable cost to the Nation.

"Second. That the supply of surface water furnished by the Spring Valley Water Co. is adequate neither in quality nor in quantity."

Answer. Mr. Freeman, the expert for the city, in his report, page 16, says: "The present quality of the water furnished by the Spring Valley Water Co. is, I believe, thoroughly wholesome and safe." Here is a flat contradiction of Mr. Pinchot. As to quantity nobody doubts that it is desirable for San Francisco ultimately to supplement its existing supply, but this need not be done at the sacrifice of the Hetch Hetchy Valley, which Mr. Pinchot in his testimony before the House committee admits is "one of the great wonders of the world." San Francisco has abundant water in the near-by Coast Range to serve it for 40 or 50 years. According to Mr. Freeman and the Army board the Hetch Hetchy plan is to provide for a time 50 years thereafter.

"Third. That the injury to the Hetch Hetchy by substituting a lake for the present swampy floor of the valley, all due allowances being made for whatever reduction in the height of the walls there may be, is altogether unimportant compared with the benefits to be derived from its use as a reservoir."

Answer. This is Mr. Pinchot's way of minimizing the immense and permanent benefits derived by the people from great natural scenery.

✦ CHAPTER 3

Who Controls
America's Natural
Resources? Water
Rights, Public
Lands, and the
Contest over the
Hetch Hetchy
Valley

According to John Muir the present floor of the valley is not swampy, and the beauty of the valley, all that gives it character and charm, will be destroyed by making of it a municipal water tank. Mr. Pinchot is measuring the value of our noblest scenery in dollars and cents. He has never shown any feeling for the conservation of great scenery, nor has he ever given any championship to the higher uses of such wonderlands as resorts for pleasure and repose, the inspiration of beauty and the cultivation of health. We believe the Creator's masterpieces should not be tinkered by engineers or politicians.

"Fourth. That the sanitary regulations included in the bill absolutely dispose of the plea, untenable at all times, that what San Francisco is asking for is control of half of Yosemite Park instead of merely the Hetch Hetchy reservoir."

Answer. This is very much like saying of a man that while his heart, lungs, stomach, and alimentary canal are in diseased condition, the rest of his body is in perfect health. The Tuolumne River, which runs through the Hetch Hetchy, drains a watershed that must be controlled by San Francisco if that valley is to be used as a reservoir. The bill would virtually prohibit camping within 300 feet from any stream. The watershed is a perfect network of streams, and this regulation would prevent campers from free access to the wonderful Tuolumne Cascades, which in many places are not 300 feet distant from sheer walls. With due respect to Mr. Pinchot, his argument on this point is a quibble. It would be the old story of the tent and the camel's head.

"Fifth. That much of the opposition has its root in the unwillingness of waterpower and transportation interests in and around San Francisco to see the city get possession of the large power it will develop if the grant goes through."

Answer. This statement, in my judgment, is entirely without foundation. The movement to oppose the bill, with which more than three-fourths of the members of the Sierra Club of San Francisco and many other organizations throughout the country have been connected, has had no relation whatever to such interests as Mr. Pinchot mentions. The endeavor to make this bill appear a measure to save San Francisco from a monopoly or from vicious commercial interests is without basis in fact. The president of the so-called monopoly is for the bill. In all the discussion of this question no one has yet mentioned, as far as I know, a single instance of opposition by commercial interests. Why are they not named? Even if there were such opposition it would not affect the conclusive objections to the scheme from the point of view of national policy.

"Sixth. That the public welfare will be immensely better served by the joint use of Hetch Hetchy for beauty and for utility than by depriving the future millions around San Francisco Bay of the use of a valley—a use which will not destroy its beauty—rather than by keeping it untouched for the benefit of the very small number of comparatively well-to-do to whom it will be accessible."

Answer: This is Mr. Pinchot's private opinion and contains no argument whatever. He entirely ignores the vast utility of beauty. Man does not live by bread alone. The beauty of Hetch Hetchy would be destroyed by flooding its floor and substituting an ugly dam and reservoir, and its continued use for the purpose to which it was dedicated will in no way deprive the future millions around San Francisco of water. When Mr. Pinchot speaks of keeping it untouched for the benefit of a very small number of comparatively well-to-do to whom it will be accessible, he makes an argument which would have dedicated the Yosemite Valley itself to San Francisco's use as a water supply. . . .

Source 8 from the Raker Act, 19 December 1913, available through the Library of Congress American Memory digital collection (memory.loc.gov).

8. Excerpt of the Raker Act, December 19, 1913.

Be it enacted by the Senate and House of Representatives of the United States of America in Congress assembled, That there is hereby granted to the city and county of San Francisco, a municipal corporation in the State of California, all necessary rights of way along such locations and of such width, not to exceed two hundred and fifty feet, as in the judgment of the Secretary of the Interior may be required for the purposes of this Act, in, over, and through the public lands of the United States in the counties of Tuolumne, Stanislaus, San Joaquin, and Alameda, in the State of California, and in, over, and through the Yosemite National Park and the Stanislaus National Forest, or portions thereof, lying within the said counties, for the purpose of constructing, operating, and maintaining aqueducts, canals, ditches, pipes, pipe lines, flumes, tunnels, and conduits for conveying water for domestic purposes and uses to the city and county of San Francisco and such other municipalities and water districts as, with the consent of the city and county of San Francisco, or in accordance with the laws of the State of California in force at the time application is made, may hereafter participate in the beneficial use of the rights and

◆ CHAPTER 3

Who Controls
America's Natural
Resources? Water
Rights, Public
Lands, and the
Contest over the
Hetch Hetchy
Valley

privileges granted by this Act; for the purpose of constructing, operating, and maintaining power and electric plants, poles, and lines for generation and sale and distribution of electric energy; also for the purpose of constructing, operating, and maintaining telephone and telegraph lines, and for the purpose of constructing, operating, and maintaining roads, trails, bridges, tramways, railroads, and other means of locomotion, transportation, and communication, such as may be necessary or proper in the construction, maintenance, and operation of the works constructed by the grantee herein; together with such lands in the Hetch Hetchy Valley and Lake Eleanor Basin within the Yosemite National Park, and the Cherry Valley within the Stanislaus National Forest, irrespective of the width or extent of said lands, as may be determined by the Secretary of the Interior to be actually necessary for surface or underground reservoirs, diverting and storage dams; together with such lands as the Secretary of the Interior may determine to be actually necessary for power houses, and all other structures or buildings necessary or properly incident to the construction, operation, and maintenance of said water-power and electric plants, telephone and telegraph lines, and such means of locomotion, transportation, and communication as may be established; together with the right to take, free of cost, from the public lands, the Yosemite National Park, and the Stanislaus National Forest adjacent to its right of way, within such distance as the Secretary of the Interior and the Secretary of Agriculture may determine, stone, earth, gravel, sand, tufa, and other materials of like character actually necessary to be used in the construction, operation, and repair of its said water-power and electric plants, its said telephone and telegraph lines, and its said means of locomotion, transportation, or communication, under such conditions and regulations as may be fixed by the Secretary of the Interior and the Secretary of Agriculture, within their respective jurisdictions, for the protection of the public lands, the Yosemite National Park, and the Stanislaus National Forest: *Provided*, That said grantee shall file, as hereinafter provided, a map or maps showing the boundaries, location, and extent of said proposed rights of way and lands for the purposes hereinabove set forth: *Provided further,* That the Secretary of the Interior shall approve no location or change of location in the national forests unless said location or change of location shall have been approved in writing by the Secretary of Agriculture. . . .

Sources 9–11 are photographs of the Hetch Hetchy Valley, Before and After Construction of the O'Shaughnessy Dam.

9. Hetch Hetchy Valley prior to Damming, Early 1900s.

National Park Service

10. The Reservoir at Hetch Hetchy, after Damming.

Alexander McClearn/Alamy

◆ CHAPTER 3

Who Controls
America's Natural
Resources? Water
Rights, Public
Lands, and the
Contest over the
Hetch Hetchy
Valley

11. O'Shaughnessy Dam, Hetch Hetchy Reservoir, circa 1930s.

Source 12 from the Bay Area Water Supply and Conservation Agency (bawsca.org).

12. Diagram of the Hetch Hetchy Regional Water System.

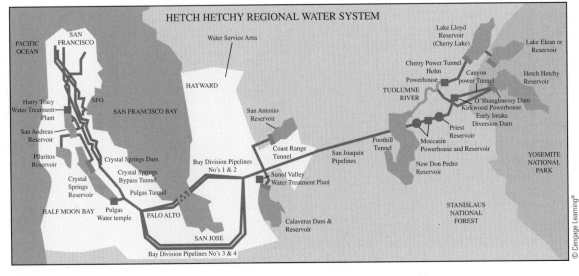

Questions to Consider

The Hetch Hetchy controversy affords a rich opportunity for you and your classmates to engage in historical debate. This can either be an oral, in-class debate or take place online. The central question for this chapter is Why did John Muir and Gifford Pinchot strongly disagree about the use of water and land? As you come to understand what lay behind their points of view and, ultimately, why the Hetch Hetchy proposal was approved by the U.S. government, you can evaluate a related, equally important question: What were the consequences of these struggles over water and land?

Each student should choose a distinct point of view in the debate over Hetch Hetchy, drawing especially on Sources 1–7. Muir and Pinchot were, of course, the most important advocates in this contest. But, as the evidence reveals, many other individuals and constituencies weighed in on the decision. Muir, for example, represented the viewpoints of tourists visiting national parks and of preservationists, among others. Pinchot, meanwhile, reflected the interests of industrialists, city planners, foresters, and conservationists. Politicians held firm (and contradictory) ideas, too. As you compile a list of varied points of view, keep in mind that oftentimes people who agree on a general policy sometimes develop their support for very different reasons. For example, San Francisco political leaders lobbying for the dam project had one set of priorities that might or might not have dovetailed with working-class residents of San Francisco who wanted safe drinking water or with industrialists hoping to expand into the city. Likewise, not all preservationists shared Muir's reverence for nature. Some, as you can see from the evidence, even supported the Hetch Hetchy proposal. Where a person lived—in Washington, D.C., in San Francisco, or near Yosemite—and how one earned a living could shape perspective. The documents from Scott Ferris (Source 6) and William Borah (Source 7) will be particularly illuminating as you begin to recreate the contest over Hetch Hetchy.

Once you have determined the range of opinions and decided on the best way to debate them in your class, return again to the evidence. Consider not only the substance of what advocates said and wrote but the political and rhetorical moves they made. How did Congressmen approach Gifford Pinchot and how did he act in return? What tactics did John Muir adopt in his public appeals to save Hetch Hetchy? What is implied, or even left unsaid, in the evidence?

After fully debating the differing reactions to the Hetch Hetchy proposal—in person, online, or however your class decides is best—turn to the remaining five sources. Now you can move from understanding the disagreements to evaluating the consequences. This should spark an even more thought-provoking and wide-ranging discussion. The excerpt from the Raker Act (Source 8) provides insight about what was legally approved, which reveals a great

[87]

✦ CHAPTER 3

Who Controls
America's Natural
Resources? Water
Rights, Public
Lands, and the
Contest over the
Hetch Hetchy
Valley

deal about the consequences of the decision. The photographs (Sources 9–11) offer visual evidence. Depending on your point of view, however, you might see very different things in those photographs. The diagram of the Hetch Hetchy Regional Water System (Source 12) will allow you to bring your class debate about the consequences of the Hetch Hetchy project into the present. Remember, the consequences of Hetch Hetchy were short-term and long-term, ecological and economic, personal and political.

Finally, consider one last issue. To what degree were you, individually and as a group, able to evaluate this controversy in the context of the Progressive Era? How much did present-day opinions about economic development or environmentalism influence your perceptions of the contest over Hetch Hetchy?

✦

Epilogue

Civil Engineer Michael O'Shaughnessy oversaw the Hetch Hetchy project, and a 430-foot-high dam across the Tuolumne River still bears his name. Flooding the Hetch Hetchy Valley to carry safe and reliable water more than 160 miles to San Francisco eventually became a twenty-year-long enterprise. It involved building over sixty miles of tunnels and 250 miles of pipelines as well as multiple reservoirs, smaller dams, and hydroelectric plants. At least eighty-nine workers lost their lives on the project.

Today, the Hetch Hetchy Regional Water System carries 260 million gallons of water every day—water that helped turn San Francisco into one of America's greatest cities. The Bay Area and Silicon Valley are home to a remarkably robust economy, a diverse and healthy population, and a lucrative investment base and tourist destination. San Francisco has some of the purest and safest water in the entire nation. The San Francisco Public Utilities Commission praises the fact that "our delicious tap water comes from pristine snowmelt in Hetch Hetchy Reservoir in Yosemite National Park." In 2010, in an effort to promote water conservation during a state-wide drought, San Francisco installed bottle-refilling stations across the city to provide "free access to high-quality Hetch Hetchy tap water while on the go."[10]

From time to time, Californians have debated restoring the Hetch Hetchy Valley, but the financial costs, water supply implications, and environmental consequences have always won out. The difficulties in going back on the Hetch Hetchy project have always seemed insurmountable.

However, the Hetch Hetchy project proved to be incredibly influential going forward. After Hetch Hetchy,

10. "Drink Tap" page of the SFPUC website: www.sfwater.org. Accessed February 2014.

Americans recalculated the costs of such massive building and extraction projects in the country's national parks and forests.

In the 1940s, politicians from some western states proposed damming part of the Colorado River in the Echo Park district of Dinosaur National Monument. The Echo Park Dam, they argued, would provide their region with efficient hydroelectric power and the resulting reservoirs would promote population growth and tourism. Leaders in the National Park Service and in the Sierra Club stood firm together against what they called during Congressional debates a second Hetch Hetchy. The environmentalists succeeded, not only in reversing the precedent of Hetch Hetchy and thwarting the Echo Park project but also in shaping national policy for decades to come. A formidable coalition of environmental groups, led by the Sierra Club and Wilderness Society, fostered a renewed commitment to national parks within the larger American population. Politicians expanded legal protections of publicly held lands, including the 1964 Wilderness Act.[11]

The question of how to best supply water to the American West remained a pressing issue, however, so the damming project was altered, not abandoned. The resulting system, the Colorado River Storage Project, today provides hydroelectric power, water, and flood control to parts of Wyoming, Colorado, New Mexico, Utah, and Arizona. The cost to the ecology of the river and the environment of the wider region has been steep.

The best-laid plans of engineers, politicians, and conservationists have not kept parts of the American West from suffering in the twenty-first century from increasingly severe droughts and growing water stress (a lack of steady access to adequate renewable water supplies). California has been especially hard hit. California Governor Jerry Brown officially declared in 2015 a drought state of emergency and the state maintains a website monitoring what they recognize as a drought "disaster" and promoting a multitude of conservation efforts.[12]

The problem is growing and global. Only around 1 percent of the Earth's water supply is suitable for human consumption—the rest is either saltwater (97 percent) or locked in ice. Population growth, droughts, and global warming all impinge on this essential and precious natural resource. Researchers anticipate that in the coming decades, as our demand for drinking water outpaces our supply, competition for water will play an increasingly central role in geopolitics. Scholars at the Massachusetts Institute of Technology, for example, calculate that by 2050 more than half of the world's population will live in water-stressed areas.

---

11. The act, signed by President Lyndon Johnson, created the National Wilderness Preservation System. Today, this act protects over one hundred million acres of undeveloped public lands where, according to the law, "man himself is a visitor who does not remain." For more on Echo Park, see Mark W. T. Harvey, *A Symbol of Wilderness: Echo Park and the American Conservation Movement* (Albuquerque: University of New Mexico Press, 1994).

12. The website is www.ca.gov/drought. Given the agricultural production of California, their drought shapes food prices nationally.

4

Homogenizing a Pluralistic Nation: Propaganda During World War I

◆

The Problem

One week after Congress approved the war declaration that brought the United States into World War I,[1] President Woodrow Wilson signed Executive Order 2594, which created the Committee on Public Information, a government agency designed to mobilize public opinion behind the war effort. Wilson selected forty-one-year-old journalist and political ally George Creel to direct this committee's efforts. By war's end in late 1918, Creel's committee had a staff of over 150,000 full-time employees and volunteers who had affected the lives of nearly every man, woman, and child in the United States. "There was no part of the great war machinery that we did not touch," Creel boasted, "no medium of appeal that we did not employ."[2]

Although Creel himself opposed government-imposed censorship and repression of information and opinions, the Committee on Public Information did construct a system of *voluntary* censorship, while employing all the appeals and tools used by private agencies in the relatively new field of mass advertising. In addition, the Committee strongly urged ethnic Americans to abandon their Old World ties and become "Unhyphenated Americans." During the twenty months that the United States was at war, the committee produced millions of press releases, books, pamphlets, scripts for speeches

1. Wilson delivered his war message on April 2, 1917. The Senate declared war on April 3 and the House of Representatives followed suit on April 6.

2. Walton Rawls, *Wake Up, America: World War I and the American Poster* (New York: Abbeville Press, 1988), p. 137.

by "Four Minute Men," and films.[3] In addition, the nation's best artists and illustrators donated their talents to the committee by producing full-color posters that played a major propaganda role, and moving picture stars such as Charlie Chaplin, Mary Pickford, and Douglas Fairbanks appeared at huge rallies to sell war bonds.[4] In all, then, U.S. citizens were almost literally inundated with propaganda commissioned by the Committee on Public Information as well as by news stories, films, songs, and other types of mass communication that the committee oversaw and approved.

Why did the federal government believe that such a massive propaganda appeal by the Committee on Public Information was necessary? For one thing, since the war broke out in Europe in 1914, the Wilson administration had promised that the United States would remain neutral and noninvolved, a policy that was supported strongly by the American people. It was feared, therefore, that a relatively swift shift from neutrality to full engagement would not be supported. Also, a number of well-known and respected Americans

(including Senators Robert La Follette of Wisconsin and George Norris of Nebraska, industrialists Andrew Carnegie and Henry Ford, and reformer Jane Addams) as well as practically the entire American left (led by socialist leader Eugene Debs) vehemently opposed American involvement and might affect public opinion. Finally, many government officials feared that large ethnic blocs of Americans would not support the U.S. entry into the conflict. In 1920 (the census closest to America's entry into the war) the Bureau of the Census estimated that there were over two million people who had been born in Germany or in one of the other Central Powers. It was also reported that the nation contained over one million people who had been born in Ireland, many of whom were vehemently anti-British and thus might be expected to side with Germany and its allies. Could such a heterogeneous society be persuaded to support the war effort voluntarily? Could Americans of the same ethnic stock as the enemies be rallied to the cause?[5]

The purpose of the Committee on Public Information was to use every means at its disposal to garner support for the U.S. war effort. Not only did the committee create its own propaganda, but it also either discouraged or banned outright speeches, news reports, editorials, and films that expressed conflicting opinions.

3. The "Four Minute Man" speeches originally were intended to be used at moving picture theaters during the roughly four minutes that the reels were being changed. They soon expanded to civic clubs, theaters, and so forth. Approximately seventy-five thousand volunteers (men and women, in spite of their name) delivered over seven million of these talks, written by the Committee on Public Information.

4. The committee engaged 279 artists to create several hundred poster designs. Some of the best-known illustrators were James Montgomery Flagg, Charles Dana Gibson, Joseph Christian Leyendecker, Haskel Coffin, and Alonzo Earl Foringer. Female illustrators included Lucille Patterson and Laura Brey.

5. The statistics for Ireland included a comparatively modest number from Northern Ireland. There were, however, over three million native-born Americans who had one or both parents of Irish birth.

◆ CHAPTER 4

Homogenizing a
Pluralistic Nation:
Propaganda
During World
War I

Although examples of propaganda are nearly as old as society itself, by World War I the combination of government propaganda and modern communications technology made the manipulation of collective attitudes and opinions considerably more pervasive and doubtless more effective than earlier efforts. Indeed, some liberal intellectuals began to fear that propaganda techniques exploited latent prejudices, created a kind of mob psychology, and used lies and half-truths to sway the crowd. For these increasingly concerned individuals, the word *propaganda* itself began to take on sinister connotations. Thus Socialist leader Eugene V. Debs was not completely alone when he recognized the "irony of free speech suppressed by a nation allegedly fighting for democracy." Yet these doubters and worriers were in the distinct minority, and the Committee on Public Information for the most part not only successfully marshaled American public opinion in support of the war effort, but in doing so helped create a climate of mass fear and suspicion.[6]

In this chapter, you will be examining and analyzing the propaganda techniques of a modern nation at war. The Evidence section contains material sponsored or commissioned by the Committee on Public Information (posters, newspaper advertisements, and excerpts from speeches by Four Minute Men) as well as privately produced works (song lyrics and commercial film advertisements) that either were approved by the committee or tended to parallel its efforts. After examining the evidence, you will work to answer the following questions:

1. How and why did the U.S. government attempt to mobilize the opinions of a diverse American public in support of a united war effort?

2. What were the consequences of this effort?

On a larger scale, you should be willing to ponder other questions as well, although they do not relate directly to the evidence you will examine. To begin with, is government-sponsored propaganda during wartime a good thing? When it comes into conflict with the First Amendment's guarantees of freedom of speech, which should prevail? **Finally, is there a danger that government-sponsored propaganda can be carried too far? Why do you think that was (or was not) the case during World War I?**

---

6. For three especially interesting studies of propaganda during World War I, see J. Michael Sproule, *Propaganda and Democracy: The American Experience of Media and Mass Persuasion* (Cambridge: Cambridge University Press, 1997), esp. pp. 1–14; Brett Gary, *The Nervous Liberals: Propaganda Anxieties from World War I to the Cold War* (New York: Columbia University Press, 1999), esp. pp. 1–23; and Philip M. Taylor, *Munitions of the Mind: A History of Propaganda from the Ancient World to the Present Era* (Manchester, UK: Manchester University Press, 2003), esp. pp. 177–185.

Background

By the early twentieth century, the United States had worldwide economic interests and even had acquired a modest colonial empire, but many Americans wanted to believe that they were still insulated from world affairs and impervious to global problems. Two great oceans seemed to protect the nation from overseas threats, and the enormity of the country and comparative weakness of its neighbors appeared to secure it against all dangers. Let other nations waste their people and resources in petty wars over status and territory, Americans reasoned. The United States should stand above such greed or insanity, and certainly should not wade into foreign quagmires.

To many Americans, Europe was especially suspect. For centuries, European nations had engaged in an almost ceaseless round of armed conflicts— wars for national unity, territory, or even religion or empire. Moreover, in the eyes of many Americans, these bloody wars appeared to have solved little or nothing, and the end of one war seemed to be but a prelude to the next. Ambitious kings and their plotting ministers seemed to make Europe the scene of almost constant uproar, an uproar that many Americans saw as devoid of reason and morality. Nor did it appear that the United States, as powerful as it was, could have any effect on the unstable European situation.

For this reason, most Americans greeted news of the outbreak of war in Europe in 1914 with equal measures of surprise and determination not to become involved. They applauded President Wilson's August 4 proclamation of neutrality, his statement (issued two weeks later) urging Americans to be impartial in thought as well as in deed, and his insistence that the United States continue neutral commerce with all the belligerents. Few Americans protested German violation of Belgian neutrality. Indeed, most Americans (naively, as it turned out) believed that the United States both should and could remain aloof from the carnage in Europe.

However, many factors pulled the United States into the conflict that later became known as World War I.[7] America's economic prosperity to a large extent rested on commercial ties with Europe. In 1914, U.S. trade with the Allies (England, France, and Russia) exceeded $800 million, whereas trade with the Central Powers (Germany, Austria, and Turkey) stood at approximately $170 million. Much of the trade with Great Britain and France was financed through loans from American banks, something President Wilson and Secretary of State William Jennings Bryan openly discouraged because both men believed that those economic interests might eventually draw the United States into the conflict. Indeed, Wilson and Bryan probably were correct. Nevertheless,

7. Until the outbreak of what became known as World War II, World War I was referred to as the Great War.

◆ CHAPTER 4

Homogenizing a
Pluralistic Nation:
Propaganda
During World
War I

American economic interests were closely tied to those of Great Britain and France. Thus a victory by the Central Powers might damage U.S. trade. As Wilson drifted to an acceptance of this fact, Bryan had to back down.

A second factor pulling the United States into the war was the deep-seated feelings of President Wilson himself. Formerly a constitutional historian (Wilson had been a college professor and university president before entering the political arena as a reform governor of New Jersey), Wilson had long admired the British people and their form of government. Although technically neutral, the president strongly, though privately, favored the Allies and viewed a German victory as unthinkable. Moreover, many of Wilson's key advisers and the people close to him were decidedly pro-British. Such was the persuasion of the president's friend and closest adviser, Colonel Edward House, as well as that of Robert Lansing (who replaced Bryan as secretary of state)[8] and Walter Hines Page (ambassador to England). These men and others helped reinforce Wilson's strong political opinions and influence the president's changing position toward the war in Europe. Hence, although Wilson asked Americans to be neutral in thought as well as in deed, in fact he and his principal advisers were neither. More than once, the president chose to ignore British violations of America's

neutrality. Finally, when it appeared that the Central Powers might outlast their enemies, Wilson was determined to intercede. It was truly an agonizing decision for the president, who had worked so diligently to keep his nation out of war.

A third factor pulling the United States toward war was the strong ethnic ties of many Americans to the Old World. Many Americans had been born in Europe, and an even larger number were the sons and daughters of European immigrants. Although these people considered themselves to be, and were, Americans, some retained emotional ties to Europe that they sometimes carried into the political arena—ties that could influence America's foreign policy.

Finally, as the largest neutral commercial power in the world, the United States soon became caught in the middle of the commercial warfare of the belligerents. With the declaration of war, both Great Britain and Germany threw up naval blockades. Great Britain's blockade was designed to cut the Central Powers off from war materiel. American commercial vessels bound for Germany were stopped, searched, and often seized by the British navy. Wilson protested British policy many times, but to no effect. After all, giving in to Wilson's protests would have deprived Britain of its principal military asset: the British navy.

German's blockade was even more dangerous to the United States, partly because the vast majority of American trade was with England and France. In addition, however, Germany's chief method of blockading the Allies was the use of the

---

8. Bryan resigned in 1915, in protest over what he considered Wilson's too sharp note to Germany over the sinking of the passenger liner *Lusitania*. Wilson called the act "illegal and inhuman." Bryan sensed that the Wilson administration was tilting away from neutrality.

submarine, a comparatively new weapon in 1914. Because of the nature of the submarine (lethal while underwater, not equal to other fighting vessels on the surface), it was difficult for the submarine to remain effective and at the same time adhere to international law, such as the requirement that sufficient warning be given before sinking an enemy ship.[9] In 1915, hoping to terrorize the British into making peace, Germany unleashed its submarines in the Atlantic with orders to sink all ships flying Allied flags. In March, a German submarine sank the British passenger ship *Falaba*. Then on May 7, 1915, the British liner *Lusitania* was sunk with a loss of more than one thousand lives, 128 of them American. Although Germany had published warnings in American newspapers specifically cautioning Americans not to travel on the *Lusitania*, and although it was ultimately discovered that the *Lusitania* had gone down so fast (in only eighteen minutes) because the British were shipping ammunition in the hold of the passenger ship, Americans were shocked by the Germans' actions on the high seas. Most Americans, however, continued to believe that the United States should stay out of the war and approved of Wilson's statement, issued three days after the *Lusitania* sank to the bottom, that "there is such a thing as a man being too proud to fight."

9. International laws governing warfare at sea, as well as neutral shipping during wartime, were written in the mid-eighteenth century, more than one hundred years before the submarine became a potent seagoing weapon.

Yet a combination of economic interests, German submarine warfare, and other events gradually pushed the United States toward involvement. In early February 1917, Germany announced a policy of unrestricted submarine warfare against all ships—belligerent and neutral alike. Ships would be sunk without warning if found to be in what Germany designated as forbidden waters. Later that month, the British intercepted a secret telegram intended for the German minister to Mexico stationed in Mexico City. In that telegram, German foreign secretary Arthur Zimmermann offered Mexico a deal: Germany would help Mexico retrieve territory lost to the United States in the 1840s if Mexico would make a military alliance with Germany and declare war on the United States in the event that the United States declared war on Germany. Knowing the impact that such a telegram would have on American public opinion, the British quickly handed the telegram over to Wilson, who released it to the press. From that point on, it was but a matter of time before the United States would become involved in World War I.

On March 20, 1917, President Wilson called his cabinet together at the White House to advise him on how to proceed in the deteriorating situation with Germany. Wilson's cabinet officers unanimously urged the president to call Congress into session immediately and ask for a declaration of war against Germany. When the last cabinet member had finished speaking, Wilson said, "Well, gentlemen, I think there is no doubt as to what your advice is. I thank you," and dismissed

✦ CHAPTER 4

Homogenizing a
Pluralistic Nation:
Propaganda
During World
War I

the meeting without informing the cabinet of his own intentions.

Yet even though Wilson had labored so arduously to keep the United States out of the war in Europe, by March 20 (or very soon after) his mind was made up: the United States must make war on Germany. Typing out his war message on his own Hammond portable typewriter, Wilson was out of sorts and complained often of headaches. The president, devoted to peace and Progressive reform, was drafting the document he had prayed he would never have to write.

The evening before the president was to deliver his message to Congress and ask for a declaration of war against Germany, he had a meeting with Frank Cobb, the editor of the *New York World*. As Cobb later remembered, Wilson unburdened himself to his friend and said in part:

> It [war] would mean that we should lose our heads along with the rest and stop weighing right and wrong. It would mean that a majority of people . . . would go war-mad, quit thinking, and devote their energies to destruction. . . . [T]hey'll forget there ever was such a thing as tolerance. . . . Conformity would be the only virtue.[10]

The next day President Wilson appeared in person before a joint session of Congress and delivered his war message. Two days later the Senate approved a war declaration by a vote of 82–6. The House of Representatives followed suit on April 6 by a vote of 373–50. The fifty-six votes in the Senate and House against the declaration of war essentially came from three separate groups: senators and congressmen with strong German and Austrian constituencies, isolationists who maintained that the United States should not become involved on either side, and some Progressive reformers who believed that the war would divert America's attention from political, economic, and social reforms.[11]

As noted earlier, at the outset of the U.S. entry into the war, the Wilson administration feared that the ethnically diverse American public might not unite in support of the nation's involvement in the Great War. Without a decisive event to prompt the war declaration (some Americans even suspected the Zimmermann telegram was a British hoax), would the American people support the war with sufficient unanimity? No firing on Fort Sumter or blowing up of the battleship *Maine* would force America's entrance into this war, nor would the *Lusitania* sinking, which had occurred two years before the 1917 war declaration. Without the obvious threat of having been attacked, would the American

---

10. Excerpt of a conversation between President Wilson and Frank Cobb on the evening of April 1, 1917, in Henry Steele Commager and Allan Nevins, *The Heritage of America* (Boston: Little, Brown, 1951), pp. 1086–1087. Some historians do not believe that this conversation took place, and that Wilson's statements were created later by Cobb.

11. Interestingly, Jeannette Rankin (Republican, Montana), the first woman elected to Congress, was the only member of that body who voted against both America's entry into World War I and World War II. During the Vietnam War, she led a demonstration against that conflict in front of the U.S. Capitol Building.

people rally to the colors to defeat a faraway enemy? Could isolationist and noninterventionist opinion, very strong as late as the presidential election of 1916, be overcome? Could an ethnically heterogeneous people stand together in time of war? To bind together a diverse people behind the war effort, President Wilson created the Committee on Public Information.

The Method

For George Creel and the Committee on Public Information, the purposes of propaganda were very clear:

1. Unite a multiethnic, pluralistic society behind the war effort.
2. Attract a sufficient number of men to the armed services and elicit universal civilian support for those men.
3. Influence civilians to support the war effort by purchasing war bonds or by other actions (such as limiting personal consumption or rolling bandages).
4. Influence civilians to put pressure on other civilians to refrain from antiwar comments, strikes, antidraft activities, unwitting dispersal of information to spies, and other public acts that could hurt the war effort.

To achieve these ends, propaganda techniques had to be used with extreme care. For propaganda to be effective, it would have to contain one or more of the following features:

1. Portrayal of American and Allied servicemen in the best possible light
2. Portrayal of the enemy in the worst possible light
3. Portrayal of the American and Allied cause as just and the enemy's cause as unjust
4. Message to civilians that they were involved in the war effort in important ways
5. Communication of a sense of urgency to civilians

In this chapter, you are given the following six types of World War I propaganda to analyze, some of it produced directly by the Committee on Public Information and some produced privately but examined and approved by the committee:

1. One popular song, perhaps the most famous to come out of World War I, performed in music halls and vaudeville houses (Source 1). Although the Committee on Public Information did not produce

◆ CHAPTER 4

Homogenizing a
Pluralistic Nation:
Propaganda
During World
War I

this kind of material, it could—and did—discourage performances of "unpatriotic" popular songs.

2. Three newspaper and magazine advertisements produced directly by the Committee on Public Information (Sources 2–4).

3. Eleven posters commissioned by the committee to be used for recruiting, encouraging the purchase of liberty bonds and liberty loans, calling for sacrifices by civilians, and urging unity and patriotism (Sources 5–15).

4. Two cartoons, one an editorial cartoon and the other a prizewinning cartoon in a contest sponsored by a U.S. Army publication (Sources 16 and 17).

5. Two excerpts from speeches by Four Minute Men and one poem by a Four Minute Man (Sources 18–20).

6. Material concerning committee or commercial feature films, including suggestions to theater owners on how to advertise the film *Kultur,* two film advertisements, and one still photograph used in advertising the film *The Kaiser, the Beast of Berlin* (Sources 21–24).

As you examine the evidence, you will see that effective propaganda operates on two levels. On the surface, there is the logical appeal for support to help win the war. On another level, however, certain images and themes are used to excite the emotions of the people for whom the propaganda is designed. As you examine the evidence, ask yourself the following questions:

1. For whom was this piece of propaganda designed?

2. What was this piece of propaganda trying to get people to think? To do?

3. What logical appeals were being made?

4. What emotional appeals were being made?

5. What might have been the results—positive and negative—of these kinds of appeals?

In songs, speeches, advertisements, and film reviews, are there key words or important images? Where there are illustrations (ads, posters, and cartoons), what facial expressions and images are used? Finally, are there any common logical and emotional themes running through government-sponsored propaganda during World War I? How did the United States use propaganda to mobilize public opinion during the war?

The Evidence

Source 1 from George M. Cohan, "Over There," 1917.

1. "Over There"

Johnnie, get your gun,
Get your gun, get your gun,
Take it on the run,
On the run, on the run.
Hear them calling you and me,
Every son of liberty.
Hurry right away,
No delay, no delay.
Make your daddy glad
To have had such a lad.
Tell your sweetheart not to pine,
To be proud her boy's in line.

Chorus (repeat chorus twice)
Over there, over there,
Send the word, send the word over there—
That the Yanks are coming,
The Yanks are coming,
The drums rum-tumming
Ev'rywhere.
So prepare, say a pray'r,
Send the word, send the word to beware.
We'll be over, we're coming over,
And we won't come back till it's over
Over there.

◆ CHAPTER 4

Homogenizing a
Pluralistic Nation:
Propaganda
During World
War I

Sources 2–4 from James R. Mock and Cedric Larson, *Words That Won the War: The Story of the Committee on Public Information* (Princeton: Princeton University Press, 1939), pp. 64, 169, 184.

2. "Spies *and* Lies" Advertisement Urging Americans to Report the Enemy.

Spies *and* Lies

German agents are everywhere, eager to gather scraps of news about our men, our ships, our munitions. It is still possible to get such information through to Germany, where thousands of these fragments—often individually harmless—are patiently pieced together into a whole which spells death to American soldiers and danger to American homes.

But while the enemy is most industrious in trying to collect information, and his systems elaborate, he is *not* superhuman—indeed he is often very stupid, and would fail to get what he wants were it not deliberately handed to him by the carelessness of loyal Americans.

Do not discuss in public, or with strangers, any news of troop and transport movements, or bits of gossip as to our military preparations, which come into your possession.

Do not permit your friends in service to tell you—or write you—"inside" facts about where they are, what they are doing and seeing.

Do not become a tool of the Hun by passing on the malicious, disheartening rumors which he so eagerly sows. Remember he asks no better service than to have you spread his lies of disasters to our soldiers and sailors, gross scandals in the Red Cross, cruelties, neglect and wholesale executions in our camps, drunkenness and vice in the Expeditionary Force, and other tales certain to disturb American patriots and to bring anxiety and grief to American parents.

And do not wait until you catch someone putting a bomb under a factory. Report the man who spreads pessimistic stories, divulges—or seeks—confidential military information, cries for peace, or belittles our efforts to win the war.

Send the names of such persons, even if they are in uniform, to the Department of Justice, Washington. Give all the details you can, with names of witnesses if possible—show the Hun that we can beat him at his own game of collecting scattered information and putting it to work. The fact that you made the report will not become public.

You are in contact with the enemy *today*, just as truly as if you faced him across No Man's Land. In your hands are two powerful weapons with which to meet him—discretion and vigilance. *Use them.*

COMMITTEE ON PUBLIC INFORMATION
8 JACKSON PLACE, WASHINGTON, D. C.

George Creel, *Chairman*
The Secretary of State
The Secretary of War
The Secretary of the Navy

Contributed through Division of Advertising   *United States Gov't Comm. on Public Information*

3. "Bachelor of Atrocities" Advertisement for Fighting the Enemy by Buying Liberty Bonds.

Bachelor *of* Atrocities

IN the vicious guttural language of Kultur,[12] the degree A. B. means Bachelor of Atrocities. Are you going to let the Prussian Python strike at your Alma Mater, as it struck at the University of Louvain?[13]

The Hohenzollern[14] fang strikes at every element of decency and culture and taste that your college stands for. It leaves a track so terrible that only whispered fragments may be recounted. It has ripped all the world-old romance out of war, and reduced it to the dead, black depths of muck, and hate, and bitterness.

You may soon be called to fight. But you are called upon right now to buy Liberty Bonds. You are called upon to economize in every way. It is sometimes harder to live nobly than to die nobly. The supreme sacrifice of life may come easier than the petty sacrifices of comforts and luxuries. You are called to exercise stern self-discipline. Upon this the Allied Success depends.

Set aside every possible dollar for the purchase of Liberty Bonds. Do it relentlessly. Kill every wasteful impulse, that America may live. Every bond you buy fires point-blank at Prussian Terrorism.

BUY U. S. GOVERNMENT BONDS FOURTH LIBERTY LOAN

Contributed through Division of Advertising

United States Gov't Comm. on Public Information

This space contributed for the Winning of the War by
A. T SKERRY, '84, and CYRILLE CARREAU, '04.

Appeal to the Symbols of Education
Two Graduates of New York University Contributed the Space for This CPI Advertisement in Their "Alumni News"

National Archives

12. Germans often asserted that they had *Kultur*, or a superior culture, in contrast to *civilization*, which they viewed as weak and effeminate.

13. The *University of Louvain*, in Belgium, was pillaged and partially destroyed by German troops. Some professors were beaten and others killed, and the library (containing 250,000 books and manuscripts, some irreplaceable) was totally destroyed. The students themselves were home for summer vacation.

14. *Hohenzollern* was the name of the German royal family since the nation's founding in 1871. It had been the Prussian royal family since 1525.

◆ CHAPTER 4

Homogenizing a
Pluralistic Nation:
Propaganda
During World
War I

4. Advertisement Appealing to History Teachers, April 4, 1917.

The Committee on Public Information
Established by Order of the President, April 4, 1917

Distribute free *except as noted* the following publications :

I. Red, White and Blue Series :

No. 1. How the War Came to America (English, German, Polish, Bohemian, Italian, Spanish and Swedish).

No. 2. National Service Handbook (primarily for libraries, schools, Y. M. C. A.'s, Clubs, fraternal organizations, etc., as a guide and reference work on all forms of war activity, civil, charitable and military).

No. 3. The Battle Line of Democracy. Prose and Poetry of the Great War. Price 25 cent. Special price to teachers. Proceeds to the Red Cross. Other issues in preparation.

II. War Information Series :

No. 1. The War Message and Facts Behind it.

No. 2. The Nation in Arms, by Secretaries Lane and Baker.

No. 3. The Government of Germany, by Prof. Charles D. Hazen.

No. 4. The Great War from Spectator to Participant.

No. 5. A War of Self Defense, by Secretary Lansing and Assistant Secretary of Labor Louis F. Post.

No. 6. American Loyalty by Citizens of German Descent.

No. 7. Amerikanische Bürgertreue, a translation of No. 6.

Other issues will appear shortly.

III. Official Bulletin :

Accurate daily statement of what all agencies of government are doing in war times. Sent free to newspapers and postmasters (to be put on bulletin boards). Subscription price $5.00 per year.

Address Requests to

Committee on Public Information, Washington, D. C.

What Can History Teachers Do Now?

You can help the community realize what history should mean to it.

You can confute those who by selecting a few historic facts seek to establish some simple cure-all for humanity.

You can confute those who urge that mankind can wipe the past off the slate and lay new foundations for civilization.

You can encourage the sane use of experience in discussions of public questions.

You can help people understand what democracy is by pointing out the common principle in the ideas of Plato, Cromwell, Rousseau, Jefferson, Jackson and Washington.

You can help people understand what German autocracy has in common with the autocracy of the Grand Mogul.

You can help people understand that democracy is not inconsistent with law and efficient government.

You can help people understand that failure of the past to make the world safe for democracy does not mean that it can not be made safe in the future.

You can so teach your students that they will acquire "historical mindedness" and realize the connection of the past with the present.

You can not do these things unless you inform yourself, and think over your information.

You can help yourself by reading the following :
"History and the Great War" bulletin of Bureau of Education.

A series of articles published throughout the year in THE HISTORY TEACHER'S MAGAZINE.

You can obtain aid and advice by writing to
The National Board for Historical Service, 1133 Woodward Building, Washington, D. C.

United States Bureau of Education, Division of Civic Education, Washington, D. C.

Committee on Public Information, Division of Educational Co-operation, 10 Jackson Place, Washington, D. C.

The Committee on Patriotism through Education of the National Security League, 31 Pine Street, New York City.

Carnegie Endowment for International Peace, 2 Jackson Place, Washington, D. C.

National Committee of Patriotic and Defense Societies, Southern Building, Washington, D. C.

The World Peace Foundation, 40 Mount Vernon St., Boston, Mass.

American Association for International Conciliation, 407 West 117th Street, New York City.

The American Society for Judicial Settlement of International Disputes, Baltimore, Md.

The Editor, THE HISTORY TEACHER'S MAGAZINE, Philadelphia.

Source 5 from *The James Montgomery Flagg Poster Book,* introduction by Susan E. Meyer (New York: Watson-Guptill Publications, 1975).

5. World War I's Most Famous Poster (James Montgomery Flagg).

◆ CHAPTER 4

Homogenizing a
Pluralistic Nation:
Propaganda
During World
War I

Source 6 from Peter Stanley, *What Did You Do in the War, Daddy?* (Melbourne: Oxford University Press, 1983), p. 55.

6. "Destroy This Mad Brute" (H. R. Hopps).

Source 7 from Anthony Crawford, *Posters in the George C. Marshall Research Foundation* (Charlottesville: University of Virginia Press, 1939), p. 30.

7. "Joan of Arc Saved France" (Haskell Coffin).

Source 8 from Walton Rawls, *Wake Up, America: World War I and the American Poster* (New York: Abbeville Press, 1988), p. 129.

8. "Our Boys Need Sox" (Anonymous).

◆ CHAPTER 4

Homogenizing a
Pluralistic Nation:
Propaganda
During World
War I

Sources 9 and 10 from Joseph Darracott, ed., *The First World War in Posters* (New York: Dover Publications, 1974), pp. 30, 56.

9. "Weapons for Liberty" (Joseph Christian Leyendecker).

10. "The Greatest Mother in the World" (Alonzo Earl Foringer).

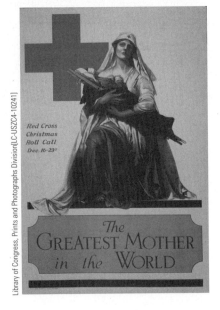

Sources 11–13 from Rawls, *Wake Up, America,* pp. 199, 150, 232.

11. "You buy a Liberty Bond" (G. R. Macauley).

◆ CHAPTER 4

Homogenizing a
Pluralistic Nation:
Propaganda
During World
War I

12. "Here He Is, Sir" (Charles Dana Gibson).

13. "Americans All" (Howard Chandler Christy).

✦ CHAPTER 4

Homogenizing a
Pluralistic Nation:
Propaganda
During World
War I

Source 14 from Special Collections, University of Tennessee Library.

14. "Jewish Welfare Board" (Sidney Reisenberg).

Source 15 from a private collection. Used with permission.

15. "Colored Man Is No Slacker" (Anonymous).

◆ CHAPTER 4

Homogenizing a
Pluralistic Nation:
Propaganda
During World
War I

Source 16 from John Higham, *Strangers in the Land: Patterns of American Nativism,* 1860–1925 (New Brunswick, N.J.: Rutgers University Press, 1955), p. 210.

16. *New York Herald* Editorial Cartoon: German American Dr. Karl Muck, Conductor of the Boston Symphony Orchestra, Needed a Police Escort When He Conducted a Concert in March 1918 in New York City.[12]

W. A. Rogers, New York Herald, March 1918.

12. Dr. Karl Muck, a native of Germany and conductor of the Boston Symphony Orchestra since 1912, was accused of sympathizing with the enemy for conducting German music. When he declined a request to lead the orchestra in "The Star Spangled Banner," he was arrested and imprisoned in Georgia for the duration of the war. After the war he was deported to Germany, where he lived until his death in 1940.

Source 17 from Rawls, *Wake Up, America*, p. 234.

17. "Pershing's Crusaders" Film Poster (Anonymous).

◆ CHAPTER 4

Homogenizing a
Pluralistic Nation:
Propaganda
During World
War I

Source 18 from *The New York Times*, January 6, 1918.

18. Hines's Prizewinning Cartoon in the 1918 *Trench and Camp* Cartoon Contest.[13]

The New York Times

13. *Trench and Camp* was a weekly publication of the U.S. Army for its thirty-two training centers in the United States. For this prizewinning cartoon, Frank Hines won a wristwatch. In the cartoon, the American soldier is holding a *pickelhaube*, a German spiked helmet.

19. Excerpt from a Speech by a Four Minute Man.

Ladies and Gentlemen:

I have just received the information that there is a German spy among us—a German spy watching *us.*

He is around here somewhere, reporting upon you and me—sending reports about us to Berlin and telling the Germans just what we are doing with the Liberty Loan. From every section of the country these spies have been getting reports over to Potsdam[17]—not general reports but details—where the loan is going well and where its success seems weak, and what people are saying in each community.

For the German government is worried about our great loan. Those Junkers[18] fear its effect upon the German *morale.* They're raising a loan this month, too.

If the American people lend their billions now, one and all with a hip-hip-hurrah, it means that America is united and strong. While, if we lend our money half-heartedly, America seems weak and autocracy remains strong.

Money means everything now; it means quicker victory and therefore less bloodshed. We are *in* the war, and now Americans can have but *one* opinion, only *one* wish in the Liberty Loan.

Well, I hope these spies are getting their messages straight, letting Potsdam know that America is *hurling back* to the autocrats these answers:

For treachery here, attempted treachery in Mexico, treachery everywhere— *one billion.*

For murder of American women and children—*one billion more.*

For broken faith and promise to murder more Americans—*billions and billions more.*

And then we will add:

In the world fight for Liberty, our share—*billions and billions and billions and endless billions.*

Do not let the German spy hear and report that *you* are a slacker.

17. *Potsdam* (a suburb of Berlin) was where the Kaiser lived.
18. *Junkers* were the Prussian nobility.

◆ CHAPTER 4

Homogenizing a
Pluralistic Nation:
Propaganda
During World
War I

20. Part of a Speech by a Four Minute Man.

German agents are telling the people of this . . . race[19] through the South that if they will not oppose the German Government, or help our Government, they will be rewarded with Ford automobiles when Germany is in control here. They are told that 10 negroes are being conscripted to 1 white man in order that the Negro race may be killed off; and that the reason Germany went into Belgium was to punish the people of that country for the cruel treatment of the negroes in the Congo.

21. "It's Duty Boy," a Poem Read by Four Minute Men.

My boy must never bring disgrace to his immortal sires—
At Valley Forge and Lexington they kindled freedom's fires,
John's father died at Gettysburg, mine fell at Chancellorsville;
While John himself was with the boys who charged up San Juan Hill.
And John, if he was living now, would surely say with me,
"No son of ours shall e'er disgrace our grand old family tree
By turning out a slacker when his country needs his aid."
It is not of such timber that America was made.
I'd rather you had died at birth or not been born at all,
Than know that I had raised a son who cannot hear the call
That freedom has sent round the world, its precious rights to save—
This call is meant for you, my boy, and I would have you brave;
And though my heart is breaking, boy, I bid you do your part,
And show the world no son of mine is cursed with craven heart;
And if, perchance, you ne'er return, my later days to cheer,
And I have only memories of my brave boy, so dear,
I'd rather have it so, my boy, and know you bravely died
Than have a living coward sit supinely by my side.
To save the world from sin, my boy, God gave his only son—
He's asking for my boy, to-day, and may His will be done.

19. At the front lines in France, Germans barraged America's African American soldiers with leaflets urging them to desert (none did). One of those propaganda leaflets said, in part, "Do you enjoy the same rights as the white people do in America . . . or are you rather not treated over there as second-class citizens?" As to the charge of discrimination against African Americans by draft boards, there were numerous complaints that African Americans found it almost impossible to get exemptions from military service. In the end, about 31 percent of the African Americans who registered were called into service, as opposed to 26 percent of the registered whites. To counteract German propaganda, prominent African Americans were sent to France to lecture to the African American troops.

Source 22 from *The Moving Picture World*, September 28, 1918.

22. Promotional Tips to Theater Managers, 1918.

ADVERTISING AIDS FOR BUSY MANAGERS
"KULTUR."

William Fox Presents Gladys Brockwell in a Typical Example of the Brutality of the Wilhelmstrasse to Its Spy-slaves.

Cast.

Countess Griselda Von Arenburg,
                            Gladys Brockwell
Eliska ....Georgia Woodthorpe
René de Bornay................William Scott
Baron von Zeller ....Willard Louis
Archduke Franz Ferdinand ....Charles Clary
Danilo ....Nigel de Brullier
The Kaiser ....William Burress
Emperor Franz Josef.........Alfred Fremont

Directed by Edward J. Le Saint.

The Story: The Kaiser decides that the time is ripe for a declaration of war, and sends word to his vassal monarch of Austria. René de Bornay is sent by France to discover what is being planned. He meets the Countess, who falls in love with him. She sickens of the spy system and declares that she is done with it, but is warned that she cannot withdraw. She is told to secure René's undoing, but instead procures his escape and in her own boudoir is stood against the wall and shot for saving the man whom she loves better than her life.

Feature Gladys Brockwell as Countess Griselda Von Arenburg and William Scott as René de Bornay.

Program and Advertising Phrases: Gladys Brockwell, Star of Latest Picture, Exposing Hun Brutality and Satanic Intrigue.
How An Austrian Countess Gave Her All for Democracy.
She Was an Emperor's Favorite Yet She Died for World Freedom.
Story of an Emperor's Mistress and a Crime That Rocked the World.
Daring Exposure of Scandals and Crimes in Hun Court Circles.
Astonishing Revelations of Hun Plots to Rape Democracy.

Advertising Angles: Do not offer this as a propaganda story, but tell that it is one of the angles of the merciless Prussian spy system about which has been woven a real romance. Play up the spy angle heavily both in your newspaper work and through window cards with such lines as "even the spies themselves hate their degradation." Miss Brockwell wears some stunning and daring gowns in this play, and with these special appeal can be made to the women.

The Moving Picture World

✦ CHAPTER 4

Homogenizing a
Pluralistic Nation:
Propaganda
During World
War I

23. Advertisement for the Feature Film *The Kaiser, the Beast of Berlin* (1918), Described by Some as the Most Famous "Hate Picture."

National Archives

24. Still Photograph from *The Kaiser, the Beast of Berlin* (1918). Used in Advertising.

Questions to Consider

Keep in mind that the "target audience" of the Committee on Public Information propaganda was America's civilian population, those men and women who were expected to support military enlistments, buy liberty bonds and liberty loans, report suspicious or unpatriotic individuals, cut back on consumption of food, fuel, and other commodities needed for the war effort, and support civilian unity and patriotism. To achieve these goals, the committee virtually bombarded the civilian population with propaganda.

Source 1, George M. Cohan's enormously popular song, "Over There," was familiar to almost every American in 1917 to 1918. What is the song urging young men to do? What emotions are the song's lyrics trying to arouse? How would you interpret the lines, "Make your daddy glad" and (speaking of sweethearts) "To be proud her boy's in line"? Recordings of the song "Over There" are readily available. As you listen to the song, how does it make you feel?

The advertisements shown in Sources 2–4 were produced by the Committee on Public Information. How are the Germans portrayed in the "Spies and Lies" ad (Source 2)? In "Bachelor of Atrocities" (Source 3)? Source 4 is an appeal to history teachers. Did the Committee on Public Information ask history teachers to "tilt" their treatments of the past? If so, how? Were there any dangers inherent in the kinds of activities the committee was urging on patriotic Americans?

In some ways, poster art (Sources 5–15) is similar to editorial cartoon art (Sources 16 and 17), principally because the artist has only one canvas or frame on which to tell his or her story. Yet the poster must be more arresting than the cartoon, must convey its message rapidly, and must avoid ambiguities and confusion. Posters commissioned or approved by the Committee on Public Information were an extremely popular form of propaganda during World War I. Indeed, so popular were the posters of James Montgomery Flagg (1877–1960) that he helped sell $1,000 of liberty bonds by performing (in his case, painting posters) in front of the New York Public Library.

Source 5, Flagg's Uncle Sam poster, probably is the most famous poster ever created. The idea was taken from a British poster by Alfred Leete, and Flagg was his own model for Uncle Sam. The poster is still used by the U.S. Army. What feeling did the poster seek to elicit? [13]

The poster "Destroy This Mad Brute" by illustrator H. R. Hopps is a classic example of a recruiting appeal. How is the enemy portrayed? What darker emotions or fears does the poster hope to elicit?

A surprisingly large percentage of the posters were appeals to women

13. For a photograph of Flagg painting a recruiting poster on the steps of the New York Public Library, see his autobiography, *Roses and Buckshot* (New York: G.P. Putnam's Sons, 1946), facing p. 159.

(Sources 7, 8, 10, and 12). How are women portrayed in each poster? What are American women expected to contribute to the war effort (consider especially the emotions in Source 12)? Do these four posters tell you anything about World War I era gender roles and stereotypes? As you examine Alonzo Earl Foringer's poster "The Greatest Mother in the World" (Source 10), what famous statue does that poster remind you of? Do you think Foringer hoped that those who saw the poster would make that connection?

The posters in Sources 7, 9, and 11 are appeals to civilians to purchase liberty bonds and liberty stamps. What appeal does each poster make? Do the posters attempt to elicit deeper emotions?

Sources 13–15 are extremely interesting in light of the government's fears and the role President Wilson assigned to the Committee on Public Information. What emotion does the extraordinary "Americans All!" poster (Source 13) attempt to elicit? What is the poster's intended "message"? How do Sources 14 and 15 seek to bolster that message? If the goal of the committee was to *unite* Americans behind the war effort, why do you think it chose to target appeals to specific groups?

The eleven posters in this chapter (Sources 5–15) are but a small fraction of the hundreds of posters that were created during World War I. They are, however, representatives of the many different themes and appeals used in the posters. You may examine the vast number of posters in the Library of Congress's American Memory Collection. Simply click on

Prints and Photographs Online Catalog, then Posters: World War I. Also, the Wolfsonian Museum at Florida International University has published a catalog of its recent exhibit *Myth and Machine: Art and Aviation in the First World War* focused on how artists from many countries dealt with the horrifying potential of new machines of war. Not a few of these artists also drew and/or painted posters. See http://shop.wolfsonian.org/mythsandmachine.espn.

On cartoons (Sources 16 and 17), nineteenth-century New York political boss William Marcy ("Boss") Tweed once exclaimed, "Let's stop these damn pictures. I don't care so much what the papers say about me—my constituents can't read; but damn it, they can see the pictures!" The editorial cartoon from the *New York Herald* (Source 16) is fairly self-explanatory. What emotions does the cartoon seek to elicit? What actions, intended or unintended, might have resulted from those emotions? Frank Hines's prizewinning cartoon (Source 17) seeks to tap very different emotions, primarily in men. Compare the cartoon to Cohan's lyrics (Source 1) and the recruiting poster (Source 6).

Sources 18–20, speeches and a poem by Four Minute Men, also were published in the Committee on Public Information's *Bulletin*, which was distributed to all volunteer speakers. Not a few of the "Four Minute Men" were women, but most of them delivered their speeches to women's organizations. All speakers received certificates from President Wilson after the war. What appeals are made in Source 18? How are appeals to African Americans (Source 19) similar or different?

◆ CHAPTER 4

Homogenizing a
Pluralistic Nation:
Propaganda
During World
War I

Compare to the poster in Source 15. The poem in Source 20 is particularly painful to read. Why is that so? How can this poem be compared to Sources 1, 12, and 17?

From 1917 to 1918, the American film industry and the Committee on Public Information produced over 180 feature films, 6 serials, 72 short subjects, 112 documentaries, 44 cartoons, and 37 liberty loan special films. Unfortunately, the vast majority of those motion pictures no longer are available, principally because the nitrate film stock on which the films were printed was extremely flammable and subject to decomposition.[14]

No sound films were produced in the United States before 1927. Until that time, a small orchestra or (more prevalent) a piano accompanied a screening. What dialogue there was—and there was not much—was given in subtitles.

The advertising tips for the film *Kultur* (Source 21) suggest a number of phrases and angles designed to attract audiences. What are the strongest appeals suggested to theater owners?

Do those same appeals also appear in the song, advertisements, posters, cartoons, and speeches?

Sources 22 and 24 are advertisements for *The Kaiser, the Beast of Berlin*, produced in 1918. What appeal do the advertisements intend to make? How effective do you think such an appeal would be? Source 23, however, is an advertisement for a government-produced film. Note the committee's seal at the upper right of the advertisement. How is the appeal in Source 23 similar to or different from that in Source 24? How are Germans depicted in Source 21? How can Source 21 be compared with Sources 6 and 7? How can Source 22 be compared with those sources as well?

You must now summarize your findings and return to the central questions: How did the United States use propaganda to mobilize public opinion in support of the nation's participation in World War I? What were the consequences—positive and negative—of the mobilization of public opinion?

◆

Epilogue

The creation of the Committee on Public Information and its subsequent work show that the Wilson administration had serious doubts concerning

whether the American people, multiethnic and pluralistic as they were, would support the war effort with unanimity. And, to be sure, there was

---

14. In 1949, an improved safety-based stock was introduced. Those films that do survive, except in private collections, are in the Library of Congress; the American Film Institute Library in Beverly Hills, California; the Academy of Motion Picture Arts and

Sciences in Los Angeles; the Museum of Modern Art in New York; the National Archives in Washington, D.C.; the New York Public Library; and the Wisconsin Center for Theater Research in Madison.

opposition to American involvement in the war, not only from socialist Eugene Debs and the left but also from reformers Robert La Follette, Jane Addams, and others. As it turned out, however, the Wilson administration's worst fears proved groundless. Americans of all ethnic backgrounds overwhelmingly supported the war effort, sometimes rivaling each other in patriotic ardor. How much of this unanimity can be attributed to patriotism and how much to the propaganda efforts of the Committee on Public Information will never really be known. Yet, for whatever reason, it can be said that the war had a kind of unifying effect on the American people. Women sold liberty bonds, worked for agencies such as the Red Cross, rolled bandages, and cooperated in the government's effort to conserve food and fuel. Indeed, even African Americans sprang to the colors, reasoning, as did the president of Howard University, that service in the war might help them achieve long-withheld civil and political rights. For his part, African American leader W. E. B. DuBois counseled that blacks should "forget about special grievances and close ranks with our own fellow white citizens."

However, this homogenization was not without its price. Propaganda was so effective that it created a kind of national hysteria, sometimes with terrible results. Vigilante-type groups such as the American Protective League, the American Defense Society, the National Security League, and others often shamefully persecuted German Americans, lynching one German American man of draft age for not being in uniform (the man was physically ineligible, having only one eye) and badgering German American children in and out of school.[15] Many states forbade the teaching of German in schools, and a host of German words were purged from the language (sauerkraut became liberty cabbage, German measles became liberty measles, hamburgers became liberty steaks, frankfurters became hot dogs). The city of Cincinnati even banned pretzels from saloons. In such an atmosphere, many Americans lived in genuine fear of being accused of spying or of becoming victims of intimidation or violence. In a society intent upon homogenization, being different could be dangerous.

Former president Theodore Roosevelt begged his onetime rival President Woodrow Wilson to be allowed to rouse a U.S. Army company, even though he was in poor health. Wilson refused the plea, after which Roosevelt toured the country calling for 100 percent unhyphenated Americans. "This is a nation," he roared, "not a polyglot boardinghouse.":

> There can be no divided allegiance here. Any man who says he is an American but something else also, isn't an American at all. We have room but for one flag, . . . room but for one language. . . .[16]

15. The mother of one of the authors of this volume, who was ten years old in 1917, was chased home from school by rock-throwing boys because she was of German descent.

16. Thomas G. Dyer, *Theodore Roosevelt and the Idea of Race* (Baton Rouge: Louisiana State University Press, 1980), quoted on p. 134. See also Patricia O'Toole, *When Trumpets Call: Theodore Roosevelt After the White House* (New York: Simon and Schuster, 2005), pp. 363, 365. Roosevelt died on January 6, 1919.

✦ CHAPTER 4

Homogenizing a
Pluralistic Nation:
Propaganda
During World
War I

During such hysteria, one would expect the federal government in general and the Committee on Public Information in particular to have attempted to dampen the more extreme forms of vigilantism. However, it seemed as if the government had become the victim of its own propaganda. Using the 1917 Espionage Act, Postmaster General Albert Burleson censored the mail, looking for examples of treason, insurrection, or forcible resistance to laws, and used his power to suppress all socialist publications, all anti-British and pro-Irish mail, and anything that he believed threatened the war effort. One movie producer Robert Goldstein was sentenced to ten years in prison for releasing his film *The Spirit of '76* (about the American Revolution) because it portrayed the British in an unfavorable light.[17] Socialist party leader Eugene Debs was given a similar sentence for criticizing the war in a speech in Canton, Ohio, on June 16, 1918. Debs announced at the outset of his remarks that he might be arrested for what he had to say, and then declared that "the working class who fight all the battles, the working class who make the supreme sacrifices, the working class who freely shed their blood and furnish the corpses, have never yet had a voice in either declaring war or making peace. It is the ruling class that invariably does both." As he entered prison, Debs stated, "I thank the capitalist masters for putting me here. They know where I belong under their criminal and corrupt system. It is the only compliment they should pay me."[18] Left-wing Industrial Workers of the World (IWW) was falsely accused of advocating draft evasion and was the victim of considerable violence, and many of its leaders were either imprisoned or deported. At the same time, thousands of Germans, Austrians, and Hungarians were taken from their homes without trial and were whisked away to Ellis Island, which had been converted into a prison. Freedom of speech, press, and assembly were violated countless times, and numerous lynchings, whippings, and tar-and-featherings occurred. Excesses by both government and private individuals were as effective in *forcing* homogeneity as were the voluntary efforts of American people of all backgrounds.[19]

Once the hysteria had begun, it is doubtful whether even President

17. The constitutionality of the Espionage Act was upheld by the Supreme Court in *Schenck v. United States* (249 U.S. 47) a year after the war was over. Writing for the unanimous court, Justice Oliver Wendell Holmes, Jr. used the phrase "clear and present danger" to temporarily set aside the First Amendment in wartime. See John J. Patrick, *The Supreme Court of the United States, A Student Companion* (New York: Oxford University Press, 3rd ed., 2006), pp. 309–310. The court case regarding the film *The Spirit of '76* had the improbable title *United States v. The Spirit of '76*.

18. Ernest Freeberg, *Democracy's Prisoner: Eugene V. Debs, the Great War, and the Right to Dissent* (Cambridge, MA: Harvard University Press, 2008), p. 2. In 1921 Debs's sentence was commuted by President Warren Harding. *ibid.*, pp. 72–77, 289–296.

19. On Ellis Island see Frederick C. Howe, *Confessions of a Reformer*, quoted in Commager and Nevins, *The Heritage of America*, pp. 1088–1092.

Wilson could have stopped it. Yet Wilson showed no inclination to do so, even stating that dissent was not appreciated by the government. Without the president to reverse the process, the hysteria continued unabated. The 1918 Sedition Act expanded the Espionage Act by making it a crime to criticize the Constitution, the flag, or the country's military forces, and so on.

Before the outbreak of World War I, anti-immigrant sentiment had been growing, although most Americans seem to have believed that the solution was to Americanize the immigrants rather than to restrict their entrance into the country. But the drive toward homogenization that accompanied America's war hysteria acted to increase cries for restricting further immigration and to weaken champions of the "melting pot." As restriction advocate Madison Grant wrote in 1922, "The world has seen many such [racial] mixtures and the character of a mongrel race is only just beginning to be understood at its true value . . . . Whether we like to admit it or not, the result of the mixture of two races . . . gives us a race reverting to the more ancient, generalized and lower type." Labor leaders, journalists, and politicians called for immigration restrictions, and a general immigration restriction (called the National Origins Act) became law in 1924.

This insistence on homogenization also resulted in the Red Scare of 1919, during which Attorney General A. Mitchell Palmer violated many people's civil liberties in a series of raids, arrests, and deportations directed largely against recent immigrants. As seen, the efforts to homogenize a pluralistic nation could have an ugly side.

As noted in the Problem section of this chapter, some liberal intellectuals were both shocked and frightened by the relative ease with which the Committee on Public Information was able to manipulate public opinion and create a climate of mass patriotic hysteria. How, they asked, could "the people" be trusted if they could be swayed and stampeded so easily? And yet, open criticism of the government or the American people themselves still could be dangerous. As one minor example, noted historian Charles Beard resigned from Columbia University in protest over the firings of antiwar faculty members. As a result, sales of Beard's books plummeted.[20]

As Americans approached World War II, some called for a revival of the Committee on Public Information. Yet President Franklin Roosevelt rejected this sweeping approach. The Office of War Information was created, but its role was a restricted one. Even so, as you will see in Chapter 7, Japanese Americans were subjected to relocation and humiliation in one of the most shameful episodes of recent American history. (See Chapter 7.) And although propaganda techniques were

20. On liberals' fear, see Walter Lippmann's columns in the November and December 1919 issues of *Atlantic Monthly*, cited in Gary, *Nervous Liberals*, p. 2. On Beard, see Sproule, *Propaganda and Democracy*, p. 14.

✦ CHAPTER 4

Homogenizing a
Pluralistic Nation:
Propaganda
During World
War I

sometimes more subtle, they never-theless displayed features that would cause Americans to hate their enemies and want to destroy them. Japanese people especially were portrayed as barbaric. In general, however, a different spirit pervaded the United States during World War II, a spirit generally more tolerant of American pluralism and less willing to stir Americans into an emotional frenzy.

And yet the possibility that propaganda will create mass hysteria and thus endanger the civil rights of some Americans is present in every national crisis, especially in wartime. In the "total wars" of the twentieth century, in which civilians played as crucial a role as soldiers (in factories, military training facilities for soldiers, and in shipping men and materiel to the front), the mobilization of the home front was a necessity. But could that kind of mobilization be carried too far? After 9/11, such a danger has been ever-present.

5

A "Revolution in Manners and Morals": Women's Changing Roles in the 1920s

◆

The Problem

In 1931, Frederick Lewis Allen, who worked as a writer and editor for popular American magazines, published a sweeping, lively history of the 1920s. *Only Yesterday* became a runaway bestseller. The book explored the end of the Great War, the Red Scare, presidential politics, and the origins of the Great Depression. Allen also devoted one chapter of his book to what he called "The Revolution in Manners and Morals." "The shock troops" of this particular rebellion, he wrote, were "the sons and daughters of well-to-do American families, who knew little about Bolshevism and cared distinctly less, and their defiance was expressed not in obscure radical publications or in soap-box speeches, but right across the family breakfast table into the horrified ears of conservative fathers and mothers."[1]

1. Frederick Lewis Allen, *Only Yesterday: An Informal History of the 1920s* (New York: Harper & Row, 1931).

Before the 1920s, Allen explained to his readers, Americans—by which he meant middle- and upper-class white families—lived according to a very precise code of manners and morals. First and foremost, "Women were the guardians of morality." Girls grew up looking forward to "a romantic love match which would lead them to the altar and to living-happily-ever-after; and until the 'right man' came along they must allow no male to kiss them." He allowed as how some men "would succumb to the temptations of sex, but only with a special class of outlawed women; girls of respectable families were supposed to have no such temptations."

The Great War was scarce over, Allen lamented, before young women and men began "making mincemeat of this code." "Innumerable families," he continued, "were torn with dissension over cigarettes and gin and all-night automobile rides. Fathers and mothers

◆ CHAPTER 5

A "Revolution
in Manners and
Morals": Women's
Changing Roles in
the 1920s

lay awake asking themselves whether their children were not utterly lost."

According to Allen, this radical and distressing change came from the same source as the now cast-aside moral code of the older generation: women. Once women got the right to vote, he argued, they followed that sense of equality with greater zeal for education, which led them to jobs previously held only by men. "With the job," Allen wrote, "came a feeling of comparative economic independence. With the feeling of economic independence came a slackening of husbandly and parental authority."

Other factors propelled "the revolution in manners and morals" along, including automobiles, magazines, and movies; Freudian psychology and preoccupation with sexuality; and fascination with and secrecy of drinking alcohol that developed during the Prohibition Era.[2] Each of these influences, Allen explained, "was played upon by all the others; none of them could alone have changed to any great degree the folkways of America; together their force was irresistible." Allen makes clear, however, that new ideals of womanhood lay at the heart of these revolutionary changes.

In the 1920s "new women" shortened their skirts and the sleeves of their dresses, discarded their corsets, put on makeup, and smoked cigarettes—all of which, Allen concluded, outwardly displayed the transformation in American culture. Among the most distressing of changes: premarital sex was no longer uncommon. Or, as Allen scornfully wrote, "the prostitute was faced for the first time with an amateur competition of formidable proportions."

The 1920s were marked by profound changes in women's rights and roles in American society and contentious debates over those changes. Clearly, Frederick Lewis Allen was no fan of the new ideals of womanhood. But many women and men were, or else the changes would not have taken place. In this chapter, you will enter those debates in order to answer the central question: **What did advocates and critics of "new womanhood" believe was at stake in their debates over women's roles in the 1920s?**

2. In 1920, the Eighteenth Amendment to the U.S. Constitution prohibited the manufacture, sale, transportation, and importation of alcoholic beverages. The nationwide ban was repealed in 1933, with the Twenty-First Amendment. Imagined by advocates as a method of moral and social improvement, the Prohibition Era, in fact, experienced escalations in violence from organized crime and the underground liquor trade.

Background

The debates that raged over the proper roles of American women in the 1920s had a long, complicated history. During their lengthy battle for women's voting rights, suffragists were sharply divided over tactics. Should suffragists focus on changing state constitutions, or should they concentrate their efforts on a federal amendment? Should they use direct protests or should they try to persuade lawmakers through more indirect lobbying techniques? They were also divided over issues of race and class. Middle- and upper-class white women headed most of the national women's rights organizations, including the National American Woman Suffrage Association (NAWSA). Should those feminists reach out to immigrant women? What role, if any, should working-class women have in the movement? What about African American women? Would their inclusion in the suffrage movement alienate southern white women and southern legislators? In some northern industrial cities, leading suffragists did cooperate with immigrant and working-class women. In a few of these cities, African American women were also included in suffrage activities. However, national leaders were always aware of the "race question" and usually they opted to direct their efforts at securing the civil rights of white middle- and upper-class women.

Successful ratification of the Nineteenth Amendment in 1920, making it unconstitutional to deny voting rights based on sex, brought its own complications. Some women concluded that the struggle for women's rights was completed by the passage of this amendment. For many leaders in the NAWSA, the recognition of women's voting rights—seventy-two years in the making—seemed like a dream come true. Its goal met, the NAWSA changed its name to the League of Women Voters (LWV) and began pursuing a new mission, which the organization continues nearly a hundred years later: to encourage informed and active participation in government and increased understanding of public policy issues. But membership in the LWV was far smaller than the NAWSA.

To their disappointment, national women's rights leaders saw the female solidarity fostered during the long fight for suffrage—at least among middle-class white women—wane as women entered the voting booth. Women turned out to be as diverse in their political agendas and as readily factionalized as men. The biggest change, though, was the relative political disinterest of the rising generation of women. Politics struck many young women in the 1920s as boring; LWV efforts to promote voter awareness and turnout seemed out of step with the youth culture.

The National Women's Party (NWP), under the leadership of Alice Paul, took a more broad-based and controversial approach than did the LWV. Far from sanguine about women's place in America after the Nineteenth Amendment, Paul and her followers were

✦ CHAPTER 5

A "Revolution
in Manners and
Morals": Women's
Changing Roles in
the 1920s

dismayed at the continued marginalization of women. While women's voting rights had been secured, they certainly had not attained legal equality. In the 1920s many states continued to pay husbands the wages their wives earned (as well as the earnings of minor children). Women were often excluded from serving on juries and holding certain public offices. Schools and professions still discriminated based on gender. Women were barred from certain jobs and routinely (and legally) paid less for their labor. In many jurisdictions, mothers had no legal claim to their children in the case of divorce—and it was often harder for a woman to get a divorce than a man. Widows did not automatically inherit spousal property, whereas widowers did. The NWP thus committed itself to "the removal of all forms of the subjection of women."

In 1921 the NWP began to campaign for an Equal Rights Amendment (ERA) to the Constitution, which would abolish all forms of gender inequality in the United States. The proposed amendment declared that "men and women shall have equal rights throughout the United States and every place subject to its jurisdiction."[3] This had far wider intent and implications than the language of the Nineteenth Amendment, which read: "The right of citizens of the United States to vote shall not be denied or abridged by the United States or by any State on account of sex."

The NWP agenda of complete equality between the sexes faced a number of vexing obstacles. The organization weakened its base of support by refusing to protest the disfranchisement of black women and men in the South. Jim Crow laws limited the franchise by race, regardless of gender; neither African American men nor women could vote in most southern elections. Explaining her organization's refusal to intercede in this patently discriminatory electoral system, Alice Paul maintained that segregation was a "race" problem, not a gender issue. The NWP also took positions that put the organization at odd with working-class women. In the 1920s, female factory workers enjoyed certain protections in industries: limited hours and exclusion from some forms of physical labor, for example, which, to the women working these jobs, seemed essential to their health and continued employment. NWP leaders countered that such protective legislation depicted women as weak and inferior. The fight over "female jobs" and the fitness of women for "male jobs" continued throughout the twentieth century. But more generally, the idea of full equality between the sexes struck many Americans as profoundly troubling.

Advocates of women's equality were caricatured as barren, disgruntled, and frigid scolds. One critics of the ERA suggested that a far better idea would be "to take charge of the old maids and teach them how to acquire a husband and have babies of their own."[4]

3. For more information on Alice Paul and the National Women's Party, see Catherine H. Adams and Michael L. Keene, *Alice Paul and the American Suffrage Campaign* (Urbana: University of Illinois Press, 2007).

4. Quoted in Sarah M. Evans, *Born for Liberty: A History of Women in America* (New York: Free Press, 1997), p. 194. Evans offers a full and thoughtful overview of American women's history.

The LWV—alongside many other women's groups in the 1920s—actually opposed the ERA. The amendment was so broad, they maintained, that it would remove certain essential, hard-earned legal protections that women enjoyed. Although there was some concern about the ERA eradicating alimony and allowing women to be drafted during wartime, the real problem lay in protective labor laws for women in the various states. Whereas the NWP saw such laws as *restrictive* of women's rights, the LWV viewed them as *protective* of women's special "nature."

For all these reasons, women's reform initiatives were generally weaker and more fragmented in the 1920s than in the pre-World War I era. But there were some successes during the decade. The Sheppard-Towner Maternity Act (1921) provided federal funding to states for improved maternal and infant health care measures. Another breakthrough came in the form of the Cable Act (1930), which allowed American women who married foreign citizens to retain their U.S. citizenship, rather than automatically losing it as they had previously. Many women also became politically active on the municipal and state levels of government, as well as working to create female networks and a place for themselves within national party politics.

As the struggles over women's rights continued in the 1920s, they both underlay and were eclipsed by the contest over proper womanhood. The decade was characterized by many serious social and cultural strains. Anti-immigrant sentiment increased, culminating in a new quota system that drastically limited immigration from southern and eastern Europe. The decade also saw the resurgence of the Ku Klux Klan (KKK), a terrorist group that emerged during the Reconstruction Era (1865–1877). In its second incarnation, the KKK gained popularity in urban areas and outside the South. The group's commitment to white supremacy expanded to target Jews, Catholics, and immigrants, in addition to African Americans. The revived Klan enforced "100% Americanism" through intimidation and violence, and in the 1920s grew to at least 3 million and perhaps as many as 8 million members nationwide.[5] A series of race riots occurred just after World War I, as the near epidemic of lynching African American men continued to rage across the South. While during the 1920s the intellectual leader Marcus Garvey promoted pride in African heritage and Black Nationalism (known as Garveyism), and the Harlem Renaissance showcased black writers, artists, and intellectuals, most African Americans endured abject poverty and political disfranchisement in the rural South. Two famous trials of the decade—the Sacco and Vanzetti case against Italian anarchists convicted of committing a murder during a payroll robbery and the Scopes case involving a teacher found guilty of breaking Tennessee state law by teaching evolution—highlighted the social and cultural strains inherent in

5. Women also joined the 1920s-era KKK. Historian Kathleen M. Blee investigated the Women's Ku Klux Klan (WKKK)—which drew nearly a half million members in the 1920s—in *Women and the Klan: Racism and Gender in the 1920s* (Berkeley: University of California Press, 1992).

◆ CHAPTER 5

A "Revolution
in Manners and
Morals": Women's
Changing Roles in
the 1920s

the conflict between the older values of rural and small-town America and the newer values of twentieth-century modernism.[6]

But perhaps nowhere were the cultural and social strains of the decade more evident than in the fierce debates about the proper place of women in American society. There was no doubt in the minds of contemporary observers that new ideas about women's "nature" were emerging and women's experiences were changing as a result. A great deal of public debate swirled around these changes.

One powerful image of the "new woman" that emerged in the 1920s was the flapper, with her short skirt and bobbed hair. These clothing and hairstyle shifts started first among urban young women. But the movies, department stores, and mail-order catalogs made these fashions desirable and available to women across the country. Women who cultivated this flapper self-image often went much further than these superficial changes, however. They embraced modernity and freedom and often criticized feminism as old-fashioned even as they also rejected Victorian attitudes toward sexuality—the "code" for which Frederick Lewis Allen grieved.

"New women" reimagined their educations, careers, marriages, and

6. Edward J. Larson's *Summer of the Gods: The Scopes Trial and America's Continuing Debate Over Science and Religion* (New York: Basic Books, 1997) offers rich insight into the trial and cultural divisions in this era. UCLA maintains the Marcus Garvey Papers projects. To learn more about Garvey, visit www.international.ucla.edu/africa/mgpp/.

maternity. In the 1920s, one in four American women worked outside the home. That pattern had emerged over the prior twenty years, but the 1920s were different. Magazines and movies now glamorized working women as sophisticated and alluring. And women took on new jobs, too, as secretaries, lawyers, professors, and writers.

The expansion of higher education and particularly of coeducation—an innovation at American colleges and universities in the early twentieth century—trained women for this new world of work. Collegiate coeducation also fostered familiarity between young women and men and advanced a different youth culture than any earlier generation of Americans had experienced. New courtship values emerged from this youth culture, encouraging young people to seek passion and sexual gratification. Smoking and drinking in public, dating casually and in cars, and dancing late into the night in jazz clubs became increasingly commonplace among young people—to the dismay and alarm of many members of the older generation.

Although some of the conduct of the new youth culture seemed shocking, the underlying values—individualism, conspicuous consumption, and innovation—were embraced by many middle-class Americans in the 1920s, including the daughters and wives of businessmen, skilled laborers, and professionals. Even for white women who remained in traditional roles as wives and mothers, then, the 1920s brought profound changes.

Experts, primarily social scientists such as sociologists, psychologists, economists, political scientists, home economists, and anthropologists, attempted to help American women negotiate this new age. Their approaches grew out of the Progressive Era. Beginning in the late nineteenth century, researchers began investigating the societal consequences of massive immigration, rapid industrialization, and widespread urbanization. These new social scientists, who worked in universities and government service, borrowed some of their methods from the natural sciences but focused their works on society. Gathering data, interviewing individuals, and compiling statistics provided the material with which progressive-minded researchers could inform citizens and shape public policy. Social scientists thus saw their work as forming the basis for important economic, social, and political reforms.

Leading social scientists published their research findings and recommendations not only in scholarly journals but also in popular middle-class books and magazines. In the 1920s, such popular advice literature proliferated, particularly regarding American women, with promises to help women negotiate the overwhelming changes occurring in America. But there was a problem: these authorities often disagreed about *how* or even *whether* changes in women's roles should occur.

Debates among experts about proper womanhood reached into the most intimate parts of women's lives. A whole host of experts—some formally trained and some not—counseled women on how to act in their relationships, the workplace, and their homes.

Experts weighed in on women's bodies, their health and reproduction, and their true "nature." Promoting female health was of particular concern at American colleges and universities, where girls became women. Social science studies shaped academics at coeducational institutions as well as university-led programs relating to student life. Physical education, tailored to meet the needs of female students, was very important and carefully monitored. Motherhood was increasingly managed, too, from guidance about healthful pregnancy to infant nutrition to toddlers' playtime. As more women pursued careers, maternal roles within families became another powerful topic of inquiry.

No one pushed the debate about motherhood further than Margaret Sanger. Sanger was a nurse, a sex educator, and an early advocate for contraceptive rights. At a time when it was a federal crime to send contraceptives or even writings about contraception across state lines, Sanger opened the first birth control clinic in the United States.[7] In fact, she coined the term "birth control." Her organization, the American Birth Control League, founded in 1921, later became

7. The Comstock Act, a federal law passed in 1873, banned writing about birth control, distributing contraceptives, and mailing information about contraception. You can research Margaret Sanger's writings and learn about her life through the Margaret Sanger Papers Project at New York University (www.nyu.edu/projects/sanger) and the Margaret Sanger Papers at the Five Colleges Archives & Manuscripts Collection (http://asteria.fivecolleges.edu/findaids/sophiasmith/mnsss43_main.html).

✦ CHAPTER 5

A "Revolution
in Manners and
Morals": Women's
Changing Roles in
the 1920s

(and remains) the Planned Parenthood Federation of America. Sanger lobbied for "voluntary motherhood" and the widespread use of contraception to "lift motherhood to the plane of a voluntary, intelligent function." Eventually, Sanger's efforts led to the scientific development of a cheap, safe, and entirely female-controlled contraceptive that became so popular that it was and is still known simply as "The Pill." In the 1920s, however, Sanger's work was highly controversial—indeed illegal. Some Americans championed Sanger as an exemplar of modern womanhood, while others excoriated her as dangerous and even diabolical.

In this chapter you will read part of Margaret Sanger's book *Woman and the New Race*, as well as selections from the vast social science and advice literature from the 1920s and reports from a typical midwestern university about student life. And you will consider several photographs of college students from that decade. Just from the diversity of these sources you can start to see the pervasiveness and power of the debates over women's roles. Appreciating the prevalence of these intense disagreements is the first step to understanding what advocates and critics of "new womanhood" believed was at stake in their debates over women's roles in the 1920s.

✦

The Method

In this chapter you will be engaging a wider diversity of evidence than in the earlier chapters, including photographs, social science studies and advice, and a university annual report. As you seek to answer the central question in the chapter, you will also need to engage in critical analysis of the evidence available to you. This, of course, is always the case for historians. But when working through very different types of evidence, the task can get more challenging. Some background information on the primary sources is therefore in order.

The first grouping of evidence (Sources 1–7) depicts college life in the 1920s, first with an annual report from the University of Illinois and then with

a series of photographs. As you study the report in particular, remember the audience and the intentions behind the annual report. It remains the case at most public universities and colleges that administrators create annual reports on the actions and accomplishments of their divisions. Such reports are eventually compiled for submission to a board of trustees and made available publicly. Historians using such evidence must therefore keep in mind that the authors are self-reporting and that the reports are for a public audience.

Consider next the photographs. Start with the rare photograph of female students at a Howard University football game (Source 4). Study their clothing and accessories, their hairstyles, their proximity to each other and to the men at the game, their physical comportment, and their apparent interaction with the photographer. In some regards, they are quite typical of university women in this era: they are well-to-do female students enjoying a quintessential experience with college athletics. What general images of womanhood are they projecting? What do they share in common with the college women in the other photographs? As you seek out patterns and make assessments about images of womanhood in the 1920s, keep in mind the class dimensions of college attendance in the 1920s. And weigh issues of race, too. Consider the particular distinctiveness of Howard University and the women in this photograph. In the 1920s, Howard ranked at the top of historically black universities in the United States. In that era, most colleges and universities prohibited the admission of African American students and the hiring of black faculty. (None of the pictures show racially integrated campuses, although gender relations and roles seem quite open and fluid.) As a result of racism and segregation, Howard's faculty consisted of many of the foremost intellectuals in the country. These prominent scholars attracted to Howard classes filled with the best and brightest students from across the nation. The prestige and competitiveness of Howard meant that many students came from elite, prominent families. So, the women in this photograph are privileged in important regards. Besides the fur worn by the women in the foreground, what other hints of their economic backgrounds do you see? What might their class, race, and admission to Howard reveal about the roles they fulfill and the ideals of womanhood they embrace? Employ the same kind of speculation and analysis with the other photographs, making sure to notice parallels as well as significant differences.

Next, in Sources 8–15, you will turn to evidence generated from the social science literature of the early twentieth century. Historians who use this evidence to understand the 1920s do so with caution. Although these writers and researchers truly believed themselves to be objective, the great majority came from middle- or upper-class backgrounds. Most were white Protestants whose families had lived in the United States for many generations. Most of them had been directly or indirectly involved in various urban reform activities. These scholars and experts chose which problems they studied and made interpretations that were shaped by their backgrounds. Thus, we certainly cannot say that the social science literature of this era was objective. This does not mean that such evidence is worthless to the historian. Rather it must be read with nuance and care and with a thoughtful appreciation of the context of its production. None of the evidence available to historians is perfect, after all. Every form of primary source comes with both virtues and problems. Part of your job is to avoid taking any primary source literally or at face value. Rather, approach evidence critically, aware of its imperfections and limits with regard to answering historical questions.

◆ CHAPTER 5

A "Revolution
in Manners and
Morals": Women's
Changing Roles in
the 1920s

The final two pieces of evidence (Sources 16 and 17) may present an additional challenge: the present influencing interpretations of the past. Today, many Americans hold strong views about contraception and reproductive rights. Margaret Sanger was the central figure in the fight for the legalization and use of birth control in the United States. Her book and the cover of the magazine she edited are vigorous advocacy pieces about an issue that was highly controversial and provocative. In addition to critically evaluating these two primary sources, you may have to turn that same skill on yourself. Do your personal attitudes toward contraception and reproductive rights influence your reaction to this historical evidence?

Keep in mind all this information about the evidence as you focus your investigation on three specific tasks.

1. Understand the *message* of each source. What does it depict, criticize, praise, or advocate? What issues are revealed?
2. Identify underlying *assumptions* in each source. What is implied in the source? What subtle messages, what subtext, do you detect? What recurrent themes and perceptions do you see linking the individual pieces of evidence?
3. Determine what the primary sources reveal about the *debates* surrounding women's changing roles during the 1920s. What controversies do you see when looking at the sources collectively? What changes are supported and regretted? What did the creators of the evidence seem to think were the most important issues confronting women in the 1920s? What image of proper womanhood did they ascribe to? What did they understand to be the foundations of women's health, happiness, and success?

Working through these tasks while developing a critical appraisal of the primary sources will allow you to develop a thoughtful answer to this chapter's central question: What did advocates and critics of "new womanhood" believe was at stake in their debates over women's roles in the 1920s?

The Evidence

Source 1 from "The President's Report for the Year 1926–1927," *University of Illinois Bulletin* 25, no. 29 (20 March 1928), pp. 104–105, 114, 116–118.

1. Excerpts from the University of Illinois President's Annual Report, Academic Year 1926–1927.

PHYSICAL EDUCATION FOR WOMEN[8]

The following report of work in physical education for women, has been condensed from the report submitted to the Director by Miss Louise Freer, in charge of this division of the departmental organization:

The required courses for freshmen and sophomores constitute the most important part of the work of physical education for women. Our aim is to develop in the individual an interest in her health and a desire to maintain and improve it. It is comparatively easy to supervise the program of the girl who is assigned to individual gymnastics, but our problem is with the large percentage of students who may have difficulties or abnormalities not serious enough to put them into the corrective class and yet need advice and correction. Following the medical and physical examination, posture pictures were taken and a conference held by the instructor with each student in her class; a second conference is held at the end of the semester and in special cases, additional conferences. Every freshman is required to take a course in gymnastics.[9] Students registering in this course take six weeks of outdoor sports and the rest of the semester is devoted to gymnastics, which we are trying to make a laboratory course in hygiene.

Individual gymnastics are included in the required work for students who have been assigned to special work by the Health Service. In addition to the regular number of cases we have tried this year to put in one group, girls who are not in need of individual work but who the Medical Advisor feels should have more moderate exercise than is given in the regular classes. The aim of individual gymnastics is to give such specialized work that the student may be

8. Illinois Industrial University, precursor to the University of Illinois, was founded in 1868. The first female students enrolled in the fall of 1870.
9. Gymnastics had a wider meaning in the 1920s than it does today. Then, it was more akin to calisthenics or fitness training. Sometimes gymnastics involved synchronized exercises, but it was not the specialized and competitive sport we associate with gymnastics today.

◆ CHAPTER 5

A "Revolution
in Manners and
Morals": Women's
Changing Roles in
the 1920s

transferred to regular gymnastics as soon as possible or to take care of those students not able to take the regular physical education work, who might otherwise be out of all physical exercise. The following shows the alphabetical distribution of cases in remedial gymnastics according to total registration:

Accidents (strains, infections, sprains)	21
Amenorrhea[10]	5
Anemia	2
Appendicitis	28
Asthma	2
Bronchitis	3
Constipation	20
Circulatory disturbances	4
Dislocation (congenital dislocation of hip)	2
Dysmenorrhea	60
Feet	25
Fatigue	25
Heart	88
Hernia	2
Kidney trouble	2
Menorrhagia	16
Overweight	16
Posture	33
Post Operatives	20
Paralysis (congenital)	1
Paralysis (infantile)	3
Rheumatism	5
Scoliosis	15
Thyroid conditions	22
Viceroptosis and pelvic displacements	8
Underweight	18

Each case in individual gymnastics is given particular training in posture. A special diet group of freshmen for over and underweight is carried on in cooperation with the dietetics division of the Department of Home Economics. The students are registered in the corrective work, reporting one period a week to the diet lecture and two periods a week for exercise. A special diet is worked out with each student. . . .

DISCIPLINE

As chairman of the Committee on Discipline for Men I have had contact, as in the past, with the moral irregularities of undergraduates. For some time we have been working under the proctor system and in regular class

10. Along with dysmenorrhea and menorrhagia, amenorrhea was a term for irregular menstruation.

exercises each instructor has been given the responsibility of overseeing his own examinations. Wherever it has been managed seriously and with an adequate number of proctors I believe the system has materially reduced cribbing. Where the instructor does not take it seriously, as in some cases he does not, cribbing has increased.

In general, our moral conditions are satisfactory. They are more satisfactory, I believe, if I may judge from my visit to other campuses similar to ours, than in many other places. There is, however, everywhere a tendency to more social freedom and less conventionality. Chaperons at social functions are given less attention than they have ever been in my recollection. Smoking among both sexes is, I am sure, on the increase. We have stood out against it here but not with complete success.

ORGANIZATIONS

We have, all told, approximately one hundred social and professional fraternities for men about the campus, who live in their own houses, and this number is on the increase. It is easier to control and to direct students in an organization than to do the same thing with those outside; and for that reason we have encouraged the formation of such organizations. . . .

OFFICE OF THE DEAN OF WOMEN

The Office of the Dean of Women has striven to reflect in the lives of the students of the campus its underlying purpose of service and counsel, so that they would think and speak of it in those terms, rather than as a disciplinary post.

THE HOUSING OF UNDERGRADUATE WOMEN

During the first semester of the past year 2,892 women were enrolled in the University and 2,720 registered the second semester. They were housed as follows: in the University residence halls, 346; in organized houses (sororities, church and cooperative houses, and McKinley Hall), 987; in town homes, 941; and with parents, 446.

The residence halls have had a most successful year under the guidance of the social directors and business management. There is always a much larger number of applicants from the State of Illinois than there are rooms to fill, which is mute evidence of the cultural and financial advantages of the residence halls. The social directors were able to bring these two largest units on our campus to sixth and eighth places in the scholarship list of our forty-five organized houses.

◆ CHAPTER 5

A "Revolution
in Manners and
Morals": Women's
Changing Roles in
the 1920s

The three cooperative houses this year have accommodated thirty-four women students. These students, by membership in any of the three cooperative houses, are able to reduce their living expenses to approximately one-half the regular expenses of University life. In these homes the members can make their own home-life and do their own housework, buying the food and serving the meals. This requires only one extra hour a day on the part of the student. These houses are under chaperonage, as are the other organized houses. . . .

Thirty-two sororities maintain and operate sorority houses, 806 young women being accommodated in these homes. Each house is supervised by a chaperon selected by the young women, who must first be approved by the Office of the Dean of Women. The total number of chaperons for the organized houses is forty-five. These women are carefully selected and are mature and refined. . . .

Besides carrying on the work of its usual seventeen committees, such as the welfare work for the cooperative house fund, the weekly Wednesday teas, attendance at which numbered at times eight hundred, the Woman's League centered its activities largely this spring around the national convention of Women's Self-Governing Associations of all the colleges and universities of the country, held at the University of Illinois. One hundred sixty-five official delegates were present.

Added emphasis has been given the Woman's Group System of the Woman's League during the past year, in order to encourage equal participation of the young women in the groups in the college life of the campus with those in the organized houses. Through athletics and participation in the Stunt Show, more active interest has been fostered. In the scholarship reports it was gratifying to report the splendid average of the groups in comparison with the general women's average. The group maintaining the highest average was made up almost entirely of students working for their room and board in town homes.

The Citizenship Committee of the Woman's League has been active in its efforts to interest the University women, especially the seniors, in their responsibility toward affairs of the State and Nation. This year's work culminated in a trip to Springfield to see the Legislature in session.

Over the week-end of May 7–9, 1927, the traditional celebration of Mother's Day brought more than fifteen hundred mothers of students to our campus. The Mothers' Association is growing in interest as well as in numbers.

The spiritual life of the University women is fostered by the Young Women's Christian Association, and also by the religious foundations, which contribute largely to the religious as well as the social campus life. . . .

Source 2 courtesy of Underwood Archives/Archive Photos/Getty Images.

2. Students at the State College for Women Practicing Their Tennis Serve, New Jersey, circa 1922.

Source 3 courtesy of John Graudenz/Ullstein bild/Getty Images.

3. Students at Smith College Practicing Archery, circa 1928.

◆ CHAPTER 5

A "Revolution
in Manners and
Morals": Women's
Changing Roles in
the 1920s

Source 4 from Howard University Press.

4. Women in the Stands at a Howard University College Football Game, circa 1920.

Howard University

Source 5 courtesy of Chicago History Museum/Archive Photos/Getty Images.

5. Women in the Social Sciences Quadrangle on the University of Chicago Campus, 1928.

Chicago History Museum/Archive Photos/Getty Images

Source 6 courtesy of University of Pennsylvania.

6. Delta Sigma Theta Sorority, Gamma Chapter, University of Pennsylvania's First Black Sorority, Organized 1918. Image circa 1920s.

University of Pennsylvania

Source 7 courtesy of Reed College Digital Archives.

7. Student Council at Reed College, Portland, Oregon, 1922.

Reed digital collection

◆ CHAPTER 5

A "Revolution
in Manners and
Morals": Women's
Changing Roles in
the 1920s

Source 8 from *Happy, Healthy Womanhood* (New York: Social Hygiene Press, 1920), pp. 3–5, 11–13, 15–16.

8. The United States Public Health Service on Healthy Living and Sexual Restraint.

HEALTHY, HAPPY WOMANHOOD

Throughout France and in many different countries of the world there stands the statue of a great, heroic Frenchwoman, Joan of Arc. This humble peasant girl of Brittany, aroused by the misfortunes of her countrymen, helped to free them from the hands of a foreign foe. But today she has come to represent far more than this. She has come to stand for the woman with a vision, the woman who is seeking to do her part in the betterment of the world. Wherever her figure appears, it is always looking forward, the light of a great purpose in her eyes, the will for a large achievement in the lines of her face. As she raises her standard aloft there seem to gather behind it innumerable hosts of those who would follow her lead. A daughter of war-ridden fifteenth-century France, she nevertheless symbolizes the woman of the twentieth century, eager to take a part in the work of the world and in the great life-giving enterprises of peace.

HEALTH, THE FOUNDATION

You who aspire to take part in the work of the world should assure yourself of good health. Without it all other preparation may be in vain. Today, in addition to the more familiar duties of the home, new occupations in factory and office are open to you. In many fields you may now compete with men. But only if you possess good health—a vigorous body and a clear brain—can you expect to undertake the new and trying work successfully. No matter how thoroughly you are trained, such training will be of little value unless it rests upon a foundation of good health.

Good health is even more important from the point of view of motherhood. In some of the war-ravaged countries of Europe more than half of the babies who are born die during the first year of life. Thousands of others begin their lives under tremendous handicaps. Why? Largely because the strength of the mothers has been sapped by food shortage and over-work so that they cannot give their babies proper nourishment. The dream of these mothers of chubby, rosy-cheeked babies, who were to have been their joy, has vanished. Upon healthy womanhood depends to a large extent happy motherhood.

Physical fitness during youth is the best foundation for healthy, happy womanhood. It is an asset of which you may rightly feel proud. With health, you can look forward to the time when you can participate actively in the work of the world; with health, happy motherhood becomes a well-grounded hope for the future.

BEAUTY AND POPULARITY

Besides fitting you more effectively for your life's work, good health will incidentally increase your beauty and attractiveness. True beauty comes from within; it cannot be put on from without. Good health gives such beauty, a beauty that will wear. Its foundation is health of mind and body; its expression is a sparkling eye, a clear complexion, a graceful body, an active brain.

Every girl wants to be popular with her companions. Today the popular girl is the girl who glows with life, who can swim and dance and play outdoor games, who has plenty of energy for fun when she has finished her daily tasks. Good health, since it produces high spirits, vitality, cheerfulness, and leadership, will help to make you popular. Every girl likes to enjoy herself. She likes to go to parties and picnics, to find the real joys of living. Physical fitness, by enlarging your opportunity for enjoyment and your power to enjoy, makes more such occasions possible.

HOW FITNESS IS ATTAINED

Plenty of physical exercise, fresh air, sufficient sleep, frequent bathing, three well-balanced meals a day, erect carriage, and comfortable clothing will help to make you strong and well. . . .

MISUSE OF SEX

After centuries of experience, the marriage of one man with one woman has come to be considered the best method of carrying on the life of the race. Through such a relationship the sex instinct finds its most wholesome satisfaction. A man and a woman who bring children into the world of whom they are unwilling to take care, endanger their own happiness as well as the welfare of the community. They miss the finer joys of human love, and fail to appreciate what such love may mean in their lives.

More than this. Indulgence in sex relations among persons who are not married to each other exposes them to a serious physical danger. They are likely to become infected with a venereal disease. These diseases are called syphilis (pox) and gonorrhea (clap). They are germ diseases.

To the man a venereal disease may mean lifelong suffering, unless by proper treatment the germs are destroyed. Syphilis often causes heart disease, paralysis, and some forms of insanity. Gonorrhea may cause

◆ CHAPTER 5

A "Revolution
in Manners and
Morals": Women's
Changing Roles in
the 1920s

blindness, chronic rheumatism, incurable disorders of the sex organs, and inability on the man's part to become a father.

A man who has one of these diseases is likely to give it to his wife. While syphilis affects her much as it does a man, gonorrhea often afflicts her even more seriously. Many operations upon women's reproductive organs are made necessary by gonorrhea. Many women are lifelong invalids as a result of this disease. Some die. Many babies are blinded at birth by gonorrhea in the mother. Fortunately, simple medical treatment given the baby immediately after birth will prevent blindness of this kind. Syphilis causes many miscarriages (the birth of babies before they can live outside the mother's body). Many babies are defective in various ways because of syphilis.

It is important to remember, however, that these results—blindness, sores, invalidism, and operations upon women—are often due to causes other than syphilis and gonorrhea. . . . Syphilis and gonorrhea can be cured if treated by a competent physician. There are many good clinics for those who cannot afford a private physician. If the treatment is not thorough and continued long enough, the disease may reappear years after the patient believes the cure to be complete. This is especially true when the infected person relies on patent medicines or "quack" doctors. Advertising doctors seldom cure and generally do more harm than good.

Because the sex instinct, which may bring the individual the greatest joy, is sometimes misused, a girl should exercise great care in the choice of the men with whom she associates. Chance acquaintances often invite girls on automobile rides, to movies and cafés with the intention of leading them into sex relations. Such invitations should be refused. A girl does not wish to be considered an easy mark, or to put herself in a position where a man may take advantage of her. . . .

A CHALLENGE TO THE PRESENT

In the development of America, women have made a splendid record. Three hundred years ago when the Pilgrims landed on the stern and rock-bound New England coast it was the women—the Anns and the Priscillas—who kept hope and faith alive as the number of graves beneath the Plymouth corn fields grew and grew. During pioneer days in solitary log cabins, women shared with their husbands the constant danger of attack from hostile Indians. They were not spared when the redskins descended upon the settlements with tomahawk and torch, as the stories of Ann Hutchinson, Hannah Dustin, and many others indicate. At the time of the Revolution, Molly Pitcher, taking her husband's place in the fighting when he was grievously wounded, was not the only woman who showed courage and endurance. Through the terrible winter at Valley Forge, when the cause of Washington and Jefferson seemed all but lost, women in homes from Massachusetts to Georgia helped to keep the light of liberty burning. Women bore their share of the burden in the settlement of the lands across the Alleghenies, in the fertile valleys of the Ohio and the Mississippi. And in the tragic days of the Civil War, in homes north and south, in hospitals and on battlefields, women took their part earnestly and courageously. Never in any period of the country's history have they been found wanting.

Today the opportunities for woman's development and her ability to contribute toward the creation of a better world are greater than ever before. At last all activities of life are open to her. She is now free to choose the part she will play in the world's work. Whatever part it may be, good health is essential. Only because the women of pioneer days possessed clear minds and vigorous bodies were they able to take such an active part in the settlement of this country. Their record is a challenge to you, a woman of the new century. But only as you are similarly qualified can you in the home and in the larger world outside meet this challenge of a glorious past by your achievement.

Source 9 from John Watson, "The Weakness of Women." Reprinted with permission from the July 6, 1927, issue of *The Nation*.

9. John Watson on the Sex Adjustment of Modern Women.

These women were too modern to seek happiness; they sought what? Freedom. So many hundreds of women I have talked to have sought freedom. I have tried to find out diplomatically but behavioristically what they mean. Is it to wear trousers? Is it to vote—to hold office—to work at men's trades—to take men's jobs away from them—to get men's salaries? Does their demand for this mystical thing called freedom imply a resentment against child-bearing—a resentment against the fact that men's sex behavior is different from women's (but not so much anymore)? I rarely arrive at a reasonable answer. . . . When a woman is a militant suffragist the chances are, shall we say, a hundred to one that her sex life is not well adjusted. Marriage as such brings adjustment in only approximately 20 per cent of all cases, so poorly have men and women been taught about sex. Among the 20 per cent who find adjustment I find no militant women, I find no women shouting about their rights to some fanciful career that men—the brutes—have robbed them of. They work—they work like a man (than which nothing better can be said about work)—they often quietly achieve careers. Most of the terrible women

✦ CHAPTER 5

A "Revolution
in Manners and
Morals": Women's
Changing Roles in
the 1920s

one must meet, women with the blatant views and voices, women who have to be noticed, who shoulder one about, who can't take life quietly, belong to this large percentage of women who have never made a sex adjustment.

Source 10 from Alyse Gregory, "The Changing Morality of Women," *Current History* 19 (1923), pp. 298, 299.

10. Alyse Gregory on Sex and the New Woman.

Alyse Gregory was a feminist, a statistical researcher for the Carnegie Educational Foundation, a "new" woman herself.

Then suddenly all was changed again. The war [World War I] was over and women were admonished to hurry once more home and give the men back their jobs. It was too late. The old discipline had vanished in the night. There was neither an avenging God nor an avenging father to coerce women back into their old places at the family board. They took flats or studios and went on earning their livings. They filled executive offices, they became organizers, editors, copywriters, efficiency managers, artists, writers, real estate agents, and even in rare instances brokers. . . . However unwilling one may be to acknowledge it, girls began to sow their wild oats. Women of the aristocratic upper classes and the poorest women had never followed too rigidly the cast-iron rules of respectability because in neither instance had they anything to lose by digressing. But for the first time in the memory of man, girls from well-bred, respectable middle-class families broke through those invisible chains of custom and asserted their right to a nonchalant, self-sustaining life of their own with a cigarette after every meal and a lover in the evening to wander about with and lend color to life. If the relationship became more intimate than such relationships are supposed to be, there was nothing to be lost that a girl could not dispense with. Her employer asked no questions as to her life outside the office. She had her own salary at the end of the month and asked no other recompense from her lover but his love and companionship. Into the privacy of her own snug and pleasant rooms not even her mother or her oldest brother could penetrate, for she and she alone, unless perhaps one other, carried the only key that would fit the lock.

Profoundly shocking as such a state of affairs may seem to large numbers of people, there is no use pretending that it does not exist. There are too many signs abroad to prove that it does. Ministers may extol chastity for women from pulpit rostrums and quote passages from the Old and New Testaments to prove that purity and fidelity are still her most precious assets, but this new woman only shrugs her shoulders and smiles a slow, penetrating, secret smile.

Source 11 from S. Dana Hubbard, *Facts About Marriage Every Young Man and Woman Should Know* (New York: Claremont Printing Company, 1922), pp. 2–5.

11. S. Dana Hubbard on Choosing a Spouse.

S. Dana Hubbard was a physician from New York who wrote extensively about sex education, including pamphlets on "Sex Education for Young Men" and "Facts about Motherhood."

Marriage naturally implies motherhood. There is no nobler word in any language than MOTHER. The young mother with her first born is a picture of joy and accomplishment that fills us with wonder and approbation. If there is a perfect home atmosphere—"the rallying place of affections"— every one does the utmost to make this place the happiest on earth.

There is a definite physical side to marriage, and if all husbands and wives were experts in gentleness and kindness the world would be spared many tragedies.

Maternity neither dims nor diminishes the energy, nor the intellectual faculties of the mother. On the contrary it acts positively on the virtues necessary for a proper membership in human society.

Marriage is the beginning and the summit of all earthly civilization.

The union of a young man and woman in the holy tie of matrimony is the most important step in life. The entire future of both depends upon whether this step is taken seriously and after proper contemplation, because success and happiness depends upon wise selection. Marriage carries with it responsibilities far greater than the average person realizes.

Some marry for a home, some marry for money, some for position, some simply because it is fashionable. Foolish people. The person that marries for money, as the wag says humorously, earns it often times before he gets it.

Marriage should be only for love. Happy married life must be built upon mutual trust and devotion, not forgetting that there will be both happiness and trial and that come what may it is a case of mutual sacrifice and helpfulness.

No undertaking in life should cause more careful consideration and if ever an undertaking which affects both health and is worthy of seeking advice and the opinion of others' happiness nothing should be overlooked in making this step.

◆ CHAPTER 5

A "Revolution
in Manners and
Morals": Women's
Changing Roles in
the 1920s

The man a woman should marry should be healthy, clean minded and strong, not a weakling—because the husband will be the father of the children and the offspring inherit mental and physical traits of the parents. Don't help perpetuate bad traits and bad character. You cannot go against nature in heredity.

Don't marry a man who cannot provide you with a home. Insist upon your own home, be it ever so humble a beginning. "Tall oaks from acorns grow." Boarding with either your or his family is unwise. Living in furnished rooms may ruin your life or his.

While it is a delicate subject for a woman to discuss, yet the matter of children is often times a stumbling block. Don't marry a man who does not want children, such a man will not want you very long. If he loves and love truly, he will be eager to be the father of your babies.

In contemplating marriage, health is the first consideration. Have a careful understanding on this point. Insist upon both yourself and himself undergoing a careful medical examination to ascertain your fitness for marriage and parenthood. Never take this for granted. If too delicate for you to undertake have your parent or guardian do so for you. This test is for your protection, because many men "sowing wild oats" before marriage contract disease and so very few of them have their disease cured. If you do not insist upon this test you may some day find yourself without children, or else the mother of weak, puny, diseased children.

If you are averse to having children, don't marry. You will be committing a sin that Nature will punish you for as surely as God exists. The world holds no more cowardly murderers than those who are involved in committing abortions to prevent child birth.

Do not allow your fiancé any liberties with your person before marriage. He may be only testing you to learn if he can have them, but many engagements are ruined by this foolish mistake. Most men figure that if one man can have liberties before marriage other men can have similar liberties after marriage. Confirmed libertines on many occasions have proposed marriage only to deceive and obtain special privileges and this is one of the surest methods of ruining women, especially young women.

If the man you are about to marry loves and respects you, he will not ask you to degrade yourself by being his prostitute before marriage. Should you not refuse, he will surely bring this up in your family bickerings and "twit" you about your weakness, that is if he will marry you after you have allowed him to ruin you.

It is the woman's right to name the wedding day—insist upon doing this. Have a confidential talk with your parents, especially your mother or some other married woman about the obligations of the marriage relation as it affects the wife or mother.

There may be instances when elopements or run-away marriages are advisable but outside of the romance these are dangerous occasions for both man and woman. The vast majority of such hasty unions turn out badly.

Be sure the marriage license is legal. That the person performing the ceremony is duly authorized. Don't take any one's word for these facts but make certain. Make them prove it. This is emphasizes to save girls from being victimized by "fake" marriages.

Never marry a chronic alcoholic, you never reform him. Never marry a drug addict. He will lower you to his level and you will never elevate him. Such experiments are failures from the first. If you decide to marry, do so, long engagements are not advisable. The engagement period is a strain on both man and woman. Extravagances that most people can ill afford are usual during this period and it is money wasted that would be most useful in your new home.

Arrange your wedding day according to your menstrual cycle. Ten days after or ten days before. This will save you some embarrassment.

In marrying, make no reservations. If there are reservations it were best not to marry. Wait for the man you are willing to share not only your heart but all your worldly possessions. . .

Source 12 from Ernest Groves and Gladys Hoagland Groves, *Wholesome Marriage*, pp. 100, 101, 206–209, 214. Copyright 1927 by Houghton Mifflin Company; copyright renewed © 1955 by Gladys Hoagland Groves. Reprinted by permission of Houghton Mifflin Company. All rights reserved.

12. Ernest and Gladys H. Groves on How to Have a Happy Marriage, 1927.

LIFE PARTNERSHIP. What is the secret of those marriages in which the wedding day seems to be a turning-point that brings the man to the straightaway leading to business success? It would be well to know, if the knowledge could be used to help those for whom the marriage ceremony is but a milestone in a long, slow, uphill climb to financial security.

The answer lies in the reactions of the newly married couple to their new relationship. Normally the man is very proud of his responsibility for the welfare of his family. He takes his business much more seriously than he did before, for now he has two mouths to feed instead of one. It would never do to lose his job, or even to miss an expected promotion.

◆ CHAPTER 5

A "Revolution
in Manners and
Morals": Women's
Changing Roles in
the 1920s

The young husband "settles down" to his work, determined to make good if it is in him. He is somewhat helped in the settling-down process by the strange, new fact that he is no longer in constant fear of losing his sweetheart. She is his "for keeps" now, and his only anxiety is to be able to do his part well in the establishment of the home life they are entering upon.

This means money, a steady stream of it that can be depended on and promises to grow larger in time. So the young man throws himself into his work whole-heartedly, and the stuff he is made of shows. That is his side of the story. . . .

Of course the wife who helps her husband on to success makes the home life restful and refreshing. Dissatisfaction finds no quarters within the four walls of the house, be it two-room flat or rambling country homestead. Good housekeeping is not enough to turn the trick, but it is an indispensable card. Singleness of purpose, alertness of mind, and a broad outlook on life are all needed.

Then the wife does not put her embroidery, bridge, and tea parties above her husband's peace of mind. She does her best to keep the home life pleasant, that her man may be in tip-top condition for his work outside. Turning and twisting to save a penny, she sees to it that the family lives within its income, so that her husband will not be worried by unpaid bills, when he is trying to increase his earning capacity. Above all she has faith in her husband's ability to better his condition.

Source 13 from Lorine Pruette, "The Married Woman and the Part-Time Job," in *The Annals: Women in the Modern World*, pp. 302, 303, 306. Copyright 1929 by Sage Publications. Reprinted by permission of Sage Publications.

13. Lorine Pruette's Critique of Domesticity, 1929.

Dr. Lorine Pruette was an economist whose dissertation "Women and Leisure" was published in 1924. Married and divorced twice, Pruette became a freelance consultant in order to try to adapt to her husbands' academic career moves.

The worst thing that can be said for the American home is that it ruins so many of its members. It is a disheartening and disillusioning business to survey the middle-aged married women of the country. They have been permanently damaged as persons by the disintegrating influences of the modern home and family life. Conversely, they contribute to the further disintegration of the institution to which they have given their lives.

It is only the rare woman who can pass without deterioration through many years of uninterrupted domesticity. . . . Schemes for coordination and cooperation in women's activities appear predicated on the idea that wives, when freed from minor household responsibilities, will find their satisfactions in helping their husbands get ahead in their vocations. This implies a subordination of self unfashionable in an age where the emphasis is on self-expression and uncommon among the individualistic American women of today. . . .

Not only does part-time employment of the married woman offer the opportunity for the development of a new home life, it lessens or destroys the appalling economic risk taken by every woman who today marries and devotes herself to the traditional role of wife. There is no security in domesticity. It is heart-breaking to see the middle-aged woman, trained for nothing except the duties of the home, venture out into the industrial world. Divorce, death or loss of money may put her in this position, where she has so little to offer organized industry and so much to suffer. The married woman who lets herself go upon the easy tide of domesticity is offering herself as a victim in a future tragedy.

Source 14 from Willystine Goodsell, *Problems of the Family* (New York: Century Company, 1928), pp. 281, 282.

14. Married Women and Academia, 1928.

Sociology professor Dr. Willystine Goodsell taught at Teachers College, Columbia University.

In one of the issues of the *Journal of the Association of Collegiate Alumnae*, there appeared a few years ago a brief article entitled "Reflections of a Professor's Wife." With her husband, the writer had spent several years in the graduate school of a university where both had earned their doctor's degrees. Then the equality in work and the delightful companionship ceased. The man was appointed assistant professor in a state university at a small salary; and the woman, who had eagerly looked forward to a similar appointment in the same institution, was brought face to face with the ruling, by no means uncommon, which prohibited wives of faculty members from teaching in the university. The comments of the professor's wife, after years spent in housekeeping, are worth quoting, for they reflect the feelings of many other women caught in a similar net of circumstance:

"After an expenditure of several thousand dollars and the devotion of some of the best years of my life to special study, I was cut off from any opportunity to utilize this training. And unless I could earn enough money

◆ CHAPTER 5

A "Revolution
in Manners and
Morals": Women's
Changing Roles in
the 1920s

to pay some one else to do the housework, I was doomed to spend a large part of my time in tasks which a woman with practically no education could do. However, accepting the situation, I put on my apron and went into the kitchen, where for six years I have cooked a professor's meals and pondered over the policy of our university. Can it be in the divine order of things that one Ph.D. should wash dishes a whole life time for another Ph.D. just because one is a woman and the other a man?"

Source 15 from *The Unadjusted Girl* by William Isaac Thomas, pp. 72, 73. Copyright © 1923 by William I. Thomas. Copyright © renewed 1951 by William I. Thomas. Reprinted with permission of Little, Brown, and Co., Inc.

15. W. I. Thomas, Case 37: A Married Woman's Despair, 1923.

William Isaac Thomas was one of the pioneers in social psychology and the sociological case study. His earliest work centered on immigrant families; later he turned his attention to issues of gender and sexuality. He is particularly noted for the sociology construct known as the Thomas theorem: "If men define situations as real, they are real in their consequences."

My husband's career, upon which I spent the best years of my life, is established favorably; our children are a joy to me as a mother; nor can I complain about our material circumstances. But I am dissatisfied with myself. My love for my children, be it ever so great, cannot destroy myself. A human being is not created like a bee which dies after accomplishing its only task. . . .

Desires, long latent, have been aroused in me and become more aggressive the more obstacles they encounter. . . . I now have the desire to go about and see and hear everything. I wish to take part in everything—to dance, skate, play the piano, sing, go to the theatre, opera, lectures and generally mingle in society. As you see, I am no idler whose purpose is to chase all sorts of foolish things, as a result of loose ways. This is not the case.

My present unrest is a natural result following a long period of hunger and thirst for non-satisfied desires in every field of human experience. It is the dread of losing that which never can be recovered—youth and time which do not stand still—an impulse to catch up with the things I have missed. . . . If it were not for my maternal feeling I would go away into the wide world.

Source 16 from "The Birth Control Review," November 1923.

16. Cover Art, "Birth Control Review," November 1923.

BIRTH CONTROL REVIEW

Edited by Margaret Sanger

TWENTY CENTS A COPY   NOVEMBER, 1923   TWO DOLLARS A YEAR

Official Organ of
THE AMERICAN BIRTH CONTROL LEAGUE, INC., 104 FIFTH AVENUE, NEW YORK CITY

◆ CHAPTER 5

A "Revolution
in Manners and
Morals": Women's
Changing Roles in
the 1920s

Source 17 from Margaret Sanger, *Woman and the New Race* (New York: Truth Publishing Company, 1920), pp. 1, 2–3, 4–5, 7, 8.

17. Excerpts from Margaret Sanger, *Woman and the New Race.*

The most far-reaching social development of modern times is the revolt of woman against sex servitude. The most important force in the remaking of the world is a free motherhood. Beside this force, the elaborate international programmes of modern statesmen are weak and superficial. Diplomats may formulate leagues of nations and nations may pledge their utmost strength to maintain them, statesmen may dream of reconstructing the world out of alliances, hegemonies and spheres of influence, but woman, continuing to produce explosive populations, will convert these pledges into the proverbial scraps of paper; or she may, by controlling birth, lift motherhood to the plane of a voluntary, intelligent function, and remake the world. . . .

Only in recent years has woman's position as the gentler and weaker half of the human family been emphatically and generally questioned. Men assumed that this was woman's place; woman herself accepted it. . . .

Woman's acceptance of her inferior status was the more real because it was unconscious. She had chained herself to her place in society and the family through the maternal functions of her nature, and only chains thus strong could have bound her to her lot as a brood animal for the masculine civilizations of the world. In accepting her role as the "weaker and gentler half," she accepted that function. In turn, the acceptance of that function fixed the more firmly her rank as an inferior.

Caught in this "vicious circle," woman has, through her reproductive ability, founded and perpetuated the tyrannies of the Earth. Whether it was the tyranny of a monarchy, an oligarchy or a republic, the one indispensable factor of its existence was, as it is now, hordes of human beings—human beings so plentiful as to be cheap, and so cheap that ignorance was their natural lot. Upon the rock of an unenlightened, submissive maternity have these been founded; upon the product of such a maternity have they flourished. . . .

Woman's passivity under the burden of her disastrous task was almost altogether that of ignorant resignation. She knew virtually nothing about her reproductive nature and less about the consequences of her excessive child-bearing. It is true that, obeying the inner urge of their natures, *some* women revolted. They went even to the extreme of infanticide and abortion. Usually their revolts were not general enough. They fought as individuals, not as a mass. In the mass they sank back into blind and hopeless subjection.

They went on breeding with staggering rapidity those numberless, undesired children who become the clogs and the destroyers of civilizations.

Today, however, woman is rising in fundamental revolt. . . . Millions of women are asserting their right to voluntary motherhood. They are determined to decide for themselves whether they shall become mothers, under what conditions and when. . . .

War, famine, poverty and oppression of the workers will continue while woman makes life cheap. They will cease only when she limits her reproductivity and human life is no longer a thing to be wasted.

Two chief obstacles hinder the discharge of this tremendous obligation. The first and the lesser is the legal barrier. Dark-Age laws would still deny to her the knowledge of her reproductive nature. Such knowledge is indispensable to intelligent motherhood and she must achieve it, despite absurd statutes and equally absurd moral canons.

The second and more serious barrier is her own ignorance of the extent and effect of her submission. Until she knows the evil her subjection has wrought to herself, to her progeny and to the world at large, she cannot wipe out that evil. . . .

The first step is birth control. Through birth control she will attain to voluntary motherhood. Having attained this, the basic freedom of her sex, she will cease to enslave herself and the mass of humanity. Then, through the understanding of the intuitive forward urge within her, she will not stop at patching up the world; she will remake it. . . .

◆

Questions to Consider

The Evidence section in this chapter is grouped according to broad thematic categories. The first grouping (Sources 1–7) centers on the college experiences of middle- and upper-class young women, both white and African American. Source 8 (guidance offered to this generation of young women) connects the first grouping with the second (Sources 8–15), which consists of expert advice from the social science tradition. These sources cover several interrelated topics, including courtship, sexuality and marriage, work in and outside the home, and motherhood. Finally, the last two pieces of evidence (Sources 16 and 17) derive from the controversial campaign for birth control. There is some unavoidable overlap between the divisions, with one influencing and leading into another. Sanger, for example, speaks

◆ CHAPTER 5

A "Revolution
in Manners and
Morals": Women's
Changing Roles in
the 1920s

to issues of female sexuality and maternal duties. The photographs of college students reflect new ideas about relationships between men and women. But the structuring of the evidence should help you to get a better handle on the debates surrounding new womanhood in the 1920s.

Start by taking notes on the intended message of each individual source as it relates to the central question in the chapter. The cover art from "Birth Control Review," depicting a woman chained to the ground by a ball marked "unwanted babies," will perhaps be the easiest to immediately understand. Other evidence will require deeper consideration but you still should be able to discern what each source says about perceptions of womanhood and women's proper roles. In the case of texts, ask yourself: What are the most important issues to these authors? What roles do they believe women should fill? With the photographs, consider both the subject and the photographer. Why was the photograph taken? What do the subjects' clothes and poses say?

Each grouping of evidence invites its own particular questions. What was the college experience like for women in the 1920s? How did men and women interact in a university setting? What did Americans in the 1920s believe constituted a good marriage? How did they imagine couples should relate to one another? Should women work outside the home? What were the benefits and costs of mothers working? Was motherhood essential to women's purpose and happiness?

Now, look closer at the subtle messages, the subtexts within the sources. In contemporary America, we generally understand that gender is socially constructed. But in the 1920s, Americans were deeply concerned about women's "nature." In fact, this is one of the most contested concepts in the sources you are investigating. Sometimes an argument about what was "natural" for women was expressly stated, but in other instances it was assumed or implied. Review the evidence to explore the contested meaning of women's "nature" in the 1920s. Looking at this kind of recurrent theme within the varied sources will help you to see the more subtle messages. Women's health, for example, was of great concern—a fact most evident in the University of Illinois annual report. But look closely: see how often the evidence returns to considerations of women's health, how much importance is assigned to health, and what people believed made women healthy. What can you learn about the controversy over women's changing roles by studying attitudes toward women's health? Apply the same technique to other recurrent themes you see in the evidence: female sexuality, male-female relationships, women's careers, and the responsibilities of mothers.

Now you should be ready to offer some conclusions. What were the most important ways in which women's roles were changing in the 1920s? Why did Americans in the 1920s find women's changing roles so controversial? What foundational beliefs—about manhood and womanhood, about sexuality and families, about education and careers—were being challenged by those changes? And, finally, what did advocates and critics of "new womanhood" believe was at stake in their debates over women's roles in the 1920s?

Epilogue

For all practical purposes, the Great Depression, which you will turn to in the next chapter, ended the fascination with debating the "new woman" and replaced it with sympathy and concern for the "forgotten man." Even though women suffered no less than men during the years of the Great Depression, women who worked, especially married women, were perceived as taking jobs away from unemployed men. In the hard times of the 1930s, people clung to traditional male and female roles: men should be the breadwinners, and women should stay home and take care of the family. Women's fashions changed just as dramatically. Clothing became more feminine, hemlines dropped, and hairstyles were no longer short and boyish.

Yet women, including married women, continued to move into paid employment throughout the 1930s, and women's roles within their families continued to transform. During the 1930s, the age of marriage rose, the number of children women bore decreased, and the percentage of women who intentionally remained childless increased.

Birth control was not only frequently used, as demographic patterns indicate, but also became widely accepted during the 1930s. In fact, many scholars point to the Great Depression as a turning point in legitimizing contraception. Couples lacking the wherewithal to support the children they already had sought ways to limit their family size, and doctors, legislators, and judges followed their lead. Beginning in the 1930s, court rulings and legislative action gradually undercut the Comstock Law and more and more doctors tried to provide their patients with birth control information and devices. In 1930, the American Birth Control League ran fifty-five birth control clinics. By 1938, that number had grown past 500. The *Ladies Home Journal* conducted a survey that same year, which found that 79 percent of American women approved of birth control.

Divorce rates had steadily increased in the early twentieth century; by 1924, one in every seven marriages legally ended, and the national rate of divorce was fifteen times higher than it had been fifty years before. The Great Depression reversed that

♦ CHAPTER 5

A "Revolution
in Manners and
Morals": Women's
Changing Roles in
the 1920s

demographic pattern: as fewer couples could afford legal fees, the rate of legal divorces dropped.[11] Desertion rates, however, soared. Men humiliated at their inability to provide for their families sometimes abandoned them. Suicides among men increased during the 1930s for the same reason.

When the U.S. entry into World War II brought about the end of the Great Depression, millions of women went to work in factories and shipyards, motivated by patriotism and a desire to aid the war effort. But in the 1950s, women workers, replaced by returning World War II veterans, were once again urged to stay at home and concentrate on fulfilling traditional roles as wives and mothers. Women's educational achievements and age of marriage dropped in the 1950s; the white middle-class birthrate nearly doubled. Fashions changed from knee-length tailored suits and dresses and "Rosie the Riveter" pants to puff-sleeved, tiny-waisted, full-skirted dresses.

The resistance to changes in women's roles so prominent in the 1920s was replicated in the 1960s and 1970s. The development and widespread use of the birth control pill, the passage of Title IX in 1972 and the consequent expansion of women's athletics, the legalization of abortion following the 1973 *Roe v. Wade* Supreme Court case,

and the influx of young women into graduate and professional programs all seemed to challenge both women's traditional roles in the family and men's role as breadwinners. In the 1960s and 1970s the gay rights movement emerged, and older assumptions about sexuality were questioned and, in many cases, rejected.

These changes, coupled with the perceived radicalism of a renewed call for women's full equality with men, sparked a conservative backlash. Feminists in the 1960s and 1970s revived the idea of broad-based gender equality, which they called women's liberation. They got as far as congressional passage of Alice Paul's dream of an Equal Rights Amendment to the Constitution before stalling in the state ratification campaigns. In a savvy and relentless crusade against the 1970s campaign for the ERA, Phyllis Schlafly painted feminists as dangerous outsiders. Some of her charges echoed criticisms from the 1920s: "See for yourself the unkempt, the lesbians, the radicals, the socialists."[12]

During the Civil Rights Movement, African American women played pivotal roles in the struggle for justice only to find their equality sometimes questioned by mainstream leaders, student protest organizations, and the

---

11. John D'Emilio and Estelle B. Freedman, *Intimate Matters: A History of Sexuality in America* (New York: Harper and Row, 1988), 248; Steven Mintz and Susan Kellogg, *Domestic Revolutions: A Social History of American Family Life* (New York: Free Press, 1988), pp. 108–110, 136–137.

12. Now in her nineties, Schlafly remains an icon of conservative politics. Her work continues as well. She writes a syndicated newspaper column, delivers a daily radio address, and leads the various initiatives of Eagle Forum: http://www.eagleforum.org.

Black Power movement. They were asked to make coffee for meetings, for example, rather than plan strategy. At the same time, African American women became targets for sexual assaults as part of the pro-segregation violence waged in the Deep South.[13]

In the second half of the twentieth century, then, the most intimate parts of women's lives—their sexuality, their bodies, and their family relationships—became increasingly politicized. Nowhere was this more pronounced than in the decades-long struggle over the legality of abortion. In the early twenty-first century, this fight increasingly moved from the federal courts and U.S. Congress to the individual states: opponents to legalized abortion focused more on passing strict state regulations that were tantamount to bans than on their long-standing campaign to overturn *Roe v. Wade*. The tactics have changed, but the intensity of the debate remains the same. In the controversy over reproductive rights and a host of other issues—from the ordination of women as ministers and priests to policing sexual assaults on college campuses—Americans across the political spectrum continue to contest the proper roles of women. In no small measure, the struggle has been intense because conservatives and progressives often share a common conviction: the roles women fill in American society shape our families and our nation's future.

13. Danielle L. McGuire, *At the Dark End of the Street: Black Women, Rape, and Resistance—A New History of the Civil Right Movement from Rosa Parks to the Rise of Black Power* (New York: Knopf, 2010).

Understanding Rural Poverty During the Great Depression

✦

The Problem

It is difficult today to comprehend the deprivation and desolation Americans endured in the 1930s. Because of the Great Depression, one-fourth of Americans could not find work: they lost their homes, their farms, and their life savings. The Great Plains were also crippled by an unprecedented ecological disaster, the Dust Bowl. Families faced staggering levels of poverty, homelessness, and hunger. Government then provided almost none of today's "safety net" social services. Churches and philanthropic societies were overwhelmed with calls for aid—health care, clothing, shelter, and food—that they could not begin to meet.

Desperate times called for desperate measures, and so tens of thousands of hungry, destitute Americans directly appealed to the new president, Franklin Roosevelt, and his wife, Eleanor. Mrs. Roosevelt received 300,000 pieces of mail in the first year of her husband's administration—far more than any other first lady. And President Roosevelt received three times the amount of mail of any previous president.[1]

Most Americans who appealed to Franklin or Eleanor Roosevelt felt ashamed of their need. Writers often begged the president and first lady not to disclose their identity, believing they would lose the respect of their neighbors if their circumstances became common knowledge. Children and adolescents numbered among the letter writers, and they also pleaded for privacy.[2] Like their parents, young people worried about friends and neighbors learning about the extent of their family's plight; some feared their parents might punish them for revealing their destitution.

1. Robert Cohen, ed., *Dear Mrs. Roosevelt: Letters from Children of the Great Depression* (Chapel Hill: University of North Carolina Press, 2002), p. 5.
2. The term "teenager" was not commonly used in the 1930s. Most young people writing to Eleanor Roosevelt were in the teenage years, not young children. For more about young people during this era, see Richard Reiman, *The New Deal and American Youth: Ideas and Ideals in a Depression Decade* (Athens: University of Georgia Press, 1993).

We know very little, then, about a young man named "E. B." who wrote Eleanor Roosevelt in the winter of 1934: he was sixteen years old; his family had fallen on very hard times; and he lived in Double Springs, Alabama, in the northwest part of the state.[3] With debts skyrocketing and farm prices plummeting, E. B.'s parents were about to lose their farm. The family might have been able to hold on—E. B. was willing to work as hard as he could to support his brothers and sisters—but both his parents were "in very bad Health." His father and a sister had recently required surgery so, he explained, "We owe lots of Hospital Bills." Only a bit of time stood between his family and homelessness—unless, E. B. hoped, the Roosevelts came to their aid.

E. B. and his family supported the political vision of President Roosevelt. But he wished the help that Roosevelt had campaigned on providing to impoverished Americans could get to Double Springs a bit quicker: "We know it is for the poor people good. But," he poignantly added, "it seems it hasn't reached us yet much." E. B. was not asking for money to pay his relatives' medical bills. Rather, he needed clothes for himself and his siblings. Winter had arrived, and E. B. did not know where else to turn. We can conclude one other thing

3. E. B. did not identify by gender. The authors infer that the person who wrote the letter was a boy, because girls tended to self-identify in their letters to Eleanor Roosevelt and because of other tonal hints in the text. But this is speculation. The letter is reprinted in Source 5, so you can decide for yourself.

from the letter. Since it was dated December 27, 1934, Christmas must have been very bleak for E. B. and his siblings.

Tens of thousands of appeals for food, clothing, money, and sympathy flooded the White House during the 1930s, and for good cause. Nationally, unemployment stood at 25 percent for most of the decade. In some areas of the country that figure could be double or higher. Between 1929 and 1932 farm prices in the United States fell by half, and the net income of farm families dropped by 66 percent. In his second inaugural address, President Roosevelt observed that one-third of the nation remained "ill-housed, ill-clad, and ill-nourished." It was no exaggeration.

President Roosevelt also said in that same speech: "The test of our progress is not whether we add more to the abundance of those who have much; it is whether we provide enough for those who have little." His plan to aid the poor and to raise Americans out of the economic devastation of the Great Depression, known as the New Deal, was radical and controversial.

New Deal proponents understood that if the United States was going to help the E.B.'s of the world, their living conditions could not be concealed. Americans of all classes would have to truly understand—to see and feel— what poor families faced in order to be moved to support New Deal legislation.

A host of efforts were undertaken to sway public opinion in favor of government programs that were very controversial at the time, including rural electrification and Social Security. One of the most powerful tools for creating support for these and other New Deal programs was photography. The Historical Section of the Farm Security Administration (FSA) sent professional photographers into rural America to document the lives of people like E. B. of Double Springs, Alabama. These powerful images graphically captured rural poverty, dislocation, and suffering. They remain iconic today.

In this chapter, you will analyze letters sent from poor children and adolescents to Eleanor Roosevelt alongside photographs taken by FSA employees in order to address two related issues: **What did the Great Depression mean to rural Americans? How did FSA photographs build support for the New Deal?**

✦

Background

Contrary to popular perception, the stock market crash of 1929 did not cause the Great Depression. October 29, 1929, certainly dealt a blow to America's economy; within a month the stock market lost half its value. But the trouble ran much deeper. "Black Tuesday" revealed those underlying problems and portended what lay ahead for Americans.

Economists in the 1930s debated the causes of the Great Depression, and historians continue that debate today. There is no firm consensus, but scholars point to a number of interrelated issues. The United States was shifting from an economy built around heavy industry (coal, railroads, steel) to one increasingly dependent on consumerism (cars, clothes, radios)—which was more volatile. When the stock market collapsed, so did consumer purchasing. Banks were virtually unregulated and they often failed— leaving many investors and savers with no money and no recourse—even

in periods of economic stability.[4] The federal government generally did not regulate corporations either, despite their sometimes suspect and erratic fiscal dealings. The American economy was weakened by European downturns, particularly in Germany in the wake of the Great War.

Republican Herbert Hoover was president in 1929–1933, and he believed that government intervention in the faltering economy would destroy American capitalism. Hoover was at first bewildered and then defensive about the rapid downward spiral of the nation's economy in 1930. President Hoover, like many Americans at the time, believed in the basic soundness of unregulated capitalism, and he prized

4. The Federal Deposit Insurance Corporation (FDIC), created as a part of the New Deal in 1933, protects bank deposits from such failures, as of 2015 up to $250,000 per depositor, per account. Since its implementation in January 1934, the FDIC proudly and accurately proclaims, "No depositor has lost a single cent of insured funds as a result of a failure." www.fdic.gov.

individualism as a core American value. In Hoover's mind, federal intervention compromised both. While he tried to get corporations, bankers, and industrial leaders to cooperate to stabilize the economy, government intervention was antithetical to his political philosophy.

Between late 1929 and when President Franklin D. Roosevelt took office in March 1933, every sector of the nation's economy was in a virtual free fall: farm prices, wages, exports, imports, and gross national product (GNP). Bank failures and farm foreclosures skyrocketed, followed inevitably by joblessness and homelessness.

The poorest Americans were hit hardest: tenant and sharecropping families in the South, migrant workers in the West, rural farmers across the whole country. Recurrent droughts worsened by overfarming turned the Great Plains into a "Dust Bowl." Terrifying dust storms blotted out the sun, suffocated livestock, and buried some farms in dust.[5]

Private charities and churches simply could not meet the pervasive and continuing needs of all these people. Nor could municipalities: many cities faced bankruptcy as their tax base collapsed. Only eight states offered any sort of unemployment insurance. Increasingly Americans looked to the federal government as their last, best hope.

Franklin Roosevelt was swept into office in a landslide victory in 1932. He won 89 percent of the electoral vote and carried every state in the South, Midwest, and West, losing only six states, all in the Northeast.[6] Roosevelt had campaigned on a "New Deal" for Americans—and he undertook a massive number of governmental innovations during his first one hundred days in office. On his first day on the job, President Roosevelt declared a national bank holiday, temporarily forbidding investors from pulling their money out of banks, which was causing the banks to fail. Under the Emergency Banking Act, the Secretary of the Treasury exercised the authority to determine when banks could reopen or, if they were insolvent, how they might be reorganized. The Emergency Banking Act passed both houses of Congress in a single day with the support of all but seven members of the U.S. Senate.

New Deal legislation sought to provide immediate relief for the needy and to ensure the nation's long-term recovery. The president and Congress created reforms focused on banking, business, the stock market, unemployed workers, farmers, and young people. In his fireside radio chats, as well as in his other speeches, President Roosevelt consistently reassured the American public that the country's economic institutions remained sound and that the nation would recover.

5. To learn more about the environmental history of the 1930s, start with Donald Worster's path-breaking book, *Dust Bowl: The Southern Plains in the 1930s* (New York: Oxford University Press, 1979). The Library of Congress holds a rich collection of photographs and sound recordings relating to the Dust Bowl. Some of those materials are available at http://www.loc.gov/collection/todd-and-sonkin-migrant-workers-from-1940-to-1941/about-this-collection/.

6. Hoover won Pennsylvania, Delaware, Connecticut, Vermont, New Hampshire, and Maine.

Meanwhile, he listened to a wide range of expert opinions, remained open to experimentation and innovative ideas, and led his administration by the example to "above all, try something."

Like her husband, First Lady Eleanor Roosevelt worked tirelessly to mitigate the effects of the Great Depression. With boundless energy, she traveled throughout the country, observing conditions firsthand and reporting back to her husband. She hosted a weekly radio show in which she discussed the pressing issues of the day, and she wrote a daily column syndicated in seventy-five newspapers. She was also one of the few New Dealers deeply committed to civil rights for African Americans. Although critics sometimes ridiculed her nontraditional behavior, to millions of Americans Eleanor Roosevelt represented the heart of the New Deal. She embraced liberal activism and redefined the role of first lady—and, as a result, many Americans loved her.

Among the myriad of problems the Roosevelt administration tackled, the plight of farmers proved particularly challenging. To meet the unusual European demand for farm products during World War I, American farmers, both small freeholders and commercial planters, had overexpanded. Many mortgaged their land and borrowed money to buy expensive new equipment and expand production. However, few family farms profited during the relatively prosperous decade of the 1920s, and they were terribly situated to weather the economic turmoil of the Great Depression.

Unfortunately, the New Deal's Agricultural Adjustment Act benefited mainly owners of large commercial farms. Intended to reduce agricultural production and thus improve the prices all farmers received for their goods, the act unintentionally encouraged large farmers to accept payment for reducing their crops, use the money to buy machinery, and evict the sharecroppers and tenants who had been working their land. Explaining to Dorothea Lange, one of the FSA photographers, why his family was traveling to California, one tenant farmer simply said they had been "tractored out." With no land of their own to farm, sharecroppers and tenants packed their few belongings and families into old trucks and cars and took to the road looking for seasonal agricultural work. In so doing, they joined thousands of other farm families who had been foreclosed on and displaced by the Dust Bowl. These Dust Bowl refugees—small farmers, tenants, and sharecroppers—competed for jobs with Mexican Americans working as migrant laborers on the West Coast. (The novel and film *The Grapes of Wrath* presented a vivid and profoundly influential tale of one such family's heartbreaking move west.[7]) For those left behind, especially in the poverty-stricken areas of the rural Midwest and South, conditions were almost as terrible as in the migrant camps.

To aid these impoverished farm families, President Roosevelt created the Resettlement Administration (RA). The RA bought barren land and put

7. John Steinbeck won the Pulitzer Prize in 1940, and John Ford won an Academy Award for best director that same year for his film adaptation of the novel.

it to nonagricultural use, including for state and national parks, and moved small farmers to more fertile ground. In 1935, the RA became the FSA. Rexford Tugwell, an economics professor from Columbia University, headed the RA/FSA. Tugwell hired one of his former graduate students, an economist named Roy Stryker, to direct the Historical Section of the agency.

Stryker's charge was to "show the city people what it's like to live on the farm." To that end, he hired a group of photographers to travel around the country and visually document the difficulties faced by small farmers, tenants, and sharecroppers. Stryker's team included Dorothea Lange, Walker Evans, Arthur Rothstein, Marion Post Wolcott, Gordon Parks, Russell Lee, John Vachon, Ben Shahn, Carl Mydans, and Theodor Jung. For nine years these photographers crossed the United States, and they took over eighty thousand Depression-era pictures.[8] Stryker made the photographs widely available to national magazines like *Look* and *Life* and to newspaper editors. The Historical Section also organized traveling exhibits and encouraged authors to use the photographs in their articles and books. Through Stryker's efforts, FSA photographs shaped how Americans perceived the Great Depression in rural America.

This photography program represented one part of an innovative partnership between government and the arts during the 1930s. New Deal programs also supported the arts through the Work Projects Administration (WPA) and by commissioning post office murals and sponsoring films. Collectively, these undertakings intended to both put Americans back to work and build support for New Deal legislation. In particular, FSA leaders wanted to mobilize public opinion in support of their projects, including model migrant camps, health clinics, and federal relief for the poorest families.

The photographers did not simply document the Great Depression. They chose their subjects, carefully composed the photographs, and sometimes cropped the images. But, as the prominent environmental writer T. H. Watkins explained, "the essential truth of the images remained undiminished by manipulation, and they became the icons that still speak to Americans of what the Great Depression was like with a heightened reality and incomparable immediacy."[9]

Like the young people who wrote to Eleanor Roosevelt, the FSA photographers had a particular perspective and agenda. Both the letter writers and the picture takers wanted to generate a response, the former on a personal level, the latter nationally. Closely studying the kind of subjects the photographs portrayed and the kind of life the letters described will enable you to understand the central issues in this chapter: What did the Great Depression mean for rural Americans? How did FSA photography build support for the New Deal?

8. After 1941, FSA photographers were increasingly assigned to chronicle American mobilization for the war effort. The FSA was transferred to the Office of War Information in late 1942.

9. T. H. Watkins, *The Hungry Years: A Narrative History of the Great Depression in America* (New York: Henry Holt, 1999), p. 452.

The Method

By the turn of the twentieth century, technological advances had made using cameras and developing photographs easier, but both the equipment and developing methods were incredibly cumbersome by today's standards. Then, like now, people were fascinated by photography. Talented amateurs spent hours taking pictures of their relatives, friends, and homes. Professional photographers cataloged the milestones of family life: weddings, anniversaries, first communions, and service in the military. These print photographs are an important source of evidence for social historians trying to reconstruct how Americans lived in the past. (The future of today's digital photographs remains questionable, especially given the ephemeral platforms for sharing them.)

Documentary photography was different than taking personal and family pictures. It had a particular purpose in this era: reform. During the late nineteenth and early twentieth centuries, middle-class Americans, particularly Progressives, became increasingly concerned about the growing number of poor families who depended on the labor of children to supplement their meager standard of living. Jacob Riis, the author of *How the Other Half Lives* (1890), and Lewis Hine, in his work for the National Child Labor Committee, photographed the working conditions of children in urban and industrial settings to document the ill effects of child labor. These photographs were used to persuade the public to support the strict regulation or abolition of child labor.

Roy Stryker understood the power of photography. Before he began working for the FSA, he and Rexford Tugwell had collaborated on an economics textbook that relied heavily on photographs. He brought that experience into his leadership of the Historical Section of the FSA. Stryker also made sure, before sending his photographers out, that they understood the economy and region they were documenting. The dozen or so talented photographers whom Stryker hired were relatively young (most were in their twenties or thirties) and came from a variety of backgrounds. Many of the photographers, including Dorothea Lange, Walker Evans, Carl Mydans, Marion Post Wolcott, and Theodor Jung, were either established professionals or serious amateurs. Others took their first professional photographs for the Historical Section: Ben Shahn and Russell Lee had been painters, and Arthur Rothstein and John Vachon were unemployed college students. All the photographers were white except Gordon Parks, a twenty-nine-year-old African American fashion photographer who joined the Historical Section in 1941. Parks never photographed farmers while at the FSA; instead, he sensitively documented the lives of African Americans and racial discrimination in Washington, D.C.

Documentary photography is a tricky medium for historians. The images appear "real"—not subject to the artist's interpretation in the same way as a painting or a movie. But documentary photography is neither neutral nor objective. Complete objectivity would be impossible even if it were desirable. As soon as a photographer frames a picture, poses a subject, or develops a negative, elements of manipulation and interpretation enter the image-making process. Further personal interpretation may be introduced in the cropping and printing of a photograph as well as in the selection of one image over another of the same subject. In an effort to educate viewers about the dire poverty afflicting rural America, FSA photographers sought to document the suffering of their subjects in images that also portrayed their dignity and resolve. For example, for the photograph in Source 12, an image of a man and his children running toward shelter, Arthur Rothstein darkened the sky to re-create what it looked like during a dust storm (he could not photograph the actual storm). In 1936 Dorothea Lange, who had been a successful portrait photographer before she joined the FSA, took six photos of one California migrant mother and several of her children. Lange posed the family and kept moving in closer and closer until she captured the image that she thought best conveyed both the suffering and the nobility of this migrant mother. Clearly, she was successful: this moving, archetypal image (Source 20) hangs in the Museum of Modern Art.

Personal letters, while a very different kind of source from photographs, present some similar complications for historians. The young people who wrote to Eleanor Roosevelt about their individual experiences conveyed, on the surface, a greater truth about the Great Depression than can be found in statistics or government policy. These children offer a unique— and uniquely compelling—perspective on life in rural America. As with all written evidence, however, one must pay careful attention to both the author and the audience.

First Lady Eleanor Roosevelt's position of power, wealth, and prominence meant that most correspondents used great deference when writing to her. The public image she cultivated also influenced their perception of her as approachable and sympathetic. The young people wanted immediate help with specific financial problems, which shaped both what and how they wrote. The dynamic between a humble, poor, rural child and a powerful, rich, benevolent woman likely encouraged these children to present their situation in a particular style. It might also lead them to exaggerate their faith in her ability to solve their problems. (Roosevelt's office sent a form letter reply to the thousands upon thousands of correspondents; occasionally the first lady would add a particular piece of advice or sympathy.)

When analyzing the evidence in this chapter, then, remember that neither personal letters nor documentary photographs offered an unbiased view of the Great Depression. Instead, both the letters and the photographs were intended to appeal to their audiences' emotions. And that response needed to be strong enough to inspire action. As you read these letters and study these photographs, you will need to be specific about *what* is portrayed, *how* you react, and *why* you respond that way.

These sources, while not wholly objective, nonetheless tell us a great deal about rural life during the Great Depression.

Pay attention to the information offered in the letters and photographs, the details within the story or picture. What do these specifics tell you about the depth of poverty and desperation confronting rural Americans? Consider, then, the messaging of the photographic evidence in particular: how did FSA photographers, either intentionally or inadvertently, present life in rural Americans to build support for the New Deal?

The Evidence

Sources 1–6 from *Dear Mrs. Roosevelt: Letters from Children of the Great Depression* by Robert Cohen. Copyright © 2002 by the University of North Carolina Press. Used by permission.

1. Letter from a Fifth Grader in Petroleum, West Virginia, to Eleanor Roosevelt, February 1934.

To keep these young people's voices authentic, spelling and grammar have not been corrected.

February 26, 1934
Petroleum, West Virginia
Dear Mrs. Roosevelt,

I just wondered If you ever received a letter from a little girl like me. I am eleven years old the 24 of March. This is my fifth year in school. I think I will soon be ready for sixth Grade. I have got five perfect certificates and one gold star of honor. I have . . . a hard way of getting what edication I have. But I expect to keep on trying. I have to walk two mile and a half to school through the mud. My Father is almost blind. We have no income of any form. Father has never recieved one cent of the money that the unemployed is supposed to get. We sure could use it. We have been told by many people that you was very kind to the poor and neady. So I thought I would ask you if you would or could send me a few things to wear. I wear size 12 year old dresses and a 14 year old coat. I am four feet and six inches tall and weigh 80 pounds. I also would like to have a pair of shoes size 3½ wide weidth. I would be the happiest person in the world. If I would recieve a package from you for my birthday. You would never miss this small amount I have asked for. My relation helped to put President Roosevelt where he is. I dont ask for anything fine just serviceable. I do hope you will fix me up a little package and mail to me at once. My friends will be surprised.

Mrs Roosevelt please dont have this printed or broadcasted, as some of my people have radios and all take papers and I dont want any of them to know I asked you to send me the things. But God knows I will remember you. And you surely will be rewarded. I send you my love and best wishes.

2. Letter from a Sixteen-Year-Old in Royse City, Texas, to Eleanor Roosevelt, September 1934.

Royse City, Texas
Sept. 6, 1934
Dear Friend:

Well I don't suppose you know who I am. but I'm a 16 year old motherless girl that has to work hard for all she gets. I have a brother & a sister & daddy We are working at day labor for a living and don't get much of that to do. In the winter I could piece quilts if I had any scraps. We are trying to keep off the relief this winter so we are keeping every penny we can to buy groceries this winter, Whether we have sufficient clothes or not. We haven't even enough furniture. We haven't any bedsteads, a stove, or cabinet. some of our Neighbors are letting us use their stove, cabinet, & one bedstead. I thought you might have some old clothes, coats, and shoes. or any kind of clothing you could send to us. I have read so much about your kindness I know if you have any you will send them. I would send some money for postage but haven't any. Address to your loving friend Miss D. H.

3. Letter from E. B., a Sixteen-Year-Old from Double Springs, Alabama, to Eleanor Roosevelt, December 1934.

Double Springs, Ala.
Dec 27, 1934
Dear Mrs. Roosevelt,

I know you get letters like this almost every day. But here is one I hope and pray will be answer. I live in Ala. on a farm, and it seem mighty hard for us.

we have so much sickness in our home We have a farm. But it seems if there isn't something done we will lose it. We owe lots of Hospital Bills. Wasnt for that we would Be in a better shape. My father and one of my sister had a operation the same year. My mother and father is in very bad Health. I am the oldest child at home and I am only 16. Mrs. Roosevelt if you please will send us a few dollars not to pay our debts. But to get us a few clothes to wear. if you can't send us none, please answer my letter and tell me why you can't. if you possible can just send us a little bit. don't never think it will be wasted for it won't. I am sure it would be put to good use. we want to thank your Husband Mr. Roosevelt for his good plan he has planned for us poor people. We know it is for the poor people good. But it seems it hasn't reached us yet much. Mrs. Roosevelt this is my first time to write any one for any money. or any of the familie. But I know you are very very rich. And we have to work hard. I don't dread working if we could only get one thing much for what we raise. Now if you please will send us a few dollars and it will grately Be appirshed. And we never can and never will thank you enough for it. Please answer my letter.

Your friend that lives in Ala.
E. B.

4. Letter from Miss R. S. and Miss M. J. M. of Twila, Kentucky, to Eleanor Roosevelt, May 1934.

Twila, Kentucky
May 16, 1934
Dear President & Wife:

It is indeed a great pleasure to write to the most beloved President and First Lady that the United States has ever had.

We are two girls age 17 years and have just finished our Junior Course at Wallins High School, Wallins Creek, Ky.

We had our hearts set on going to Knoxville, Tenn. this summer to take a beauty course, but as our fathers are miners and the mines here in the South-eastern coal fields have closed down it now looks impossible to obtain the necessary finance.

As the closest Beauty training school is in Knoxville, Tennessee it will be necessary to pay board buy uniforms, books, and other necessities, we would also have to pay for our training. So wont you please help us? We are not begging for money, we are just asking for a small loan. You can judge for yourself how much it would take to finance both of us.

Mr. & Mrs. Roosevelt we are two 100% girls and if you care to find out what kind of girls we are we refer you to:

Mr. L. P. M.—Principal of
Wallins High School Wallins Creek, Ky.
also
Miss M. L. J., Teacher Wallins High School
Wallins Creek, Ky.

As soon as we have finished our training and recieved our first pay we will begin sending small payments to you.

Won't you please give this, careful consideration? As the Summer Session begins May 28th. Please let us know at once if you can Help us.

Thanking you,
Miss R. S., Miss M. J. M

5. Letter from a Young Woman in Wachapreague, Virginia, to Eleanor Roosevelt, June 1934.

Wachapreague, Va.
June 20, 1934
Dear Mrs. Roosevelt,

Please don't consider this a foolish idea but, I knew no other to call on for help than the one who has been a mother to the country, regardless of color or creed.[10]

Mrs. Roosevelt, I am eager for an education. I have worked out since I was 11 yrs. old. I missed four school terms out of school, and graduate from high school at the age of 19 yrs.

I want to enter college in September. I have'nt a dime, and I cannot find work. What shall I do? To whom shall I turn to for help if you fail me? Mrs. Roosevelt I feel that you can help me and I feel that you will.

I am willing to work for you night and day to pay you for all that you do for me. Help me if you can.

The school that I have made application for is West Virginia State Teachers College, Institute, W. Virginia.

I want to make a woman of my self. I want to be some body. Help me in any way that you can. I'll do any kind of honest work and I have had lots of experience.

I have a good reccomendation. Please, Mrs. Roosevelt, may I count on you to help me? I am sick at heart.

10. B. A. G. was an African American woman. Eleanor Roosevelt's support for civil rights inspired African American youth to write her and to anticipate her empathy.

I graduated in "33" and I have been out of school all this winter.
I hope to hear from you at once please.

Sincerely yours
B. A. G.

6. Letter from a Fifteen-Year-Old Polio Patient from Chicago, Illinois, to Eleanor Roosevelt, November 1935.

Chicago, Ill.
Nov. 6, 1935
My dear Mrs. Roosevelt,

I am a little girl, fifteen years old. I was stricken with infantile paralysis last August 15—My legs are paralyzed—I am heart broken. I was going into my second year in High School—I am enclosing my picture, also the clipping about you—I think you are the most wonderful woman, and also our dear President to help so much in this sad world of ours. I get so lonely and depressed some days—then I think of President Roosevelt & all the great things he has done and he also suffered from this dreadful disease—I only hope some day I may get to Warm Springs—I pray dear God will soon help me walk again—Mrs. Roosevelt please write me a little letter, it would make me so happy—My best wishes to you and yours.

Love
V. F.

Source 7 from the United States Farm Security Administration, Historical Section, Library of Congress, Washington, D.C.

7. Abandoned Farm Home, Ward County, North Dakota, 1940 (John Vachon).

Vachon, John/Library of Congress

Source 8 from F. Jack Hurley, *Portrait of a Decade: Roy Stryker and the Development of Documentary Photographs in the Thirties* (Baton Rouge: Louisiana State University Press, 1972), p. 8.

8. Drought-Stricken Farm, Mills, New Mexico, 1935 (Dorothea Lange).

Dorothea Lange/Library of Congress

Source 9 from the United States Farm Security Administration, Historical Section, Library of Congress, Washington, D.C.

9. "Tractored-out" Farm, Hall County, Texas, 1938 (Dorothea Lange).

Dorothea Lange/Library of Congress

Sources 10 and 11 from Robert K. Reid, ed., *Back Home Again: Indiana in the Farm Security Administration Photographs, 1935–1943* (Bloomington: Indiana University Press, 1987), pp. 10, 2.

10. Eroded Farm Land, Martin County, Indiana, 1938 (Arthur Rothstein).

Arthur Rothstein/Library of Congress

11. Soil Erosion on an Indiana Farm, Brown County, Indiana, 1935 (Theodor Jung).

Theodor Jung/Library of Congress

Sources 12 and 13 from the United States Farm Security Administration, Historical Section, Library of Congress, Washington, D.C.

12. Farm Family from Cimarron County, Oklahoma, 1936 (Arthur Rothstein).

Arthur Rothstein, 1915–1985/Library of Congress Prints and Photographs Division[LC-DIG-ppmsc-00241]

13. Family on the Road in Oklahoma, 1939 (Dorothea Lange).

Dorothea Lange/Library of Congress

Sources 14 and 15 from F. Jack Hurley, *Portrait of a Decade: Roy Stryker and the Development of Documentary Photographs in the Thirties* (Baton Rouge: Louisiana State University Press, 1972), pp. 111, 135.

14. Plowing in the Shenandoah Valley of Virginia, Undated (Marion Post Wolcott).

Marion Post Wolcott/Library of Congress

15. West Virginia Coal Miner's Child Carrying Home Kerosene for Lamps, Undated (Marion Post Wolcott).

Wolcott, Marion Post/Library of Congress

Sources 16 and 17 from the United States Farm Security Administration, Historical Section, Library of Congress, Washington, D.C.

16. Migrant Family Living in an Abandoned Truck Bed, Tennessee, 1936 (Carl Mydans).

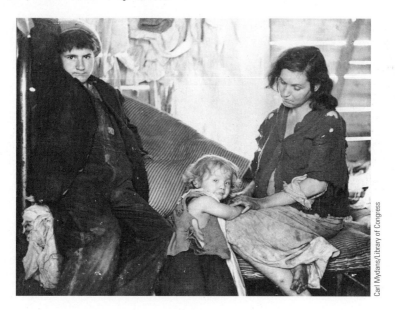

Carl Mydans/Library of Congress

17. Migrants from Oklahoma, Living in California, 1936 (Dorothea Lange).

Dorothea Lange/Library of Congress

Sources 18 and 19 from Robert K. Reid, ed., *Back Home Again: Indiana in the Farm Security Administration Photographs, 1935–1943* (Bloomington: Indiana University Press, 1987), pp. 11, 12.

18. Home of Ross Lundy Family, Martin County, Indiana, 1938 (Arthur Rothstein).

Arthur Rothstein/Library of Congress

19. Mrs. Lundy and Daughter Inside Their Home, Martin County, Indiana, 1938 (Arthur Rothstein).

Arthur Rothstein/Library of Congress

Sources 20 through 25 from the United States Farm Security Administration, Historical Section, Library of Congress, Washington, D.C.

20. Migrant Mother, Nipomo, California, 1936 (Dorothea Lange).

21. Mexican Migrant Worker's Home, Imperial Valley, California, 1937 (Dorothea Lange).

22. Home of Fruit Packing Plant Workers, Berrien, Michigan, 1940 (John Vachon).

John Vachon/Library of Congress

23. Christmas Dinner, Iowa Tenant Farmer's Home, 1936 (Russell Lee).

Russell Lee/Library of Congress

24. Cotton Pickers, Pulaski County, Arkansas, 1935 (Ben Shahn).

Ben Shahn/Library of Congress

25. FSA Client Family, Beaufort, South Carolina, 1936 (Carl Mydans).

Carl Mydans/Library of Congress

Source 26 from F. Jack Hurley, *Portrait of a Decade: Roy Stryker and the Development of Documentary Photographs in the Thirties* (Baton Rouge: Louisiana State University Press, 1972), p. 57.

26. Agricultural Workers and Children, Gee's Bend, Alabama, 1937 (Arthur Rothstein).

Arthur Rothstein/Library of Congress

Sources 27 and 28 from the United States Farm Security Administration, Historical Section, Library of Congress, Washington, D.C.

27. Plantation Owner and Workers, Clarksdale, Mississippi, 1936 (Dorothea Lange).

Dorothea Lange/Library of Congress

28. Owner of the General Store, Bank, and Cotton Gin, Wendell, North Carolina, 1939 (Marion Post Wolcott).

Marion Post Wolcott/Library of Congress

◆

Questions to Consider

Begin your analysis with the letters written to First Lady Eleanor Roosevelt (Sources 1 through 6). What motivated these young people to write the first lady? Think both about the economic circumstances within their homes *and* about the New Deal policies her husband, President Franklin Roosevelt, advanced.

What do these letters tell you about the effects of the Great Depression on family life? What particular economic and familial difficulties did these children confront? How did they and their families respond? What values and attitudes did these young people convey? What response do the letters evoke?

What can you learn from these letters about the United States in this era? What do the letters tell you about banks, health care, class tensions, environmental changes, educational institutions, and politics?

How did the letter writers perceive Eleanor Roosevelt and her husband? Do you think the age of the writers shaped their perceptions? For example, did they reveal some youthful naïveté in their understanding of how government worked and what the New Deal would mean for their families? What does the absence of criticism in the letters to Eleanor Roosevelt tell you about these writers in particular and American political culture in general? (A contemporary corollary to these letters might be emails sent from citizens to their senators or representatives. Today we are much less deferential to and much more cynical about government officials.)

Now turn to the visual sources. The photographs in Sources 7 through 11 depict what happened to the once-fertile farmlands of America's plains and prairies. How would you describe these pictures to someone who had not seen them? What happened to the land and the people who lived there? What response do these landscapes evoke?

Sources 12 through 27 show farm families, sharecroppers, and migrant workers caught in the financial crush of the 1930s. What message do they send about the need for a "New Deal"? What values and attitudes did the subjects of these photographs seem to convey? What response do these photographs evoke?

The great majority of FSA photographs captured the lives of white Americans. What does this tell you about the program? Sources 24 through 27 depict African Americans. What do these images reveal about the living conditions of black southerners? What do they indicate about the economic and social relationships between poor black agricultural workers and white property owners (particularly Source 27)? Compare the images of black and white families and farmers. What similarities and what differences do you see in family life, economic circumstance, attitude of the subjects, and composition of the photographs?

Sources 27 and 28 depict relatively affluent white men. How are they portrayed? What response do they evoke, especially in contrast to images 12–26?

Use these photographs collectively as a window into the Great Depression and New Deal policies. If a picture is worth a thousand words, what story is told by these pictures? The photographers intended to portray Americans both greatly in need of government aid and worthy of it. Did they succeed? Collectively, what do these FSA photographs tell you about the agenda of the Historical Section?

Compare the letters to Eleanor Roosevelt with the FSA photographs.

Do they tell a similar story? In what ways do the two types of sources diverge? Generally speaking, which do you think more accurately depicts the experiences of rural Americans during the Great Depression: the FSA photographs or the young peoples' letters? What are the strengths and weaknesses of the two types of evidence?

Finally, return to the two central and interrelated questions in this chapter: What did the Great Depression mean to rural Americans? How did FSA photographs build support for the New Deal?

Epilogue

The images captured by FSA photographers brought shocking views of rural poverty to the attention of all Americans. Most of the photographers had never been in southern states, and the grim circumstances rural families endured as well as the harsh effects of Jim Crow laws appalled them— reactions they conveyed in their photography. (Stryker understood the political perils of displaying too much sympathy for blacks, however, so he carefully chose the images the FSA exhibited.) In the early 1940s, several of the photographers left the FSA. Walker Evans quit to work with James Agee on a magazine assignment that evolved into their renowned book, *Let Us Now Praise Famous Men*. Dorothea Lange began to document the experiences of Japanese Americans interred

during World War II.[11] But long after the FSA photographers moved on to other projects, their pictures of the Great Depression continued to shape government policy and public opinion.

Many middle-class white Americans had been unaware of the living and working conditions of families caught in the sharecropping or tenant farmer system. They found especially grievous the photographs of women and children. Homeless families living in cars, camping out, or on the road looking for work particularly distressed

11. *Let Us Now Praise Famous Men* was first published in 1941. Many of Lange's photographs of the internment camps were censored. See Linda Gordon and Gary Y. Okihiro, eds., *Impounded: Dorothea Lange and the Censored Images of Japanese American Internments* (New York: W.W. Norton, 2006).

middle-class Americans, who believed that home and family provided stability for the nation. The FSA images thus led some Americans to question their faith in unchecked capitalism.

President Roosevelt's New Deal sought to alleviate the financial crises facing Americans by recasting the relationship between government and economy. Through initiatives such as banking and securities regulation, funding of public works projects, and Social Security, the federal government could promote financial stability for the nation and economic security for its citizens. Roosevelt believed that by protecting families from the gravest consequences of the Great Depression he was defending the American home and American democracy. Roosevelt's critics insisted that his programs undermined personal responsibility and individual freedom. The president responded to his opponents by challenging Americans to read the Bill of Rights and weigh whether they had lost any freedoms. In a fireside chat in June 1934, he confidently proclaimed, "The record is written in the experiences of your own personal lives." While this certainly did not convince his political opponents, Roosevelt easily won reelection. In fact, in 1936, he triumphed in the most lopsided presidential election in U.S. history, winning 523 electoral votes to his opponent's eight and carrying every state but Vermont and Maine. At the height of his presidency, Roosevelt enjoyed a popularity exceeded only by George Washington.

Yet the economic crisis continued into Roosevelt's second term of office.

Indeed, in the fall of 1937 the "Roosevelt Recession" saw sharper declines in stock prices and industrial production and greater losses in jobs than in 1929. In 1939, nine million Americans remained unemployed, and the epidemic of rural poverty continued. On the other hand, banking and securities exchange were regulated and stabilized; the Social Security Administration protected senior citizens and children; programs such as the Tennessee Valley Authority (TVA) brought electricity to rural America.

In 1940, Franklin Roosevelt won an unprecedented third term. In his third inaugural address Roosevelt famously defined the "Four Freedoms": freedom of speech, freedom of religion, freedom from fear, and freedom from want. The U.S. government, he maintained, should be equally dedicated to defending all. In 1944, Roosevelt was again reelected, and in his State of the Union Address that year, he outlined an economic bill of rights, including:

The right to a useful and remunerative job in the industries or shops or farms or mines of the nation;

The right to earn enough to provide adequate food and clothing and recreation;

The right of every farmer to raise and sell his products at a return which will give him and his family a decent living;

The right of every businessman, large and small, to trade in an atmosphere of freedom from unfair competition and domination by monopolies at home or abroad;

The right of every family to a decent home;

The right to adequate medical care and the opportunity to achieve and enjoy good health;

The right to adequate protection from the economic fears of old age, sickness, accident, and unemployment;

The right to a good education.

But the second half of Franklin Roosevelt's remarkable four-term presidency differed sharply from his first two terms, and the economic bill of rights never reached fruition. Throughout President Roosevelt's third term and into his fourth, international events towered over domestic concerns. The Japanese attack on Pearl Harbor on December 7, 1941, and the subsequent U.S. entry into World War II marked a turning point in Roosevelt's presidency—and in the nation's history. Ironically, the war that overshadowed Franklin Roosevelt's domestic agenda also solved it. America's participation in World War II finally brought an end to the Great Depression. Farmers and their sons went off to war, while wives and daughters headed to factories as the nation's economy was mobilized to defeat the Axis powers. Victory in 1945 shepherded in a period of unprecedented prosperity and power for the United States.

In the twenty-first century, Americans continue to struggle with the economic, political, and philosophical questions raised by the New Deal. We still contest the proper relationship between citizens and the federal government, and we disagree over the roles government should play in the economy. While Social Security—a highly controversial part of Roosevelt's New Deal—tends to be supported by the great majority of U.S. citizens and by national leaders of both the Republican and Democratic parties, other parts of the New Deal legacy are more provocative. Some Americans believe unemployment programs and food stamps provide essential protections to our society, while others believe such program compromise individual liberties. National debates over both the Economic Stabilization Act of 2008, passed under President George W. Bush, and the 2010 Affordable Care Act, advanced by President Barack Obama, turned on many of the same lingering divisions over New Deal–style government programs. Three quarters of a century later, fundamental questions about the merits of President Franklin Roosevelt's new vision of the American Republic remain at the forefront of our national politics.

The American Judicial System and Japanese Internment During World War II: *Korematsu v. United States* (323 U.S. 214)

◆

The Problem

On May 30, 1942, a young man who identified himself as Clyde Sarah was apprehended by police in San Leandro, California, as he was smoking a cigarette outside a drugstore. The man told police that he had been born in Las Vegas, was of Spanish Hawaiian descent, that his parents were deceased, and that he was waiting outside the drugstore for his girlfriend.[1]

Under further interrogation, however, "Clyde Sarah" confessed that he actually was Fred Toyosaburo Korematsu, a Nisei[2] who had been born in Oakland, California, in 1919, that his Issei parents were still very much alive, and that he had forged his Selective Service (draft) card and undergone a crude facial surgery procedure in an effort to conceal his Japanese identity. Apparently his plan had been to leave California, where anti-Japanese feeling after Pearl Harbor was particularly high, and relocate with his girlfriend Ida Boitano (an Italian American) to somewhere in the Midwest.

1. The best treatment of Korematsu's background, arrest, and trials is in Peter Irons, *Justice at War* (New York: Oxford University Press, 1983), esp. pp. 93–96. See also Roger Daniels, *"Korematsu v. United States* Revisited," in Annette Gordon-Reed, ed., *Race on Trial: Law and Justice in American History* (New York: Oxford University Press, 2002), pp. 139–159.

2. An *Issei* is a person of Japanese extraction who was living in the United States but who was born in Japan. The Immigration Act of 1924 made Issei ineligible to become American citizens. A *Nisei* is a person of Japanese extraction who was born in the United States to Issei parents and therefore was an American citizen. *Sansei* are those of the third generation, children of Nisei.

Before Fred Korematsu could put his plan into operation, however, the U.S. government began moving against all Japanese, citizens and aliens alike, living on the West Coast. Citing "military necessity," General John DeWitt, commander of the recently established Western Defense Command (WDC), issued a military order prohibiting all Japanese persons, Issei and Nisei alike, from leaving Military Area Number 1 (the entire Pacific Coast). Three days later, however, DeWitt announced that a total evacuation "was in prospect for all Japanese" and that all Japanese would be required to report to one of sixteen "assembly centers" for relocation in one of the ten "relocation centers" for the duration of the war.[3] Korematsu, therefore, was caught in a trap: one order prohibited him from leaving San Leandro, whereas the following announcement predicted that all Japanese would be evacuated. While his parents and three brothers had reported to their designated assembly centers at Tanforan (south of San Francisco), Fred Korematsu instead decided to stay where he was, hoping that his forged draft card and plastic surgery would prevent his arrest and forced evacuation. The police, however, acting on a tip from either the druggist who sold him the pack of cigarettes on May 30 or from his girlfriend, seized Korematsu and turned him over to the military for either imprisonment or internment.

West Coast attorneys for the American Civil Liberties Union (ACLU)[4] began searching for Japanese American citizens who were willing to be represented by the ACLU in cases testing the constitutionality of the mass imprisonment of approximately 112,000 people, even though no charges ever were filed against the vast majority of detainees, roughly 62.5 percent of whom were American citizens, supposedly protected by the Bill of Rights. Fearing even harsher treatment than they already had received, however, the vast majority of Japanese Americans refused, and ultimately only four individuals allowed the ACLU to represent them, and Fred Korematsu did so only hesitantly.[5] Found guilty in September 1942 of violating the military's exclusion order, he was sentenced to five years' probation. Korematsu's appeal reached the U.S. Supreme Court in October 1944,

---

3. The WDC consisted of the states of Arizona, California, Idaho, Montana, Nevada, Oregon, and Utah. Eighty percent of all Issei and Nisei living in the WDC resided in California. See Gen. J. L. DeWitt, *Final Report: Japanese Evacuation from the West Coast, 1942* (Washington: Government Printing Office, 1943), pp. 80–81. For assembly and relocation centers see *ibid.*, pp. 151–289. For photographs see *ibid.*, pp. 433–509; Linda Gordon and Gary Y. Okihiro, eds., *Impounded: Dorothea Lange and the Censored Images of Japanese American Internment* (New York: W. W. Norton, 2006).

4. The ACLU was established in 1917 and was originally called the National Civil Liberties Bureau. It provided legal advice and services for conscientious objectors and those prosecuted under the 1917 Espionage Act and the 1918 Sedition Act.

5. Besides Korematsu, the other three were Min Yasui (Portland, Oregon; violation of curfew order), Gordon Hirabayashi (senior at University of Washington; refused to register for evacuation or to obey the curfew order), and Mitsuye Endo (former clerical worker in the California Department of Motor Vehicles; dismissed for being a Japanese American and then refused to obey the evacuation order).

◆ CHAPTER 7

The American
Judicial System
and Japanese
Internment During
World War II:
*Korematsu v.
United States* (323
U.S. 214)

by which time any danger of a Japanese invasion of the West Coast was highly unlikely. The decision in *Korematsu v. United States* was handed down on December 18, 1944, with Justice Hugo Black selected by Chief Justice Harlan Stone to write the majority opinion.

Your task in this chapter is to read carefully the arguments of the prosecution and defense attorneys, the Supreme Court's majority opinion written by Justice Hugo Black together with the concurring opinion of Justice Felix Frankfurter, and the three dissenting opinions of Justices Owen Roberts, Frank Murphy, and Robert Jackson. Some footnotes have been added by the authors to clarify certain points made and occasionally to provide important facts and background. Having read the opinions, together with the Background section of this chapter and relevant material in your textbook, answer the following questions:

1. What constitutional issues were involved in *Korematsu v. United States*?
2. What were the principal arguments of the prosecuting and defense attorneys?
3. How did the majority and concurring opinions deal with the facts of the case as well as with the constitutional issues? How did the wartime situation affect these opinions if at all?
4. How did the three dissenting opinions deal with the facts and the constitutional issues?
5. **In your opinion, did the facts presented support the claim that the military situation justified the temporary suspension of parts of the Constitution? Prove your points.**

A chart will help you to remember the main points as well as to keep the facts and constitutional issues straight.

Background

The case of *Fred Korematsu v. United States* (323 U.S. 214) dealt with the critically important issues of citizenship, of individual rights, and of the rights of citizens in times of war. As such, it has been included in *Landmark Supreme Court Cases: The Most Influential Decisions of the Supreme Court of the United States* (New York: Checkmark Books, 2007), pp. 81–85, and is still studied by law students as well as by civil rights organizations. Indeed, for obvious reasons, the case is as important now as it was in 1944.

Although Fred Korematsu's difficulties began immediately after the attack on Pearl Harbor, in fact his story begins several decades before he was born. Beginning in the late nineteenth century, the comparatively small nation of Japan experienced rapid population growth, especially in the mushrooming industrial cities. To relieve population pressure, in 1886 the Japanese government for the first time permitted its citizens to emigrate. As a result, a large number of Japanese citizens sought opportunities outside their native land, especially in Korea, Southeast Asia, and the United States, where at first they were welcomed as substitutes for Chinese laborers who had become unpopular due to their efforts to organize for higher wages. Mostly young males, these Japanese immigrants to the West Coast of the United States were agricultural workers who intended to make money and return to Japan. Therefore, most had little interest in learning English, adopting American ways, or assimilating into the general population. In their minds, their home was Japan, not America. Their allegiance was to *Yamato Damashii*, the "Japanese Spirit."[6]

Yet the rapid increase in Japanese immigration (from roughly 3,000 in 1890 to 127,000 from 1901 to 1908) combined with a desire of a growing number of people to remain in the United States caused a dramatic upturn in anti-Japanese feelings.[7] Even as President Theodore Roosevelt was negotiating with the Japanese government to end the Russo-Japanese War, the city of San Francisco passed a school law that segregated all Asian children, an act that officials in Japan viewed as

a slap in the face. "The infernal fools in California . . . insult the Japanese recklessly," Roosevelt wrote to his son Kermit, "and in the event of war it will be the Nation as a whole which will pay the consequences." To cool tempers, Roosevelt negotiated a "Gentleman's Agreement" in which Japan would stop issuing passports to Japanese to immigrate to the United States if the federal government promised not to pass a Japanese exclusion law similar to the Chinese Exclusion Act of 1882.[8]

As we continue to tell Fred Korematsu's story, we must keep in mind that in late nineteenth-century United States, Japanese Americans were not the only minority groups that faced discrimination and even violence. In the American South, between 1889 and 1900 roughly 1,357 African Americans were lynched and others faced unspeakable hostility and cruelty. In 1899 in the Senate debate over whether or not to acquire the Philippine Islands, more than a few senators rose to attack the people of the Philippines as an inferior race. In the Southwest, Hispanics faced severe economic and political difficulties. In the American West, by the late nineteenth century, the majority of Native Americans lived on government reservations in poverty and misery and often were the victims of corrupt government officials and private suppliers. The U.S. government banned Indian religious and sacred ceremonies, imprisoned many "medicine men," and established

---

6. For early Japanese immigrants' desires see Page Smith, *Democracy on Trial: The Japanese American Evacuation and Relocation in World War II* (New York: Simon & Schuster, 1995), p. 53.

7. For immigration statistics see Roger Daniels, *Prisoners without Trial: Japanese Americans in World War II* (New York: Hill and Wang, rev. ed., 2004), p. 8. Partially responsible for the change in attitude about returning to Japan was the fact that the "Gentlemen's Agreement" allowed Japanese women to come to America to join their husbands. Not a few of these women were "picture brides," who joined husbands they had never seen. *Ibid.*, p. 13.

8. For Roosevelt's typically intemperate remark see Roosevelt to Kermit Roosevelt, October 27, 1906, quoted in Morton Grodzins, *Americans Betrayed: Politics and the Japanese Evacuation* (Chicago: University of Chicago Press, 1949), p. 6.

♦ CHAPTER 7

The American
Judicial System
and Japanese
Internment During
World War II:
*Korematsu v.
United States* (323
U.S. 214)

"Indian schools" where teaching Native American languages was forbidden. Finally, immigrants from southern and eastern Europe were looked down upon and there were numerous efforts, finally successful in 1924, to restrict their entries into the United States. In all, it was an especially painful time for those who sought economic, social, and political freedom.[9]

The increase in the Japanese population in California, combined with a growing number of Japanese agricultural workers who were buying their own farms rather than continuing to work on white-owned land, led to a significant rise in efforts to stop all further immigration. In 1909, one California state senator practically predicted that within ten years Japanese in the state would outnumber whites ten to one. And a few years later, Governor William Stephens of California asserted that "the fecundity of the Japanese race far exceeds that of any other people that we have in our midst." Throughout the western states (but especially in California), anti-oriental groups such as the Oriental Exclusion League of California, the Native Sons of the Golden West, and the California Joint Immigration Committee together with associations such as the American Legion, the Grange, and the Federation of Labor began pressuring their congressmen, who in turn lobbied ener-

getically in Washington, for anti-Japanese legislation.[10]

Not waiting for the federal government to act, in 1913, California passed a law denying Japanese immigrants the right to own property. Then, in 1922, the Supreme Court ruled (in *Ozawa v. United States*, 260 U.S. 178) that a person of Japanese extraction who was living in the United States was ineligible to apply for citizenship. Finally, in 1924, in response to a wave of anti-immigrant sentiment throughout the country but to anti-Japanese feelings on the West Coast especially, Congress passed the National Origins Act of 1924, which established quotas for immigrants from all nations except those from Asia, who were entirely excluded. In Washington the Japanese ambassador resigned while in Tokyo a protester committed suicide (*harakiri*) in front of the American embassy. In the Japanese capital, July 1 was named "Humiliation Day" and was marked by "Hate America" demonstrations. A few years later, in a roundtable discussion at a Tokyo elementary school, students were asked whether they thought there would be a war between Japan and the United States. "Yes," said one discussant, "I think so. Americans are so arrogant. I'd like to show them a thing or two."[11]

10. The senator's and governor's statements are quoted in *ibid.*, p. 7. For the anti-Japanese organizations see *ibid.*, pp. 4–11.
11. For the 1913 California Alien Land Law and the 1922 *Ozawa v. United States* decision, see Smith, *Democracy on Trial*, pp. 49–50. Ozawa challenged the 1906 Naturalization Act by claiming that Japanese were white. For "Humiliation Day" protests and elementary school discussion, see Sabuto Ienaga, *The Pacific War: World War II and the Japanese* (New York: Pantheon Books, 1978), p. 29.

9. For lynchings see Arthur F. Raper, *The Tragedy of Lynching* (Chapel Hill: University of North Carolina Press, 1933), p. 480. For the Philippine debate see *Congressional Record*, 55th Cong., 3rd Sess., vol. 32, pp. 436–1481. For other minorities see Madison Grant, *The Passing of the Great Race* (New York: Charles Scribner's Sons, 4th ed., 1922), pp. 16–18, 89–90.

The *Ozawa* decision and the National Origins Act of 1924 did not cause anti-Japanese feelings in the United States to subside. Japan's economic and population increases made it increasingly difficult to produce enough food or secure critical raw materials, especially oil and iron. An increasing number of Japanese came to believe that most of the nation's problems had military solutions. And if those "solutions" would be bloody, the gains would more than offset the sacrifices.

On September 18, 1931, Japan began its conquest of Manchuria, a 585,000-square-mile region in northernmost China. Southern Manchuria fell to Japanese troops within forty-eight hours, and the remainder of the area was subdued weeks afterward. Soon the Japanese military established the puppet government of Manchukuo (their new name for Manchuria) and began relocating approximately 500,000 people (including twenty-five thousand farmers and fifty thousand teenagers) from Japan to the new Japanese province. Ultimately, the plan called for the resettlement of one million Japanese households (five million people), which would relieve population pressures in Japan as well as provide for the growth of food and the extraction of natural resources in Manchukuo. Other nations were outraged, and the League of Nations protested vigorously. But the League was toothless, and Japan responded by withdrawing from the League of Nations. The United States, not a member of the League, also protested, but mired in its own depression with up to 25 percent of the work force unemployed and with isolationist feeling running high, the nation similarly did nothing.[12]

Convinced by American inaction that it could move with impunity in the Pacific, Japan was determined to fashion an empire that would include Manchukuo, parts of China, Southeast Asia, and the western Pacific, an empire that Japan called the Greater East Asia Co-Prosperity Sphere. Using a minor incident at the Marco Polo Bridge just south of Beijing, Japan initiated a full-scale invasion of China. As the war in China deteriorated into a bloody stalemate, Japan began indiscriminately bombing civilians in order to terrorize them into surrendering.[13] In response, President Franklin Roosevelt delivered an angry speech in Chicago on October 5, 1937:

> It seems to be unfortunately true that the epidemic of world lawlessness is spreading. When an epidemic of physical disease starts to spread, the community approves and joins in a quarantine of the patients in order to protect the health of the community.... War is a contagion....[14]

12. On increased Japanese militarism see Ienaga, *The Pacific War*, pp. 6, 28. On the conquest of Manchuria, see Henry L. Stimson, *The Far Eastern Crisis: Recollections and Observations* (New York: Harper and Row, 1936), Appendix 2, pp. 267–270. On the Japanese resettlement plans, see Akira Iriye, *Power and Culture: The Japanese American War, 1941–1945* (Cambridge: Harvard University Press, 1981), p. 3.
13. It is generally thought that Japanese naval officer Nakajima Chikuhei was the first to advocate bombing civilians to terrorize them to surrender. See Haruo Tohmatsu and H. P. Willmott, *A Gathering Darkness: The Coming of War to the Far East and the Pacific, 1921–1942* (Lanham, MD: Rowman & Littlefield, 2004), p. 75.
14. Samuel I. Rosenman, ed., *The Public Papers and Addresses of Franklin D. Roosevelt* (New York: Harper & Brothers, 1950), vol. 6, pp. 407–408.

◆ CHAPTER 7

The American
Judicial System
and Japanese
Internment During
World War II:
*Korematsu v.
United States* (323
U.S. 214)

But the American public thought the president's message was too belligerent. In Japan, however, diplomat Yosuke Matsuoka announced

> Japan is expanding. And what country in its expansion era has ever failed to be trying to its neighbors? Ask the American Indian or the Mexican how excruciatingly trying the young United States used to be once upon a time.[15]

Clearly the United States and Japan appeared to be on a collision course toward what many historians now believe was "a war that neither nation desired, but one that neither could avoid." As the United States put increasing economic pressure on Japan in an effort to arrest Japanese expansion, Japan became convinced that only a quick war with America could achieve its demographic and economic goals. The result was Japan's surprise attack on Pearl Harbor in Hawaii, the home of the U.S. Navy's Pacific Fleet, which in 1940 had been moved from San Francisco to Pearl Harbor as a warning to Japanese expansionists.[16]

The days immediately following Pearl Harbor were extremely anxious ones for all Americans, but especially for people of German, Italian, and Japanese extraction. By February 16, 1942, officials had detained 2,192 Japanese, 1,393 Germans, and 264 Italians who were suspected of being spies or saboteurs. For their part, Japanese Americans rushed to proclaim their loyalty to the United States, as one Nisei probably spoke for the vast majority when he said, "It sounds bad, but we live here and our loyalty is here." At the same time the Federal Bureau of Investigation (FBI), with previously signed warrants but often with no warrants at all, began rounding up approximately 1,500 Japanese (both Issei and Nisei) that the FBI had already identified as enemy aliens. By the afternoon of December 8, when President Roosevelt signed the proclamation authorizing these arrests, almost everyone on the FBI list already was in custody.[17]

Even as the FBI sweeps became known, however, federal government officials called for calm. In an address to the U.S. Conference of Mayors, Attorney General Francis Biddle pleaded for "precautions against the undemocratic treatment of innocent, loyal aliens by the amateur detective, the super-patriot, [and] the self-appointed sentinel. The Department of Justice is determined to prevent

15. John Toland, *The Rising Sun: The Decline and Fall of the Japanese Empire, 1936–1945* (New York: Random House, 1970), p. 48. See also Hashimoto Kingoro, "Address to Young Men," in Ryusaka Tsunoda, et al., *Sources of Japanese Tradition* (New York: Columbia University Press, 1958), vol. 2, pp. 289–290.

16. Jonathan G. Utley, *Going to War with Japan, 1937–1941* (Knoxville: University of Tennessee Press, 1985), p. xii; Michael A. Barnhart, *Japan Prepares for Total War: The Search for Economic Security, 1919–1941* (Ithaca, NY: Cornell University Press, 1987), p. 21.

17. For Japanese proclamations of loyalty see *Los Angeles Times*, December 8, 9, 10, 1941. For alien arrests and Roosevelt's proclamation, see Francis Biddle, *In Brief Authority* (Garden City, NY: Doubleday & Co., 1962), pp. 206–207; *New York Times*, December 8, 1941; *Los Angeles Times*, December 11, 1941. When Germany and Italy declared war on the United States on December 11, 1941, mass internment of aliens was never considered. Of Italians, Roosevelt said, "They are a lot of opera singers." Of the Germans, however, he said, "The Germans are different, they may be dangerous." Biddle, *In Brief Authority*, p. 207.

the injustices of the World War in this respect." Biddle and others urged that employers refrain from discharging their employees "merely because they are aliens." In California Attorney General Earl Warren blocked the State Personnel Board from removing the names of job applicants who were of Japanese, German, or Italian descent.[18]

And yet, a toxic combination of the press, West Coast politicians and interest groups saw an opportunity to be rid of Japanese aliens and citizens once and for all. Even as the *Los Angeles Times* reported that the president of the city's Chamber of Commerce urged its ten thousand members to "discourage in every way possible the tendency to pass on and enlarge upon rumor and unfounded scare stories," between December 8, 1941, and February 23, 1942, that the same newspaper ran headlines like "Jap Boat Flashes Message Ashore," "Japanese Here Sent Vital Data to Tokyo," "Japs Plan Attack in April," "Caps on Japanese Tomato Plants Point to Air Base," and several others, while one editorial warned, "We Shall Not Forget This, Yellow Men." Stories of two Japanese youths who "hissed at Winston Churchill" during a movie newsreel, of Japanese language schools preaching pro-Tokyo propaganda, of a Japanese college student who predicted that "we SHALL take California" with high birth rates, and editorials urging white

Californians not to "underestimate the cunning of these little brown men" helped to create a climate of fear, suspicion, and nearly mass hysteria. Even as Attorney General Biddle was calling for calm, he received a letter from Los Angeles that stated, "No Jap should be permitted to remain in America . . . and no such opportunity as now exists may ever again be presented to us . . . to ship them back to Japan." Even the normally judicious Walter Lippmann, at the time probably America's most influential columnist, got carried away when he wrote, "the Pacific Coast is in imminent danger of a combined attack from within and without. Some parts of it may at any moment be a battlefield. And nobody ought to be on a battlefield who has no good reason for being there. There is plenty of room elsewhere for him to exercise his rights."[19]

In addition to the press's efforts to frighten Americans into calling for the removal of Issei and Nisei from Military Area Number 1 and, in some cases, all of the United States, an almost endless number of interest groups and civic associations also lobbied Congress and the Roosevelt administration for Japanese removal. Agricultural interest groups, such as the Western Growers Protective Association and the Grower-Shipper

18. *New York Times*, January 13, 1942. In his autobiography, Biddle claimed that there "was little hysteria for the first few months after Pearl Harbor." Biddle, *In Brief Authority*, p. 209. For Warren see *New York Times*, February 8, 1942; *Los Angeles Times*, February 8, 1942.

19. *Los Angeles Times*, December 23, 28, 1941; January 6, 7, 15, 23, 1942; Daniels, *Prisoners without Trial*, p. 29. For the belief that Japanese language schools were "sources of Japanese nationalistic propaganda, cultivating allegiance to Japan," see *Hirabayashi v. United States* (320 U.S. 81), 1943 opinion of Chief Justice Harlan Stone. For the letter to Biddle see J. R. Carter to Biddle, December 13, 1941, quoted in Grodzins, *Americans Betrayed*, p. 21. On Lippmann's February 12 article see Daniels, *Prisoners without Trial*, p. 45.

♦ CHAPTER 7

The American
Judicial System
and Japanese
Internment During
World War II:
Korematsu v.
United States (323
U.S. 214)

Japanese American Family Bound for Internment Camp.

Vegetable Association, sought economic gain by the removal of competition from Japanese farmers. But also groups, such as the Lions, Elks, American Legion, Veterans of Foreign Wars, North Hollywood Home Owners, and others clearly thought they were offering their patriotic services by rooting out and removing Japanese spies, fifth columnists, and saboteurs intent on undermining West Coast military defenses and war plants. Convinced that some Issei and Nisei were loyal to the United States but others were not *and* that it was impossible to tell one from the other, to these mistaken patriots the only solution was to remove them all. As Supreme Court justice Hugo Black said years afterward in an attempt to justify his majority opinion in *Korematsu v. United States,* "They all look alike to a person not a Jap. Had they attacked our shores you'd have a large number fighting with the Japanese troops. And

a lot of innocent Japanese Americans would have been shot in the panic."[20] As the war in the Pacific went badly for the United States in the early months of 1942, the pressure on Congress and President Roosevelt to remove all Issei and Nisei from the West Coast to internment camps was overwhelming. Almost all the mayors of West Coast cities urged immediate removal. Especially bellicose was Los Angeles mayor Fletcher Bowron, who urged that all Japanese be relocated to various inland Indian reservations, and warned of the possibility of "a repetition of Pearl Harbor on the West Coast." Although the mayor's assertion (in a radio address) was both undocumented and extreme, virtually no elected officials rose to contest it. Finally, on February

20. Grodzins, *Americans Betrayed*, ch. 2, esp. p. 21; Biddle, *In Brief Authority*, p. 217. For Black's statement see *New York Times*, September 25, 1971.

National Portrait Gallery, Smithsonian Institution / Art Resource, NY

Fred Korematsu and Family

13, the combined congressional delegation of congressmen and senators from California, Oregon, and Washington adopted a report recommending "the immediate evacuation of all persons, alien and citizen, from all strategic areas and . . . that such areas shall be enlarged . . . until they shall encompass the entire area of the States of California, Oregon, Washington, and the Territory of Alaska." After a sharp debate on February 18, the House of Representatives approved the delegation's recommendation.[21]

The next day, on February 19, 1942, President Roosevelt issued Executive Order Number 9066, which authorized Secretary of War Henry Stimson and military commanders under him "to prescribe military areas in such places . . . as he or the appropriate military commander may determine, from which any and all persons may be excluded . . . .The Secretary of War is hereby authorized to provide for residents of any such area who are excluded therefrom, such transportation, food, shelter, and any other accommodations as may be necessary." According to Attorney General Francis Biddle, "I do not think he [Roosevelt] was much concerned with the gravity or implications of this step. He was never theoretical about things. What must be done to defend the country must be done."[22]

The removal of Issei and Nisei fell to Lt. Gen. John DeWitt. DeWitt was willing to round up and incarcerate Japanese noncitizens (Issei)

21. For Bowron see *Congressional Record*, 77th Cong. 2nd Sess., vol. 88 pt. 8, pp. A653–654; *Los Angeles Times*, February 6, 1942; Grodzins, *Americans Betrayed,* pp. 100–106. For congressional delegation see Grodzins, *Americans Betrayed*, pp. 76–90; *Los Angeles Times*, January 31, February 14, 1942.

22. For Executive Order 9066 see *Congressional Record*, 77th Cong. 2nd Sess., House Report 2124; *Los Angeles Times*, February 21, 1942. For Biddle's opinion see Biddle, *In Brief Authority*, p. 219.

✦ CHAPTER 7

The American
Judicial System
and Japanese
Internment During
World War II:
*Korematsu v.
United States* (323
U.S. 214)

but hesitated to remove U.S. citizens of Japanese extraction (Nisei and Sansei). On December 26, 1941, he told his superior, Major General Allen Gullion, "An American citizen, after all, is an American citizen. And while they may not be loyal, I think we can weed the disloyal out and lock them up if necessary."[23]

But DeWitt was not strong-willed and would be relieved and retired before the war was over. He was aware that Lt. General Walter Short and Rear Admiral Husband Kimmel, the military commanders at Pearl Harbor on December 7, had been charged by a presidential commission of inquiry with dereliction of duty and were attempting to retire before their trials commenced. DeWitt was terribly afraid that he would face Short's and Kimmel's fate if any Japanese invasion or act of treachery occurred on his watch. Even before Roosevelt's Executive Order, DeWitt made plans for mass removals. Yet in his 600+ page *Final Report: Japanese Evacuation from the West Coast, 1942* (Government Printing Office, 1943), DeWitt attempted to justify removal and internment as "impelled by military necessity." But in that same report he purposely withheld crucial evidence that cast doubt on his claim, evidence that years later would prove extremely

embarrassing. By that time DeWitt was dead.[24]

To oversee the evacuation as well as to establish the assembly and relocation centers, Roosevelt's Executive Order Number 9102 created the War Relocation Authority and selected as its head the Agriculture Department's Director of Information Milton Eisenhower, the youngest brother of General Dwight Eisenhower. Eisenhower's original plan was for all the evacuees to go to an assembly center, after which they would be settled individually in houses near their jobs, which Eisenhower thought would be on farms. But his comparatively gentle plan was greeted by a firestorm of opposition and he was forced to retreat. Governors in the western states almost unanimously wanted a concentration camp-style relocation for Japanese Americans. And while he tried to make the evacuation process and the relocation centers as humane as possible, Eisenhower wrote to his former boss at the Agriculture Department, "I feel most deeply that when the war is over and we consider calmly this unprecedented migration of 120,000 people, we as Americans are going to regret

23. Transcript of telephone conversation between DeWitt and Gullion, December 26, 1941, quoted in Roger Daniels, *The Decision to Relocate the Japanese Americans* (Philadelphia: J. B. Lippincott, 1975), p. 18. In January 1942 DeWitt told a Justice Department official that any proposal for mass evacuation was "damned nonsense." Biddle, *In Brief Authority*, p. 215.

24. On Short and Kimmel see *Los Angeles Times*, February 8, 1942. On DeWitt shifting his position see Daniels, *The Decision to Relocate*, pp. 18–20. On DeWitt's 1943 attempt at justification see *Final Report: Japanese Evacuation from the West Coast, 1942* (Washington: Government Printing Office, 1943), esp. pp. vii, 3–24. DeWitt's tampering with the historical record was not unique. In 1942, Supreme Court Justice Owen Roberts reported that "a Japanese fifth column had aided the attackers" at Pearl Harbor, a patently false assertion. Daniels, *Prisoners without Trial*, p. 37.

the avoidable injustices that may have been done." In that sense Eisenhower was prophetic.[25]

Fred Korematsu sought to evade the evacuation process through forged identification and plastic surgery. But he was apprehended almost immediately. While awaiting trial, however, he was allowed to work outside the relocation center as a welder and, because of that skill, he was never without employment. His case reached the Federal District Court for the Northern District of California on September 8, 1942, less than four months after his arrest.[26]

The Method

It has been said that the wheels of justice grind exceedingly slowly. Surely this was true in the case of Fred Korematsu. Arrested on May 30, 1942, he appeared before Judge Adolphus St. Sure in the Federal District Court for the Northern District of California in September 1942 and was found guilty of having violated the Civilian Exclusion Order Number 34. But as St. Sure later put it, "I did not wish to send that man to jail," and therefore sentenced Korematsu to a five-year term of probation. In a surprising move, however, the judge never actually imposed the sentence, thus leaving Fred Korematsu in a state of legal limbo: he had been found guilty and yet no sentence had been ordered.[27]

Korematsu's attorneys filed an appeal to the Ninth Circuit Court of Appeals on March 27, 1943. But since no sentence ever had been imposed, the Court of Appeals was unsure whether or not it had any jurisdiction to hear the appeal and begged the U.S. Supreme Court to rule on that issue, which it did on June 1, 1943, ruling that the Court of Appeals did indeed have jurisdiction to hear Korematsu's appeal. Finally *Korematsu v. United States* was back in the hands of the Court of Appeals, which in December 1943 confirmed the district court's initial judgment.

26. Korematsu's trial would have taken place earlier than that except the original judge, Martin Welsh, went on vacation.

25. Irons, *Justice at War*, pp. 69–74. On Eisenhower's misgivings see his letter to Secretary of Agriculture Claude Wilkins, April 1, 1942, quoted in Roger Daniels, *Concentration Camps USA: Japanese Americans and World War II* (New York: Holt, Rinehart & Winston, 1972), p. 91.

27. Irons, *Justice at War*, pp. 152–154. Although St. Sure set Korematsu's bail at $2,500, which was quickly posted, a military policeman refused to release him and Korematsu was escorted under armed guard back to the Tanforan Assembly Center. *Ibid.*, p. 154.

◆ CHAPTER 7

The American
Judicial System
and Japanese
Internment During
World War II:
*Korematsu v.
United States* (323
U.S. 214)

Predictably the case at last arrived in the U.S. Supreme Court once again, which on December 18, 1944, issued its majority and dissenting opinions. It had taken over two and a half years for Fred Korematsu's case to reach the Supreme Court for what everyone assumed would be a final judgment, which in fact it wasn't. Ironically, the day before the Court announced its decision, the federal government announced that loyal Japanese Americans would no longer be interned and would be released.

Review the central questions you are required to answer:

1. What constitutional issues were involved in *Korematsu v. United States*?
2. What were the principal arguments of the prosecuting and defense attorneys?
3. How did the majority and concurring opinion deal with the facts of the case as well as with the constitutional issues? How did the wartime situation affect these opinions if at all?
4. How did the three dissenting opinions deal with the facts and the constitutional issues?
5. In your opinion, did the facts presented support the claim that the military situation justified the temporary suspension of parts of the Constitution? Prove your points.

Keep in mind that the business of the Supreme Court is not conducted in the same ways that other judicial hearings are held. No witnesses, examination, or cross-examinations take place. Instead, the attorneys for each side are given a predetermined amount of time to present their statements, to be followed by questions from the justices. The Court then retires and some days (or weeks) later the justices assemble for a conference in which there is a good deal of give and take, a vote taken, and the assignment by the chief justice to one of the justices to write the majority opinion. Other justices are free to write concurring or dissenting opinions, which become a part of the Court's record. Needless to say, between the hearing of the case and the conference, a good deal of lobbying and private conversations may take place. Of the several thousand cases the Supreme Court is asked to hear each year, it can only hear a small fraction of them, usually cases that the Court believes deal with important constitutional issues. Therefore, although the Court did not have to hear the appeal of Fred Korematsu, it chose to do so based on the above criterion.

Read carefully the arguments of the prosecuting and defense attorneys and the Court's majority opinion (by Justice Black), the concurring opinion (Justice Frankfurter), and the three dissenting opinions (by Justices Roberts, Murphy, and Jackson). Make an outline of the general arguments of each attorney and each Supreme Court justice. Due to space limitations, only portions of the transcript are reproduced in the Evidence section.

For the complete opinions, note that *Korematsu v. United States* has been assigned the numbers 323 U.S. 214. A law school library or a law firm's office would have the Court cases. *Korematsu v. United States* is in volume 323, the U.S. standing for Supreme Court, beginning on page 214. District Court rulings also have volume and page numbers, with F. Supp. in the middle denoting a District Court. For the Circuit Court of Appeals, in the middle of the citation is F. 2nd. Armed with those codes, you will be able to find any federal case in American history.[28]

◆

The Evidence

Sources 1 through 3 from *Cases Argued and Decided in the Supreme Court of the United States, October Term,* 1944 (Washington, D.C.: Government Printing Office, 1945), pp. 194–215.

1. Solicitor General Charles Fahy, for Appelee.

The President authorized and Congress ratified the exclusion of persons from the Pacific Coast military areas, which was within the combined war powers of the President and Congress.

At the time of the issuance of the evacuation order and Civilian Exclusion Order No. 34 under it, there was a rational basis for the military decision to evacuate as a group all persons of Japanese ancestry. In time of war, evacuation has been held to be a reasonable method of removing potentially dangerous persons from critical military areas. The evacuation of all persons of Japanese ancestry from military areas as a group was not, at the time and under the circumstances, a denial of due process. . . .

2. Brief of the States of California, Oregon, and Washington as *Amici Curiae*,[29] on Behalf of Appelee.

Although in most circumstances racial distinctions are irrelevant, the facts and circumstances pertaining to the Japanese population of the Pacific coast when considered in the light of a threatened attack by Japan and the danger of espionage and sabotage, afforded a reasonable basis for dealing with all persons of Japanese ancestry in the area as a group. Restrictions

28. For example, *Brown v. Board of Education* is located at 347 U.S. 483; *Miranda v. Arizona* is at 384 U.S. 436; *Bush v. Gore* is at 531 U.S. 98; *Roe v. Wade* is at 410 U.S. 113. In pre–Civil War Supreme Court cases, the name in the middle is the Court reporter. Therefore *Marbury v. Madison* is 1 Cranch 137 and *Dred Scott v. Sandford* is 19 How 393.

29. An *amici curiae* is a friend of the Court—a person invited to advise the Court on a matter of law in a case to which he/she is not a party, in this case a friend of the government.

◆ CHAPTER 7

The American
Judicial System
and Japanese
Internment During
World War II:
*Korematsu v.
United States* (323
U.S. 214)

placed upon that group, if reasonable in the light of these dangers, would not constitute an unlawful discrimination in violation of the "due process" requirements of the Fifth Amendment.

The individual rights which were affected by the evacuations are of the highest order, but these rights, precious and valuable as they are, are not absolute and must at times be temporarily curtailed in the exercise of the war power which is the paramount and fundamental right of the public person, the Nation, to defend itself. Self-preservation is the first law of national life and the Constitution itself provides the necessary powers in order to defend and preserve the United States (Hughes, "War Powers Under the Constitution," "American Bar Association Reports," 1917, p. 248).

In view of the foregoing considerations, we respectfully submit that petitioner's conviction and the judgment of the court below should be affirmed.

3. Wayne M. Collins, Counsel for the Appellant, Brief for the Appellant.[30]

This is an appeal by Fred Toyosaburo Korematsu, a civilian and native-born American citizen, from a judgment of conviction against him in the District Court below for an alleged violation of the provisions of Public Law No. 503 (18 USCA sec. 97a). He was adjudged guilty and placed on probation for five years because, in the exercise of his constitutional rights of national and state citizenship, he resisted unlawful military orders issued by John L. DeWitt, a Lt. Gen., U.S.A., which were designed to banish him from his home and imprison him in a concentration camp set up for him simply because in his line of ancestry there are to be found a few persons who, either by the accident of birth or residence, may be asserted to have owed in the dim past a temporal allegiance to a long forgotten Mikado. Branded a criminal and impoverished by his own government which he ever has been ready and willing to defend with his own life he is compelled to prosecute his appeal *in forma pauperis.*[31]

[Here Collins accused General DeWitt of believing that all Japanese Americans were "an enemy race" and that their "racial strains are undiluted" (from DeWitt's own Final Report*). DeWitt also stated that "112,000 potential enemies, of Japanese extraction, are at large today. There are indications that these are organized and ready for concerted action," an accusation which, Collins, argued could easily be refuted.]*

30. There were also two *amici curiae* briefs supporting Mr. Korematsu, one by the American Civil Liberties Union and one by the Japanese American Citizens' League.
31. *In forma pauperis:* In the United States, the term refers to someone who is without the funds to pursue the normal costs of a lawsuit or a criminal defense.

Who is this DeWitt to say who is and who is not an American and who shall and who shall not enjoy the rights of citizenship? . . . General DeWitt let Terror out to plague these citizens but closed the lid on the Pandora box and left Hope to smother. It is your duty to raise the lid and revive Hope for these, our people, who have suffered at the hands of one of our servants. Do this speedily as the law commands you. History will not forget your opinion herein.

Sources 4 through 8 from *Korematsu v. United States* (323 U.S. 214–248).

4. Mr. Justice Black Delivered the Opinion of the Court. Vote 6–3.

It should be noted, to begin with, that all legal restrictions which curtail the civil rights of a single racial group are immediately suspect. That is not to say that all such restrictions are unconstitutional. It is to say that courts must subject them to the most rigid scrutiny. Pressing public necessity may sometimes justify the existence of such restrictions; racial antagonism never can.

Exclusion Order No. 34, which the petitioner knowingly and admittedly violated, was one of a number of military orders and proclamations, all of which were substantially based upon Executive Order No. 9066, 7 Fed. Reg. 1407. That order, issued after we were at war with Japan, declared that "the successful prosecution of the war requires every possible protection against espionage and against sabotage to national-defense material, national-defense premises, and national-defense utilities. . ."

One of the series of orders and proclamations, a curfew order, which like the exclusion order here was promulgated pursuant to Executive Order 9066, subjected all persons of Japanese ancestry in prescribed West Coast military areas to remain in their residences from 8 p.m. to 6 a.m. As is the case with the exclusion order here, that prior curfew order was designed as a "protection against espionage and against sabotage." In *Hirabayashi v. United States,* 320 U.S. 81, we sustained a conviction obtained for violation of the curfew order. . . .

[Hirabayashi v. United States was the first case that tested the constitutionality of Executive Order 9066 and a supporting Act of Congress. The Court found Hirabayashi guilty of violating the curfew order, which the Court ruled was a legitimate exercise of the government's war powers.]

◆ CHAPTER 7

The American
Judicial System
and Japanese
Internment During
World War II:
*Korematsu v.
United States* (323
U.S. 214)

We upheld the curfew order as an exercise of the power of the government to take steps necessary to prevent espionage and sabotage in an area threatened by Japanese attack. . .

[Here Black wrote that evacuations, while more serious, are similar to curfews, which it was ruled to be within the rights of a nation at war. He also rejected the argument that, by the time of the hearing, any danger of invasion or sabotage had passed.]

We are not unmindful of the hardships imposed by [war] upon a large group of American citizens. But hardships are part of war, and war is an aggregation of hardships. All citizens alike, both in and out of uniform, feel the impact of war in greater or lesser measure. Citizenship has its responsibilities as well as its privileges, and in time of war the burden is always heavier. Compulsory exclusion of large groups of citizens from their homes, except under circumstances of direst emergency and peril, is inconsistent with our basic governmental institutions. But when under conditions of modern warfare our shores are threatened by hostile forces, the power to protect must be commensurate with the threatened danger. . . .

[Here Justice Black addressed Korematsu's claim that he was caught in a trap—forbidden by one order to leave and by another to stay in San Leandro, which was within Military Area Number1. But Black ruled that the Exclusion Order automatically voided the "freeze order."]

It is said that we are dealing here with the case of imprisonment of a citizen in a concentration camp solely because of his ancestry, without evidence or inquiry concerning his loyalty and good disposition towards the United States. Our task would be simple, our duty clear, were this a case involving the imprisonment of a loyal citizen in a concentration camp because of racial prejudice. Regardless of the true nature of the assembly and relocation centers—and we deem it unjustifiable to call them concentration camps with all the ugly connotations that term implies—we are dealing specifically with nothing but an exclusion order. To cast this case into outlines of racial prejudice, without reference to the real military dangers which were presented, merely confuses the issue. Korematsu was not excluded from the Military Area because of hostility to him or his race. He *was* excluded because we are at war with the Japanese Empire, because the properly constituted military authorities feared an invasion of our West Coast and felt constrained to take proper security measures, because they decided that the military urgency of the situation demanded that all citizens of Japanese ancestry be segregated from the West coast temporarily, and finally, because Congress, reposing its confidence in this time of war in our military leaders—as inevitably it must—determined that they should have the power to do just this. There was evidence of disloyalty on the part of some, the military authorities considered that the need for action was great, and time was short. We cannot—by availing ourselves of the calm perspective of hindsight—now say that at that time these actions were unjustified.

Affirmed

5. Mr. Justice Frankfurter, Concurring.

According to my reading of Civilian Exclusion Order No. 34, it was an offense for Korematsu to be found in Military Area No. 1, the territory wherein he was previously living, except within the bounds of the established Assembly Center of that area. Even though the various orders issued by General DeWitt be deemed a comprehensive code of instructions, their tenor is clear and not contradictory. They put upon Korematsu the obligation to leave Military Area No. 1, but only by the method prescribed in the instructions, i.e., by reporting to the Assembly Center. I am unable to see how the legal considerations that led to the decision in *Hirabayashi v. United States*, 320 U.S. 81, fail to sustain the military order which made the conduct now in controversy a crime. And so I join in the opinion of the Court, but should like to add a few words of my own.

The provisions of the Constitution which confer on the Congress and the President powers to enable this country to wage war are as much part of the Constitution as provisions looking to a nation at peace. And we have had recent occasion to quote approvingly the statement of former Chief Justice Hughes that the war power of the Government is "the power to wage war successfully."

Therefore, the validity of action under the war power must be judged wholly in the context of war. That action is not to be stigmatized as lawless because like action in times of peace would be lawless. To talk about a military order that expresses an allowable judgment of war needs by those entrusted with the duty of conducting war as "an unconstitutional order" is to suffuse a part of the Constitution with an atmosphere of unconstitutionality. . . .

6. Mr. Justice Roberts, Dissenting.

I dissent, because I think the indisputable facts exhibit a clear violation of Constitutional rights.

This is not a case of keeping people off the streets at night as was *Hirabayashi v. United States*, 320 U.S. 81, nor a case of temporary exclusion

◆ CHAPTER 7

The American
Judicial System
and Japanese
Internment During
World War II:
*Korematsu v.
United States* (323
U.S. 214)

of a citizen from an area for his own safety or that of the community, nor a case of offering him an opportunity to go temporarily out of an area where his presence might cause danger to himself or to his fellows. On the contrary, it is the case of convicting a citizen as a punishment for not submitting to imprisonment in a concentration camp, based on his ancestry, and solely because of his ancestry, without evidence or inquiry concerning his loyalty and good disposition towards the United States. If this be a correct statement of the facts disclosed by this record, and facts of which we take judicial notice, I need hardly labor the conclusion that Constitutional rights have been violated. . . .

[Here Roberts recited a chronology of all the Executive Orders, military orders, and Acts of Congress, some of which were in conflict with others, thus making it impossible for Korematsu to obey them all.]

As I have said above, the petitioner, prior to his arrest, was faced with two diametrically contradictory orders given sanction by the Act of Congress of March 21, 1942. The earlier of those orders made him a criminal if he left the zone in which he resided; the later made him a criminal if he did not leave.

I had supposed that if a citizen was constrained by two laws, or two orders having the force of law, and obedience to one would violate the other, to punish him for violation of either would deny him due process of law. And I had supposed that under these circumstances a conviction for violating one of the orders could not stand.

We cannot shut our eyes to the fact that had the petitioner attempted to violate Proclamation No. 4 and leave the military area in which he lived he would have been arrested and tried and convicted for violation of Proclamation No. 4. The two conflicting orders, one which commanded him to stay and the other which commanded him to go, were nothing but a cleverly devised trap to accomplish the real purpose of the military authority, which was to lock him up in a concentration camp. The only course by which the petitioner could avoid arrest and prosecution was to go to that camp according to instructions to be given him when he reported at a Civil Control Center. We know that is the fact. Why should we set up a figmentary and artificial situation instead of addressing ourselves to the actualities of the case?. . .

Again it is a new doctrine of constitutional law that one indicted for disobedience to an unconstitutional statute may not defend on the ground of the invalidity of the statute but must obey it though he knows it is no law and, after he has suffered the disgrace of conviction and lost his liberty by sentence, then, and not before, seek, from within prison walls, to test the validity of the law.

Moreover, it is beside the point to rest [the] decision in part on the fact that the petitioner, for his own reasons, wished to remain in his home. If, as is the fact, he was constrained so to do, it is indeed a narrow application of constitutional rights to ignore the order which constrained him, in order to sustain his conviction for violation of another contradictory order.

I would reverse the judgment of conviction.

7. Mr. Justice Murphy, Dissenting.

This exclusion of "all persons of Japanese ancestry, both alien and non-alien," from the Pacific Coast area on a plea of military necessity in the absence of martial law ought not to be approved. Such exclusion goes over "the very brink of constitutional power" and falls into the ugly abyss of racism.

In dealing with matters relating to the prosecution and progress of a war, we must accord great respect and consideration to the judgments of the military authorities who are on the scene and who have full knowledge of the military facts. The scope of their discretion must, as a matter of necessity and common sense, be wide. And their judgments ought not to be overruled lightly by those whose training and duties ill-equip them to deal intelligently with matters so vital to the physical security of the nation.

At the same time, however, it is essential that there be definite limits to military discretion, especially where martial law has not been declared. Individuals must not be left impoverished of their constitutional rights on a plea of military necessity that has neither substance nor support. Thus, like other claims conflicting with the asserted constitutional rights of the individual, the military claim must subject itself to the judicial process of having its reasonableness determined and its conflicts with other interests reconciled. "What are the allowable limits of military discretion, and whether or not they have been overstepped in a particular case, are judicial questions."

The judicial test of whether the Government, on a plea of military necessity, can validly deprive an individual of any of his constitutional rights is whether the deprivation is reasonably related to a public danger that is so "immediate, imminent, and impending" as not to admit of delay and not to permit the intervention of ordinary constitutional process to alleviate the danger. Civilian Exclusion Order No. 34, banishing from a prescribed area of the Pacific Coast "all persons of Japanese ancestry, both alien and non-alien," clearly does not meet that test. Being an obvious racial discrimination, the order deprives all those within its scope of the equal protection of the laws as guaranteed by the Fifth Amendment. It further

✦ CHAPTER 7

The American
Judicial System
and Japanese
Internment During
World War II:
*Korematsu v.
United States* (323
U.S. 214)

deprives these individuals of their constitutional rights to live and work where they will, to establish a home where they choose and to move about freely. In excommunicating them without benefit of hearings, this order also deprives them of all their constitutional rights to procedural due process. Yet no reasonable relation to an "immediate, imminent, and impending" public danger is evident to support this racial restriction which is one of the most sweeping and complete deprivations of constitutional rights in the history of this nation in the absence of martial law. . . .

That this forced exclusion was the result in good measure of this erroneous assumption of racial guilt rather than bona fide military necessity is evidenced by the Commanding General's Final Report on the evacuation from the Pacific Coast area.[32] In it he refers to all individuals of Japanese descent as "subversive," as belonging to "an enemy race" whose "racial strains are undiluted," and as constituting "over 112,000 potential enemies . . . at large today" along the Pacific Coast. In support of this blanket condemnation of all persons of Japanese descent, however, no reliable evidence is cited to show that such individuals were generally disloyal, or had generally so conducted themselves in this area as to constitute a special menace to defense installations or war industries, or had otherwise by their behavior furnished reasonable ground for their exclusion as a group. . . .

I dissent, therefore, from this legalization of racism. Racial discrimination in any form and in any degree has no justifiable part whatever in our democratic way of life. It is unattractive in any setting but it is utterly revolting among a free people who have embraced the principles set forth in the Constitution of the United States. All residents of this nation are kin in some way by blood or culture to a foreign land. Yet they are primarily and necessarily a part of the new and distinct civilization of the United States. They must accordingly be treated at all times as the heirs of the American experiment and as entitled to all the rights and freedoms guaranteed by the Constitution.

8. Mr. Justice Jackson, Dissenting.

Korematsu was born on our soil, of parents born in Japan. The Constitution makes him a citizen of the United States by nativity and a citizen of California by residence. No claim is made that he is not loyal to this country.

32. Here Justice Murphy is referring to General DeWitt's *Final Report: Japanese Evacuation from the West Coast.* Written by DeWitt in 1943, the report was not released to the public until early 1944.

There is no suggestion that apart from the matter involved here he is not law-abiding and well disposed. Korematsu, however, has been convicted of an act not commonly a crime. It consists merely of being present in the state whereof he is a citizen, near the place where he was born, and where all his life he has lived.

Even more unusual is the series of military orders which made this conduct a crime. They forbid such a one to remain, and they also forbid him to leave. They were so drawn that the only way Korematsu could avoid violation was to give himself up to the military authority. This meant submission to custody, examination, and transportation out of the territory, to be followed by indeterminate confinement in detention camps.

A citizen's presence in the locality, however, was made a crime only if his parents were of Japanese birth. Had Korematsu been one of four—the others being, say, a German alien enemy, an Italian alien enemy, and a citizen of American-born ancestors, convicted of treason but out on parole—only Korematsu's presence would have violated the order. The difference between their innocence and his crime would result, not from anything he did, said, or thought, different than they, but only in that he was born of different racial stock.

Now, if any fundamental assumption underlies our system, it is that guilt is personal and not inheritable. Even if all of one's antecedents had been convicted of treason, the Constitution forbids its penalties to be visited upon him, for it provides that "no attainder of treason shall work corruption of blood, or forfeiture except during the life of the person attainted." But here is an attempt to make an otherwise innocent act a crime merely because this prisoner is the son of parents as to whom he had no choice, and belongs to a race from which there is no way to resign. If Congress in peace-time legislation should enact such a criminal law, I should suppose this Court would refuse to enforce it. . . .

Of course the existence of a military power resting on force, so vagrant, so centralized, so necessarily heedless of the individual, is an inherent threat to liberty. But I would not lead people to rely on this Court for a review that seems to me wholly delusive. The military reasonableness of these orders can only be determined by military superiors. If the people ever let command of the war power fall into irresponsible and unscrupulous hands, the courts wield no power equal to its restraint. The chief restraint upon those who command the physical forces of the country, in the future as in the past, must be their responsibility to the political judgments of their contemporaries and to the moral judgments of history. . . .

✦ CHAPTER 7

The American
Judicial System
and Japanese
Internment During
World War II:
*Korematsu v.
United States* (323
U.S. 214)

Questions to Consider

By the time *Korematsu v. United States* finally reached the U.S. Supreme Court in October 1944, it had been heard once by a Federal District Court and twice by the Ninth Circuit Court. In all the hearings, the central issue was whether serious military danger allowed the federal government to violate some of Fred Korematsu's constitutional rights. Before you analyze the five opinions in the Evidence section of this chapter, you will want to consult the U.S. Constitution to determine which of Korematsu's rights had been violated.

In presenting the government's case, Solicitor General Charles Fahy argued that both the president's authorization and Congress's ratification of the evacuation of all persons of Japanese ancestry was both reasonable and constitutional. Where in the Constitution was the government given such powers? Did Fahy (or the Amici Curiae of the states of California, Oregon, and Washington) *prove* that such actions were necessary? How could it have been done?[33]

---

33. *Korematsu v. United States* was the first case in which the Supreme Court used the "strict scrutiny" test to review a law that classified people on the basis of race. The test established a standard for determining whether equal protection rights and fundamental rights had been violated. The government must prove that the law it made is substantially related to a compelling government interest. *Landmark Supreme Court Cases*, p. 547.

Fred Korematsu's attorney Wayne M. Collins chose to attack General DeWitt, claiming that his racial prejudice caused him to "step over the line" and exceed his orders and his powers. Did he prove his points? Collins asserted that Korematsu was arrested, tried, and convicted *not* because he was an enemy but solely because he was a Japanese American. How significant, then, was the face that he purposely broke a law . . . *unless* the law was unconstitutional. Was Collins able to establish that point?

Writing the Court's majority opinion, Justice Hugo Black (1886–1971) spoke directly to the issue above. In Black's view, what was the "military necessity" (the phrase that Gen. John DeWitt used to justify his military orders)? Who should determine whether (or not) there is such a "military necessity"?

You already are familiar with *Hirabayashi v. United States* (320 U.S. 81). How did Justice Black use that earlier decision as a precedent?

Clearly there were Japanese and Japanese Americans living in the United States who were loyal to Japan. Recall the FBI roundups in December 1941. How did Justice Black justify Korematsu's arrest and evacuation even though there was no proof that he was disloyal, as Black admitted? Following his reasoning, were there any limits to government powers in times of war or imminent danger?

In an earlier hearing of the case, Fred Korematsu's attorneys argued that he was caught between two military orders and that if he obeyed one he would automatically violate the other. How did Justice Black address that issue?

Finally Justice Black dealt with the accusation that, since the military orders and acts of Congress applied only to people of Japanese ancestry, they were by definition acts of racial discrimination. How did Justice Black address that issue?

In his concurring opinion, Justice Felix Frankfurter (1882–1965) agreed with the majority opinion that *Hirabayashi v. United States* was in fact a precedent for the case under consideration. In addition, what did Justice Frankfurter add? See the opinion of former chief justice Charles Evans Hughes (1862–1948).[34]

The three dissenting justices (Owen Roberts [1875–1955], Frank Murphy [1890–1949], and Robert Jackson [1892–1954]) all agreed that Fred Korematsu—as well as all people on the West Coast of Japanese ancestry—had been the victims of racial discrimination. And yet, each dissenting opinion went beyond that assertion to attack the majority opinion. How did each Justice argue that the decisions of the lower courts should be overturned? In other words, each of the dissenting justices had his own reasons for disagreeing with the majority opinion of Justice Black. What were those individuals' points?

<hr/>

Epilogue

One would have thought that the Supreme Court's decision in *Korematsu v. United States* and the denial of Korematsu's attorneys' appeal on February 12, 1945, would have finally closed the door on this painful chapter in American history. But this was not to be the case. Almost since the beginning of the war, First Lady Eleanor Roosevelt had urged fellow Americans "to prove that in a time of stress we can still live up to our beliefs and maintain the civil liberties we have established as the rights of human beings everywhere." Not long after the denial of Korematsu's appeal, the *Columbia University Law Review* and the *Yale University Law Journal* both published stinging criticisms of the government's denial of constitutional rights to Japanese *Issei* and *Nisei* living on the West Coast. In the Yale

34. According to historian Roger Daniels, Justices Black, Frankfurter, and Douglas, and Chief Justice Harlan Stone should have recused themselves in all cases affecting Japanese Americans, since Black and Douglas had social contacts with General DeWitt, and Frankfurter and Stone because they had advised the government about these cases. See Daniels, "*Korematsu v. United States* Revisited," no. 29, p. 147.

◆ CHAPTER 7

The American
Judicial System
and Japanese
Internment During
World War II:
*Korematsu v.
United States* (323
U.S. 214)

publication, professor Eugene Rostow
wrote

Our war-time treatment of Japanese
aliens and citizens of Japanese descent
. . . has been hasty, unnecessary, and
mistaken. . . . It was calculated to
produce both individual injustice and
deep-seated social maladjustments of
a cumulative and sinister kind.[35]

Nor was it known until much later
that Japanese *Issei* and *Nisei* were
not the only people interned as enemy
aliens. Roughly eleven thousand
German Americans and three hundred
Italian Americans also were interned in
camps for either all or part of the war.

Even more shocking was the fact
that numerous Latin American countries with a history of anti-Semitism
rounded up numerous Jews (who were
accused of being enemy aliens) who
were taken to the Panama Canal Zone
from which they were transported
by the United States to internment
camps in Georgia, Florida, Oklahoma,
and Texas. In addition, some Jews of
German and Italian descent who were
living on the West Coast were collected
and shipped to camps.[36]

After nearly a half-century of anti-
Asian prejudice, a brutal war in the
Pacific, and war hysteria on the home
front, anti-Japanese feelings, especially on the West Coast, were slow to
die. Soon after Hiroshima and Naga-
saki, the *Chicago Defender*, a weekly
newspaper with a national circulation
of primarily African American readers,
reported the results of a public opinion
poll of mostly white Americans, which
revealed that a twelve to one margin
favored "dropping more atomic bombs
on Japan." In an angry reaction, the
newspaper asked," Would the people
have voted 12 to 1 for the use of the
bomb against Germany or any other
white race?"[37]

Gradually, however, as Americans
began to learn about the internment
camps, more than a few were overcome by a wave of shame. Indeed, well
before the end of the war, the Roosevelt
administration secretly began conversations about closing the ten retention
centers, but may have hesitated due to
a combination of the fear of the negative reaction and perhaps also fear of
anti-Japanese violence and race riots.
By war's end, an undetermined number
of internees had been "furloughed."

Attempts by the Japanese Americans after the war to recover their property proved only partially successful. In
1948, Congress passed and President

35. For Eleanor Roosevelt see Gold, *Korematsu
v. United States*, pp. 32–33. See Eugene Rostow,
"The Japanese American Cases—A Disaster,"
in *The Yale Law Journal,* vol. 54, no. 3 (June
1945), pp. 489–533; and Nanette Dembitz,
"Racial Discrimination and the Military
Judgment: The Supreme Court's Korematsu
and Endo Decisions," in *Columbia Law Review,*
vol. 45, no. 2 (March 1945), pp. 175–239.
36. For Jewish internees see Harvey
Strum, "Jewish Internees in the American
South, 1942–1945," in *American Jewish
Archives*—http://americanjewisharchives.
org/publications/journal/PDF/1990 42 01 00
strum.pdf.

37. African Americans were the only significant ethnic group of Americans who
opposed the treatment of people of Japanese
ancestry. See Harry Paxton Howard, "Americans in Concentration Camps," in *Crisis*
September 1942), pp. 281–284, 301–302;
and *Negro Digest* (September 1944), quoted in Gordon & Okihiro, *Impounded,*
p. 82.

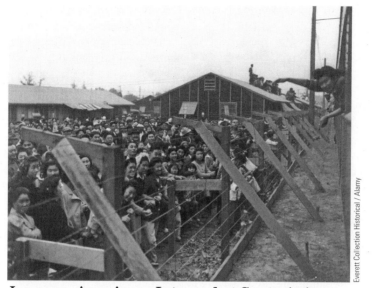

Everett Collection Historical / Alamy

Japanese Americans Interned at Santa Anita Race Track, ca. 1942–1945.

Harry Truman signed the Japanese American Claims Act that appropriated $38 million to assist claimants to recover their property. But this was estimated to be only about one-third of what would have been necessary. Was the government afraid of stirring up anti-Japanese prejudice?[38]

Then, in 1951, Hollywood released the commercial film *Go for Broke,* about the 442nd Regimental Combat Team, a unit of all-volunteer Nisei that distinguished itself during World War II in Italy, France, and Germany, receiving 18,000 decorations including 21 Medals of Honor, 52 Distinguished Service Crosses, 560 Silver Stars, 4,000 Bronze Stars, and an astounding 9,486 Purple Hearts. Slowly Americans came to understand that the vast majority of Japanese Americans had been loyal men and women who supported their country in the war.[39]

In the latter half of the twentieth century, as Japan became the U.S. strongest ally in the Pacific, opinions about Japanese Americans shifted markedly. Also in 1973 a very popular book was published, co-authored by a woman who was seven years old when the family was moved into an internment camp, and her husband. Jeanne Wakatsuki Houston's and James Houston's book *Farewell to*

38. On the 1948 Claims Act, in 1988, President Ronald Reagan signed the Civil Liberties Act, which provided for a $20,000 "redress payment" to each of the sixty thousand surviving internees, including Fred Korematsu.

39. For the 442nd and the one hundredth Battalion, see Commission on Wartime Relocation and Internment of Civilians, *Personal Justice Denied: The Report* (Washington, D.C.: Government Printing Office, December 1982), pp. 256–260.

◆ CHAPTER 7

The American
Judicial System
and Japanese
Internment During
World War II:
*Korematsu v.
United States* (323
U.S. 214)

Manzanar told the story of the camps through the eyes of a young child, and many Americans were moved by her remembrances.[40]

Then, in 1976, President Gerald Ford repealed President Roosevelt's Executive Order Number 9066, a symbolic gesture but one that was appreciated by the approximately 700,000 Americans of Japanese ancestry. In 1980, Congress and President Jimmy Carter created the Commission on Wartime Relocation and Internment of Civilians, an independent federal commission to study the events surrounding the internment of American citizens and to "recommend appropriate remedies."

As the Commission's report was being compiled, legal historian and attorney Peter Irons at the University of California, San Diego, discovered in the Justice Department files that General DeWitt had falsified information about Issei and Nisei on the West Coast immediately following the attack on Pearl Harbor. DeWitt knew, from reports by the FBI, the Office of Naval Intelligence, and the Federal Communications Commission, that accusations of espionage, planned sabotage, and information sent to the Japanese military from the West Coast all were false. Therefore, DeWitt's attempt in his *Final Report* to justify his military orders and proclamations on the grounds of "military necessity" simply was deceitful. Worse, by 1944 when *Korematsu v. United States* at last arrived at the Supreme Court, the government knew

it was not true and purposely had withheld evidence from the Court, an action that both Justices Murphy and Jackson may have suspected.[41]

Before the Commission's report was completed, Professor Irons approached Fred Korematsu, who had not spoken of his tribulations for forty years, and asked him if he would be willing to have his case reopened. Korematsu agreed, and Irons and a team of Japanese American attorneys had the case retried in the Federal District Court on the grounds of *coram nobis* (that the earlier conviction should be vacated or overturned due to "errors of the most fundamental character").

The judge hearing the case was Marilyn Hall Patel, a recent Carter appointee. The government had responded by offering a full pardon, but if it had been accepted it would have meant that Fred Korematsu was guilty of the charges, and therefore he refused the offer. The Commission's report was available, stating that the internment was a "grave injustice" and there was no "military necessity" for the internment. Rather, it was the result of "race prejudice, war hysteria and a failure of political leadership."[42]

Fred Korematsu stood and made a brief statement to the court, immediately after which Judge Patel handed down her verdict, warning that *Korematsu v. United States* "stands as a constant caution that in times of war or

40. Jeanne Wakatsuki Houston and James D. Houston, *Farewell to Manzanar* (Boston: Houghton Mifflin, 1973). Jeanne was seven years old in 1941, and was eleven when the camps finally closed.

41. Daniels, *Prisoners without Trial*, pp. 90–92.
42. For the offer of a pardon, see the film "Of Civil Wrongs and Rights: The Fred Korematsu Story" (2000). For the findings see Commission on Wartime Relocation and Internment of Civilians, *Personal Justice Denied: The Report* (Washington: Government Printing Office, December 1982), p. 18.

Bettmann/Corbis

**A Barber near Seattle Points to an
Anti-Japanese Sign in His Shop.**

declared military necessity our institutions must be vigilant in protecting constitutional guarantees."[43]

It was over. Not fully understanding, Fred Korematsu asked Irons, "What happened?" "You won," Irons replied.[44]

In his senior years Korematsu became something of a folk hero. He met Rosa Parks, another famous protester, and other luminaries. In 1998, he was awarded the Presidential Medal of Freedom by President Clinton.[45]

Fred Korematsu lived long enough to understand that Americans had not learned that in times of war the government and its citizens must take care to avoid "racial profiling" and to protect the constitutional rights of all its citizens. After 9/11/01, he continued to express concerns about the civil liberties in times of mass hysteria. He died in 2005, at the age of eighty-six.

43. Daniels, *Prisoners without Trial,* p. 100.
44. "Of Civil Wrongs and Rights."
45. *New York Times,* April 1, 2005.

The 1960 Student Campaign for Civil Rights

◆

The Problem

In 1954, the U.S. Supreme Court issued one of the most significant decisions in American judicial history. The case began with a father, World War II veteran Oliver Brown, who wanted his daughter, Linda, to attend the elementary school closest to the family home. The Browns lived in Topeka, Kansas—a state whose laws strictly mandated racial segregation, including in restaurants, movie theaters, and the public schools. Linda walked six blocks through a railroad yard to meet the bus that carried her to school; Sumner Elementary School stood just a few blocks in the other direction from her house, but Linda Brown could not attend there because she was African American. By 1952, Mr. Brown had been joined by other parents in Topeka, and their suit, in turn, was combined with cases in four other jurisdictions, collectively challenging the constitutionality of racially segregated public schools. In 1952, the Supreme Court heard opening arguments and the justices issued their decision in May 1954.

Brown v. Board of Education of Topeka was, then, not solely one man's fight for his child's education. It included two hundred plaintiffs and represented the culmination of years of effort and scores of cases brought by the National Association for the Advancement of Colored People (NAACP) legal defense team. Thurgood Marshall served as Chief Counsel for the NAACP. Building on the intellectual and legal foundation laid by his predecessor and mentor, Charles Hamilton Houston, Marshall led the NAACP's strategy to upend legalized racial segregation in the United States. A dozen lawyers on the NAACP team meticulously planned the case: litigating in jurisdictions outside the Deep South, carefully choosing the particular school districts to challenge, selecting a veteran as the first named plaintiff, and commissioning psychological studies of the effects of segregation on children. Marshall successfully argued the *Brown* case before the

Supreme Court.[1] He and his team had previously won cases centered on graduate and professional education in segregated public universities in Missouri, Oklahoma, and Texas. While powerful precedents, these lawsuits necessarily applied to a very small percentage of the population: the consequences of those cases could not compare with *Brown v. Board of Education.*

In the wake of the *Brown* decision, African Americans, particularly in the South, where segregation was especially pervasive and grinding, rejoiced. But hopes for a transformed South were soon dashed. The 1955 U.S. Supreme Court decision known as *Brown II*, in which the Court declared that desegregation should proceed with "all deliberate speed," inadvertently opened the door to southern resistance. In 1956, 101 representatives in the U.S. Congress signed a "southern manifesto," including the entire congressional delegations from Alabama, Arkansas, Georgia, Louisiana, Mississippi, South Carolina, and Virginia. Initially drafted by South Carolinian Strom Thurmond, the document rebuked the "unwarranted exercise of power by the Court" and blamed the Supreme Court justices for undermining the

"amicable relations" between black and white southerners. Southern politicians also responded to *Brown* with hundreds of state and municipal laws antithetical to the Supreme Court decision. Pro-segregationists unleashed a wave of violence intended to intimidate African Americans and their white sympathizers. The year after the *Brown* verdict, Emmett Till, a fourteen-year-old boy from Chicago, visiting relatives in the rural community of Money, Mississippi, was kidnapped, tortured, and murdered. His alleged offense: whistling at a white woman. In 1957, President Dwight D. Eisenhower had to send one thousand soldiers from the 101st Airborne Division to quell civil unrest after nine African American students desegregated Central High School in Little Rock, Arkansas.[2]

Inspired by both the momentum of *Brown* and the backlash it spawned, the NAACP and the Southern Christian Leadership Conference (SCLC), led by Martin Luther King, Jr., worked with community groups to organize several campaigns, most famously the Montgomery Bus Boycott in 1955. Despite national attention on the *Brown* decision, the Emmett Till lynching, and the Little Rock Nine, to a large degree the burgeoning Civil Rights Movement had stalled by the end of the 1950s. Many conservative

1. Marshall won twenty-nine of thirty-two cases he argued before the Supreme Court and later became the first African American to serve on the nation's highest court. For a full explanation of the *Brown* case and its history, see Richard Kluger, *Simple Justice: The History of Brown v. Board of Education and Black America's Struggle for Equality,* (New York: Knopf, 1975). For Marshall's career, see Juan Williams, *Thurgood Marshall: American Revolutionary* (New York: Crown, 1998).

2. For firsthand accounts of the Little Rock crisis, see Daisy Bates, *The Long Shadow of Little Rock: A Memoir* (Fayetteville: University of Arkansas Press, 2007, reprint); Melba Pattillo Beals, *Warriors Don't Cry: A Searing Memoir of the Battle to Integrate Little Rock's Central High* (Washington Square Press, 1995, reprint).

black and white leaders urged the gradual dismantling of segregation and the pursuit of justice through the federal courts—both protracted processes.

In the early weeks of 1960, however, an unlikely cohort of eighteen-year-old college students in North Carolina revived the movement. Ezell Blair, Jr., Franklin McCain, Joseph McNeil, and David Richmond were freshmen at North Carolina Agricultural and Technical College (A&T) when they launched the student sit-in movement at the segregated lunch counter of a Woolworth's store in Greensboro, North Carolina, on February 1, 1960. Within a week three hundred students from A&T, Bennett College (an African American women's school), and Dudley High School joined in the campaign. Sit-ins spread like wildfire, to Winston-Salem, Raleigh, and Charlotte, North Carolina, to Nashville, Tennessee, and to Richmond, Virginia.[3]

No individual or organization in particular led the students—they operated as grassroots campaigns. Student activists founded the Student Nonviolent Coordinating Committee (SNCC) in April 1960, and members led community-organizing efforts and conducted protests across the South. But unlike the SCLC and the NAACP, SNCC operated in a decentralized manner, in terms of meeting style (everyone spoke as long as he or she wanted), strategy (set at the local level), and decision-making (through group consensus). While SNCC provided a forum for and advice to local protest organizers, the organization did not direct the student movement. African American college students typically led the efforts, and high schoolers, white classmates, and members of their communities joined them. By springtime, student sit-ins against segregation were sweeping the South and transforming the Civil Rights Movement. The students launched immediate, personal, and peaceful confrontations of segregation, which diverged from the approaches of long-standing organizations such as the NAACP. Their approach forced police and political leaders to decide whether or not they would defend the rights of the protestors. The student body president of Knoxville College in Tennessee captured the convictions of the student activists when he insisted: "We do not intend to wait placidly for those rights which are already legally and morally ours to be meted out to us one at a time."[4]

In this chapter, you will investigate the student-led protests that gave new life to the Civil Rights Movement in the early 1960s. What special skills, distinctive points of view, or unique approaches did college students bring to that movement? What did they seek to accomplish and how did they

3. Digital technology makes sources from this era—both the student-led part of the Civil Rights Movement and the advocacy of the NAACP, SCLC, CORE, and other organizations—easily accessible. Excellent websites for Civil Rights history sources include the Civil Rights Movement Veterans site maintained by Tougaloo College (crmvet. org), the Martin Luther King, Jr., Research and Education Institute at Stanford University (kinginstitute.stanford.edu), and the Civil Rights Digital Library (crdl.usg.edu/).

4. Quoted in William B. Wheeler, *Knoxville, Tennessee: A Mountain City in the New South* (Knoxville: University of Tennessee Press, 2005), p. 125.

pursue their aims? Studying the ambitions and tactics of young civil rights advocates, with a particular eye on generation and education, will enable you to answer the central question in this chapter: **What changes did students seek in the Civil Rights Movement and why?**

Background

In the wake of the Civil War, when the federal government forbade the continuation of racial slavery, white southerners faced a potentially radically transformed world. For a few years after the war, the U.S. military occupied the former Confederate states, and martial law ensured that African American men exercised their civil rights. But this transformation of the South did not long stand.

By 1877, Reconstruction had collapsed. In the North, white Americans, including many who opposed slavery, balked at continuing the federal commitment to racial equality. The majority of Americans lost interest in militarily occupying the South, which was expensive and controversial, and other national events took center stage. In the South, a vicious campaign of intimidation backed up by murder waged by the paramilitary wing of the Democratic Party, the Ku Klux Klan (KKK), overthrew Reconstruction governments. In "redeemed" state governments white Democrats wrested political power from black and white Republican politicians. They then revised all the southern state constitutions and passed a host of laws aimed at revoking the civil rights of African American citizens and reducing black men and women to a status as close to slavery as possible.

From the 1880s, former slaveholders dominated the Democratic Party, and they used the "redeemed" state governments to revive the hierarchical society of the Old South. Laws restricted the jobs African Americans could hold and where they could live. "Antimiscegenation" laws prohibited interracial marriages.[5] Several southern states required African Americans to contract their labor on an annual basis. It was a crime to leave a job without permission. Vagrancy laws criminalized the physical movement of black families. Parchman Farm Prison, in Mississippi, became a vehicle—a profitable one at that—for forcing black men into lifelong servitude.[6]

The post-Reconstruction justice system worked in tandem with sharecropping to disfranchise poor black as well as poor white southerners. Republican politicians debated redistributing land during the Reconstruction era, but ultimately rejected the idea. Former

5. The U.S. Supreme Court ended race-based marriage prohibitions in the *Loving v. Virginia* case in 1967. For this case, see Peter Wallenstein, *Race, Sex, and the Freedom of Marry: Loving v. Virginia* (Lawrence: University Press of Kansas, 2014).
6. For more on Parchman, see David Oshinsky, *Worse Than Slavery: Parchman Farm and the Ordeal of Jim Crow Justice* (New York: Free Press, 1997).

slaveholders kept their property, which left former slaves with few work opportunities besides agriculture. Sharecropping, the dominant system for agricultural production from the 1880s to the 1930s, was supposed to allow African Americans a chance at eventual landownership and economic autonomy. In theory, poor black (and white) families grew cotton for rich white landowners who provided them cotton seed, tools, and shelter. At the end of the year, the landowner sold the crop, kept his due, and split the profit with his laborers. If sharecropping families worked hard and lived frugally, in time, they could buy their own land and be independent. But that was only the theory. In practice, landowners routinely and systematically manipulated the arithmetic; sharecropping families seldom, if ever, finished the year with a profit. Laws prohibited their moving so long as a debt remained. So, for decades poor black and white southerners lived in abject poverty, beholden to wealthy white planters who controlled the land, the economy, and the law. Sharecropping and Democrat-dominated state governments thereby recreated a social order similar to that of the Old South: large landholders held sway over government and the economy, which left most white and black southerners impoverished and disfranchised. As you saw in Chapter 1, this racial agenda thwarted the alternative vision of a progressive, industrialized "New South" that could move out of the shadow of plantation agriculture and slavery.

The most important legal innovation to emerge in the South after the 1870s was the legal system known as "Jim Crow." These laws (the term derived from a minstrel show) racially segregated the South. Because slavery had so starkly defined the lives of black and white southerners, there was little reason to compel physical separation in the antebellum era. But after the United States defeated the Confederacy and outlawed slavery, white political elites desperately sought to redefine the lines between black and white southerners. Racial divisions became particularly pressing after "redemption" because the economic and political status of black and white nonelites was so similar. Jim Crow became the elites' best tool.

Hundreds of state and municipal laws physically separated black southerners from their white neighbors. African Americans could not drink from the same water fountains as white people; they entered restaurants and businesses through separate doors; they sat in the balcony at movie theaters; if they appeared in court, they swore on a separate Bible; pools, libraries, and even cemeteries were segregated. But for white southerners, perhaps the most important and meaningful part of the Jim Crow system was the public school system.

Both black and white southerners had long understood the power of education. The famous abolitionist Frederick Douglass maintained that learning changed his life and set him on the path toward self-liberation. During the era of slavery, southern states outlawed literacy among slaves; whites who taught slaves to read were themselves guilty of a crime. Education was power, and it was rigidly protected in the early twentieth century, just as it had been before the Civil War.

In terms of race, public education in the American South changed little between the 1880s and the 1950s. During Reconstruction, former slaves worked with the Freedman's Bureau to build and subsidize schools for African American students. But southern state legislatures consistently fought funding these schools. African American children attended poorly financed, rigidly segregated schools. Certainly teachers in African American schools were dedicated, but textbooks, transportation, physical spaces, and faculty salaries were all far inferior to those in all-white schools. Higher education was segregated as well. African American applicants were barred from attending whites-only state universities, even though their taxes supported those institutions.

One consequence of this segregated educational system was the growth of black colleges and universities. To avoid integration, many states funded (albeit parsimoniously) institutions such as North Carolina A&T, which attracted middle-class African American students like the Greensboro Four. Private institutions of higher education, such as Fisk University in Nashville, also emerged out of the efforts of black and white community leaders. Some universities and colleges, such as Tuskegee Institute in Alabama, focused heavily on practical education, training African American men and women in teaching, agriculture, and skilled trades. Under the leadership of Booker T. Washington, Tuskegee emphasized economic uplift and self-reliance.[7] Other universities,

including North Carolina A&T, focused on mathematics, business, and military science, in addition to agriculture. (When North Carolina created A&T they simultaneously chartered North Carolina A&M—now North Carolina State University—for white students.) Alongside black-owned newspapers and black churches, these colleges and universities became not only powerful symbols of African American culture but also leading centers for activism in the early twentieth century.

Strictly racialized education was not illegal in the United States—the Supreme Court actually sanctioned racial segregation in the *Plessy v. Ferguson* case of 1896. According to the decision in that case, segregation did not violate the Constitution. The case centered specifically on railroad cars. Homer Plessy was a passenger on a Louisiana train in the 1890s. Told to move to the car reserved for African American travelers, he refused. Fined twenty-five dollars, he refused to pay and was arrested. Plessy sued over the arrest and his case eventually reached the Supreme Court. Seven of nine justices voted to uphold the Louisiana law segregating railroad cars, finding that since the train provided "separate but equal" accommodations, the Fourteenth Amendment to the Constitution, which guaranteed equal protection and rights to all citizens, had not been violated. Justice John Marshall Harlan issued the only dissenting opinion, proclaiming, "Our Constitution is colorblind." None of his fellow justices concurred, and state government leaders quickly interpreted the ruling to apply to all public accommodations.

7. For more on Washington, see Robert J. Norrell, *Up from Slavery: The Life of Booker T. Washington* (Cambridge: Harvard University Press, 2009).

While codified in law, segregation was also policed by vigilante violence, orchestrated by white supremacists, including those involved in reviving the KKK, and by economic and political retribution at the hands of members of the White Citizens' Councils. The Citizens' Councils, another network of white supremacists, shared nearly all the views of KKK members. They spurned parading in sheets and hoods, however, and preferred political intimidation, educational activism, and economic retaliation—firing people from their jobs, for example, cutting off their credit, or boycotting their businesses. Both KKK and Citizens' Councils members exerted tremendous sway in local and state politics in every part of the South. White and African American southerners who violated Jim Crow faced swift retribution: against their livelihoods and their lives.

While lynching was not solely a southern phenomenon, most lynchings occurred in the region, and the overwhelming majority of victims were African American men. The violence was intentionally gruesome and widely publicized. A few examples from the pervasive pattern illustrate the vicious reaction generated by challenges to white supremacy. In Atlanta in 1899, Sam Hose, a young farmer, was accused of killing a white man (which he had unintentionally done during an argument) and raping the victim's wife (which he had not). As railroads ferried Atlantans to the community where he sat in jail, a lynch mob overwhelmed the authorities. They stripped Hose naked and chained him to a tree. While thousands of spectators cheered, white men took turns cutting off his ears,

fingers, and genitals. Still alive, Hose was set on fire. The mob dismembered his burned corpse, and members of the crowd gathered up body parts as souvenirs.[8] Emmett Till was lynched in 1955 by J. W. Milam and Roy Bryant, who, by their own admission, kidnapped him from his uncle's home, brutally beat him, shot him in the head, and threw his body in the Tallahatchie River. Milam and Bryant were tried for kidnapping and murder and exonerated by an all-white jury which deliberated only sixty-seven minutes. In June 1963, Byron De La Beckwith shot Medgar Evers, field secretary for the NAACP, in the driveway of his Jackson, Mississippi, home. During the murder trial, as Evers' widow, Myrlie Evers, testified, the Governor of Mississippi, Ross Barnett, walked into court and shook De La Beckwith's hand. An all-white jury found De La Beckwith not guilty.[9] Such was the justice system under Jim Crow—and the risk to African Americans who crossed the color line.

The young people who started the sit-in protests knew the stakes. Ezell Blair, Jr., remembered watching the news coverage of the Emmett Till lynching. Pictures from his open casket funeral appeared in *Jet* magazine in 1955, and journalists reported the story around the world. As a young child, Blair also watched the KKK parade through his neighborhood—a common experience in the Jim Crow South.[10]

8. Norrell, *Up from History*, pp. 160–161.
9. De La Beckwith was retried in Mississippi in 1994 and convicted.
10. *February One* (film documentary), Video Dialog, 2003. For the larger sweep of the Civil Rights Movement, *Eyes on the Prize* (PBS, 1987 and 1990) remains a signal achievement in documentary filmmaking.

Although racial violence and segregation pervaded the South between the 1880s and the 1950s, a number of changes occurred in the 1940s and the 1950s that launched a broad-based, revolutionary challenge to this way of life.[11] The NAACP legal defense team was only one part of that organization's advocacy for equality. During the first half of the twentieth century, the NAACP also waged a decades-long antilynching campaign and organized lobbying operations and social protests in pursuit of equal rights. Over one million African American men served in the armed forces during World War II. The hypocrisy of fighting fascism abroad while over twelve million U.S. citizens were denied basic human rights at home was not lost on the black community or on some American politicians. President Harry Truman ordered the U.S. military desegregated in 1948; within a few years integration was accomplished, including at primary and secondary schools on military bases. On one level, the Cold War presented an ideological obstacle to challenging America's racial order. White southerners disparaged anyone who questioned segregation

as a communist and routinely used red-baiting to discredit civil rights activists. Other Americans, however, saw that racial discrimination presented the Soviet Union with a powerful and credible tool for criticizing American values. Segregation damaged America's reputation abroad and posed a risk to national security. International relations thus raised the stakes in the contest over civil rights.

The international human rights movement likewise influenced American domestic politics. By midcentury, the movement for Indian liberation led by Mahatma Gandhi was exerting a profound effect on many African Americans, including Martin Luther King, Jr. Gandhi pioneered nonviolent civil disobedience; he believed that by directly, peacefully, and relentlessly confronting inequality, justice could be won.

Finally, the power of television should not be overlooked. Television emerged as a dominant cultural force in the United States when viewership skyrocketed in the 1950s. In 1950, less than 10 percent of American households owned television sets; by 1960, over 85 percent did. Television was so influential that many political commentators attribute John Kennedy's victory over Richard Nixon in the 1960 election to Nixon's poor performance in the nation's first televised presidential debate. Network news cameras brought the Little Rock Nine at Central High School, Emmett Till's funeral, and the student sit-ins into Americans' living rooms.

Despite these changes and the *Brown* decision, in the 1950s most African American parents, hoping to

---

11. Scholars have also explored the many challenges to the South's—and the nation's—racial order in the decades before the Civil Rights Movement. See, for example, John Egerton, *Speak Now against the Day: The Generation before the Civil Rights Movement in the South* (Chapel Hill: University of North Carolina Press, 1995); and Glenda Elizabeth Gilmore, *Defying Dixie: The Radial Roots of Civil Rights, 1919–1950* (New York: W. W. Norton, 2008). For a model study of student led anti-segregation activism outside the South, see Stefan M. Bradley, *Harlem vs. Columbia: Black Student Power in the Late 1960s* (Urbana: University of Illinois Press, 2009).

protect their children, continued to teach them how to negotiate Jim Crow, not challenge it. Adults warned children never to approach whites, to drop their eyes when they met on the street. Where one went, what one said, even one's body language could be deadly. By 1960, though, young people were increasingly dubious of their parents' generation and values. Even the brilliant, systematic legal strategy of the NAACP struck many young people as too slow and too accommodating. Many in the rising generation viewed gradual challenges to segregation with skepticism. As Franklin McCain remembered, he and his friends "trusted no one over eighteen." The older generation, he believed, had its chance to change the system and failed to take it—the rising generation believed they could do better.

Ezell Blair, Jr., grew up in Greensboro, the son of a teacher, and became friends with Franklin McCain at Dudley High School when McCain's family moved from Washington, D.C. David Richmond was a track star and the most popular student at Dudley. In the fall of 1959, Richmond, Blair, and McCain enrolled in A&T, where they met and became fast friends with Joseph McNeil, a quiet, deeply intellectual physics major. When McNeil returned to Greensboro in January 1960 after spending Christmas break with his family in New York, he was refused service at the bus station. It was a breaking point for McNeil and his friends. Over the course of the following weeks, the four men carefully planned their next move. On February 1, they dressed in their Sunday best, met outside the university library, and headed downtown.

✦

The Method

Certain moments in U.S. history— the creation of the Constitution, the Allied victory in World War II—are rightly celebrated. Americans take pride in marking those parts of their nation's past. The Civil Rights Movement has become one of those justifiably honored eras. It required a great deal of courage, resolve, and talent to wage that fight for social justice, to push America toward "a more perfect union." Americans collectively remember it as a noble era, and the leaders of the movement are honored in public spaces, including roads,

parks, and statues.[12] While historians can, some might say should, share in celebrating the high points in the nation's past, our job also involves explaining the context, significance, and implications of these eras.

12. It took fifteen years of lobbying for the U.S. government to designate Martin Luther King, Jr., Day as a national holiday. The Senate debates in 1983 were especially rancorous; Senator Jesse Helms claimed Dr. King was a communist and tried to filibuster the legislation. Seventeen more years passed before every state honored the holiday. South Carolina became the last to recognize the day as an official paid holiday for all state employees: in 2000.

The young people who risked their lives to secure justice for their communities will likely appeal to you, perhaps even inspire you. When they started the sit-in movement, they were the same age as the average college student taking a U.S. history survey course today. In this chapter, you will move through celebration and toward understanding.

Use the evidence in this chapter to cultivate a deeper understanding of the student sit-in movement. Certainly the Jim Crow laws are self-evident explanations of why African Americans resented segregation. But why did resentment produce this particular kind of resistance on campuses such as North Carolina A&T and Fisk University in 1960? How—and why—was the student campaign different from the efforts by the NAACP and other civil rights organizations? How did age, class, geographic location, and perspective shape college students' agendas and their actions? In sum, what changes did students seek in the Civil Rights Movement and why?

As you seek to deepen your understanding of these issues, interviews with sit-in leaders provide one kind of evidence. The student leaders explain their actions and intentions, but they also tell us a great deal about the context of their movement. Read these accounts closely: what assumptions and values underlay their accounts? How important was personal experience versus organizations in mobilizing these students? What new ideas did they bring to the Civil Rights Movement?

The photographs from early sit-ins, the materials circulated by student leaders, and the music of the movement all offer additional context. What image did the organizers project? Why did they project such an image? What image did the opposition project? What philosophy did the students embrace? What attitude did they convey in their songs and organizational literature? How did the student movement fit in—or fail to do so—with the mainstream Civil Rights Movement? What challenge did they pose to mainstream movement leaders? How did they benefit movement leaders?

Coverage in the *New York Times* and the *Washington Post* reveals how quickly both the sit-in protests and national awareness of them spread. Like the interviews, these journalistic accounts also provide information about the background, societal implications, and larger meaning of the student protests. Consider these articles carefully, paying attention to clues about the changes forged by the student protesters. What was innovative and controversial about their actions?

A second important issue you should consider as you read this evidence is the role of historical memory. You will notice that the interviewees speak in the past tense; they were interviewed years after the passage of the Civil Rights Act (1964) and Voting Rights Act (1965), when they were well past their collegiate years. As you consider those narratives as well as the 1990 photograph of the Greensboro Four (Source 18) and statue in their honor (Source 19), think about historical memory. How might subsequent experiences have shaped the way the sit-in leaders remembered (and were remembered for) their roles in the Civil Rights Movement? Why do we as a society collectively remember and commemorate certain parts of our past and ignore others?

♦

The Evidence

Source 1 from American Public Media, "Remembering Jim Crow" documentary and website: http://americanradioworks.publicradio.org/features/remembering/laws.html.

1. Compilation of Typical Jim Crow Statutes.

EDUCATION

Florida: The schools for white children and the schools for negro children shall be conducted separately.

Kentucky: The children of white and colored races committed to reform schools shall be kept entirely separate from each other.

Mississippi: Separate schools shall be maintained for the children of the white and colored races.

Mississippi: Separate free schools shall be established for the education of children of African descent; and it shall be unlawful for any colored child to attend any white school, or any white child to attend a colored school.

New Mexico: Separate rooms shall be provided for the teaching of pupils of African descent, and such pupils may not be admitted to the school rooms occupied and used by pupils of Caucasian or other descent.

North Carolina: School textbooks shall not be interchangeable between the white and colored schools, but shall continue to be used by the race first using them.

ENTERTAINMENT

Alabama: It shall be unlawful to conduct a restaurant or other place for the serving of food in the city, at which white and colored people are served in the same room, unless such white and colored persons are effectually separated by a solid partition extending from the floor upward to a distance of seven feet or higher, and unless a separate entrance from the street is provided.

Alabama: It shall be unlawful for a negro and white person to play together or in company with each other at any game of pool or billiards.

Alabama: Every employer of white or negro males shall provide for such white or negro males reasonably accessible and separate toilet facilities.

Georgia: All persons licensed to conduct a restaurant, shall serve either white people exclusively or colored people exclusively and shall not sell to the two races within the same room or under the same license.

Georgia: It shall be unlawful for any amateur white baseball team to play on any vacant lot or baseball diamond within two blocks of a playground devoted to the Negro race, and it shall be unlawful for any amateur colored baseball team to play baseball within two blocks of any playground devoted to the white race.

Georgia: All persons licensed to conduct the business of selling beer or wine . . . shall serve either white people exclusively or colored people exclusively and shall not sell to the two races within the same room at any time.

Louisiana: All circuses, shows, and tent exhibitions, to which the attendance of more than one race is invited shall provide not less than two ticket offices and not less than two entrances.

Virginia: Any public hall, theatre, opera house, motion picture show or place of public entertainment which is attended by both white and colored persons shall separate the white race and the colored race.

HEALTH CARE

Alabama: No person or corporation shall require any white female nurse to nurse in wards or rooms in hospitals, either public or private, in which negro men are placed.

Louisiana: The board of trustees shall maintain a separate building, on separate grounds, for the admission, care, instruction, and support of all blind persons of the colored or black race.

Mississippi: There shall be maintained by the governing authorities of every hospital maintained by the state for treatment of white and colored patients separate entrances for white and colored patients and visitors, and such entrances shall be used by the race only for which they are prepared.

LIBRARIES

Texas: Negroes are to be served through a separate branch or branches of the county free library, which shall be administered by a custodian of the negro race under the supervision of the county librarian.

North Carolina: The state librarian is directed to fit up and maintain a separate place for the use of the colored people who may come to the library for the purpose of reading books or periodicals.

MARRIAGE

Arizona: The marriage of a person of Caucasian blood with a Negro shall be null and void.

Florida: All marriages between a white person and a negro, or between a white person and a person of negro descent to the fourth generation inclusive, are hereby forever prohibited.

Florida: Any negro man and white woman, or any white man and negro woman, who are not married to each other, who habitually live in and occupy in the nighttime the same room, shall each be punished by imprisonment not exceeding 12 months, or by fine not exceeding five hundred dollars.

Maryland: All marriages between a white person and a negro, or between a white person and a person of negro descent, to the third generation, inclusive . . . are forever prohibited, and shall be void.

Mississippi: The marriage of a white person with a negro or mulatto or person who shall have one-eighth or more of negro blood, shall be unlawful and void.

Wyoming: All marriages of white persons with Negroes, Mulattos, Mongolians, or Malaya hereafter contracted in the State of Wyoming are, and shall be, illegal and void.

SERVICES

Georgia: No colored barber shall serve as a barber to white women or girls.

Georgia: The officer in charge shall not bury, or allow to be buried, any colored persons upon ground set apart or used for the burial of white persons.

Source 2 from Trenholm State Technical College, accessed through Alabama State Archives at http://www.alabamamoments.alabama.gov/sec59ps.html.

2. Alabama Voter Questionnaire and Literacy Test.

Southern states required African Americans to pass literacy tests in order to register to vote. As the following source demonstrates, the tests were both exacting and vague. To thwart potential voters, by 1964 Alabama had created a hundred different tests. Prospective voters chose at random from a binder. In many locales, the paperwork was so rigidly timed that no one could actually complete the form. Whites bypassed these requirements through grandfather clauses (if your grandfather was a registered voter, you could vote) and voucher programs (if a registered voter vouched for you, you could vote).

APPLICATION FOR REGISTRATION

I, _____, do hereby apply to the Board of Registrars of _____ County, State of Alabama, to register as an elector under the Constitution and laws of the State of Alabama, and do herewith submit answers to the interrogatories propounded to me by said board.

_____

(Applicants Full Name)

QUESTIONNAIRE

1. State your name, the date and place of your birth, and your present address

    _____

2. Are you single or married? _____ (a) If married, give name, resident and place of birth of your husband or wife, as the case may be: _____

3. Give the names of the places, respectively, where you have lived during the last five years; and the name or names by which you have been known during the last five years: _____

4. If you are self-employed, state the nature of your business: _____

    A. If you have been employed, by another during the last five years, State the nature of your employment and the name or names of such employer or employers and his or their addresses: _____

5. If you claim that you are a bona fide resident of the State of Alabama, give the date on which you claim to have become such bona fide resident: _____ (a) When did you become a bona fide resident of _____ County: _____ (b) When did you become a bona fide resident of _____ Ward or Precinct _____

6. If you intend to change your place of residence prior to the next general election, state the facts: _____

7. Have you previously applied for and been denied registration as a voter? _____ (a) If so, give the facts: _____

8. Has your name been previously stricken from the list of persons registered? _____

9. Are you now or have you ever been a dope addict or a habitual drunkard?

    _____

    (A) If you are or have been a dope addict or habitual drunkard, explain as fully as you can: _____

10. Have you ever been legally declared insane? _____ (a) If so, give details: _____

11. Give a brief statement of the extent of your education and business experience: _____

12. Have you ever been charged with or convicted of a felony or crime or offense involving moral turpitude? _____ (a) If so, give the facts: _____

13. Have you ever served in the Armed Forces of the United States Government? _____

    (a) If so, state when and for approximately how long: _____

14. Have you ever been expelled or dishonorable discharged from any school or college or from any branch of the Armed Forces of the United States, or of any other Country? _____ If so, state facts: _____

15. Will you support and defend the Constitution of the United States and the Constitution of the State of Alabama? _____

16. Are you now or have you ever been affiliated with any group or organization which advocates the overthrow of the United States Government or the government of any State of the United States by unlawful means? _____ (a) If so, state the facts: _____

17. Will you bear arms for your county when called upon it to do so? _____ If the answer is no, give reasons: _____

18. Do you believe in free elections and rule by the majority? _____

19. Will you give aid and comfort to the enemies of the United States Government or the Government of the State of Alabama? _____

20. Name some of the duties and obligations of citizenship: _____

    (A) Do you regard those duties and obligations as having priority over the duties and obligations you owe to any other secular organization when they are in conflict? _____

21. Give the names and post office addresses of two persons who have present knowledge of your bona fide residence at the place as stated by you: _____

Insert Part III (5)

(The following questions shall be answered by the applicant without assistance.)

1. What is the chief executive of Alabama called?
2. Are post offices operated by the state or federal government?

3. What is the name of the president of the United States?
4. To what national lawmaking body does each state send senators and representatives?

Instructions "A"

The applicant will complete the remainder of this questionnaire before a Board member and at his instructions. The Board member shall have the applicant read any one or more of the following excerpts from the U.S. Constitution using a duplicate form of this Insert Part III. The Board member shall keep in his possession the application with its inserted Part III and shall mark thereon the words missed in reading by the applicant.

EXCERPTS FROM THE CONSTITUTION

1. "The right of the people to be secure in their persons, houses, papers, and effects, against unreasonable searches and seizures, shall not be violated, and no warrants shall issue, but upon probable cause supported by oath or affirmation, and particularly describing the place to be searched, and the person or things to be seized."
2. "Representatives shall be apportioned among the several states according to their respective numbers, counting the whole number of persons in each state, excluding Indians not taxed."
3. "Treason against the United States, shall consist only in levying war against them, or in adhering to their enemies, giving them aid and comfort."
4. "The senators and representatives before mentioned, and the members of the several legislatures, and all executive and judicial officers, both of the United States and of the several states, shall be bound by oath or affirmation, to support this constitution."

Instructions "B"

The Board member shall then have the applicant write several words, or more if necessary to make a judicial determination of his ability to write. The writing shall be placed below so that it becomes a part of the application. If the writing is illegible, the Board member shall write in parentheses beneath the writing the words the applicant was asked to write.

HAVE APPLICANT WRITE HERE, DICTATING WORDS FROM THE CONSTITUTION

Signature of Applicant _____

3. Franklin McCain Discusses the Greensboro Sit-In.

The planning process was on a Sunday night, I remember it quite well. I think it was Joseph who said, "It's time that we take some action now. We've been getting together, and we've been, up to this point, still like most people we've talked about for the past few weeks or so—that is, people who talk a lot, in fact, make very little action." After selecting the technique, then we said, "Let's go down and just ask for service." It certainly wasn't titled a "sit-in" or "sit-down" at that time. "Let's just go down to Woolworth's tomorrow and ask for service, and the tactic is going to be simply this: we'll just stay there." We never anticipated being served, certainly, the first day anyway. "We'll stay until we get served." And I think Ezell said, "Well, you know that might be weeks, that might be months, that might be never." And I think it was the consensus of the group, we said, "Well, that's just the chance we'll have to take."

What's likely to happen? Now, I think that was a question that all of us asked ourselves. . . . What's going to happen once we sit down? Of course, nobody had the answers. Even your wildest imagination couldn't lead you to believe what would, in fact, happen.

Why Woolworth's?

They advertise in public media, newspapers, radios, television, that sort of thing. They tell you to come in: "Yes, buy the toothpaste; yes, come in and buy the notebook paper. . . . No, we don't separate your money in this cash register, but, no, please don't step down to the hot dog stand. . . ." The whole system, of course, was unjust, but that just seemed like insult added to injury. That was just like pouring salt into an open wound. That's inviting you to do something.

. . . We did make purchases of school supplies and took the patience and time to get receipts for our purchases, and Joseph and myself went over to the counter and asked to be served coffee and doughnuts. As anticipated, the reply was, "I'm sorry, we don't serve you here." And of course we said, "We just beg to disagree with you. We've in fact already been served; you've served us already and that's just not quite true." The attendant or waitress was a little bit dumbfounded, just didn't know what to say under the circumstances like that. And we said, "We wonder why you'd invite us in to serve us at one counter and deny service at another. If this is a private club or private concern, then we believe you ought to sell membership cards and sell only to persons who have a membership card. If we don't have a card, then we'd know pretty well that we shouldn't come in or even attempt to come in." That didn't go over too well, simply because I don't really think she understood what we were talking about, and for the second reason, she had no logical response to a statement like that. And the only thing that an individual in her case or position could do is, of course, call the manager. [Laughs] Well, at this time, I think we were joined by Dave Richmond and Ezell Blair at the counter with us, after that dialogue.

Were you afraid at this point?

Oh hell yes, no question about that. [Laughs] At that point there was a policeman who had walked in off the street, who was pacing the aisle . . . behind us, where we were seated, with his club in his hand, just sort of knocking it in his hand, and just looking mean and red and a little bit upset and a little bit disgusted. And you had the feeling that he didn't know what the hell to do. You had the feeling that this is the first time that this big bad man with the gun and the club has been pushed in a corner, and he's got absolutely no defense, and the thing that's killing him more than anything else—he doesn't know what he can or what he cannot do. He's defenseless. Usually his defense is offense, and we've provoked him, yes, but we haven't provoked him outwardly enough for him to resort to violence. And I think this is just killing him; you can see it all over him.

People in the store were—we got mixed reactions from people in the store. A couple of old ladies . . . came up to pat us on the back sort of and say, "Ah, you should have done it ten years ago. It's a good thing I think you're doing."

These were black ladies.

No, these are white ladies.

Really?

Yes, and by the same token, we had some white ladies and white men to come up and say to us, "Nasty, dirty niggers, you know you don't belong here at the lunch counter. There's a counter—" There was, in fact, a counter downstairs in the Woolworth store, a stand-up type counter where they sold hot dogs. . . .

[237]

But at any rate, there were expressions of support from white people that first day?

Absolutely right. Absolutely. And I think probably that was certainly some incentive for additional courage on the part of us. And the other thing that helped us psychologically quite a lot was seeing the policeman pace the aisle and not be able to do anything. I think that this probably gave us more strength, more encouragement, than anything else on that particular day, on day one.

Unexpected as it was, the well-wishing from the elderly white women was hardly more surprising than the scorn of a middle-aged black dishwasher behind the counter. She said, "That's why we can't get anyplace today, because of people like you, rabble-rousers, troublemakers. . . . This counter is reserved for white people, it always has been, and you are well aware of that. So why don't you go on out and stop making trouble?" He has since seen the woman at, of all places, a reunion commemorating the event in which she played so unsupportive a role.

[She said] "Yes, I did say it and I said it because, first of all, I was afraid for what would happen to you as young black boys. Secondly, I was afraid of what would happen to me as an individual who had a job at the Woolworth store. I might have been fired and that's my livelihood. . . ."

It took me a long time to really understand that statement . . . but I know why she said it. She said it out of fear more than anything else. I've come to understand that, and my elders say to me that it's maturity that makes me understand why she said that some fifteen years ago.

But, moved by neither praise nor scorn, he and the others waited for the waitress to return with the manager, a career Woolworth's employee named C. L. Harris.

That was real amusin' as well [laughing] because by then we had the confidence, my goodness, of a Mack truck. And there was virtually nothing that could move us, there was virtually nothing probably at that point that could really frighten us off. . . . If it's possible to know what it means to have your soul cleansed—I felt pretty clean at that time. I probably felt better on that day than I've ever felt in my life. Seems like a lot of feelings of guilt or what-have-you suddenly left me, and I felt as though I had gained my manhood, so to speak, and not only gained it, but had developed quite a lot of respect for it. Not Franklin McCain only as an individual, but I felt as though the manhood of a number of other black persons had been restored and had gotten some respect from just that one day.

But back to Mr. Harris, who was the store manager, he was a fairly nice guy to talk to on that day. I think what he wanted to do more than anything else was to—initially—was to kill us with kindness, to say, "Fellas, you know this is just not the way we do business. Why don't you go on back to your campus? If you're just hungry, go downstairs," and that sort of thing.

We listened to him, paid him the courtesy of listening to what he had to say. We repeated our demands to him, and he ended up by saying, "Well, you know, I don't really set policy for this store. The policy for serving you is set by corporate headquarters." And of course, we found out that that was just a cop out. Corporate headquarters said, "No, it's up to local communities to set standards and set practices and that sort of thing, and whatever they do is all right with us." You know, the usual sort of game of rubber checkers.

The only reason we did leave is the store was closing. We knew, of course, we had to leave when the store was closing. We said to him, "Well, we'll have plenty of time tomorrow, because we'll be back to see you." [Laughs] I don't think that went over too well. But by the time we were leaving, the store was just crowded with people from off the streets and on the streets. . . . As a matter of fact, there were so many people standin' in front of the store, and we had to leave from the side entrance.

But back at the campus, there was just a beehive of activity. Word had spread. As a matter of fact, word was back on campus before we ever got back. There were all sorts of phone calls to the administration and to people on the faculty and staff. The mayor's office was aware of it and the governor's office was aware of it. I think it was all over North Carolina within a matter of just an hour or so.

That night they met with about fifty campus leaders to form the Student Executive Committee for Justice.

The movement started out as a movement of nonviolence and as a Christian movement, and we wanted to make that very clear to everybody, that it was a movement that was seeking justice more than anything else and not a movement to start a war. . . . We knew that probably the most powerful and potent weapon that people have literally no defense for is love, kindness. That is, whip the enemy with something that he doesn't understand.

How much was the example of Dr. King and the Montgomery Bus Boycott in your mind in that regard?

Not very much. The individual who had probably most influence on us was Gandhi, more than any single individual. During the time that the Montgomery Bus Boycott was in effect, we were tots for the most part, and we barely heard of Martin Luther King. Yes, Martin Luther King's name was well-known when the sit-in movement was in effect, but to pick out Martin Luther King as a hero. . . . I don't want you to misunderstand what I'm about to say: Yes, Martin Luther King was a hero. . . . No, he was not the individual that we had upmost in mind when we started the sit-in movement. . . .

Most journalists and historians have been quite wrong about the impetus for the first sit-in, he insists. Although all of the students had read extensively on the Montgomery movement, they were not, as has been widely reported, directly inspired by a Fellowship of Reconciliation "comic book" entitled "Martin Luther King and the Montgomery Story." They had not heard of CORE's Chicago sit-in twenty years earlier. Nor were he and the others persuaded, as one history of the sit-ins has it, to make their protest by Ralph Johns, an eccentric white NAACP member who ran a haberdashery near the campus. The subject irritates him. Dignified even in his light-hearted moments, he now becomes even more formal.

Credit for the initiation of the sit-in movement has been granted to one or two ministers, the NAACP, Ralph Johns,[13] CORE, at least a dozen people, and it's rather amusing when you do read some of these articles. I think it's a game. The same type tactic that has been used over and over and over by the white news media and the white press to discredit blacks with particular types of achievement. You don't have to look at the sit-in movement to see that. You can think of things like, well, for instance, the surveying of the laying out of the city of Washington, D.C., or the invention of the traffic signal, or the concept of Labor Day, or even Perry's expedition to the North Pole. These are the kinds of things that come into my mind when I think about the attempt to discredit the people who actually started the sit-in movement.

So what you're saying is . . . the most simple explanation applies?

Four guys met, planned, and went into action. It's just that simple.

On the second day, they were joined by over twenty other A&T students, and they kept most of the stools occupied all day. On the fourth day the first white students joined them from the University of North Carolina Women's College in Greensboro. By the second week sit-ins had spread to a half-dozen North Carolina towns.

From the Greensboro area there must have been people from six or seven university campuses who wanted to participate, who wanted to help sit-in, who wanted to help picket. We actually got to the point where we had people going down in shifts. It got to the point wherein we took all the seats in the restaurants. We had people there in the mornings as soon as the doors were open to just take every seat in the restaurant or at the lunch counter. . . .

As a manager, you've got to do something. You just can't continue to have people come in and sit around. The cash registers have to ring. What

13. Joseph McNeil's memory of Ralph Johns differs somewhat from that of Franklin McCain's.

happened is that after we started to take all of the seats in the restaurants, they started to pull the stools up in the restaurants. So we just started to stand around then and take all the standing room. . . . I think at the height of the sit-in movement in Greensboro, we must have had at least, oh, ten or fifteen thousand people downtown who wanted to sit-in, but obviously there weren't that many chairs in downtown Greensboro for people to sit in. . . .

It spread to places like the shopping centers, the drugstores in the shopping centers, the drive-ins. . . . No place was going to be left untouched. The only criteria was that if it did not serve blacks, it was certainly going to be hit. . . .

With such success came attention.

The Congress of Racial Equality offered a funny sort of help, and that kind of help was, in effect, "If you let us control the show, we'll show you how the thing is supposed to be done." And four seventeen-year-old guys were just not in the mood to let someone take their show. That was our position. Our position was, we are probably as much experts about this as anybody else. We were experts because we had had one experience already, and that's more than most people had had.

We got a lot of attention from the Communist party. [Laughs] The Communist party sent representatives down to Greensboro to assist us in any way that we deemed appropriate. If it meant actual participation, they offered to sit-in with us. If it meant you needed x number of dollars to do this, or if you needed air fare to go here or there, if you needed anything, they made it known that money was available, assistance was available. Just don't sit down here in Greensboro and want for things that you need. But you know, again, it was a Christian movement, and Christians and Communists just don't mix.

Did you avail yourself of any of that?

No, we didn't need it. Even if we had needed it, there was no reason to affiliate with the Communist party. We were in the driver's seat. . . . Remember, too, you have four guys who were pretty strong-willed, pretty bull-headed, and who were keenly aware that people would rush in and try to take over the Movement, so to speak. And we were quite aware of that, and we felt—not felt—*were* very independent. . . . As a matter of fact, we were criticized on several occasions for being too damned independent. But I still don't regret it.

Did the success that you experienced cause strains among the four of you?

Never. There was enough to go around. [Laughs] . . .

4. Joseph McNeil Remembers Greensboro.

I don't think there's any specific reason why that particular day was chosen. I had talked to a local merchant [Ralph Johns] who was extremely helpful to us in getting things rolling, in giving us some ideas. We had played over in our minds possible scenarios, and to the best of our abilities we had determined how we were gonna conduct ourselves given those scenarios. But we did walk in that day—I guess it was about four-thirty—and we sat at a lunch counter where blacks never sat before. And people started to look at us. The help, many of whom were black, looked at us in disbelief too. They were concerned about our safety. We asked for service, and we were denied, and we expected to be denied. We asked why couldn't we be served, and obviously we weren't given a reasonable answer and it was our intent to sit there until they decided to serve us. We had planned to come back the following day and to repeat that scenario. Others found out what we had done, because the press became aware of what was happening. So the next day when we decided to go down again, I think we went down with fifteen, and the third day it was probably a hundred and fifty, and then it probably mushroomed up to a thousand or so, and then it spread to another city. All rather spontaneously, of course, and before long, I guess it was probably in fifteen or twenty cities, and that's when we had our thing going.

5. John Lewis Describes the Nashville Sit-Ins.

John Lewis, born into poverty in rural Alabama, became a national leader for civil rights during his college years. The Nashville campaign began two weeks before his twentieth birthday. He went on to organize the Freedom Rides in 1961, and serve as national chairman of the Student Non-Violent Coordinating Committee (SNCC), which he helped found. Lewis has represented Georgia's Fifth Congressional District in the U.S. House of Representatives since 1987. Congressman Lewis is the last surviving speaker from the 1963 March on Washington.

We had on that first day over five hundred students in front of Fisk University chapel, to be transported downtown to the First Baptist Church, to be organized into small groups to go down to sit in at the lunch counters.

We went into the five-and-tens—Woolworth's, Kresge's, McClellan's— because these stores were known all across the South and for the most part all across the country. We took our seats in a very orderly, peaceful fashion.

The students were dressed like they were on the way to church or going to a big social affair. They had their books, and we stayed there at the lunch counter, studying and preparing our homework, because we were denied service. The managers ordered that the lunch counters be closed, that the restaurants be closed, and we'd just sit there, all day long. . . .

The first day nothing in terms of violence or disorder happened. This continued for a few more days and it continued day in and day out. Finally, on Saturday, February twenty-seventh, when we had about a hundred students prepared to go down—it was a very beautiful day in Nashville—we got a call from a local white minister who had been a real supporter of the movement. He said that if we go down on this particular day, he understood that the police would stand to the side and let a group of white hoodlums and thugs come in and beat people up, and then we would be arrested. We made a decision to go, and we all went to the same store. It was a Woolworth in the heart of the downtown area, and we occupied every seat at the lunch counter, every seat in the restaurant, and it did happen. A group of young white men came in and they started pulling and beating primarily the young women. They put lighted cigarettes down their backs, in their hair, and they were really beating people. In a short time police officials came in and placed all of us under arrest, and not a single member of the white group, the people that were opposing our sit-in, was arrested.

That was the first time I was arrested. Growing up in the rural South, you learned it was not the thing to do. To go to jail was to bring shame and disgrace on the family. But for me it was like being involved in a holy crusade, it became a badge of honor. I think it was in keeping with what we had been taught in the workshops, so it felt very good, in the sense of righteous indignation, about being arrested, but at the same time I felt the commitment and education on the part of the students.

6. Diane Nash Remembers the Nashville Campaign.

Diane Nash, a Chicago native studying at Fisk University, was twenty-two when she ran the Nashville Student Movement. With John Lewis, she was a founder of SNCC. She became a leading figure in organizing the Freedom Rides of 1961, the demonstrations in Birmingham in 1963, and the voter registration drive in Selma in 1965.

The sit-ins were really highly charged, emotionally. In our non-violent workshops, we had decided to be respectful for the opposition, and try to keep issues geared towards desegregation, not get sidetracked. The first sit-in we had was really funny, because the waitresses were nervous. They must have dropped two thousand dollars' worth of dishes that day. It was almost a cartoon. One in particular, she was so nervous, she picked up dishes and she dropped one, and she'd pick up another one, and she'd drop it. It was really funny, and we were sitting there trying not to laugh, because we thought that laughing would be insulting and we didn't want to create that kind of atmosphere. At the same time we were scared to death. . . .

After we had started sitting in, we were surprised and delighted to hear reports of other cities joining in the sit-ins. And I think we started feeling the power of the idea whose time had come. Before we did the things that we did, we had no inkling that the movement would become as widespread as it did. I can remember being in the dorm any number of times and hearing the newscasts, that Orangeburg had demonstrations, or Knoxville, or other towns. And we were really excited. We'd applaud, and say yea. When you are that age, you don't feel powerful. I remember realizing that with what we were doing, trying to abolish segregation, we were coming up against governors, judges, politicians, businessmen, and I remember thinking, I'm only twenty-two years old, what do I know, what am I doing? And I felt very vulnerable. So when we heard these newscasts, that other cities had demonstrations, it really helped. Because there were more of us. And it was very important.

The movement had a way of reaching inside you and bringing out things that even you didn't know were there. Such as courage. When it was time to go to jail, I was much too busy to be afraid.

7. C. T. Vivian Explains the Reactions to the Nashville Sit-Ins.

Reverend C. T. Vivian had trained for the ministry in Nashville and was an advisor to the students and an active participant in the movement. He was thirty-five when the protests started. He went on to become a close ally of Martin Luther King Jr. and a leading figure in the SCLC.

Now, many of the parents were afraid, thought that their children's lives would be destroyed forever because of what would be on their record. Many telephone calls were coming from everywhere. Pressure was on the college presidents and the vice presidents and staff. But students made up their minds what they were going to do. It was a great point of their own development.

The police knew that they represented the city, the merchants, the thugs, more than they represented us. Yet here is the importance of nonviolence, that they did not want to appear too demanding, too brutal. They wanted to stop us, but when we would not stop, then they had to begin to work on the thugs, because the thugs will bring out the worst of segregation in a racist society, so that it even shames the people who are themselves racists and who keep the system going. They were caught in that dilemma and they were waiting for their orders from the businessmen.

The city fathers themselves had to see their relationship to the business-men. Businessmen saw their relationship to profits. And the black people were beginning to respond all over, "What to do?" So the boycotts start, to force the businessmen to deal with the issue. As one of the businessmen put it, nobody came downtown. Blacks wouldn't come downtown, whites were afraid to come downtown, so the only people downtown were green people and there weren't many of them, all right? As a result, the businessmen began to lose money and they began to ask for a change. Remember, though, we were meeting with them, we were talking with them, trying to get them to understand, think for themselves, or react without our presence. We were constantly negotiating with them.

Source 8 from the North Carolina A&T University Archives, reproduced at: http://www.pbs.org/independentlens/februaryone/transparencies.pdf

8. Greensboro Four Letter to Fellow Students.

Dear fellow students,

For every effective organization there is a level of leadership. As far as we're concerned, this was the purpose of the Students Executive Committee for Justice. This committee is composed of the original formulators of this passive resistance movement now taking place and several other students who are quite reliable in conducting adequate guidance. And, since this committee has already drafted "plans-of-action" to accomplish this objective and possess a more detailed knowledge of what is taking place "behind the scene", we feel that the responsibility of leadership should fall upon this group of persons. We sincerely hope that you will fully agree and cooperate with us in this respect.

A movement has been made on Kress' to obtain similar results expected from Woolworth. We are requesting that the students will fully Support these movements. However, we also request that no students shall go over the heads of the committee and start another such movement in that we must concentrate our efforts toward breaking down these places and we're certain that with success, the others will eventually fall in line.

As much as we desire the full cooperation of all students, we must insist that we show *no violence* under any circumstances. The insults received cannot harm us in anyway and any assault on any student will be dealt with immediately by the police department who have promised that there will be protection for *ALL* persons with no partisanship. We are asking that you will take no weapons with you such as knives, etc., but a Bible in its place.

The agitators who are heckling our group now are organized primarily for the purpose of "picking a fight." But if this happens, all of our previous work and desire are lost. Therefore we beg that you shall completely ignore these persons and neglect the *freak* accidents. Keep a "cool" head and we're always sure of being in the right.

You are aware of the support received yesterday from the Women's College students and this is self-evidence that the Negroes *are not* alone. Let us be certain that we do not let these people down as well as ourselves by losing ground in anyway.

INSTRUCTIONS

(1) Students will wear dress attire or other pertinent clothing. (Young ladies are urged to look their best and gentlemen wear ties).
(2) All students going down will report to the Library dispatcher so as to make certain that we do not become so crowded until we hinder the stores businesses.
(3) If the persons who arrive later or after the first shift has come, they will seek to relieve those who desire to be; if not, they will quietly check with the spokesman and then leave quietly.
(4) At no time will we fight back with words or physically, but will do so by our sitting.

We must remember that we are now well known in the eyes of the world and we must do nothing to hurt the chances of the minority races nor rob the people who sympathize with us of the loyal support they are giving us.

Again we may strongly advocate, NO VIOLENCE NOR DRINKING WHILE WE ARE DOWN TOWN OR IN THE EYES OF THE PUBLIC. We know that we will receive your loyal support in our drive for justice and we hope that you will weigh this letter carefully and cooperate fully.

STUDENTS EXECUTIVE COMMITTEE

Source 9 from March 1960 leaflet, "Wanted: Picketers". Records of the Office of Chancellor - William B. Aycock Series (#40020), University Archives, Wilson Library, University of North Carolina at Chapel Hill.

9. Guidelines to Prospective Demonstrators, UNC-Chapel Hill.

PICKETING
WHY we picket—

WE DO NOT PICKET
. . . .just because we want to eat. We can eat at home or walking down the street.
. . . .just because students in many other cities are picketing.
. . . .to express our anger or resentment at anyone.
. . . .to humiliate or put anyone out of business.

WE DO PICKET
. . . .to protest the lack of dignity and respect shown us as human beings.
. . . .to enlist the support of all (whatever their color) in getting services in business places that will grant us dignity and respect.
. . . .to help the businessman make changes that will bring us closer to the Christian and Democratic practices.

WHO can picket—
We welcome picketers of any race, high school age and beyond, ONLY if they agree THAT UNDER NO CIRCUMSTANCES will they resort to violence.
We will use picketers ONLY if they agree to go through a short course of instruction on picketing.
Picketing will be done at stated hours and days decided by the Executive Committee and under the direction of a Picket Captain, trained for this work. Picketers must promise to obey the captain at all times.

REMEMBER – the teachings of Jesus, who, "when reviled, reviled no again."

SOME DOs AND DON'Ts FOR PICKETERS

DO. . . .
. . . .walk slowly and quietly—at least four feet apart.
. . . .be careful to let anyone who wishes to enter the place of business do so.
. . . .refer all incidents or jostling, abuse by word, or anything of this nature to the picket captain.
. . . .be on time at the place set by the picket captain.
. . . .leave the place of picketing promptly on being relieved.

DON'T. . . .

. . . .be boisterous, laugh or joke with other picketers or by-standers.

. . . .hold conversation with by-standers or business owner.

. . . .block the entrance or make it difficult for people to enter the business.

. . . .come to the picket line without being neatly dressed.

. . . .answer insult with insult, argument with argument, blow with blow, anger with anger.

REMEMBER—the example and teachings of Martin Luther King who refused to hate anyone, but stood in love and firmness for human dignity and respect.

Source 10 accessed through the Library of Congress. Copyright © 1960 and 1963, Ludlow Music Company, Inc., New York City, New York.

10. We Shall Overcome (Song Lyrics).

"We Shall Overcome" was a protest song that traces to early twentieth-century gospel music. During the 1950s and 1960s, it became a signal anthem of the Civil Rights Movement. The verses changed over time and sometimes varied according to the needs of the demonstrators singing it. The song title was famously invoked by President Lyndon Johnson when he addressed Congress in March 1965, after the bloody violence in Selma, Alabama, and as he called for the passage of the Voting Rights Act.[14]

"We Shall Overcome"
We shall overcome,
We shall overcome,
We shall overcome some day,
Oh, deep in my heart I do believe
We shall overcome some day.
We'll walk hand in hand,
We'll walk hand in hand,
We'll walk hand in hand some day,
Oh, deep in my heart I do believe
We shall overcome some day.
The truth will make us free, the truth will make us free,
The truth will make us free some day.

14. You can listen to these songs through the PBS "Eyes on the Prize" website at http://www.pbs.org/wgbh/amex/eyesontheprize/story/05_riders.html#music.

Oh, deep in my heart I do believe
We shall overcome some day.
The Lord will see us through, the Lord will see us through,
The Lord will see us through some day some day.
Oh, deep in my heart I do believe
We shall overcome some day.
We shall overcome, we shall overcome,
We shall overcome some day.
Oh, deep in my heart I do believe
We shall overcome some day.
We shall live in peace, we shall live in peace,
We shall live in peace some day,
Oh, deep in my heart I do believe
We shall overcome some day.
We are not afraid, we are not afraid,
We are not afraid today,
Oh, deep in my heart I do believe
We shall overcome some day.
The whole wide world around, the whole wide world around,
The whole wide world around some day,
Oh, deep in my heart I do believe
We shall overcome some day.

Source 11 from *The New York Times*, "Carolina College Students Fight Woolworth Ban on Lunch Counter Service," p. 22. Copyright © February 3, 1960 *The New York Times*.

11. "Carolina College Students Fight Woolworth Ban on Lunch Counter Service," *The New York Times*, February 3, 1960, page 22.

NEGROES IN SOUTH IN STORE SITDOWN

Carolina College Students Fight Woolworth Ban on Lunch Counter Service

GREENSBORO, N. C., Feb. 2 (UPI)—A group of well-dressed Negro college students staged a sitdown strike in a downtown Woolworth store today and vowed to continue it in relays until Negroes were served at the lunch counter.

"We believe since we buy books and papers in the other part of the store we should get served in this part," said the spokesman for the group.

The store manager, C. L. Harris, commented:

"They can just sit there. It's nothing to me."

He declined to say whether it was the policy of the store not to serve Negroes.

The Negroes, students at North Carolina Agricultural and Technical College here, arrived shortly after 10 A. M. and sat at two sections of the lunch counter.

At 12:30 P. M. the group filed out of the store and stood on the sidewalk in this city's busiest downtown street. They formed a tight circle, threw their hands into a pyramid in the center and recited the Lord's Prayer.

The spokesman said that "another shift" of students would carry forward the strike and it would continue "until we get served". . . .

Source 12 from *The New York Times*, "Raleigh is 6th Carolina City Affected – Student Action May Spread Here," p. 22. Copyright © February 11, 1960 *The New York Times*.

12. "Raleigh Is 6th Carolina City Affected," *The New York Times*, February 11, 1960, page 22.

NEGROES EXTEND STORE PICKETING

Raleigh is 6th Carolina City Affected—Student Action May Spread Here

RALEIGH, N.C., Feb. 10—Negro student demonstrations against segregated lunch counters spread today to variety stores in this state capital. It is the sixth North Carolina city to be affected.

There were no major incidents. But eggs were tossed at demonstrators at one store here. Another closed after a crowd of white onlookers had become unruly.

Officials expressed fear that the movement might build up to violence, which would mar the state's tradition of even racial relations. Some called for an end to the protest, while others urged legal action against the college students.

The chief targets of the movement appeared to be two national variety chains, S. H. Kress & Co. and F. W. Woolworth & Co.

Gordon R. Carey, field secretary for the Congress for Racial Equality, said his organization had been negotiating with the headquarters of the two concerns in New York in behalf of the students.

A New York store of each chain will likely be picketed Saturday unless satisfactory agreements are reached, he said.

Mr. Carey said the movement would spread to other North Carolina cities and also to Virginia and South Carolina. He said students planned to appear at stores in High Point, N. C., tomorrow.

Officials of the congress, an anti-segregation group founded in 1942 at the University of Chicago, and Negro student leaders of various colleges contended that the movement started spontaneously Feb. 2 in Greensboro.

The congress took part in a similar protest last year in Miami, Fla. The store on which it had concentrated finally removed its counter facilities.

The Greensboro protest was called off last Saturday night by students at the college after a bomb threat at the Woolworth store. Another bomb threat was reported at a Durham high school.

However students from other Negro schools continued "sit-in, stand-in" demonstrations at lunch counters in Fayetteville, Winston-Salem, Durham, Charlotte and Raleigh.

They were refused service at all the downtown variety stores and soda fountains in the six cities. Most stores immediately closed their lunch counters when the Negroes appeared, and a few closed their doors.

However, students continued to file in and out of the open stores in relays to sit or stand quietly at the counters. Shortly after the demonstrations developed here today, Mayor William G. Enloe issued a statement deploring the possible effects on the city's reputation.

"It is regrettable that some of our young Negro students would risk endangering Raleigh's friendly and cooperative race relations by seeking to change a long-standing custom in a manner that is all but destined to fail," he said.

Malcolm B. Seawell, State Attorney General, said the students' actions "pose a serious threat to the peace and good order in the communities in which they occur."

While there is no state law requiring segregation in eating establishments, he added, "the right of the owner of a private business to sell or to refuse to sell customers has been recognized by our [State] Supreme Court."

Negroes from Shaw University and St. Augustine's College trooped into Fayetteville Street at mid-morning. They fanned out into variety and drug stores, which shut their eating facilities.

While a group sat at a counter in a variety store, a sullen crowd of white youths gathered outside.

Some whites entered the store and began shoving the manager and his assistants. One struggled briefly with a newspaper photographer.

The store then closed and the whites and Negroes moved to another next door.

Hands-Off Policy

Spokesmen for Woolworth and Kress said here yesterday it was company policy to leave decisions to service to local mangers.

Thomas J. Mullen of Woolworth said:

"Local discretion is governing the question of closing the lunch counters. We cannot interfere with local customs."

Karl H. Helfrich, public relations director for Kress, commented:

"Our policy must abide by customs of the local community. We cannot be the leaders in a change of customs."

He said he had met "cordially" with representatives of the Committee for Racial Equality and explained the company's policy.

Source 13 from *The New York Times*, "Negroes Sitdowns Stirs Fear of Wider Unrest in South," p. 1. Copyright © Feburary 15, 1960 *The New York Times*.

13. "Negro Sitdowns Stirs Fear of Wider Unrest in South," *The New York Times*, February 15, 1960, page 1.

NEGRO SITDOWNS STIRS FEAR OF WIDER UNREST IN SOUTH

CHARLOTTE, N.C., Feb. 14—Negro student demonstrations against segregated eating facilities have raised grave questions in the South over the future of the region's race relations. A sounding of opinion in the affected areas showed that much more might be involved than the matter of the Negro's right to sit at a lunch counter for a coffee break.

The demonstrations were generally dismissed at first as another college fad of the "panty-raid" variety. This opinion lost adherents, however, as the movement spread from North Carolina to Virginia, Florida, South Carolina and Tennessee and involved fifteen cities.

Some whites wrote off the episodes as the work of "outside agitators." But even they conceded that the seeds of dissent had fallen in fertile soil.

Backed by Negro Leaders

Appeals from white leaders to leaders in the Negro community to halt the demonstrations bore little fruit. Instead of the hoped-for statements of disapproval, many Negro professionals expressed support for the demonstrators.

A handful of white students joined the protests. And several state organizations endorsed it. Among them were the North Carolina Council on Human Relations, an inter-racial group, and the Unitarian Fellowship for Social Justice, which currently has an all-white membership. Students of race relations in the area contended that the movement reflected the growing dissatisfaction over the slow pace of desegregation in schools and other public facilities.

It demonstrated, they said, a determination to wipe out the last vestiges of segregation.

Moreover, these persons saw a shift of leadership to younger, more militant Negroes. This, they said, is likely to bring increasing use of passive resistance. The technique was conceived by Mohandas K. Gandhi of India and popularized among Southern Negroes by the Rev. Dr. Martin Luther King Jr. He led the bus boycott in Montgomery, Ala. He now leads the Southern Christian Leadership Conference, a Negro minister's group, which seeks to end discrimination. . . .

There was general agreement on all sides that a sustained attempt to achieve desegregation now, particularly in the Deep South, might breed racial conflict that the region's expanding economy could ill afford.

The spark that touched off the protests was provided by four freshmen at North Carolina Agricultural and Technical College in Greensboro. Even Negroes class Greensboro as one of the most progressive cities in the South in terms of race relations. . . .

[*The story then turns to interviews conducted with Joseph McNeil and Franklin McCain, who recounted their experiences in Greensboro.*]

. . . The four students sat, coffee-less, until the store closed at 5:30 P. M. then, hearing that they might be prosecuted, they went to the executive committee of the Greensboro N. A. A. C. P. to ask advice.

"This was our first knowledge of the demonstration," said Dr. George C. Simkins, who is president of the organization. He said that he had then written to the New York headquarters of the Congress of Racial Equality, which is known as CORE. He requested assistance for the demonstrators, who numbered in the hundreds during the following days.

Dr. Simkins, a dentist, explained that he had heard of a successful attempt, led by CORE, to desegregate a Baltimore restaurant and had read one of the organization's pamphlets. CORE's field secretary, Gordon R. Carey, arrived from New York on Feb. 7. He said that he had assisted Negro students in some North Carolina cities after they had initiated the protests. The Greensboro demonstrations and the others that it triggered were spontaneous, according to Mr. Carey. All of the Negroes questioned agreed on this.

The movement's chief targets were two national variety chains, S. H. Kress & Co. and the F. W. Woolworth Company. Other chains were affected. In some cities the students demonstrated at local stores. The protests generally followed similar patterns. Young men and women and, in one case, high school boys and girls, walked into the stores and requested food service. Met with refusals in all cases, they remained at the lunch counters in silent protest. . . .

The demonstrations attracted crowds of whites. At first the hecklers were youths with duck-tailed haircuts. Some carried small Confederate battle flags. Later they were joined by older men in faded khakis and overalls.

The Negro youths were challenged to step outside and fight. Some of the remarks to the girls were jesting in nature, such as, "How about a date when we integrate?" Other remarks were not.

Negro Knocked Down

In a few cases the Negroes were elbowed, jostled and shoved. Itching powder was sprinkled on them and they were spattered with eggs.

At Rock Hill, S. C., a Negro youth was knocked from a stool by a white beside whom he sat. A bottle of ammonia was hurled through the store of a drug store there. The fumes brought tears to the eyes of the demonstrators.

The only arrests reported involved forty-three of the demonstrators. They were seized on a sidewalk outside a Woolworth store at a Raleigh shopping center. Charged with trespassing, they posted $50 bonds and were released.

The management of the shopping center contended that the sidewalk was private property.

In most cases, the demonstrators sat or stood at store counters talking in low voice, studying or starting impassively at their tormenters. There was little joking or smiling, now and then a girl giggled nervously. Some carried bibles.

Those at Rock Hill were described by the local newspaper, The Evening Herald, as "orderly, polite, well-dressed and quiet." . . .

Source 14 from "Southern Moderates Fearful Sitdowns Endanger Negro Gains," in *The Washington Post*, February 29, 1960, copyright © 1960 *The Washington Post*.

14. "Southern Moderates Fearful Sitdowns Endanger Negro Gains," *Washington Post*, February 29, 1960.

SOUTHERN MODERATES FEARFUL SITDOWNS ENDANGER NEGRO GAINS

ATLANTA, Feb. 28—The spread of the sitdown movement to the Deep South was viewed with apprehension today by Southern moderates.

Spokesmen for the moderate point of view on race relations fear that the sitdown demonstrations in Montgomery, Ala., last week may jeopardize the progress being made toward school desegregation.

It also is feared that further demonstrations in the Deep South may lead to much more serious violence than the skirmishing between white and Negro youths that has erupted in some areas.

Some Alabama segregationists are reported, on the other hand, to be eager for a showdown with Negro college students who are seeking to be served at lunch counters where only whites are now allowed to sit down and eat.

Further demonstrations are expected today in Montgomery. There are reports, too, that a sitdown is being organized in Birmingham, Ala., which is a stronghold of segregationist sentiment.

Negro students in Atlanta have considered staging a sitdown, but so far have been dissuaded from taking action by leaders of the Negro community who believe that a demonstration here would be a severe setback to the efforts now under way to desegregate the Atlanta schools.

Harold Flemings, executive director of the Southern Regional Council, noted today that the sitdown demonstrations have become much more than an economic matter now that they have been staged in the Deep South.

Fleming and other Southern moderates look upon the demonstrations as a protest against the slow progress being made in the desegregation of schools, in the expansion of employment opportunities for Negroes and delay in the enactment of civil rights legislation.

The moderates believe that a Southern filibuster in the Senate against legislation protecting the right of Negroes to vote will only goad the student demonstrators into taking new action.

Although the sitdown movement is only a month old, demonstrations have already been held in 23 cities in North Carolina, Virginia, South Carolina, Tennessee, Florida and now Alabama. They began in Greensboro, N. C., on Feb. 1.

The movement has spread so quickly that none of the Negro organizations has even been able to coordinate the demonstrations, which have been directed against variety or dime stores operated by national chains.

As the Southern Regional Council noted in a report on the movement it made public Saturday, it has been "spontaneous and contagious."

Fleming said that the Negro students have resisted adult direction of the movement. This resistance is widely considered to be a manifestation of the impatience of Southern youths with the slow progress in the adjudication of civil rights questions. . . .

. . . The Rev. Martin Luther King, the Negro minister who led the successful bus boycott in Montgomery four years ago, is looked upon as the spiritual American father of the sitdown demonstrations, which are traced further to the passive resistance philosophy of India's Gandhi.

Although the Rev. Mr. King has made speeches in North Carolina in support of the sitdown movement, neither he nor his Southern Christian Leadership Council has succeeded in taking over the leadership of the demonstrations.

Some Negro leaders are talking about organizing boycotts against the variety stores, and in Winston-Salem, N. C., 300 Negroes decided on Saturday to urge other members of their race not to patronize the stores where they are not allowed to sit down and eat.

Boycotts are difficult to conduct, it is pointed out, and many of the Negroes need the stores as much as the stores need trade from the Negro community.

Negro leaders are aware that even the highly publicized Montgomery bus boycott did not break down desegregation on the buses. It was a U.S. Supreme Court decision which finally ended segregation on Montgomery buses.

Source 15 courtesy of Jack Moebes, CORBIS.

15. Left to right, David Richmond, Franklin McCain, Ezell Blair, Jr., Joseph McNeil, Greensboro, February 1960.

Jack Moebes/CORBIS

16. Students at the Greensboro Woolworth's Lunch Counter, including Joseph McNeil and Franklin McCain (First and Second from Left), February 1960.

Jack Moebes/Corbis

Source 17 courtesy of Gerald Holly/*The Tennessean*.

17. Nashville Students at the Previously Segregated Greyhound Terminal Lunch Counter, Including Diane Nash (Third from Left), May 1960.

Gerald Holly/The Tennessean

Source 18 courtesy of AP Photo/Chuck Burton.

18. Joseph McNeil, Jibreel Khazan (formerly Ezell Blair, Jr.), Franklin McCain, and David Richmond at the Woolworth's Lunch Counter, 1990.

AP Images/Chuck Burton

Source 19 courtesy of Smithsonian/Getty images.

19. Monument to Greensboro Four, North Carolina A&T University, Unveiled February 1, 2001.

Smithsonian/Getty images

◆

Questions to Consider

To gain a deeper understanding of this phase of the Civil Rights Movement and to understand what changes students sought in the Civil Rights Movement and why, you must appreciate the context in which the protests occurred. Review the documents for clues about the background and motivations of the student sit-ins.

What laws were the students challenging? Why did they challenge those laws in this particular way? Why did they follow some laws and rules—restricting the number of protestors so as to not impede sales, for example—and ignore others? What was different about their challenge to segregation laws from that of national organizations such as the NAACP?

How important was Christianity to the student-led sit-ins? In what ways did religious faith shape their campaign for desegregation?

What impact did class, locale, and stage of life exert in the student campaign? What role did black students from outside the South, including Diane Nash and Joseph McNeil, play in shaping the campaigns? Does it matter that the protests occurred in cities with black colleges and universities, while the majority of African Americans lived in rural regions of the South? How might the perspective of these students—mostly middle class and well educated—have been different from the perspectives of working-class and poor black southerners? How might the college experience shape ideals and activism? What generational

tensions do you observe in the evidence? Why would college students see segregation in a different light than their parents and other adults?

How would you describe the students themselves? How did they physically conduct themselves at the sit-ins? What did they reveal about themselves in their music and organizational literature? What were they conveying with that presentation of self?

Now locate the 1960 student sit-ins in the context of the struggle against segregation and compare their campaign to other parts of the Civil Rights Movement. What were the students' philosophical beliefs? Why and how did they adhere to nonviolence? What did nonviolence achieve? What were its limitations? Why and how did students practice direct action? What did they achieve by this approach? What were its limitations?

What events and ideas shaped the values and attitudes of the students? How important was Gandhi, Martin Luther King, the Cold War, Little Rock, and Montgomery? How important were existing national organizations, including the NAACP and SCLC? What did the students think about the NAACP, Dr. King and the SCLC, and southern "moderates"? What does this tell you about the politics of civil rights activism in 1960?

The student sit-ins caught national leaders in the Civil Rights Movement by surprise. How did leaders within the mainstream Civil Rights Movement respond to the student sit-ins? How did southern whites respond? What about the national news media? What did the reactions—from civil rights leaders, white liberals, both black and white locals, and the national press—reveal about the student campaign? Overall, in what ways did the student campaign differ from other, earlier desegregation efforts? What parts of the earlier Civil Rights Movement did the students adopt? What did they reject? How did the student sit-ins change the struggle for civil rights in America?

What challenges did the student movement pose to established institutions (local police, mayors and civic leaders, governors of states, and federal officials)? How did the students' tactics challenge and expand government's role in guarding citizens' rights?

Once you have understood what changes students sought in the Civil Rights Movement and why, turn to a final issue: historical memory of this

pivotal moment in U.S. history. When they were interviewed, what did the former student leaders stress as important to remember? Why did they say they participated in the movement? Do you think their opinions would have changed over time? If so, why and in what ways? Here it might be useful to compare the picture taken at Woolworth's in 1960 (Source 16) with the photograph of the Greensboro Four taken in 1990 (Source 18).

Now move from personal memory to collective memory. Why do we as a society commemorate certain events and people and not others? What does the statue of the Greensboro Four (Source 19), which was based on a photograph of the men taken in 1960 (Source 15), convey about the collective memory of the Greensboro sit-ins? What important parts of the story does it *not* tell? What parts of the Civil Rights Movement do we as a nation honor? What parts do we ignore?

Epilogue

None of the Greensboro Four moved into national leadership positions in the Civil Rights Movement. Ezell Blair, Jr. (now Jibreel Khazan) became an educator, and lives in New Bedford, Massachusetts. Joseph McNeil retired from the Air Force Reserve at the rank of Major General, and he enjoyed a distinguished career in finance. Franklin McCain worked as a chemist, and spent most of his career in Charlotte, North Carolina. He served

on the board of trustees for both North Carolina A&T and Bennett College before his death in January 2014. Unlike his three friends, David Richmond did not graduate from A&T, and he alone stayed in Greensboro, where resentment for his activism cast a long shadow. He struggled to find employment, and died in 1990 at the age of forty-nine—but not before the four friends commemorated the thirtieth anniversary of their famous campaign (Source 18). The portion of the Woolworth's counter where they sat is now housed at the Smithsonian Institution in Washington, D.C.

Several of the Greensboro Four's peers did emerge as national figures, most notably U.S. congressman John Lewis. Raised in poverty in Pike County, Alabama, Lewis was a scholarship student at American Baptist Theological Seminary in 1960 when he joined Diane Nash, C. T. Vivian, and others in leading the Nashville student protest movement. Lewis went on to organize the Freedom Rides that began in 1961. His bus was firebombed by the KKK and he was brutally beaten. He also served as chairman of SNCC, and at the age of twenty-three he was the youngest person to speak at the 1963 March on Washington, in which Dr. Martin Luther King, Jr., gave his famous "I Have a Dream" speech. In 1965, Lewis suffered a fractured skull while being beaten on the Edmund Pettus Bridge, during the Selma, Alabama, campaign for voting rights.

The student protests launched in 1960 redefined the Civil Rights Movement. Sit-ins, wade-ins (at public pools), kneel-ins (at segregated churches), and similar protests spread across the South and the nation. The student movement laid the foundation for Freedom Summer, when, in 1964, over one thousand volunteers, mostly college students, both black and white, moved to Mississippi to create Freedom Schools and register black voters. They were joined by doctors, who provided poor children with medical care, and lawyers, who waged the fight for racial equality in the state courts. Mississippi

convulsed. Hundreds of young people were arrested, scores were brutally beaten, and at least three—James Chaney, Andrew Goodman, and Michael Schwerner—were murdered in Mississippi that summer. The television networks carried it all on the nightly news.

The student movement against segregation also had a profound effect on this generation of Americans. Their tactics were adopted by opponents of the Vietnam War, feminists, leaders of the American Indian Movement (AIM), and waves of New Left groups. That young people designed and populated these movements gave that generation a distinct identity and a powerful voice in civic life.

It is a complicated matter to assess the success of the student campaign for civil rights. In many regards, the mid-1960s, when student protests were most pervasive and effective, marked the zenith of the Civil Rights Movement. In spite of all the violence, the 1963 March on Washington, the 1964 Civil Rights Act, and the 1965 Voting Rights Act seemed to fulfill a century-long quest for black equality. Exactly one hundred years after the end of slavery, the U.S. federal government finally, officially rejected the idea that African Americans were second-class citizens. And yet civil rights did not ensure equality. De facto segregation continued, as did economic disparities, educational inequities, and racial discrimination.

The mainstream movement, centered around Dr. King and the philosophy of nonviolent direct action, was met by brutal violence, and not just the fire hoses in Birmingham and the rocks and clubs in Selma. Murder became an all-too-frequently employed political tactic. Medgar Evers, the NAACP field secretary, was gunned down outside his Mississippi home on June 12, 1963, the same summer as the March on Washington. Two weeks after the March on Washington, on a Sunday morning, a bomb ripped through the Sixteenth Street Baptist Church in Birmingham, Alabama, killing four girls and deeply wounding the appeal of the nonviolent movement. President Kennedy was assassinated that November in Dallas. Malcolm X was murdered in February 1965. Robert Kennedy was shot and killed in June of 1968, while campaigning for the presidency.

By the mid-1960s, Black Power, with its focus on African American self-reliance and encouragement of self-defense increasingly resonated with young African Americans who were tired of acting passively while they were being brutalized and frustrated by the slow pace of social change.[15] Huey Newton and Bobby Seale founded the Black Panthers in Oakland, California, in 1966. That same year Stokely Carmichael, a new leader in SNCC, promoted Black Power within that organization and broadened its focus to include antiwar activism. SNCC changed its name in 1969 to the Student National Coordinating Committee. Movement leaders also increasingly moved their campaigns north, to fight slums and ghettos and redress economic disparities. While

King's SCLC also expanded its agenda, the organization remained resolute in its passive resistance philosophy, even in the darkest days of the movement.

The assassination of Martin Luther King, Jr., on April 4, 1968, spawned riots in over one hundred American cities. The night before he died Dr. King gave what, in retrospect, many considered a prophetic last public address to an audience in Memphis:

"Well, I don't know what will happen now. We've got some difficult days ahead. But it doesn't matter with me now. Because I've been to the mountaintop. And I don't mind. Like anybody, I would like to live a long life. Longevity has its place. But I'm not concerned about that now. I just want to do God's will. And He's allowed me to go up to the mountain. And I've looked over. And I've seen the promised land. I may not get there with you. But I want you to know tonight, that we, as a people, will get to the promised land. And I'm happy, tonight. I'm not worried about anything. I'm not fearing any man. Mine eyes have seen the glory of the coming of the Lord."

King was shot just after 6:00 p.m. the next evening, as he stood on the balcony of the Lorraine Motel.[16] Though the SCLC continued its efforts under the leadership of Reverend Ralph Abernathy, the movement became increasingly fragmented. The election of Richard Nixon and escalation of the Vietnam War diverted national attention from civil rights, as did antiwar activism.

15. To see how this played out in rural Alabama, see Hasan Kwane Jeffries, *Bloody Lowndes: Civil Rights and Black Power in Alabama's Black Belt* (New York: New York University Press, 2009).

16. The Lorraine Motel is now the site of the National Civil Rights Museum.

On August 28, 2008, on the forty-fifth anniversary of Dr. King's address at the 1963 March on Washington, Barack Obama accepted the Democratic Party nomination for president. On January 20, 2009, Obama was sworn in as the forty-fourth president of the United States. John Lewis sat on the stage. Historians, including those who disagreed with the Democratic president's policies and opposed his candidacy, generally agreed that President Obama's election held great historical meaning: it signified a turning point in the nation's long, fraught racial history and was an event in which all Americans could take pride.

But scholars are also quick to caution that the election (and 2012 reelection) of an African American president did not mark the end of the country's centuries-long troubling history with racial discrimination and violence. In the summer and fall of 2014, protests yet again arose in many cities across the United States, prompted by the deaths of unarmed African American men in Ferguson, Missouri, and New York City at the hands of police officers who were exonerated of all criminal wrongdoing. The mass incarceration of people of color, a vast and widening wealth gap between black and white families, and persistent inequities in public education all remain of great concern to U.S. citizens committed to civil rights and social justice.

A Generation in War and Turmoil: The Agony of Vietnam

◆

The Problem

When the middle-class readers of *Time* magazine went to their mailboxes in January 1967, they were eager to find out who the widely read newsmagazine had chosen as "Man of the Year." To their surprise, they discovered that the "inheritors"—the whole generation of young people under twenty-five years of age—had been selected as the major newsmakers of the previous year. *Time*'s publisher justified the selection of an entire generation by noting that, in contrast to the previous "silent generation," the young people of the late 1960s were dominating history with their distinctive lifestyles, music, and beliefs about the future of the United States.

Those who wrote to the editor about this issue ranged from a writer who thought the selection was a long-overdue honor to one who called it an "outrageous choice," from a correspondent who described contemporary young people as "one of our best generations" to one who believed the choice of a generation was "eloquent nonsense." Furthermore, many writers

were frightened or worried about their children, and some middle-aged correspondents insisted that they themselves belonged to the "put-upon" or "beaten" generation.

There is no doubt that there was a generation gap in the late 1960s, a kind of sharp break between the new generation of young people comprising nearly half the population and their parents. The first segment of the so-called baby-boom generation came to adulthood during the mid- to late 1960s,[1] a time marked by the high point of the civil rights movement, the rise of a spirit of rebellion on college campuses, and a serious division over the U.S. participation in the Vietnam War. For most baby boomers, white and black alike, the war was the issue that

1. Although the birthrate began to climb during World War II (from 19.4 births per one thousand in 1940 to 24.5 per one thousand in 1945), the term *baby boom* generally is used to describe the increase in the birthrate between 1946 and the early 1960s.

concerned them most immediately, for this was the generation that would be called on to fight or to watch as friends, spouses, or lovers were called to military service.

Your tasks in this chapter include identifying and interviewing at least one member of the baby-boom generation (preferably born between 1946 and 1956)[2] about his or her experiences during the Vietnam War era. Then, using your interview, along with those of your classmates and those provided in the Evidence section of this chapter, determine the ways in which the baby-boom generation reacted to the Vietnam War. **On what issues did baby boomers agree? On what issues did they disagree? Finally, how can a study of people of the same generation help historians understand a particular era in the past?**

✦

Background

The year 1945 was the beginning of one of the longest sustained economic booms in American history. Interrupted only a few times by brief recessions, the boom lasted from 1945 to 1973. And although there were still pockets of severe poverty in America's deteriorating inner cities and in some rural areas such as Appalachia, most Americans had good cause to be optimistic about their economic situations.

The pent-up demand of the Depression and war years broke like a tidal wave that swept nearly every economic indicator upward. Veterans returning from World War II rapidly made the transition to the civilian work force or used the GI Bill to become better educated and, as a result, secure better jobs than they had held before the war. Between 1950 and 1960, real wages increased by 20 percent, and disposable family income rose by a staggering 49 percent. The number of registered automobiles more than doubled between 1945 and 1955, and the American automobile industry was virtually unchallenged by foreign competition. At the same time, new home construction soared, as thirteen million new homes were built in the 1950s alone—85 percent of them in the new and mushrooming suburbs.[3]

New homes were financed by new types of long-term mortgage loans that required only a small down payment (5 to 10 percent) and low monthly payments (averaging $56 per month for a tract house in the suburbs). And these new homes required furniture and

2. A person born during the late 1950s to early 1960s would technically be considered a baby boomer but would probably have been too young to remember enough to make an interview useful.

3. There were 114,000 housing starts in 1944. In 1950, housing starts had climbed to nearly 1.7 million.

appliances, which led to sharp upturns in these industries. Between 1945 and 1950, the amount spent on household furnishings and appliances increased 240 percent, and most of these items were bought "on time" (that is, on installment plans).[4] Perhaps the most coveted appliance was a television set, a product that had been almost non-existent before the war. In 1950 alone, 7.4 million television sets were sold in the United States, and architects began designing homes with a "family room," a euphemism for a room where television was watched.

This new postwar lifestyle could best be seen in America's burgeoning suburbs. Populated to a large extent by new members of the nation's mush-rooming middle class, suburbanites for the most part were better educated, wealthier, and more optimistic than their parents had been. Most men com-muted by train, bus, or automobiles back to the center city to work, while their wives remained in the suburbs, having children and raising them. It was in these suburbs that a large per-centage of baby boomers were born.

Sociologist William H. Whyte called America's postwar suburbs the "new melting pot," a term that referred to the expectation that new middle-class suburbanites should leave their various class and ethnic character-istics behind in the cities they had abandoned and become homogeneous. Men were expected to work their way up the corporate ladder, tend their carefully manicured lawns, become accomplished barbecue chefs, and serve their suburban communities as Boy Scout leaders or Little League coaches. For their part, women were expected to make favorable impres-sions on their husbands' bosses (to aid their husbands in their climb up the corporate ladder), provide trans-portation for the children to accepted after-school activities (scouts, athlet-ics, music and dance lessons), and make a happy home for the family's breadwinner. Above all, the goal was to fit in with their suburban neighbors. Thus suburbanites would applaud the 1956 musical *My Fair Lady*, which was based on the premise that working-class flower seller Eliza Doolittle would be accepted by "polite society" as soon as she learned to speak properly.

The desire for homogeneity or con-formity would have a less beneficial side as well. The Cold War and the McCarthy era meant that the demand for homogeneity could be enforced by the threat of job loss and ostracism. In addition, many suburban women had met their husbands in college and hence had had at least some col-lege education.[5] But the expectation that they be primarily wives and mothers often meant that they were

---

4. Between 1946 and 1956, short-term con-sumer credit rose from $8.4 billion to almost $45 billion, most of it to finance automobiles and home furnishings. The boom in credit card purchases ("plastic money") did not occur until the 1960s.

5. One mid-western women's college boasted that "a high proportion of our graduates marry successfully," as if that was the chief reason for women to go to college in the first place. Indeed, in many cases it was. See Elaine Tyler May, *Homeward Bound: Ameri-can Families in the Cold War Era* (New York: Basic Books, 1988), p. 83.

discouraged from using their education in other ways. As a result, one survey of suburban women revealed that 11 percent of them felt that they experienced a "great deal of emotional disturbance." At the same time, men were expected to be good corporate citizens and good team players at work. It was rumored that IBM employees began each day by gathering together, facing the home office, and singing the praises of IBM and its executive vice president C. A. Kirk (to the tune of "Carry Me Back to Old Virginny"):

> Ever we praise our able leaders,
> And our progressive C. A. Kirk is one of them,
> He is endowed with the will to go forward,
> He'll always work in the cause of IBM.

Finally, homogeneity meant that suburbanites would have to purchase new cars, furniture, television sets, and so on, to be like their neighbors (it was called "keeping up with the Joneses"), even though monthly payments already were stretching a family's income pretty thin.

There was an underside to the so-called affluent society. Indeed, many Americans did not share in its benefits at all. As middle-class whites fled to the suburbs, conditions in the cities deteriorated. Increasingly populated by the poor—African Americans, Latin American immigrants, the elderly, and unskilled white immigrants—urban areas struggled to finance essential city services such as police and fire protection. Poverty and its victims could also be found in rural areas, as Michael Harrington pointed out in his classic study *The Other America*,

published in 1962. Small farmers, tenants, sharecroppers, and migrant workers not only were poor but often lacked any access to even basic educational opportunities and health care facilities.

Young people who lacked the money or who were not brought up with the expectation of earning a college degree tended to continue in more traditional life patterns. They completed their education with high school or before, although some attended a local vocationally oriented community college or trade school for a year or two. They often married younger than their college counterparts, sought stable jobs, and aspired to own their own homes. In other words, they rarely rejected the values of their parents' generation.

The baby boomers began leaving the suburbs for college in the early 1960s. Once away from home and in a college environment, many of these students began questioning their parents' values, especially those concerned with materialism, conformity, sexual mores and traditional sex roles, corporate structure and power, and the kind of patriotism that could support the growing conflict in Vietnam. In one sense, they were seeking the same thing that their parents had sought: fulfillment. Yet to the baby boomers, their parents had chased false gods and a false kind of fulfillment. Increasingly alienated by impersonal university policies and by the actions of authority figures such as college administrators, political leaders, and police officers, many students turned to new forms of religion, music, and dress and to the use of drugs to set themselves apart from the older generation. The term *generation gap* could be heard across the American land-scape as bewildered, hurt, and angry parents confronted their children, who (in the parents' view) had "gotten everything." Nor could the children seem to communicate to their confused parents how bankrupt they believed their parents' lives and values actually were. In the midst of this generational crisis, the Vietnam War was becoming a major conflict.

The Japanese defeat of Western colonial powers, particularly Britain and France, in the early days of World War II had encouraged nationalist movements[6] in both Africa and Asia. The final surrender of Japan in 1945 left an almost total power vacuum in Southeast Asia. As Britain struggled with postwar economic dislocation and, within India, the independence movement, both the United States and the Soviet Union moved into this vacuum, hoping to influence the course of events in Asia.

Vietnam had long been a part of the French colonial empire in Southeast Asia and was known in the West as French Indochina. At the beginning of World War II, the Japanese had driven the French from the area. Under the Leadership of Vietnamese nationalist and Communist Ho Chi Minh, the Vietnamese had cooperated with American intelligence agents and fought a guerrilla-style war against the Japanese. When the Japanese were finally driven from Vietnam in 1945, Ho Chi Minh declared Vietnam independent. In his declaration, he borrowed liberally from Thomas Jefferson's "Declaration of Independence":

> All men are created equal. They are endowed by their Creator with certain inalienable rights; among them are life, liberty, and the pursuit of happiness.[7]

The Western nations, however, did not recognize this declaration. At the end of World War II, France wanted to reestablish Vietnam as a French colony. But, seriously weakened by war, France could not reassert itself in Vietnam without assistance. At this point, the United States, eager to gain France as a postwar ally and member of the North Atlantic Treaty Organization, and viewing European problems as being more immediate than problems in Asia, chose to help the French reenter Vietnam as colonial masters. From 1945 to 1954, the United States gave more than $2 billion in financial aid to France so that it could regain its former colony. U.S. aid was contingent upon the eventual development of self-government in French Indochina.

Ho Chi Minh and other Vietnamese felt that they had been betrayed. They believed that, in return for fighting against the Japanese in World War II, they would be granted their independence. Many Vietnamese viewed the reentry of France, with assistance from the United States, as a broken

6. Those in nationalist movements seek independence for their countries.

7. For the excerpt from Ho Chi Minh's declaration of independence see Mark Philip Bradley, *Vietnam at War* (Oxford, UK: Oxford University Press, 2009), quoted p. 9.

promise. Almost immediately, war broke out between the French and their westernized Vietnamese allies and the forces of Ho Chi Minh. In the Cold War atmosphere of the late 1940s and early 1950s, the United States gave massive aid to the French, who, it was maintained, were fighting against monolithic communism.

The fall of Dien Bien Phu in 1954 spelled the end of French power in Vietnam. The U.S. secretary of state, John Foster Dulles, tried hard to convince Britain and other Western allies of the need for "united action" in Southeast Asia and to avoid any use of American ground troops (as President Truman had authorized earlier in Korea). The allies were not persuaded, however. Rather than let the area fall to the Communists, President Eisenhower and his secretary of state eventually allowed the temporary division of Vietnam into two sections: South Vietnam, ruled by westernized Vietnamese formerly loyal to the French, and North Vietnam, governed by the Communist Ho Chi Minh.

Free and open elections to unify the country were to be held in 1956. However, the elections were never held because American policymakers feared that Ho Chi Minh would easily defeat the unpopular but pro-United States Ngo Dinh Diem, the U.S. choice to lead South Vietnam. From 1955 to 1960, the United States supported Diem with more than $1 billion of aid as civil war between the South Vietnamese and the Northern Vietminh (later called the Vietcong) raged across the countryside and in the villages.

President Kennedy did little to improve the situation. Facing his own Cold War problems, among them the building of the Berlin Wall and the Bay of Pigs invasion,[8] Kennedy simply poured more money and more "military advisers" (close to seventeen thousand by 1963) into the troubled country. Finally, in the face of tremendous Vietnamese pressure, the United States turned against Diem, and in 1963 South Vietnamese generals, encouraged by the Central Intelligence Agency, overthrew the corrupt and repressive Diem regime. Diem was assassinated in the fall of 1963, shortly before Kennedy's own death.

Lyndon Johnson, the Texas Democrat who succeeded Kennedy in 1963 and won election as president in 1964, was an old New Dealer[9] who wished to extend social and economic programs to needy Americans. The "tragedy" of Lyndon Johnson, as the official White House historian, Eric Goldman, saw it, was that the president was increasingly drawn into the Vietnam War. Actually, President Johnson and his military and foreign policy advisers clung to the idea that if Vietnam fell to the communists, then the rest of the Southeast Asian nations would fall one by one, like dominoes, to the communists. Thus, they believed,

8. The Berlin Wall was a barricade created to separate East Berlin (Communist) from West Berlin. The Bay of Pigs invasion was a U.S.-sponsored invasion of Cuba in April 1961 that failed. The American role was widely criticized.

9. Johnson had served in Congress during the 1930s and was a strong supporter of New Deal programs.

Vietnam was a major test of the U.S. ability to resist the spread of communism in Asia. Economist and foreign policy adviser Walt W. Rostow spoke for many when he said of Vietnam that "[it] is on this spot that we have to break the liberation war. If we don't break it here we shall have to face it again . . . .Vietnam is a clear testing ground for our policy in the world."[10]

Under Johnson, therefore, the war escalated rapidly. In 1964, the Vietcong controlled almost half of South Vietnam, and Johnson obtained sweeping powers from Congress to conduct the war as he wished. On March 8, 1965, the 9th Marine Expeditionary Brigade came ashore on the beaches north of Da Nang to meet the Vietcong, which military historian Max Boot characterized as "men of the shadows, holy warriors who wore no uniform, who shirked open battle [and] who took refuge among civilians and emerged to strike when least expected."[11] In November 1965, the U.S. Army First Cavalry Division fought the first major battle of the conflict against the North Vietnamese Army and was mauled in the thirty-four-day campaign. After a quick trip to Vietnam, Secretary of Defense Robert McNamara authored a memo to Lyndon Johnson pointing out that the United States had two options in Vietnam: (1) to withdraw "under diplomatic cover," or (2) to undertake a long war with significant American losses (one thousand per month was his estimate) with no guarantee of victory. But Johnson refused to accept McNamara's warning and increased bombing, approved the destruction of what were believed to be hiding places for the Vietcong, sprayed chemical defoliants (19.5 million gallons between 1965 and 1968) on forests, and approved Gen. William Westmoreland's request for increasing troops to over five hundred thousand American men and women by 1968.[12]

As the war effort increased, so did the doubts about it. In the mid-1960s, the chair of the Senate Foreign Relations Committee, J. William Fulbright, raised important questions about whether the Vietnam War was serving our national interest. Several members of the administration and foreign policy experts (including George Kennan, author of the original containment policy) maintained that escalation of the war could not be justified. Television news coverage of the destruction and carnage, along with reports of atrocities

---

10. Walter A. McDougall, *Promised Land, Crusader State: The American Encounter with the World Since 1776* (Boston: Houghton Mifflin, 1997), quoted p. 187.
11. The Tonkin Gulf Resolution of August 1964 gave President Johnson the power to "take all necessary measures to repel any armed attack against the forces of the United States and to prevent further aggression." On Boot's description of the Vietcong and the landing of the Marine Brigade see Max Boot, *The Savage Wars of Peace: Small Wars and the Rise of American Power* (New York: Basic Books, 2002), pp. xiv, 286–288.

12. On the Battle of Ia Drang and McNamara's memo see Lt. Gen. Harold G. Moore and Joseph L. Galloway, *We Were Soldiers Once . . . and Young—Ia Drang: The Battle that Changed the War in Vietnam* (New York: Random House, 1992), pp. xvii, 340. Years later McNamara wrote a painful confession that he should have done more to convince Johnson to end the war. For the spraying of the poisonous dioxin (which caused cancer in large numbers of Vietnamese as well as American troops) see Patrick Coffey, *American Arsenal: A Century of Waging War* (New York: Oxford University Press, 2014), pp. 238–241.

such as the My Lai massacre,[13] disillu-sioned more and more Americans. Yet Johnson continued the bombing, called for more ground troops, and offered peace terms that were completely unac-ceptable to the North Vietnamese.

Not until the Tet offensive—a coordi-nated North Vietnamese strike across all of South Vietnam in January 1968, in which the Communists temporarily captured every provincial capital and even entered Saigon (the capi-tal of South Vietnam)—did President Johnson change his mind. Two months later, Johnson appeared on national tel-evision and announced to a surprised nation that he had ordered an end to most of the bombing, asked North Vietnam to start real peace negotia-tions, and withdrawn his name from the 1968 presidential race. Although we now know that the Tet offensive was a setback for Ho Chi Minh, in the United States it was seen as a major defeat for the West, evidence that the optimistic press releases about our imminent victory simply were not true.

As the U.S. role in the Vietnam War increased, the government turned increasingly to the conscription of men for military service (the draft). Early in the war, all college men up to age twenty-six could get automatic defer-ments, which allowed them to remain in school while noncollege men (dis-proportionately poor and black) were drafted and sent to Vietnam. As the demand for men increased, however, deferments became somewhat more difficult to obtain. College students had to maintain good grades, gradu-ate student deferments were ended, and draft boards increasingly were unsympathetic to pleas for conscien-tious objector status.[14] Even so, the vast majority of college students who did not want to go to Vietnam were able to avoid doing so, principally by using one of the countless loopholes in the system such as opting for ROTC (Reserve Officers' Training Corps) duty, purposely failing physical exami-nations, getting family members to pull strings, and obtaining conscien-tious objector status. Only 12 percent of the college graduates between 1964 and 1973 served in Vietnam. Twenty-one percent of high school graduates and an even higher percentage of high school dropouts served.

As the arbitrary and unfair nature of the draft became increasingly evi-dent, President Richard Nixon finally replaced General Lewis Hershey, who had headed the Selective Service System since 1948, and instituted a new system of conscription: a lottery. In this system, all draft-age men were assigned numbers and were drafted in order from lowest to highest num-ber until the draft quota was filled. With this action, the very real threat of the draft spread to those who had previously felt relatively safe. Already divided, an entire generation had to come face to face with the Vietnam War.

13. The My Lai massacre occurred in March 1968, when American soldiers destroyed a Vietnamese village and killed many of the inhabitants, including women and children. For a recent report see Seymour M. Hersh, "The Scene of the Crime," in *The New Yorker* (March 30, 2015), pp. 52–61.

14. Conscientious objectors are those whose religious beliefs are opposed to military service, such as the Society of Friends (Quakers).

Whether by draft or lottery and whatever race or socioeconomic class, a significant majority of American troops came from the baby-boom generation. When American fighting forces were first sent to Vietnam (in 1965) eighteen-year-olds would have been born in 1947, and when American troop withdrawal took place in 1973, eighteen-year-olds would have been born in 1955. As you can see, the Vietnam War was fought primarily by baby boomers. And of the fifty-eight thousand American troops killed in Vietnam, a significant majority were twenty-three years old or younger. Interestingly, a large percentage of the opponents of the war were baby boomers too.

The Method

Historians often wish they could ask specific questions of the participants in a historical event—questions that are not answered in surviving diaries, letters, and other documents. Furthermore, many people, especially the poor, uneducated, and members of minority groups, did not leave written records and thus often are overlooked by historians.

When dealing with the comparatively recent past, however, historians do have an opportunity to ask questions by using a technique called *oral history*. Oral history—interviewing famous and not-so-famous people about their lives and the events they observed or participated in—can greatly enrich our knowledge of the past. It can help capture the "spirit of an age" as seen through the eyes of average citizens, and it often bridges the gap between impersonal forces (wars, epidemics, depressions) and personal, individual responses to them. Furthermore, oral history allows the unique to emerge from the total picture: the conscientious objector who would not serve in the army, the woman who did not marry and devote herself to raising a family, and so forth.

Oral history is both fascinating and challenging. It seems easy to do, but it is really rather difficult to do well. There is always the danger that the student may "lead" the interview by imposing his or her ideas on the subject. It is equally possible that the student may be led away from the subject by the person being interviewed.

Still other problems sometimes arise. The student may miss the subtleties in what is being said or may assume that an exceptional person is representative of many people. Some older people like to tell only the "smiling side" of their personal histories—that is, they prefer to talk about the good things that happened to them, not the bad things. Others actually forget what happened or are influenced by reading or television. Some older people cannot resist sending a message to younger people by recounting how hard it was in the past, how few luxuries they had when they were young, how far they had to walk to school, and so forth. Yet oral history, when used carefully and judiciously along with other sources, is an invaluable tool that helps historians recreate a sense of our past.

Recently, much attention has been paid—and rightly so—to protecting the rights and privacy of human subjects. For this reason, the federal government requires that an interviewee consent to the interview and be fully aware of how the interview is to be used. The interviewer must explain the purpose of the interview, and the person being interviewed must sign a release form (for one sample, see Source 1). Although these requirements are intended to apply mostly to psychologists and sociologists, historians who use oral history are included as well.

When you identify and interview an individual of the baby-boom generation, you will be speaking with a member of a *birth cohort*. A birth cohort comprises those people born within a few years of one another who form a historical generation. Members of a birth cohort experience the same events—wars, depressions, assassinations, as well as personal experiences such as marriage and childbearing—at approximately the same age and often have similar reactions to them. Sociologist Glen Elder showed that a group of people who were relatively deprived as young children during the Great Depression grew up and later made remarkably similar decisions about marriage, children, and jobs. Others have used this kind of analysis to provide insights into British writers of the post–World War I era and to explain why the Nazi party appealed to a great many young Germans.

Yet even within a birth cohort, people may respond quite differently to the same event or experience. *Frame of reference* refers to an individual's personal background, which may influence that person's beliefs, responses, and actions. For example, interviews conducted with Americans who lived during the Great Depression of the 1930s reveal that men and women often coped differently with unemployment, that blacks and whites differed in their perceptions of how hard the times were, and that those living in rural areas had remarkably different experiences from city dwellers.

In this chapter, all but one of the interviewees (Helen) belong to the generation that came of age during the Vietnam War. Thus, as you analyze their frames of reference, age will not give you any clues. However, other factors, such as gender, race, socioeconomic class, family background, values, region, and experiences, may be quite important in determining the interviewees' frames of reference and understanding their responses to the Vietnam War. When a group of people share the same general frame of reference, they are a *generational subset* who tend to respond similarly to events. In other words, it may be possible to form tentative generalizations from the interviewees about how others with the same general frames of reference thought about and responded to the Vietnam War. To assist you in conducting your own interview of a member of the baby-boom generation (or birth cohort), we have included some instructions for interviewers and a suggested interview plan.

Instructions for Interviewers

1. Establish the date, time, and place of the interview well in advance. You may wish to call and remind the interviewee a few days before your appointment.

2. State clearly the purpose of the interview *at the beginning*. In other words, if the interview is part of a class project, explain how the interview will be used in the project.

3. Prepare for the interview by carefully reading background information about the 1960s and by writing down and arranging the questions you will be asking to guide the interview.

4. Keep most of your major questions broad and general so that the interviewee will not simply answer with a word or two ("What was your job in the army?"). Specific questions such as "What did the people in your town think about the war?" are useful for obtaining more details.

5. Avoid "loaded" questions such as "Everyone hated President Lyndon Johnson, didn't they?" Instead, keep your questions neutral: "What did you think about President Lyndon Johnson and his Vietnam strategy?"

6. Save any questions involving controversial matters for last. It is better to ask them toward the end of the interview, when the interviewee is more comfortable with you.

7. Be courteous, and be sure to give the person enough time to think, remember, and answer. Never argue, even if he or she says something with which you strongly disagree. Remember that the purpose of the interview is to find out what *that person* thinks, not what you think.

8. Take notes, even if you are tape-recording the interview (with permission). Notes will help clarify unclear portions of the tape and will be essential if the recorder malfunctions or the tape is accidentally erased.

9. Obtain a signed release form. Many who use the oral history method believe that the release forms should be signed at the beginning of the interview; others insist that this often inhibits the person who is to be interviewed and therefore should not be done until the end of the session. Although students who are using the material only for a class exercise are not always held strictly to the federal requirements, it is still better to obtain a signed release. Without such a release, the tape cannot be heard and used by anyone else (or deposited in an oral history collection), and the information the tape contains cannot be published or made known outside the classroom.

10. Write up the results of your interview as soon as possible after completing it. Even in rough form, these notes will help you capture the sense of what was said as well as the actual information that was presented.

A Suggested Interview Plan

Remember that your interviewee is a *person* with feelings, sensitivities, and emotions. If you intend to tape-record the interview, ask permission first.

If you believe that a tape recorder will inhibit the person you have selected, leave it at home and rely on your ability to take notes.

The following suggestions may help you get started. People usually remember the personal aspects of their lives more vividly than they remember national or international events. That is a great advantage in this exercise because part of what you are attempting to find out is how this person lived during the 1960s. Begin by getting the following important data from the interviewee:

1. Name
2. Age in 1968
3. Race and sex
4. Where the person lived in the 1960s and what the area was like then
5. Family background (what the interviewee's parents did for a living; number of brothers and sisters; whether the interviewee considered himself or herself rich, middle class, or poor)
6. Educational background

Then move on to the aspects of the person's life that will flesh out your picture of the 1960s and early 1970s:

1. Was the person in college at any time? What was college life like during the period?
2. If the person was not in college, what did he or she do for a living? Did he or she live at home or away from home?
3. How did the person spend his or her leisure time? If unmarried, did the person go out on dates? What was dating like? Did he or she go to the movies (and if so, which ones?)

Did he or she watch much television (and if so, which shows)?

These questions should give you a fairly good idea of how the person lived during the period. Now move on to connect the interviewee with the Vietnam War:

1. Did the person know anyone who volunteered or was drafted and sent to Vietnam? How did the interviewee feel about that? Did the person lose any relatives or friends in Vietnam? What was his or her reaction to that?
2. (*Male*): Was the person himself eligible for the draft? Did he volunteer for service or was he drafted? Was he sent to Vietnam? If so, what were some memorable Vietnam experiences? What did the person's family think of his going to Vietnam? (*Female*): If you intend to interview a female who went to Vietnam as a nurse, alter the preceding questions as needed.
3. Was the person a Vietnam War protester? If so, what was that experience like? If not, did the person know any Vietnam War protesters? What did the person think of them?
4. Did the person know anyone who tried to avoid going to Vietnam? What did the person think of that?

Finally, review the national events and people of the Vietnam era and develop some questions to ask your interviewee about these events and people. As you can see in this plan, you want to guide the interview through three stages, from personal information and background to the interviewee's reactions to a widening sphere of experiences and events.

The Evidence

Source 1 is a sample permission form used by students in 2002 as part of a class project in a college class studying the period of American history from 1945 to 1980.

PERMISSION FORM

I was interviewed by _____ (Interviewer) _____ on _____ (date) _____ on my recollections of the Vietnam War era. I understand that this interview will be used in a history class at _____ (Institution) _____ for a class project on American history from 1945 to 1980.

(Signature) _____
(Date) _____

I further understand that my name will not be made public unless I give my written permission for my name to be divulged. In addition, if I give my permission for my name to be used, my interview will be collected with other interviews and saved for future historians.

(Signature)_____
(Date)_____

Sources 2 through 7 from interviews conducted by the authors; interviews 2 and 3 in 1985 and 4 through 7 in 1992. Photographs were supplied by the interviewees.

2. Photograph of John and His Family (*left to right:* John's father, John, John's mother, and John's brother).

© Cengage Learning

John

[John was born in 1951. His father was a well-to-do and prominent physician, and John grew up in a mid-western town that had a major university. He graduated from high school in 1969 and enrolled in a four-year private college. John dropped out of college in 1971 and returned home to live with his parents. He found work in the community and associated with students at the nearby university.]

My earliest memory of Vietnam must have been when I was in the seventh grade [1962–1963] and I saw things in print and in *Life* magazine. But I really don't remember much about Vietnam until my senior year in high school [1968–1969].

I came from a repressive private school to college. College was a fun place to hang out, a place where you went after high school. It was just expected of you to go.

At college there was a good deal of apprehension and fear about Vietnam—people were scared of the draft. To keep your college deferments, you had to keep your grades up. But coming from an admittedly well-to-do family, I somehow assumed I didn't have to worry about it too much. I suppose I was outraged to find out that it *could* happen to me.

No, I was outraged that it could happen to *anyone.* I knew who were going to get deferments and who weren't going to get them. And even today my feelings are still ambiguous. On one hand I felt, "You guys were so dumb to get caught in that machine." On the other, and more importantly, it was wrong that *anyone* had to go.

Why? Because Vietnam was a bad war. To me, we were protecting business interests. We were fighting on George III's side, on the wrong side of an anticolonial rebellion. The domino theory didn't impress me at all.

I had decided that I would not go to Vietnam. But I wasn't really worried for myself until Nixon instituted the lottery. I was contemplating going to Canada when my older brother got a CO.[15] I tried the same thing, the old Methodist altar boy gambit, but I was turned down. I was really ticked when I was refused CO status. I thought, "Who are you to tell me who is a pacifist?"

My father was conservative and my mother liberal. Neither one intervened or tried to pressure me. I suppose they thought, "We've done the best we could." By this time I had long hair and a beard. My dad had a hard time.

The antiwar movement was an intellectual awakening of American youth. Young people were concentrated on college campuses, where their maturing intellects had sympathetic sounding boards. Vietnam was part of that awakening. So was drugs. It was part of the protest. You had to be a part of it. Young people were waking up as they got away from home and saw the world around them and were forced to think for themselves.

I remember an argument I had with my father. I told him Ho Chi Minh was a nationalist before he was a Communist, and that this war wasn't really against communism at all. It's true that the Russians were also the bad guys in Vietnam, what with their aid and support of the North Vietnamese, but they had no business there either. When people tried to compare Vietnam to World War II, I just said that no Vietnamese had ever bombed Pearl Harbor.

The draft lottery certainly put me potentially at risk. But I drew a high number, so I knew that it was unlikely that I'd ever be drafted. And yet, I wasn't concerned just for myself. For example, I was aware, at least intellectually, that blacks and poor people were the cannon fodder in Vietnam. But I insisted that *no one,* rich or poor, had to go to fight this war.

---

15. A "CO" is a conscientious objector.

Actually I didn't think much about the Vietnamese people themselves. The image of a kid who could take candy from you one day and hand you a grenade the next. What in hell were we doing in that kind of situation?

Nor did I ever actually know anyone who went to Vietnam. I suppose that, to some extent, I bought the "damn baby napalmers" image. But I never had a confrontation with a veteran of Vietnam. What would I think of him? I don't know. What would he think of me?

Kent State[16] was a real shock to me. I was in college at the time, and I thought, "They were students, just like me." It seemed as if fascism was growing in America.

I was part of the protest movement. After Kent State, we shut down the campus, then marched to a downtown park where we held a rally. In another demonstration, later, I got a good whiff of tear gas. I was dating a girl who collapsed because of the gas. I recall a state policeman coming at us with a club. I yelled at him, telling him what had happened. Suddenly he said, "Here, hold this!" and gave me his club while he helped my date to her feet.

But there were other cops who weren't so nice. I went to the counter-inaugural in Washington in June 1973. You could see the rage on the cops' faces when we were yelling, "One, two, three, four, we don't want your f——king war!" It was an awakening for me to see that much emotion on the subject coming from the other side. I know that I wasn't very open to other opinions. But the other side *really* was closed.

By '72 their whole machine was falling apart. A guy who gave us a ride to the counter-inaugural was a Vietnam vet. He was going there too, to protest against the War. In fact, he was hiding a friend of his who was AWOL,[17] who simply hid rather than go to Vietnam.

Then Watergate made it all worthwhile—we really had those f——kers scared. I think Watergate showed the rest of the country exactly what kind of "law and order" Nixon and his cronies were after!

I have no regrets about what I did. I condemn them all—Kennedy, Johnson, Nixon—for Vietnam. They all had a hand in it. And the war was wrong, in every way imaginable. While I feel some guilt that others went and were killed and I didn't, in retrospect I feel much guiltier that I wasn't a helluva

16. Kent State: On May 4, 1970, in the midst of an antiwar rally on the campus of Kent State University in Ohio, panicked National Guard soldiers fired into a crowd of protesters. Four students, two of whom were on their way to class and were not demonstrators, were killed and eleven were wounded. The tragedy increased campus unrest throughout the nation.
17. "AWOL" is an acronym for "absent without leave."

lot more active. Other than that, I wouldn't change a thing. I can still get angry about it.

How will I explain all that to my sons? I have no guilt in terms of "duty towards country." This *real* duty was to fight *against* the whole thing. I'll tell my sons that, and tell them that I did what I did so that no one has to go.

[John chose not to return to college. He learned a craft, which he practices today. He married a woman who shared his views ("I wouldn't have known anyone on the other side, the way the country was divided"), had two children, and shared the responsibilities of child care. John and his wife are now divorced.]

3. Photograph of Mike in Vietnam.

© Cengage Learning

Mike

[Mike was born in 1948. His family owned a farm in western Tennessee, and Mike grew up in a rural environment. He graduated from high school in 1966 and enrolled in a community college not far from his home. After two quarters of poor grades, Mike left the community college and joined the U.S. Marine Corps in April 1967. He served two tours in Vietnam, the first in 1967 to 1969 and the second in 1970 to 1971.]

I flunked out of college my first year. I was away from home and found out a lot about wine, women, and song but not about much else. In 1967 the old system of the draft was still in effect, so I knew that eventually I'd be rotated up and drafted—it was only a matter of time before they got me.

My father served with Stilwell in Burma and my uncle was career military. I grew up on a diet of John Wayne flicks. I thought serving in the military was what was expected of me. The Marines had some good options—you could go in for two years and take your chances on the *possibility* of not going to Vietnam. I chose the two-year option. I thought what we were doing in Vietnam was a noble cause. My mother was against the war and we argued a lot about it. I told her that if the French hadn't helped us in the American Revolution, then we wouldn't have won. I sincerely believed that.

I took my six weeks of basic training in Parris Island [South Carolina]. It was sheer hell—I've never been treated like that in my life. Our bus arrived at Parris Island around midnight, and we were processed and sent to our barracks. We had just gotten to sleep when a drill instructor threw a thirty-two gallon garbage can down the center of the barracks and started overturning the metal bunks. We were all over the floor and he was screaming at us. It was that way for six weeks—no one ever talked to us, they shouted. And all our drill instructors geared our basic training to Vietnam. They were always screaming at us, "You're going to go to Vietnam and you're gonna f——up and you're gonna die."

Most of the people in basic training with me were draftees. My recruiter apologized to me for having to go through boot camp with draftees. But most of the guys I was with were pretty much like me. Oh, there were a few s——birds, but not many. We never talked about Vietnam—there was no opportunity.

There were a lot of blacks in the Corps and I went through basic training with some. But I don't remember any racial tension until later. There were only two colors in the Marine Corps: light green and dark green. My parents drove down to Parris Island to watch me graduate from basic training, and they brought a black woman with them. She was from Memphis and was the wife of one of the men who graduated with me.

After basic training I spent thirteen weeks in basic infantry training at Camp Lejeune [North Carolina]. Lejeune is the armpit of the world. And the harassment didn't let up—we were still called "scumbag" and "hairbag" and "whale——." I made PFC [private first class] at Lejeune. I was an 03–11 [infantry rifleman].

From Lejeune [after twenty days' home leave] I went to Camp Pendleton [California] for four-week staging. It was at Pendleton where we adjusted our training at Parris Island and Lejeune to the situation in Vietnam. I got to Vietnam right after Christmas 1967.

It was about this time that I became aware of antiwar protests. But as far as I was concerned they were a small minority of malcontents. They were the *protected*, were deferred or had a daddy on the draft board. I thought, "These people are disloyal—they're selling us down the drain."

We were not prepared to deal with the Vietnamese people at all. The only two things we were told was don't give kids cigarettes and don't pat 'em on the heads. We had no cultural training, knew nothing of the social structure or anything. For instance, we were never told that the Catholic minority controlled Vietnam and they got out of the whole thing—we did their fighting for them, while they stayed out or went to Paris or something. We had a Catholic chaplain who told us that it was our *duty* to go out and kill the Cong,[18] that they stood against Christianity. Then he probably went and drank sherry with the top cats in Vietnam. As for the majority of Vietnamese, they were as different from us as night and day. To be honest, I still hate the Vietnamese SOBs.

The South Vietnamese Army was a mixed bag. There were some good units and some bad ones. Most of them were bad. If we were fighting alongside South Vietnam units, we had orders that if we were overrun by Charley[19] that we should shoot the South Vietnamese first—otherwise we were told they'd turn on us.

I can't tell you when I began to change my mind about the war. Maybe it was a kind of maturation process—you can only see so much death and suffering until you begin to wonder what in hell is going on. You can only live like a nonhuman so long.

I came out of Country[20] in January of 1969 and was discharged not too long after that. I came home and found the country split over the war. I

18. "Cong" is short for *Vietcong,* also known as "the VC."
19. "Charley" is a euphemism for *Vietcong.*
20. "Country" means Vietnam.

thought, "Maybe there *was* something to this antiwar business after all." Maybe these guys protesting in the streets weren't wrong.

But when I got back home, I was a stranger to my friends. They didn't want to get close to me. I could feel it. It was strange, like the only friends I had were in the Marine Corps. So I re-upped[21] in the Marines and went back to Vietnam with a helicopter squadron.

Kent State happened when I was back in Vietnam. They covered it in *Stars and Stripes.*[22] I guess that was a big turning point for me. Some of the other Marines said, "Hooray! Maybe we should kill more of them!" That was it for me. Those people at Kent State were killed for exercising the same rights we were fighting for the Vietnamese. But I was in the minority—most of the Marines I knew approved of the shootings at Kent State.

Meanwhile I was flying helicopters into Cambodia every day. I used pot to keep all that stuff out of my mind. Pot grew wild in Vietnam, as wild as the hair on your ass. The Army units would pick it and send it back. The first time I was in Vietnam nobody I knew was using. The second time there was lots of pot. It had a red tinge, so it was easy to spot.

But I couldn't keep the doubts out of my mind. I guess I was terribly angry. I felt betrayed. I would have voted for Lyndon Johnson—when he said we should be there, I believed him. The man could walk on water as far as I was concerned. I would've voted for Nixon in '68, the only time I ever voted Republican in my life. I believed him when he said we'd come home with honor. So I'd been betrayed twice, and Kent State and all that was rattling around in my head.

It was worse when I got home. I came back into the Los Angeles airport and was spit on and called a baby killer and a mother raper. I really felt like I was torn between two worlds. I guess I was.

I went back to school. I hung around mostly with veterans. We spoke the same language, and there was no danger of being insulted or ridiculed. We'd been damn good, but nobody knew it. I voted for McGovern in '72—he said we'd get out no matter what. Some of us refused to stand up one time when the national anthem was played.

What should we have done? Either not gotten involved at all or go in with the whole machine. With a different attitude and tactics, we could have *won*. But really we were fighting for just a minority of the Vietnamese, the westernized Catholics who controlled the cities but never owned the

---

21. "Re-upped" means reenlisted.
22. *Stars and Stripes* is a newspaper written and published by the armed forces for service personnel.

backcountry. No, I take that back. There was no way in hell we could have won that damned war and won anything worth winning.

I went to Washington for the dedication of Vietnam Veterans Memorial. We never got much of a welcome home or parades. The dedication was a homecoming for me. It was the first time I got the whole thing out of my system. I cried, and I'm not ashamed. And I wasn't alone.

I looked for names of my friends. I couldn't look at a name without seeing myself reflected back in it [the wall].

One of the reasons I went back to school was to understand that war and myself. I've read a lot about it and watched a lot of TV devoted to it. I was at Khe Sanh and nobody could tell about that who wasn't there. There were six thousand of us. Walter Cronkite said we were there for seventy-two days. I kept a diary—it was longer than that. I'm still reading and studying Vietnam, trying to figure it all out.

[Mike returned to college, repeated the courses he had failed, and transferred to a four-year institution. By all accounts he was a fine student. After earning both bachelor's and master's degrees, he became a park ranger and was considered a valuable, respected, and popular member of his community. Presently Mike is retired, divorced, and has returned to his family's farm, which he now runs with his son. He suffers from his exposure to Agent Orange and undergoes regular chemotherapy treatments.]

4. Photograph of M. M., Boot Camp Graduation.

© Cengage Learning

M. M.[23]

[M. M. was born in 1947 and grew up in a midsize southern city. He graduated from high school in 1965. A standout in high school football, he could not get an athletic scholarship to college because of low grades. As a result, he joined the U.S. Army two months after graduating from high school to take advantage of the educational benefits he would get upon his discharge. He began his basic training in early September 1965.]

I went into the service to be a soldier. I was really gung ho. I did my basic training at Fort Gordon [Georgia], my AIT [advanced infantry training]

---

23. Since M. M.'s first name is Mike, his initials are used here to avoid confusion with Mike in Source 3.

at Fort Ord [California], and ranger school and airborne at Fort Benning [Georgia].

All of this was during the civil rights movement. I was told that, being black, I had a war to fight at home, not in Vietnam. That got me uptight because that wasn't what I wanted to do—I'd done some of that in high school.[24] I had one mission accomplished, and was looking for another.

A lot of guys I went into the service with didn't want to go to Nam—they were afraid. Some went AWOL. One guy jumped off the ship between Honolulu and Nam and drowned. Another guy shot himself, trying to get a stateside wound. He accidentally hit an artery and died. Most of us thought they were cowards.

I arrived in Nam on January 12, 1966. I was three days shy of being eighteen years old. I was young, gung ho, and mean as a snake. I was with the Twenty-fifth Infantry as a machine gunner and rifleman. We went out on search and destroy missions.

I did two tours in Vietnam, at my own request. You could make rank[25] faster in Nam and the money was better. I won two silver stars and three bronze stars. For my first silver star, I knocked out two enemy machine guns that had two of our platoons pinned down. They were drawing heavy casualties. The event is still in my mind. Two of the bronze stars I put in my best friend's body bag. I told him I did it for him.

I had a friend who died in my arms, and I guess I freaked a little bit. I got busted[26] seven times. They [the army] didn't like the way I started taking enemy scalps and wearing them on my pistol belt. I kept remembering my friend.

I didn't notice much racial conflict in Nam. In combat, everybody seemed to be OK. I fought beside this [white] guy for eleven months; we drank out of the same canteen. When I got home, I called this guy's house. His mother said, "We don't allow our son to associate with niggers." In Vietnam, I didn't run into much of that.

The Vietnamese hated us. My first day in Vietnam, Westmoreland[27] told us that underneath every Vietnamese was an American. I thought, "What drug is he on?" But they hated us. When we weren't on the scene, the enemy would punish them for associating with us. They would call out to us, "G.I. Number Ten."[28] They were caught between a rock and a hard place.

24. M. M. participated in sit-ins to integrate the city's lunch counters and movie theaters.
25. "Make rank" means to earn promotions.
26. "Busted" means demoted.
27. General William Westmoreland was an American commander in Vietnam.
28. "Number Ten" means bad or no good.

We could have won the war several times. The Geneva Convention[29] wouldn't let us, and the enemy had the home court advantage. To win, it would have taken hard soldiering, but we could have done it. America is a weak country because we want to be everybody's friend. We went in there as friends. We gave food and stuff to the Vietnamese and we found it in the hands of the enemy. We just weren't tough enough.

I got out of the Army in 1970. I was thinking about making the Army a career and was going to re-enlist. But when they wanted me to go back for a third tour in Vietnam, I got out. Hell, everybody told me I was crazy for doing two.

[M. M. used his GI Bill benefits to obtain three years of higher education: two years at 2 four-year colleges and one year at a business school. According to him, however, jobs were "few and far between." He described himself as "restless" and reported that automobile backfires still frightened him. He was married and divorced twice. In 1999, M. M. died at the age of fifty-two.]

---

29. "The Geneva Convention" refers to international agreements for the conduct of war and the treatment of prisoners. The agreements began to be drawn up in the 1860s.

5. Photograph of Helen (*left*) at an Army Hospital in Phu Bai, South Vietnam.

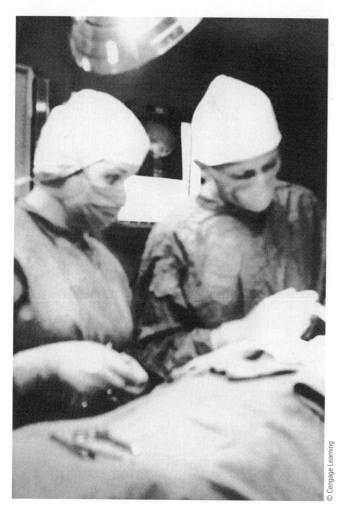

© Cengage Learning

Helen

[Helen was born in 1942 in Cleveland, Ohio, and grew up there. Since grade school, she had wanted to be a nurse. After graduation from high school, she spent three years in nurses' training to become a registered nurse. She worked for three years in the operating rooms of a major medical facility in Cleveland. In 1966, she joined the U.S. Navy.]

[289]

I joined the Navy in 1966 and reported to Newport, Rhode Island, for basic training. Our classes consisted of military protocol, military history, and physical education. There was only a passing reference made to our medical assignments and what was expected of us.

I was assigned to the Great Lakes Naval Hospital [outside Chicago]. Although I had been trained and had experience as an operating room surgical nurse, at first I was assigned to the orthopedic wards. It was there that I got my first exposure to mass casualties [from Vietnam]. Depending on the extent of their injuries, we would see patients at Great Lakes about seven to ten days after them being wounded in Vietnam.

I became attached to some of the boys—they were young, scared and badly injured. I remember a Negro who in tears asked for his leg to be taken off—he couldn't stand the smell of it anymore and had been to surgery once too often for the removal of dead tissue. He was in constant pain.

On the wards, we always kept nightlights on. If someone darkened a ward by accident, it produced a sense of terror in the patients. Many were disoriented, and a lot had nightmares.

When I made the decision to go to Vietnam, I volunteered in 1968 and requested duty aboard a hospital ship. It was necessary to extend my time on active duty in order to go. I felt I had a skill that was needed and it was something I felt I personally had to do. I didn't necessarily agree with our policy on being there, but that wasn't the point.

The median age of our troops in Vietnam was nineteen years old. It was like treating our kid brothers. I would have done as much for my own brothers. I know this sounds idealistic, but that's the way I felt then.

The troops got six weeks of staging, preparing them for duty in Vietnam. Most of the nurses were given no preparation, no orientation as to what to expect when you go into a war zone. No one said, "These are the things you'll see," or "These are the things you'll be expected to do."

I was assigned to the U.S.S. *Sanctuary,* which was stationed outside of Da Nang harbor. The *Sanctuary* was a front-line treatment facility. Casualties were picked up in the field combat areas and then brought by Medevac choppers to the ship. During our heaviest months, we logged over seven hundred patient admissions per month. That was at the height of the Tet offensive in January through March, 1968. I had just gotten to Vietnam.

It was terribly intense. There was nothing to shelter you, no one to hold your hand when mass casualties came in. If you had time to think, you'd have thought, "My God, how am I to get through this?" We dealt with multiple amputations, head injuries, and total body trauma. Sometimes injuries were received from our own people caught in crossfires. When all hell breaks loose at night in the jungle, a nineteen-year-old boy under ambush will fire at anything that moves.

How do you insulate yourself against all this? We relaxed when we could, and we put a lot of stock in friendships (the corpsmen were like our kid brothers). We played pranks and sometimes took the launch ashore to Da Nang. Occasionally we were invited to a party ashore and a helicopter came out for the nurses. The men wanted American women at their parties.

There were some people who had the idea that the only reason women were in the service was to be prostitutes or to get a man. Coming back from Vietnam, I was seated next to a male officer on the plane who said to me, "Boy, I bet you had a great time in Vietnam." I had my seat changed. When I got home and was still in uniform I was once mistaken for a police officer.

I heard a story of a Vietnamese child running up to a chopper that was evacuating casualties and tossing a grenade into it. Everyone on board was killed in a split second; both crew and casualties, because they paused to help a child they thought needed them. A soldier I knew said, "If they're in the fire zone, they get killed." War really takes you to the lowest level of human dignity. It makes you barbaric.

After Vietnam, I was stationed at the Naval Academy in Annapolis to finish out my duty. There I dealt basically with college students—measles and sports injuries. It was a hard adjustment to make.

I guess the hardest thing about nursing in Vietnam was the different priorities. Back home, if we got multiple-trauma cases from, say, an automobile accident, we always treated the most seriously injured first. In Vietnam, it was often the reverse. I remember working on one soldier who was not badly wounded, and he kept screaming for us to help his buddy, who was seriously wounded. I couldn't tell him that his buddy didn't have a good chance to survive, and so we were passing him by. That was difficult for a lot of us, went against all we'd been trained to do. It's difficult to support someone in the act of dying when you're trained to do all you can to save a life. Even today, I have trouble with patients who need amputations or who have facial injuries.

It is most important to realize that there is a great cost to waging war. Many men are living out their lives in veterans' hospitals as paraplegics or quadriplegics, who in World War II or Korea would not have survived. Most Americans will never see these people—they are hidden away from us. But they are alive.

Maybe the worst part of the war for many of these boys was coming home. The seriously wounded were sent to a military hospital closest to their own homes. Our orthopedic ward at Great Lakes Naval Hospital had forty beds, and it was like taking care of forty kid brothers. They joked around and were supportive of each other. But quite a few of them got "Dear John"[30] letters while they were there. Young wives and girlfriends sometimes couldn't deal with these injuries, and parents sometimes had trouble coping too. All these people were "casualties of war," but I believe that these men especially need our caring and concern today, just as much as they did twenty years ago.

[On her discharge from the U.S. Navy in August 1969, Helen returned to nursing. She married in 1972. She and her husband, an engineering physicist, have two children. Helen returned to school and received her B.S. degree in nursing. She is now a coordinator of cardiac surgery and often speaks and writes of her Vietnam experience. She also actively participates in a local veterans' organization. When her daughter was in high school and offered her mother's services to speak on Vietnam to a history class, she was rebuffed by the teacher, who said, "Who wants to hear about that? We lost that war!" Both Helen and her daughter (who is proud of what her mother did in Vietnam) were offended.]

30. A "Dear John" letter is one that breaks off a relationship.

6. Photograph of Nick (*right*) with Some Buddies in Vietnam.

© Cengage Learning

Nick

[Nick was born in 1946 in a midsize city. Both his parents were skilled factory workers. Nick graduated from high school in 1964 and wanted to work for the fire department, but he was too young for the civil service. He got a job at the local utility company and married in 1966. Nick was drafted in 1967. He served in the U.S. Army with the First Cavalry Division.]

I suppose I could have gotten a deferment, but I didn't know they were available. My wife was pretty scared when I got drafted, but neither of us ever imagined that I would shirk my duty.

I did my boot camp at Fort Benning [Georgia]. About 80 percent of the people in boot camp with me were draftees. A number of the draftees were black. I had worked with blacks before the Army, had many black friends, and never saw any racial problems. We were then sent to Fort Polk, Louisiana, for advanced infantry training. They had built simulated Vietnamese villages that were very similar to what we later encountered in Vietnam. Overall, we were trained pretty well, but we were still pretty scared.

I arrived in Vietnam on December 12, 1967, and was assigned to go out on "search and destroy" missions. Even though I was prepared mentally, I was still very frightened. I was wounded once when we got ambushed while we were setting up an ambush of our own. Another time I got hit with some shrapnel from a 60mm mortar. That was at 3:00 A.M. and the medics didn't arrive until 7:30.

I'm not proud of everything I did in Vietnam, but I won't run away from it either. You got so hard at seeing friends killed and things like that. We desecrated their dead, just as they did ours. We used to put our unit's shoulder patches on the VC dead (we nailed 'em on) to get credit for it.

I didn't like the Vietnamese themselves. Most of the civilians were VC sympathizers, and the South Vietnamese army just wouldn't fight. I was in some kind of culture shock. Here we were, trying to help these people, and some of them were living in grass huts. Once I asked myself, "What am I doing here?"

The highest rank I made was sergeant, but I was demoted when I caught a guy in my unit asleep on guard duty and busted him with a shotgun. I was demoted for damaging the shotgun, government property.

I got back to the States in December 1968. There were some protesters at the Seattle airport, but they just marched with signs and didn't harass us at all. Over time, I lost my hostility to the antiwar protesters, although at the time I despised them. Except for Jane Fonda[31] (who went too far), I have no bad feelings for them at all. I have a friend who threatened to run his daughter off because she had a Jane Fonda workout tape.

I'm no hero and didn't do anything special. But college students today need to know that the people who fought in that war are no less important than people who fought in World War I, World War II, or Korea.

---

31. Movie star and antiwar activist Jane Fonda organized shipments of food and medical supplies to North Vietnam and traveled to Vietnam during the war.

[Nick returned to his position with the utility company. He and his wife have two sons, born in 1969 and 1972. He never talked about Vietnam and wanted to throw his medals out, but his wife made him keep them. When his sons started asking questions, he told them about Vietnam. They convinced him to bring his medals out and display them. Since returning from Vietnam, he has never voted "and never will. . . . I have no use for politicians at all." He is now enjoying retirement although his health is deteriorating.]

7. Photograph of Robyn as a College Student.

© Cengage Learning

Robyn

[Robyn was born in 1955 and raised in a Wisconsin farming town of around fifteen hundred people. Her father owned a small construction business and, like many other men in town, had proudly served in World War II. Her mother was a high school teacher. Robyn has three sisters and three brothers, none of whom served in Vietnam.]

I remember starting to watch the war on television when I was about ten. I asked my mother, "How come they're killing each other?" She said that America was the land of freedom and that we were in Vietnam to help make the people free. As a teacher, though, she always encouraged us to think for ourselves and find our own answers.

The guys in town started going away [to Vietnam], and in a town that size, everybody knows. When my ninth-grade algebra teacher suddenly disappeared, no adults would talk about it. Later, we found out that he had received CO status. In my town, that wasn't much different from being a Communist. The peer pressure was tremendous.

I have always believed the United States is the greatest country in the world, but it's not perfect. The more I heard about the war, the more I realized something was wrong. Although only in high school, I felt obligated to let the government know that I thought it was in the wrong. And yet at no time while I was protesting the war was I *ever* against the guys fighting it. My quarrel was with how the government was running the war.

I recall one of my first "protests." I was in the high school band and we were playing "The Star-Spangled Banner" at a basketball game. Although I stood and played with the rest of the band, I turned my back to the flag. When I came home that night, my father hit me for being disrespectful. So much for the right to free speech we were fighting to protect.

When I left for college in 1973, one brother had just gotten a medical deferral, and another would soon be registering for the draft. The war was becoming more and more personal. I skipped classes to attend rallies and antiwar events, and I wrote lots of letters to politicians. When the POW-MIA bracelets[32] came out, I helped sell them. There were quite a few heated discussions with some protesters who thought that wearing a bracelet (my guy is still MIA) was contrary to the cause. In those days, I tended to "discuss" things in decibels.

My second year of college ended with me skipping classes to watch the televised returns of our POWs. I would have loved to hug each one, so this was my way of saying "Welcome home" and to bear witness. I cried the whole time—for them, for their families, and for all the agony we'd all gone through during the war. Then I dropped out of school and just "vegetated" for a year. My idealistic perceptions of humanity had been severely challenged, and I was drained.

After Vietnam, I got involved in some projects that were targeted to help Vietnam vets. One of my best and proudest experiences will always be my work at the Vietnam Veterans Memorial in Washington, D.C. I worked at the wall as a volunteer every week for almost ten years. Unlike past memorials,

32. Bracelets bearing the names of American POWs (prisoners of war) and MIAs (soldiers missing in action) were worn to remember those soldiers left behind in Vietnam and to urge the U.S. government to act on securing their return home.

this one doesn't honor the war. It's the Vietnam *Veterans* Memorial, not War Memorial, and it honors those who fought it.

I have seen firsthand its healing effects on vets and their families. And on me. At the wall, the former protester and the Vietnam veteran share something in common—our great sadness for those who were lost and those who haven't yet returned. Vietnam vets also don't seem to have the glorified view of war that older vets do.

The government's lack of support for Vietnam vets (during and after the war) might be part of the reason. If more people were aware of the other side of war, the side the vets saw, they'd have a lot more incentive to work things out. Instead of seeing war as an alternative solution, people would finally realize that war is simply the result of our failure to find a solution.

[Robyn returned to college and eventually graduated from law school. She worked in Washington, D.C., for a nonprofit education organization and as a government relations consultant. Robyn now works at a public and government relations firm. She continues to work with Vietnam veterans and, in particular, on the POW-MIA issue.]

◆

Questions to Consider

The interviews in this chapter were conducted between 1985 and 1992. As you read through the interviews, try to get a sense of the tone and general meaning of each one. Then try to establish the respective frames of reference for the interviewees by comparing and contrasting their backgrounds. From which socioeconomic class does each person come? From what region of the country? What do you know about the interviewee's parents and friends? What did the person think was expected of him or her? Why?

After high school, the interviewees' experiences diverged greatly. Eventually, Mike, M. M., and Helen enlisted in the armed services. What reason did each

of them give (if any) for enlisting? How different were their reasons? For his part, Nick was drafted. What was his reaction to being drafted?

Both John and Robyn (Sources 2 and 7) became involved in antiwar protests, but in different ways and for different reasons. Why and in what ways did each become involved? Would John and Robyn (who never met) have agreed on why the war should be opposed? On how Vietnam veterans should be treated? What do you think each would have to say about the majority of their birth cohort who *did not* oppose the war?

Return to the four veterans (Mike, M. M., Helen, and Nick). What were their feelings about the Vietnamese people? What did they believe were the reasons for American involvement in the war? What were their reactions to events of the time—the draft, antiwar protests, Kent State, and race relations in the armed services? What were their feelings about their respective roles in Vietnam? What did they think about the situation of returning veterans? Some of the interviewees seem to have made the adjustment to civilian life better than others. Can you think of why that might have been so? Finally, what do you think each of the six veterans or civilians learned from his or her personal experiences during the Vietnam War era?

Now look at the photographs closely. Are they posed or unposed? For whom might they have been intended? What image of each person is projected? How does each person help create that image?

Next consider carefully the interview that you conducted. You have done some important historical work by creating this piece of oral evidence. Now you must analyze it. What does your interview mean? In other words, how does it fit into or modify what you know about the Vietnam era? Begin by comparing and contrasting your interview with those in this chapter. Do the same with the interviews conducted by other students in your class. What major similarities and differences can you identify in the responses to the Vietnam War among members of this birth cohort? Do you see any patterns based on race, geographic region, socioeconomic class, or other factors? If so, describe and explain these patterns.

The majority of the people we interviewed had never met one another. Do you think they could meet and talk today about the Vietnam era? What might such a conversation be like?

♦

Epilogue

In the spring of 1971, fifteen thousand antiwar demonstrators disrupted daily activities in the nation's capital by blocking the streets with trash, automobiles, and their own bodies. Twelve thousand were arrested, but the protest movement across the country continued and the war dragged on. By that year, all of the four veterans who had served in Vietnam and were

interviewed for this chapter were home.[33] When they were interviewed for this chapter, Mike was thirty-seven years old, M. M. was forty-five, Helen was fifty, and Nick was forty-six. All were trying, with varied success, to put

33. When Mike, M. M., Helen, and Nick were sent home, there were still 150,000 American troops in Vietnam.

the war behind them and get on with the rest of their lives.[34]

As part of his effort to win the presidency in 1968, Richard Nixon had promised to bring "peace with honor" and announced that he had a plan for bringing the conflict to an end. And yet the war raged on for four more years, including the invasions of Cambodia in 1970 and Laos in 1971, the mining of North Vietnamese harbors, and increasing the bombing in North Vietnam in an effort to terrorize the civilian population. None of these efforts, however, was able to force the North Vietnamese to sue for peace. Finally in January 1973, an agreement was signed in Paris between the United States and North Vietnam that essentially ended the war in North Vietnam's favor. Beginning in March 1973, American troops began their withdrawal and North Vietnamese general Vo Nguyen Giap observed, "We were not strong enough to drive out a half-million American troops, but that wasn't our aim. Our intention was to break the will of the American government to continue the war."[35]

For the entire Vietnam War, approximately 2,594,000 served in the army, navy, air force, and Marines. Of that number, approximately 58,000 were killed, 153,303 wounded who required hospitalization, 23,214 totally disabled, and 1,639 missing in action (MIA). And in the years after the war, there were well over seventy thousand suicides and around seven hundred thousand veterans who required treatment for psychological trauma.[36]

As disturbing as the above statistics are, they were only a part of the cost to Americans of the Vietnam War. For one thing, the war left the army in a seriously weakened position, with extremely low morale; internal bickering, blaming, and finger pointing; discipline of army staff in Vietnam completely broken down, with widespread drug abuse, racial tensions, and even instances of "fragging." As one soldier put it, "No one wants to be the last man to die in Vietnam."[37]

In 1973, President Nixon ordered an end to the draft and the creation of an all-volunteer army. In spite of monetary incentives and widespread advertising, in 1973, the army was able to attract only 68.5 percent of volunteers necessary to meet its quota. Indeed, even with decreased quotas (as the army trimmed its numbers) and added bonuses, the goals were

34. At the time they were interviewed, John was thirty-four years old and Robyn was forty-seven.
35. On bombing, the United States delivered more explosive tonnage in Vietnam than in the entire Pacific Theater during World War II. See Patrick Coffey, *A Century of Waging War* (New York: Oxford University Press, 2014), p. 250. For Giap's remark see Boot, *The Savage Wars of Peace*, p. 316.

36. The MIA figures are for February 2015. See miafacts.org.
37. For the army's much weakened position see Richard W. Stewart, gen. ed., *American Military History, Volume II: The United States Army in a Global Era, 1917–2008* (Washington: Center of Military History, 2nd ed. 2005), p. 373. This volume is used to train would-be officers in the ROTC program. On "fragging," this is the act of throwing a fragmentation grenade into the sleeping quarters or office of a superior officer.

reached only by accepting women volunteers (fifty thousand by 1978 and eighty thousand by 1983). To be sure, there were problems that arose with men and women serving side by side, but as late as 1990, when the army was deployed to the Persian Gulf, 8.6 percent of the total force were women.[38]

Perhaps the greatest wound inflicted on Americans by the Vietnam War was the damage to the American **psyche**.[39] Buffeted by the war, urban violence, the death of Martin Luther King, Jr., Watergate, and what appeared to be a disunited society, Americans were confused, angry and disillusioned, and feared that the United States was unraveling. In one effort to reunify the different sides of the Vietnam debate, Presidents Gerald Ford and Jimmy Carter offered amnesty to those opponents of the war who hid from the draft in American cities or in Canada, invitations that a relatively small number of draft violators used.

Those American veterans who returned from Vietnam often did not recognize the nation they had fought for. Instead of the traditional homecoming parades, veterans were alternately ignored or maligned. Oftentimes they withdrew from the mainstream of society and clung together with brothers and sisters who had shared their experiences. Those who enrolled in colleges stayed clear of other students who, they feared, would look down on them. Only gradually did most of them rejoin the mainstream. But Vietnam was always with them.

Finally these men and women got their memorial. A stark, simple, shiny black granite wall engraved with the names of fifty-eight thousand war dead, the monument is located on the mall near the Lincoln Memorial in Washington, D.C. The idea came from Jan Scruggs (the son of a milkman), a Vietnam veteran who was wounded and decorated for bravery when he was nineteen years old. The winning design was submitted by twenty-year-old Maya Lin, an undergraduate architecture student at Yale University. A representational statue designed by thirty-eight-year-old Frederick Hart, a former antiwar protester, stands near the wall of names, along with a statue dedicated to the nurses who served in Vietnam. All one hundred U.S. senators cosponsored the gift of public land, and the money to build the memorial was raised entirely through 650,000 individual public contributions. Not everyone was pleased by the memorial, and some old emotional wounds were reopened. Yet more than 150,000 people attended the dedication ceremonies on Veterans Day 1982, and the Vietnam veterans paraded down Constitution Avenue. Millions of Americans have

38. The army's master plan was to create a highly technological fighting force with a small number of well-trained army regulars and increasing numbers of National Guard and army Reserve. At its numerical peak in 1968 of 1.5 million troops, by 1999 the number of army regulars had shrunk to 519,000, with 46 percent of the combat troops composed of National Guard and Army Reserve. See Stewart, *American Military History*, Vol. II, pp. 376–381.
39. Psyche (sī ´ kē): the center of thought and feelings; the soul and spirit.

viewed the monument, now one of Washington's most visited memorials.

In the years after 1973, one of the major topics of conversation and argument among the American military establishment as well as the general population was what *lessons* should be learned from the debacle that was Vietnam. Tumbling like coins out of a slot machine that was "paying off," these notions littered the landscape, books about Vietnam, and arguments from dormitory rooms to beery taverns. According to historian Robert A. Divine in his article "Vietnam Reconsidered," there have been a "plethora of opinions as to why the United States lost the Vietnam War."[40]

Through a survey of the literature and interviews of some informed individuals, the authors have identified some of the principal "lessons" of the Vietnam War. Interestingly, we went to the farm of Mike (Source 3) almost thirty years to the day after his first interview. In his opinion, the most important lesson was to "leave making war to the professionals, and keep politicians out of it." He believed that civilian leaders ought to articulate the goals of the conflict, and then "give the military a comparatively free rein." Mike then loaned us a book by Mark Woodruff (*Unheralded Victory: The Defeat of the Viet Cong and the North Vietnamese Army,* 1961–1973, published in 1999) that argued that the United States actually had won the war, but the media had convinced politicians that the opposite was true, which resulted in the general public and politicians calling for an end to the conflict.[41]

A somewhat different opinion was offered by Colonel Gregory Daddis, Professor of History at the U.S. Military Academy at West Point. He claimed (and many agree) that the key was to "gain some semblance of political support from the population," but tactics such as bombings and the uses of Agent Orange undercut the efforts to win over the civilian population. Unfortunately, Daddis believes, too many U.S. leaders, both military and civilian, "lacked the patience required for the 'long pull'." Still other historians disagree with Daddis, claiming that Vietnam was "unwinnable" because the United States backed a "corrupt and largely illegitimate South Vietnam government."[42]

Several military theorists at the Department of Defense asserted that the "growth of technology was an absolute requirement to bring about victory." They called for an "AirLandBattle," with the combined use of what was called the "big five": (1) a large tank, (2) a new infantry

40. Robert A. Divine, "Historiography: Vietnam Reconsidered," in Capps, *The Vietnam Reader,* pp. 100–115.

41. Second interview with Mike, March 10, 2015.

42. Gregory A. Daddis, *Westmoreland's War: Reassessing American Strategy in Vietnam* (New York: Oxford University Press, 2014), pp. xxi–xxii, 179, 181. See also original interview with Mike, in the Evidence section of this chapter. For the description of the South Vietnamese government as "Byzantine," see Moore and Galloway, *We Were Soldiers Once . . . and Young,* p. xvii.

Bruce Wheeler

Mike, at His Second Interview

combat vehicle, (3) a new Apache attack helicopter, (4) a new transport helicopter, and (5) a new Patriot air defense missile. But in an interview with an army sergeant who served for four tours in Iraq and presently teaches military history and leadership in an ROTC program, "once bullets start flying, technology is not so important."[43]

Some officers who saw combat in Vietnam wondered whether or not the United States should undertake "small wars" altogether. Or if America

did so, it should go all-out to achieve a total victory. As one put it, "Many of my generation, the career captains, majors and lieutenant colonels seasoned in that war vowed that when their turn came to call the shots, we would not quietly acquiesce in halfhearted warfare for half-baked reasons that the American people would not understand or support." This opinion was very close to the thinking of Gen. Colin Powell, whose "Powell Doctrine" called for six preconditions before U.S. troops would be committed to battle.[44]

43. Stewart, *American Military History*, Vol. II, pp. 383–388. *Interview with ROTC instructor*, March 13, 2015.

44. Boot, *The Savage Wars of Peace*, pp. 318–319.

There is little doubt that American military and civilian leaders vastly underestimated the strategy and tenacity of the Viet Cong and the North Vietnamese army, and at the same time vastly overestimated their own strategy and the tenacious support that the American people over time would give to the war effort. The combined deaths suffered by the Viet Cong and the North Vietnamese army was an astounding 1.1 million, and bombing raids left much of North Vietnam in rubble, with orphanages dotting the bombed-out landscape. And yet, in 1966 Ho Chi Minh stated defiantly, "The war may still last ten, twenty years or longer. Hanoi, Haiphong, and other cities and enterprises may be destroyed, but the Vietnamese people will not be intimidated!" Ho died in 1969 and did not see the victory that he was sure would come, but at war's end another North Vietnamese person asked, "Do you realize we are the only nation on earth that's defeated three out of the five permanent members of the United Nations Security Council?"[45]

As the Vietnam War drew to its painful close, not a few people blamed the press for having played a major role in the evaporation of public support for the conflict. President Nixon charged that the news media "had come to dominate domestic opinion about [the war's] purpose and conduct," an attack that probably was not true. But Mike and the ROTC instructor both criticized the press, claiming that the print journalists for the most part never went with the troops into the field and spent most of their time at press briefings and then filed critical reports. As Mike put it in his second interview, "There were no Ernie Pyles in Vietnam."[46]

According to a professor we interviewed who teaches in a journalism department at a major university, the most important aspect of the media and Vietnam was *television*. During this time, the traditional evening newscasts of the three major networks went from fifteen to thirty minutes, allowing more time for visual reporting of the war. Unlike most of the print journalists, television newspeople went into the field and brought the war into the home almost every evening. These television reporters included Homer Bigart, Bernard Fall, David Halberstam, Neil Sheehan, Malcolm Brown, Frances FitzGerald, Gloria Emerson, Morley Safer, and Ward Just. For many people in their homes, this was the first time they had seen war "up-close and personal." For their part, many military men thought that

45. For Ho's statement see Daddis, *Westmoreland's War*, p. 172. On the comment regarding the defeat of China, France, and the United States, see Christian Appy, *Patriots: The Vietnam War Remembered from All Sides* (New York: Viking Penguin, 2003), p. xviii.

46. For Nixon's charge see Daniel Hallin, *The Uncensored War: The Media and Vietnam* (New York: Oxford University Press, 1986), p. 3. For another opinion, Peter Braestrup claimed that for the most part "public opinion followed the casualty list." See his "Vietnam in Retrospect," in *Forbes Media Critic*, vol. 3, no. 1 (Fall 1995), p. 36. Ernie Pyle was a popular World War II war correspondent who lived with the troops and wrote about them. He was killed in the Pacific theater in 1945.

Americans could not tolerate casualties, what they called the "body bag syndrome." Whether it was casualties or the hard footage of television, American support for the war peaked in 1968 and began to erode after that.[47]

Finally, in an article that was both perceptive and audacious, historian Richard M. Ketchum explained the lessons of Vietnam as he saw them by comparing the Americans in Vietnam to the British in the American Revolution. Appearing in the June 1971 issue of *American Heritage*, Ketchum listed a number of obvious lessons that the arrogant British chose to ignore (1) the difficulty of apprehending the Patriot militia that would fight and then melt into the general population, (2) the cross-purposes of the aims of conquering the colonists while trying to lure them to the peace table, (3) the inability to discourage other European powers (mostly France and Spain) from aiding the rebellion, (4) the colonists who were loyal to Britain were not as powerful as the mother country had hoped, and (5) the growing opposition to the war at home. In fact, all the colonists had to do was hold on until the British simply gave up (see Giap's earlier comment). Finally, when military reverses did come, as they did at Saratoga and Yorktown, "the [British] people, wearied out with almost uninterrupted ill-success and misfortune, [called] out as loudly for peace as they had formerly done for war."[48]

At first blush, it appeared that the American military had learned the important lessons of Vietnam. In 1991 and again in 2003, the United States invaded Iraq, the first time to drive Saddam Hussein out of Kuwait and the second time to search for what it believed were "weapons of mass destruction" and to capture Osama bin Laden, the al-Qaeda leader who was the mastermind of the 9/11 attack on the World Trade Center. In both cases, heavy bombing was followed by rapidly moving infantry and tank units that overran and smashed the huge Iraqi army.[49]

But then, as our ROTC instructor put it, "Some of Vietnam's lessons did *not* carry over . . . we had to reinvent the wheel. Once we'd won, what had we won? We toppled Iraq's army, but *then what?*" And as Mike stated in his

47. Interview with professor of journalism, March 13, 2015. For the "body bag syndrome," see Boot, *The Savage Wars of Peace*, p. 329. For TV reporters see Hersh, "The Scene of the Crime," p. 55.
48. Richard M. Ketchum, "England's Vietnam: The American Revolution," in *American Heritage*, vol. 22, no. 4 (1971), pp. 6–13.

49. In the first invasion, Operation Desert Storm, American planes dropped almost ninety thousand tons of bombs and then crushed Saddam Hussein's army in an impressive one hundred days. American losses were 147 killed, 35 by friendly fire. A new feature of the first Iraq War was "smart bombs" that, while only 8 percent of all bombs dropped, did 75 percent of the damage. Coffey, *American Arsenal*, p. 273. See Roger Chickering et al., *War in the Modern World*, Volume 4 of *The Cambridge History of War* (Cambridge, UK: Cambridge University Press, 2012), pp. 569–571. On the necessity for speed, see Stewart, *American Military History*, Vol. II, p. 455. Saddam was captured on December 13, 2003.

second interview, "We're really good at defeating people militarily, but as occupiers we suck."[50]

Meanwhile, in 1989, the Soviet Union withdrew from Afghanistan where it had been fighting against the Afghan warriors the Mujahedeen. As a result, Afghanistan (which could hardly be called a nation in the traditional sense) descended into civil war. One of the Islamic extremists groups, the Taliban, in 1994 captured the capital Kabul and declared itself the legitimate government of Afghanistan. To combat terrorism and to capture Osama bin Laden (who it was believed was hiding there with Taliban protection), on October 7, 2001, President George W. Bush ordered air strikes against al-Qaeda training facilities and soon after American troops arrived in Afghanistan under the title Operation Enduring Freedom. "This crusade," Bush warned, "this war on terrorism, is going to take a while." However, like Iraq, Americans were unable to defeat the terrorists or win the loyalty of the tribesmen. To be sure, Osama bin Laden was located and killed in Pakistan on May 2, 2011, but peace and stability were still only a dream and not a reality. As historian Mary Kaldor put it, terrorists in Iraq, Afghanistan, and elsewhere "blurred the distinctions between wars, organized crime, and large-scale violators of human rights, . . . [a sort of]

degenerate warfare." As of the writing of this chapter, American troops are still in Afghanistan.[51]

As for the baby boomers, a good number have put their Vietnam-era experiences behind them, as they either enjoy or anticipate retirement and await or play with grandchildren—a new birth cohort. Many have children old enough to have served in the military in Iraq, Afghanistan, or other places where the United States is attempting to combat terrorism and bring political and social stability. Not a few baby boomers have come to fear that for the United States the Vietnam War was not a military aberration but rather a *harbinger* of guerrilla-style conflicts in which the enemy, not unlike the Vietcong, would strike suddenly at soldiers and civilians alike and then melt away into the countryside or into the civilian population (as Mike put it, "rice farmers by day, VC by night"). In such a warlike atmosphere, modern technology cannot be brought to bear so easily. Mary Kaldor called those enemies, like ISIS or others, "young men in home-made uniforms, desperate refugees and thuggish, neophyte politicians."[52]

Thus for many reasons, Vietnam is a chapter in American history that has not yet been closed. Does that era contain lessons that Americans—and historians—still need to learn?

50. Interview with ROTC instructor, March 13, 2015, and with Mike, March 10, 2015.

51. Mary Kaldor, *New and Old Wars: Organized Violence in a Global Era* (Cambridge, UK: Polity Press, 1999), pp. 1–2.
52. *Ibid.,* p. 1.

10

The Religious Revolution in Post–World War II America: The Pivotal Role of Southern California

The Problem

Dartmouth College professor and author Randall Balmer claimed that "you can tell a lot about a church . . . by looking at the automobiles in its parking lot." Therefore, when he visited Calvary Chapel in Santa Ana, California, one Sunday morning, he paid particular attention to the huge parking lot where the cars ranged from Mercedes-Benzes and Lincoln Continentals to old Ford Mavericks and dilapidated Volkswagen vans. Inside the 2,300-seat auditorium were people dressed in three-piece suits, beachwear, and everything in-between. They sang with enthusiasm and paid close attention to Pastor Chuck Smith's brief message and announcements of the myriad of weekday activities.[1]

About twenty years before Balmer's visit, the small church with only twenty-five members was on the verge of disbanding, when they invited Smith to be their pastor. Because of his energy and that of church members who embraced his vision, twenty years later Calvary Chapel had a twenty-one-acre "campus," its own radio station, and around twenty-five thousand people who

1. Randall Balmer, *Mine Eyes Have Seen the Glory: A Journey into the Evangelical Subculture in America* (New York: Oxford University Press, 1989), pp. 12–13.

attended the three Sunday morning services or the chapel's other activities.

Like many "megachurches" in Southern California and elsewhere, Calvary Chapel was nondenominational, was proudly independent, and was strongly **evangelical** (from the Greek "evangelion," which means "good news"; Christians who emphasize the importance of scripture, the need for personal conversion, and the expectation of an apocalypse). Although evangelical Christians (mostly Protestants) have been around for centuries, in the years following World War II, evangelism expanded rapidly until by the 1970s evangelical churches had become a major force in America's religious life.

Interestingly, although traditionally most evangelical churches were in the American South, the energy and power of the postwar evangelical movement came from Southern California. Also, while southern evangelicals often had carried their faith into the political arena (to support prohibition; oppose evolution; call for "blue laws" that forced stores, movie theaters, sporting events, and so on, to close on Sundays), it was in Southern California where the energy and power of evangelism made itself felt in national politics.

Your task in this chapter is to examine and analyze the evidence in order to answer the following central question: **What role did evangelism in Southern California play in the spread of that religious movement and its visibility and influence in the American social and political arenas in the late twentieth century?**

In a typical history class, men and women from all faith traditions and from no religions work together to learn about the past and solve history's puzzling questions. This chapter should be no exception, but all students must remember to respect and learn from people with different ideas and traditions than their own. We urge you to keep that in mind as you work together on this historical problem.

◆

Background

In 1990, California historian Kevin Starr observed that Los Angeles was "the Great Gatsby of American cities; it envisioned itself, then materialized that vision through sheer force of will."[2] Originally a land of sprawling *ranchos* in an almost uninhabitable

2. Kevin Starr, *Material Dreams: Southern California Through the 1920s* (New York: Oxford University Press, 1990), p. 69.

desert, real estate salespeople, land developers, Los Angeles business interests, and the Santa Fe and Southern Pacific Railroad systems initiated widespread and effective advertising campaigns to attract people to a land of comfortable climate and relaxed lifestyle. What had been a small city of only 5,000 in the 1870s was by 1900 a mushrooming metropolis of 102,000 that had serious

◆ CHAPTER 10

The Religious
Revolution in
Post–World War II
America: The
Pivotal Role of
Southern California

water problems. To meet those needs, at least temporarily, the Los Angeles Water Company constructed a 215-mile aqueduct from the Owens River into the San Fernando Valley. On November 3, 1913, a crowd of thirty thousand to forty thousand gathered with cups to take the first drinks. As the water appeared, Superintendent William Mulholland gave one of the shortest speeches on record: "There it is," Mulholland announced, "Take it."

From 1900 to 1930 the population of Los Angeles and surrounding towns virtually exploded, increasing over *tenfold*, to 1,238,048. Many of these in-migrants came from the Midwest: from Iowa, Illinois, Indiana, Ohio, Nebraska, and Missouri. A large percentage of them flocked to the Angelus Temple of Aimee Semple McPherson, which opened in 1923 and fed the new Californians an ample diet of fundamentalism and patriotism.[3] Not atypical of the eastern intellectuals' view of Los Angeles and McPherson was Baltimore editor and scold Henry Louis Mencken's comment:

> The minority of civilized Californians . . . sent out a call from Los Angeles for succor, as if they were beset by wolves—commonly lay the blame . . . upon the horde of morons that has flowed in from Iowa, Nebraska, and other cow states, seeking relief from the bitter climate of the steppes . . . and they now swarm in all the southern towns, especially

Los Angeles [where] they patronize the swamis, buy oil stock, gape at the movie folk, and pack the Methodist churches.

And in 1926 author Louis Adamic dubbed Los Angeles "a bad place, . . . a failed Jerusalem, a low-density Babylon."[4] But jobs were plentiful, and many of the in-migrants were making more money than they ever had, more than enough to buy a home, which cost a few hundred dollars, purchase their first automobile, shop in department stores, and attend the Angelus Temple. In 1919, the city issued $28 million of building permits. In 1923, it issued $200 million.[5]

Unlike most American cities, foreign-born in-migrants made up only a fraction of the population of Los Angeles—only 19 percent by 1920. Also, rural-to-urban migration within California was not significant: only 26 percent of the city's 1920 population was born in California. As a result,

---

3. Fundamentalists—a group of Protestants who believe in the Bible as factual historical record and incontrovertible prophecy.

4. H. L. Mencken, "The Champion," in *Prejudices: Fourth, Fifth, and Sixth Series* (New York: Literary Classics of the United States, 2010), originally published in 1926. See also Mencken in *American Mercury*, Vol. 13 (January 1928), p. 507; Louis Adamic, *Laughing in the Jungle*, quoted in Mark Girouard, *Cities and People: A Social and Architectural History* (New Haven: Yale University Press, 1985), p. 375; and Matthew Avery Sutton, *Aimee Semple McPherson and the Resurrection of Christian America* (Cambridge: Harvard University Press, 2007), especially. p. 30; Kevin Phillips, *The Emerging Republican Majority* (New Rochelle, NY: Arlington House, 1969), p. 443.

5. Sir Peter Hall, *Cities in Civilization* (New York: Pantheon Books, 1998), pp. 803–804. For building permits see Girouard, *Cities and People*, p. 375.

by 1920 the population of Los Angeles was comparatively homogeneous.[6]

The second major population boom for Los Angeles took place roughly between 1930 and 1970 when the number of residents more than doubled, to 2,818,061. These new in-migrants were mostly from the South. They came during the Depression and World War II in search of jobs, which were plentiful, especially during and after the war when government and defense-related industries offered good jobs with comparatively high wages. In-migrants found employment at, among others, Liberty Ships, Victory Ships, Douglas Aircraft, Hughes Aircraft, North American Aviation, Lockheed, Northrop, Vultec, Phillips, and the companies that served those industries and their employees. Also, by 1957 Los Angeles was second only to Akron in tire manufacturing and second only to Detroit in automobile assembly. By the mid-1950s, an average of seven hundred people *per day* were moving into the corridor from Los Angeles to San Diego, and by 1969 California had more southern residents than Arkansas.[7]

Los Angeles began expanding into what would later be described as the suburbs, where modest single-family homes were being built almost as fast as people could buy them. And, as would be the case later in eastern American cities, retail establishments followed their customers into the low-density sprawl. Los Angeles had an interurban transportation system earlier, but abandoned it in favor of automobile highways and freeways. And automobiles created a drive-in culture: the first drive-in market (1924), the first drive-in bank, the first McDonald brothers' fast food establishment, and so on. Parking spaces were critical to a business's success, and commercial buildings were set back far from the roads to make room for huge parking lots (Lakewood Center had enough parking spaces for twelve thousand automobiles). Large signs close to the roads advertised shopping opportunities. By the mid-1930s, 88 percent of all new retail stores in Los Angeles were opening in the suburbs. And by 1965, if California had been a nation, its economy would have been ranked *fifth* among all Western industrialized countries (United States, United Kingdom, West Germany, France, and California). In all, middle-class Southern Californians believed they were living the American dream.[8]

And yet, while most of these new in-migrants to Southern California were enjoying a standard of living that their parents could only imagine ("deck, patio, barbecue, [and] swimming pool . . . was . . . the good life, California style"),

6. Darren Dochuk, *From Bible Belt to Sunbelt: Plain-Folk Religion, Grassroots Politics, and the Rise of Evangelical Conservatism* (New York: W. W. Norton, 2011), pp. xv–xviii.

7. Hall, *Cities in Civilization,* pp. 817–836. On the economy see Lee Edwards, *The Conservative Revolution: The Movement That Remade America* (New York: The Free Press, 1999), p. 142. On jobs, Southern California ranked first in military contracts awarded, military payroll, civilian Defense Department payroll, and military retirees. Phillips, *The Emerging Republican Majority,* p. 448. See also Kevin Starr, *Golden Dreams: California in an Age of Abundance, 1950–1963* (New York: Oxford University Press, 2009), p. 218.

8. For the "good life" see Starr, *Golden Dreams,* p. 29.

◆ CHAPTER 10

The Religious
Revolution in
Post–World War II
America: The
Pivotal Role of
Southern California

beneath the surface all was not well. Although World War II was over and most of the American military men and women had come home, the fear of communism and nuclear war made a majority of middle-class Americans nervous. In 1959, a survey revealed that 64 percent of those surveyed responded that they feared nuclear war and 12 percent feared the spread of communism. In addition, those newly minted members of the middle class worried about the permanence of their status. Also, in the past most of these middle-class Americans had paid almost no taxes, and they resented the steep rise in taxes (in California the state budget increased by 87 percent between 1959 and 1965). At the same time, the children of these men and women appear to have lacked the appreciation of what their parents had accomplished and began embracing new music, new dances, new dress, and even a new vocabulary. In all, a poll revealed that almost half of all Americans surveyed feared that the United States was "beset by unrest serious enough to lead to a real breakdown." Combined with the beginnings of the civil rights crusade and what appeared to be a revolt of the young, many in the middle and lower middle class feared that their world was unwinding.[9]

It was to their churches that in-migrants often had turned and in the post–World War II era they did so again. Indeed, throughout history organized religions have provided their adherents with four very important social benefits:

1. Religion gives people a *sense of identity,* a way to define a group and offer it unity.
2. Religion offers believers an *interpretive framework* for understanding the world's past, present, and future and humans' place in that framework.
3. Organized religion contains *rules and standards* that are supposed to guide the thoughts and actions of believers.
4. Religion provides the *methods* for passing its beliefs, rules, and institutions from one generation to the next.[10]

Therefore, in the decade following World War II membership in most Christian denominations increased, from 49 percent in 1940 to 62 percent in 1956. And yet, in the next decade, for the first time in U.S. history most of the "mainline" Protestant denominations stopped growing and began to shrink.

At the same time, even as "mainline" Protestant denominations'

---

9. For middle-class fears see Albert H. Cantril and Charles W. Roll, Jr., *Hopes and Fears of the American People* (New York: Universe Books, 1971), pp. 23–32; Lowell D. Streiker and Gerald S. Strober, *Religion and the New Majority: Billy Graham, Middle America, and the Politics of the 70s* (New York: Association Press, 1972), pp. 13–18; Robert Coles and Jon Erikson, *The Middle Americans: Proud and Uncertain* (Boston: Little, Brown, 1971), pp. vi, 3–13, 43–59, etc.

10. For the four social functions served by religion see Jonathan Fox, *Ethnoreligious Conflict in the Late Twentieth Century* (Lanham, MD: Lexington Books, 2002), p. 29. In his book on California, Kevin Starr wrote that "[c]hurches and synagogues offered residents of the new communities a way of regrouping and reaffirming themselves in their new environment." Starr, *Golden Dreams*, p. 19.

memberships both shrank and aged, evangelical denominations and independent evangelical churches enjoyed dramatic growth. Between 1968 and 1993 membership in evangelical denominations (not counting independent churches) rose by 51 percent while memberships in "mainline" denominations declined by 23 percent. In Southern California evangelicals combed their neighborhoods house by house, inviting neighbors to what were then modest but soon to be impressive structures such as Pastor Chuck Smith's Calvary Chapel, and subsequent to that with impressive and well-organized revivals. These efforts in turn were followed by advertising and promotion, the use of Sunday Schools to attract "unchurched" parents, and a constant message combining religion and American patriotism.[11]

Many explanations have been offered for why most of the "mainline" denominations declined. Evangelical scholars themselves claimed that American people were "fed up with secular humanism, which has led to, among other things, drugs in public schools, sex on television, liberalism in the government, and weakness in foreign affairs." For his part, well-known Los Angeles evangelist and radio preacher Robert "Fighting Bob" Shuler (1880–1965) charged that in the "mainline" churches the "fires have gone out on their altars. They are cold, lifeless, formal, dead." Others asserted that "mainline" churches were "falling all over each other to be relevant to modern man." Still others asserted that "mainline" churches had abandoned their traditional missions and emphasized social activism in order to bring the Kingdom of God to earth. Finally, one might return to the list of the four important social benefits and measure the extent to which "mainline" denominations were meeting those needs.[12]

The emergence of postwar evangelicalism took place at about the same time as the reemergence of conservatism

11. For membership see Larry Eskridge and Mark A. Noll, eds., *More Money, More Ministry: Money and Evangelicals in Recent North American History* (Grand Rapids, MI: William B. Eerdmans Publishing Co., 2000), pp. 117–119. For tactics see Dochuk, *From Bible Belt to Sunbelt,* pp. 14–15; William Martin, *With God on Our Side: The Rise of the Religious Right in America* (New York: Broadway Books, 1996), p. 5. In addition to independent evangelical churches, there are numerous evangelical denominations, the largest of which is the Southern Baptist Convention. "Mainline" churches are the traditional principal churches, among which are Roman Catholic, United Methodist, Presbyterian USA, Disciples of Christ, Lutheran Church of America, Congregational, and others. For their national memberships see Eerdman's *Handbook of Christianity in America* (Grand Rapids, MI: William B. Eerdmans Publishing co., 1983), pp. 463–464.

12. Eskridge and Noll, *Money and Evangelicals,* p. 33; Kelley, *Why Conservative Churches Are Growing,* pp. ix–x; Richard John Neuhaus, *The Naked Public Square: Religion and Democracy in America* (Grand Rapids, MI: William B. Eerdmans Publishing Co., 1984), p. 38; Leonard Sweet, "The 1960s: The Crises of Liberal Christianity and the Public Emergence of Evangelism," in George Marsden, *Evangelism and Modern America* (Grand Rapids, MI: William B. Eerdmans Publishing Co., 1984), pp. 30–34, 40–42; Steven Miller, *The Age of Evangelism* (New York: Oxford University Press, 2014), p. 15; Grant Wacker, "Uneasy in Zion," in Marsden, *Evangelism and Modern America,* pp. 17–19. For a very different interpretation see Roger Finke and Rodney Stark, *The Churching of America, 1776–2005: Winners and Losers in Our Religious Economy* (New Brunswick: Rutgers University Press, 2nd ed. 2005), pp. 245–250.

✦ CHAPTER 10

The Religious
Revolution in
Post–World War II
America: The
Pivotal Role of
Southern California

in America, a movement with several roots. To begin with, some conservative intellectuals like Russell Kirk feared that a liberal government was embracing central planning and criticizing private property and individual freedom. To other conservatives, the principal foe was communism and an internal communist conspiracy. Still other conservatives attacked the economic ideas of British economist John Maynard Keynes who advocated central government economic planning. Largely, but by no means exclusively, in the South were those who believed the Democratic Party had put too much emphasis on supporting African American and liberal white civil rights actions. Finally, conservative Protestants viewed the "mainline" denominations as sacrificing their traditional beliefs while taking up social action. It doesn't take too much imagination to see how this multicausal American conservative movement (or movements) could become allied with evangelical Protestantism. As evangelical churches preached a unification of religion and patriotism, people involved in both movements began drawing closer together, especially as evangelicals became more critical of the liberal churches' social action theology.[13]

In order to carry out their ambitious mission, evangelical churches, both denominational and independent, had to raise considerable amounts of money—for expanding facilities, initiating, and carrying out an ambitious array of programs. For example, when visiting Calvary Chapel in Santa Ana, Randall Balmer counted at least fifty-one separate events taking place in *one week*. And evangelicals were more generous with their church donations than "mainstream" members—in 1968, the evangelical average was $608 per year as opposed to "mainstream" contributions of $329. And as for the practice of "tithing," 80 percent of all Americans who gave more than their respective tithes claimed to be "born-again" Christians.[14]

Evangelicals also used bookstores, radio stations, and television to carry their message, attract potential new members, and raise money. As early as 1945, there were 936 totally evangelistic radio stations, but by 1990 there were 1,512 totally evangelical stations (not counting five full-time cable networks), and by 1990 there were over four thousand Christian bookstores in the United States. Costs of employing this outreach doubtless were expensive, although most of them made a profit to add to denominational and nondenominational church donations. According to Michael Hamilton, not a few evangelical preachers claimed that

13. See especially George H. Nash, *The Conservative Intellectual Movement in America Since 1945* (New York: Basic Books, 1976); Edwards, *The Conservative Revolution* (1999); Mickey Edwards, *Reclaiming Conservatism: How a Great American Political Movement Got Lost—and How It Can Find Its Way Back* (New York: Oxford University Press, 2008); William A. Rusher, *The Rise of the Right* (New York: William Morrow and Co., 1984); Mary C. Brennan, *Turning Right: The Conservative Capture of the GOP* (Chapel Hill: University of North Carolina Press, 1995).

14. Balmer, *Mine Eyes Have Seen the Glory*, p. 17. For donations see Michael S. Hamilton, "More Money, More Ministry: The Financing of American Evangelicalism Since 1945," in Eskridge and Noll, *More Money, More Ministry*, p. 117.

God would "reward a generous giver with yet greater financial returns *in his life*," a promise that some people found almost irresistible. In all, nevertheless, expenses were very high for both the modest and the megachurches, and preachers were constantly on the lookout for more funding sources as well as for increased publicity to expand both their flocks and their incomes.[15]

It was at this point that significant donations began to be pledged and given by some wealthy Southern California businessmen who sympathized with evangelicals' opposition to the erosion of social norms, the rebellion of many middle-class teenagers (in their music, vocabulary, dress, and so on), the increased reliance on an expanding government to solve America's problems, and the secularization of many of the "mainline" churches. Also, these businessmen saw the opportunity to draw closer to evangelicals in order to gain control of the state's Republican Party and identify and support electable candidates for state and national offices. Included in this group were Walter Knott of Knott's Berry Farm (and major supporter of the ultraconservative John Birch Society); George Pepperdine, founder of Western Auto Supply Co. and in 1937 Pepperdine University; J. Howard Pew, president of Sun Oil Co.; wealthy Los Angeles businessman; and the city's most

powerful Republican Henry Salvatori; and others. These wealthy business leaders began searching for evangelical churches and preachers willing to carry the message of small government, individualism, strong moral standards, and anticommunism. Both the Southern California wealthy conservatives and the evangelical leaders, it was reasoned, would profit from this loose alliance.[16]

Several evangelicals worked to bring the two groups closer together. Almost by coincidence, however, the most visible person to carry the dual banners was a thirty-one-year-old who was a field evangelist for the organization established in 1945 and named Youth for Christ, a part-time radio preacher, and the president of the Northwestern Bible College in Minneapolis since 1943. In 1949, North Carolina native Billy Graham held a tent meeting revival in downtown Los Angeles called "Christ for Greater Los Angeles." Roughly seven hundred churches, almost all of them evangelical, associated themselves with the crusade, while almost no "mainline" churches participated. An

---

16. John Birch was an American Baptist missionary in China who also served as an anticommunist intelligence officer, was captured by communists, and killed. The John Birch Society, founded by Robert Welch, was an ultraconservative, anticommunist organization that was particularly strong in Southern California where there were an astounding 192 chapters in Greater Los Angeles alone. Starr, *Golden Dreams*, p. 201; Kurt Schuparra, *Triumph of the Right: The Rise of the California Conservative Movement, 1945–1966* (Armonk, NY: M.E. Sharpe, 1998), p. 49. Welch once attacked President Eisenhower for his "communist connections." Schuparra, *Triumph of the Right,* p. 51.

---

15. *Ibid.*, pp. 107–108, 114–131. Chuck Smith's *Calvary Chapel* owns a radio station: KWVE (K-wave). By 1992, Americans donated over $52 billion to religious organizations or churches. Hamilton, "More Money, More Ministry," p. 114.

◆ CHAPTER 10

The Religious
Revolution in
Post–World War II
America: The
Pivotal Role of
Southern California

estimated 350,000 people attended and three thousand recorded their "decisions for Christ." Two days before Graham's revival opened, President Truman announced that the Soviet Union had detonated a nuclear bomb. Graham had preached against communism since 1947, and he did so again in the extended eight-day crusade. Within weeks he was a national figure, America's most well-known evangelical preacher.[17]

The rise of evangelist Billy Graham to national prominence awakened many Americans to the seismic shift in American religious thought. Self-proclaimed "born-again" Christians, once mainly confined to the South, had emerged in almost every corner of the republic, and a plethora of organizations had been established to meet the needs of these people. Fairly typical was Dr. Frederick C. Schwarz's Christian Anti-Communist League

(1958) in Long Beach, California, that attracted several large contributors. Also prominent were the Christian Coalition of America, the Jesus Movement (late 1960s in Southern California and the Bay area), the Campus Crusade for Christ (1951), the American Coalition for Traditional Values, and numerous others. In 1976, both the Gallup Poll and *Newsweek* magazine labeled 1976 as "The Year of the Evangelical," due in part to the presidential campaign of born-again Christian Jimmy Carter.

Remember that your task in this chapter is to examine and analyze the evidence in order to answer the following central question: What role did evangelism in Southern California play in the spread of that religious movement and its visibility and influence in the American social and political arenas in the late twentieth century?

◆

The Method

In previous chapters, you have learned to use a wide variety of historical sources to "solve" several problems. And yet, whether that evidence is statistical charts, interview transcripts, sermons or speeches, photographs, court rulings, legislation, newspaper and magazine articles, songs, poems, advertisements, cartoons, posters, and

17. Charles T. Cook, *The Billy Graham Story: "One Thing I Do"* (Wheaton, IL: Van Kampen Press, 1954), pp. 15–21; Streiker and Strober, *Religion and the New Majority*, pp. 29–30; Martin, *With God on Our Side*, p. 29.

so forth, you have learned some basic rules on how to examine and analyze primary sources:

1. Approach all historical evidence with skepticism. Who created that piece of evidence? What biases might that person or persons have had? Remember that *all evidence* contains biases, even when it *appears* to be objective.

2. Was the person or persons who created the evidence in a good position to know about or observe what he/

she/they said? If there is another piece of evidence that directly contradicts the piece you are examining, which is closer to the truth? Can you find any *other* pieces of evidence that corroborate one or the other piece of evidence?

3. Remember that you *may not* "prove" a hypothesis (statement of opinion that answers a question) with another hypothesis. Sometimes a person may disguise a statement of opinion to make it *appear* to be a factual piece of evidence. For example, what is wrong with this historical process? Hypothesis: the United States should withdraw all its troops from foreign soil. "Evidence": the United States is an imperialist power. Can you see why you may not "prove" a hypothesis by using another hypothesis?

4. Do not add or delete parts of a piece of evidence because it does not "prove" your hypothesis. The worst accusation that can be leveled at a historian is that he or she saw some evidence that was contrary to his or her own hypothesis and so ignored it.

These rules are especially important when historians deal with especially sensitive subjects, such as religion.

Evidence must be approached dispassionately and sensitively, for, as you can see from this chapter, many people's basic worldviews and ethical codes come directly from their religious faith traditions.

Finally, keep in mind that no denomination or independent church dealt with in this chapter is a monolithic group. All evangelical and "mainline" denominations or individual churches are composed of people of all ranges of religious, social, and political opinions. Therefore, in most cases no single person can speak for all members.

As you examine each of the thirteen pieces of evidence, ask yourself the following questions:

1. What does that piece of evidence tell me?
2. How does each piece fit into the larger picture?
3. In what way does that piece of evidence help in answering the chapter's central question?

In order to help you examine and analyze the evidence, we have added certain **prompts** that are designed to assist you in understanding evidence in its historical context.

Be sure to take notes as you go along.

◆ CHAPTER 10

The Religious
Revolution in
Post–World War II
America: The
Pivotal Role of
Southern California

◆

The Evidence

Sources 1 and 2 from Roger Finke and Rodney Stark, *THE CHURCHING OF AMERICA, 1776–2005: WINNERS AND LOSERS IN OUR RELIGIOUS ECONOMY* (New Brunswick: Rutgers Univ. Press, 2005), page 159.

1. Adherents per One Thousand Population for Methodist Episcopal Church and Southern Baptist Convention, 1890–1986.

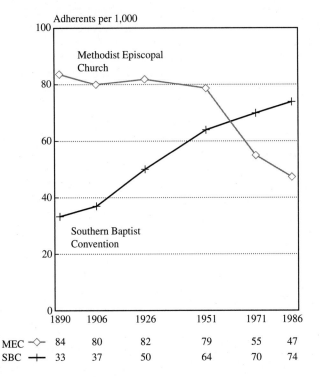

	1890	1906	1926	1951	1971	1986
MEC	84	80	82	79	55	47
SBC	33	37	50	64	70	74

2. Shares of Religious Denominations per One Thousand Church Members, 1940–2000.

	1940	1960	1980	2000	1940–2000 Percentage loss or gain
MAINLINE					
United Methodists	124.7	93.0	70.6	54.8	−56%
Presbyterian Church (USA)	41.7	36.4	24.3	16.6	−60%
Episcopal	31.4	28.6	20.7	15.3	−51%
Christian (Disciples)	25.7	15.7	8.7	5.4	−79%
United Church of Christ (Congregationalists)	26.5	19.6	12.9	9.1	−66%
EVANGELICALS					
Southern Baptists	76.7	85.0	100.9	104.9	+37%
Church of God in Christ	2.6	3.4	24.7	36.2	+1292%
Assemblies of God	3.1	4.4	7.8	9.9	+221%
Pentecostal Assemblies of the World	NA	0.4	3.7	9.9	+2375%
Church of God (Cleveland, Tenn.)	1.0	1.5	3.2	5.9	+501%
Church of the Nazarene	2.6	2.7	3.6	4.2	+63%
OTHER COSTLY RELIGIONS					
Mormons	12.0	13.0	20.9	30.8	+157%
Jehovah's Witnesses	NA	2.27	4.2	6.6	+200%

Source 3 from Rodney Stark and Charles Glock, *AMERICAN PIETY: THE NATURE OF RELIGIOUS COMMITMENT* (Berkeley, CA: Univ. of California Press, 1968), pp. 28, 33, 34, 37, 43, 99, 119.

◆ CHAPTER 10

The Religious
Revolution in
Post–World War II
America: The
Pivotal Role of
Southern California

3. 1963 Survey of Three Thousand Christians from Four Northern California Counties, On Beliefs.

Questions	Denominations							
	Congregational	Methodist	Episcopal	Disciples of Christ	Presbyterian	S. Baptist	Catholic	Sects
I know God exists	41%	60%	63%	76%	75%	99%	81%	96%
Jesus is the Son of God	40%	54%	59%	74%	72%	99%	86%	97%
Jesus was born of a Virgin	21%	34%	39%	62%	57%	99%	81%	94%
Jesus walked on water	19%	26%	30%	62%	51%	99%	71%	94%
The Bible is God's Truth	23%	39%	32%	58%	64%	61%	38%	59%
There is Life beyond Death	36%	49%	53%	64%	69%	97%	75%	94%
I say Grace at a table at least once a day	27%	24%	21%	24%	26%	20%	22%	16%
I believe my Prayers are answered	43%	47%	57%	58%	62%	87%	70%	85%

BILLY GRAHAM

Prompt: *Reread the section in the Background about the Rev. Billy Graham. Think about his rapid rise in national reputation and the nature of his message.*

Source 4 from Deborah Hart Strober and Gerald Strober, *BILLY GRAHAM: AN ORAL AND NARRATIVE BIOGRAPHY* (San Francisco: Jossey-Bass, 2006), pp. 41–42.

4. Three Interviews of Individuals Who Participated in the 1949 Los Angeles Revival.

Louis Zamperini—A former Olympic track star and prisoner of war by the Japanese during World War II

Billy Graham was unknown, except for church people, and because four well-known people were all saved in the same week—a famous broadcast cowboy,[18] a singer-songwriter; Mickey Cohen's wiretap person; and me, an Olympic athlete—Hearst in New York saw a little article about this and he called the editor of the [*Los Angeles*] *Examiner* here, and says, "Blow up Billy Graham." Otherwise, evangelism was a dirty word in those days. There were so many crooked evangelists leading up to Billy Graham, and here comes an honest, refreshing evangelist, so Hearst[19] realized that something was going on here; he realized that Billy Graham was *real*. When I talked to the editor, he said to me, "Who do you think talked to Hearst?" Meaning: God.

Howard Jones—A member of the Graham evangelistic team

I believe that it was the sovereignty of God, who for some reason known only to Himself picked Billy to do something in the field of evangelism that no other evangelist was able to do. If you go back to Los Angeles in 1949, the crowds began to dwindle. Billy told me that weariness had crept in. The team met and realized that unless God did something, the meetings would have to end. Little did they realize that a miraculous thing would happen. One morning, they awoke to find Billy's picture on the front page of the newspaper. Billy told us many times that this was the sovereign work of God—that God had touched Mr. Hearst.

18. Roy Rogers.
19. William Randolph Hearst (1863–1951) owned the nation's largest newspaper chain. He was the basis for Orson Welles's fictionalized biography *Citizen Kane* that appeared in 1941.

◆ CHAPTER 10

The Religious
Revolution in
Post–World War II
America: The
Pivotal Role of
Southern California

Gerald Beavan—Another member of the Graham team

Hearst's telegram was very crucial. Up to that point, Billy had been going to small cities; he was active in Youth for Christ and was an itinerant evangelist. In fact, the Los Angeles meeting itself wasn't that big. It wasn't one of the massive meetings he would later conduct. It was held in a tent on the corner of Washington and Hill Streets. But then Hearst, who more or less controlled the Southern California press, sent that famous message to his people and suddenly Billy became a front-page name. That certainly launched him because from that moment on we were able to go to other major cities. That is really when his nationwide crusades got started. It was terribly important.

I believe Hearst saw that here was a young man who had an important message, from God if you will, and who could express it well, and meant only good, and Hearst just decided to give Billy a boost.

Source 5 from Charles T. Cook, *THE BILLY GRAHAM STORY: "ONE THING I DO"* (Wheaton, IL: Van Kempen Press, 1954), p. 100.

5. "The Holy Spirit and Revival in Our Time," Address Delivered by Graham at the 1952 Convention of the National Association of Evangelicals in Chicago.

In the next few months we are going to be in a great political campaign in the United States. Many people have said to me, "Why do you go and talk to all these political leaders?" Do you know the reason? I sit down with them and give them the Gospel of Jesus Christ straight from the shoulder. God has opened the door, and I believe it is my duty to talk to these leaders for Christ. I've had prayer with most of them.

In the coming election campaign there's going to be the Jewish bloc, there's going to be the Roman Catholic bloc, there's going to be the labour bloc, there's going to be the Negro bloc, there's going to be the Polish bloc, there's going to be the Irish bloc. They will put on tremendous pressure. They will vote as blocs. Some of them will almost hold the balance of power. Why should not Evangelicals across America be conditioned and cultured and instructed until we, too, can make our voice known?

We need good Christian men to offer themselves for political office. One reason we don't have better men in Washington is because too few Christian men offer themselves. They are afraid. They say, "We ought not to delve in politics." God didn't say that to Daniel. Daniel lived in a country far more heathen than ours, and he was Prime Minister under seven kings in two Empires. The people are hungry for a moral crusade, and they need a Moses or a Daniel to lead them in this hour. . . .

Source 6 from *San Francisco Chronicle*, August 23, 1980, quoted in Martin, *With God On Our Side*, p. 33. The statement was originally made in 1953.

6. Billy Graham on Unions.

The Garden of Eden had "no union dues, no labor leaders, no snakes, no disease."

Source 7 from Graham, "Satan's Religion," in *AMERICAN MERCURY* (August 1954), pp. 41–46.

7. "Satan's Religion."

The Communist revolution that was born in the hearts of Marx and Engels in the middle of the nineteenth century is not going to give up or retreat. No amount of words at the United Nations or peace conferences in the Far East is going to change the mind of Communism. It is here to stay. It is a battle to the death—either Communism must die, or Christianity must die, because it is actually a battle between Christ and anti-Christ.

Has it ever occurred to you that the Devil is a religious leader, and millions are worshipping at his shrine today? While it is true that his religion is anti-Christ and anti-God, it must be classified as a religion nevertheless. And it must be an alluring one, for millions of the world's population at this hour can be counted as his devoted followers.

The name of this present-day religion is: Communism. Everything it teaches, every strategic move it makes, every philosophy it advocates is designed to strip Jehovah God of His deity, rob Him of His holiness, and reduce Him to the proportions of a heartless, shapeless, and meaningless god.

But Communism endeavors to crucify Christ upon a cross of secularism and put Him to an open shame.

Yes, like Satan, from whom they draw their inspiration, they proclaim the principles of peace, sharing and equality, but reject the only One who can impart these characteristics to a selfish, greedy world.

[321]

✦ CHAPTER 10

The Religious
Revolution in
Post–World War II
America: The
Pivotal Role of
Southern California

A war of ideologies is being waged throughout the world, a war of the secular against the spiritual. The actual battles in the areas of combat are only material manifestations of the larger battle that rages in the hearts of men throughout the earth. Will it be truth or a lie? Will we be motivated by materialistic philosophy or spiritual power? Will we be led by Jehovah God or duped by Satan? The battle lines are clearly drawn. All men of every country are being asked to choose sides. Which will it be? Christ said, "You cannot serve two masters." Joshua demanded of the Israelites long ago, "Choose you this day whom you will serve.". . .

The best defense against Communism resides in those ideals, doctrines, and principles which call for a personal faith in a personal God, belief in the Bible as the rule of faith, the regenerating grace of God, which transforms character. . . .

It is inconceivable that Communism could penetrate the barrier of a praying nation where its securities are moral and spiritual and not merely mechanical and military. Let there be more genuine prayer in our homes and churches and there will be less Communism in our capitals and statehouses. . . .

The greatest need in America today is for men and women to be born again by the Holy Spirit, by repenting of their sins, and receiving Christ as Saviour. The greatest and most effective weapon against communism today is to be born again Christian.

Source 8 from Graham, "God Before Gold," in *NATION'S BUSINESS* (September 1954), pp. 34–35, 55–56.

8. "God Before Gold."

The Apostle Paul once wrote a letter to some men in busy, bustling, commercial Rome and among other things he said: "Be . . . not slothful in business; but fervent in spirit; serving the Lord."

Thus we have the suggestion from the Scripture itself that faith and business, properly blended, can be a happy, wholesome and even profitable mixture.

Too long have many held the idea that religion should be detached from life, something aloof and apart. Still others have thought that the Christian faith and business are not compatible, that the one opposes the other. Perhaps this is true of the business of the quack, the crook and the racketeer; but it is certainly not true of legitimate business. Many or perhaps most of our traditional business axioms are fragments of scriptural truth. For example, this one: "Honesty is the best policy.". . .

Roger Babson, a businessman and well-known statistician, has said: "Statistics and economic history clearly show that the world must progress in balance. That is, materially, spiritually and socially, at approximately equal rates of growth. This means that, following a period of war or depression, prosperity can only return as people catch up spiritually. I therefore think that the principles of Christ are the only solution to our economic, political and international problems."

[Here Graham applauded the Gideons, an organization of Christian businessmen that distributes thousands of Bibles annually. Graham then concluded by citing the prophet Isaiah:]

And then as a final word to those who were interested in business and commerce, He said: "If ye be willing and obedient, ye shall eat of the good of the land."

BILL BRIGHT

Prompt: *Bill Bright (1921–2003) was born in Oklahoma, moved to California, and in 1951 founded the Campus Crusade for Christ to evangelize on college campuses, the first one being UCLA. By 1963, the organization had a staff of three hundred and was active on 108 campuses. In 1972, he was the honorary chairman of Explo '72 in Dallas (nicknamed "Godstock"), which boasted of 180,000 attendees and had an annual budget of $241 million.*[20]

Source 9 from Gill Bright, *COME HELP CHANGE THE WORLD* (Old Tappan, NJ: Fleming and Revell, 1970, pp. 27–33.

9. Bill Bright, "In the Beginning."

Though my heart was filled with praise and thanksgiving to the Lord for this remarkable revelation of what I was to do with my life, I still needed the counsel of more mature Christians. The next day I went to see one of my favorite seminary professors, Dr. Wilbur Smith, famous scholar and author

---

20. John Turner, *Bill Bright and the Campus Crusade for Christ: The Renewal of Evangelism in Postwar America* (Chapel Hill: University of North Carolina Press, 2008) and Richard Quebedeaux, *I Found It! The Story of Bill Bright and Campus Crusade* (New York: Harper & Row, 1979).

◆ CHAPTER 10

The Religious
Revolution in
Post–World War II
America: The
Pivotal Role of
Southern California

of many books. As I shared with him what God had revealed to me, he got out of his chair and paced back and forth in his office, saying again and again, "This is of God. This is of God. I want to help you. Let me think and pray about it."

The next morning when I arrived for his seven o'clock class in English Bible, Dr. Smith called me out of the classroom into a little counseling room and handed me a piece of paper on which he had scribbled these letters, "CCC." He explained that God had indeed provided the name for my vision.

Ever since that spring night experience, it has been my passion and concern to be obedient to the heavenly vision that God had given me, even going so far as to drop out of seminary with only a few units remaining before graduation. I became convinced, and remain so convinced today, that God did not want me to be ordained. Though I have a great respect and appreciation for clergy, layman status has often worked to a great advantage in my ministry with students and laymen.

The next move was to look for a board of outstanding men and women of God to advise and counsel me in the establishment of this ministry. Dr. Wilbur Smith was the first I approached. Then I asked Dr. Henrietta Mears (who had helped to introduce both Vonette and me to Christ), Billy Graham, Dick Halverson, Dawson Trotman, Cy Nelson, Dan Fuller, and Edwin Orr, to serve in this capacity. All of them readily agreed to be a part of this new facet of God's strategy. The events of the days that followed were framed in prayer and meditation. The guidance I was seeking was *where to begin*. "Lord, where do You want us to launch this ministry?" was a prayer Vonette and I and our friends uttered frequently in the spring and summer of 1951.

Increasingly, the University of California at Los Angeles was the focus of our attention. It seemed so right to begin there, at a university that in 1951 had a strong, radical minority which was exercising great influence and was causing unprecedented disturbances. Many referred to the campus as "the little Red school house." It seemed that this would be one of the most difficult campuses on which to begin, and that if our venture for Christ could succeed there, it would be likely to succeed on any campus. . . .

Our first spiritual effort was to organize a twenty-four-hour chain of prayer divided into ninety-six periods of fifteen minutes each and invite people to pray around the clock that God would do a unique thing on the UCLA campus. Next, we began to recruit and train interested students and to organize them into teams to visit the various fraternities and sororities, dormitories, and other groups on the campus. The teams would present personal testimonies of faith in Christ, explaining who Christ is, why He came and how others could know Him personally.

I remember well our first sorority meeting. It was at the Kappa Alpha Theta sorority, which was known then as the "house of beautiful women." Apparently the pledges were selected, among other reasons, for their good looks and personalities. In any event, when I finished my message and the challenge was presented to receive Christ, many girls remained behind to talk to us and ask further questions. It was a new experience for me. For more than a year we had gone into various fraternity and sorority houses on local campuses prior to the time that God gave the vision of this ministry; yet we had never seen one single person commit his life to Christ. To our knowledge, no one had ever prayed to receive Christ as a result of any of our meetings.

At the conclusion of this first sorority meeting following the vision God had given, I was amazed to see such a large group of young women standing in line to express their desire to become Christians. One after another they came (more than half of the original sixty girls present) communicating in different words, "I want to become a Christian." It was a humbling experience, seeing God work in this marvelous way. This was a dramatic confirmation to me that the vision to reach the collegians of the world was truly from God. Unsure, stepping carefully, speaking reservedly, we had been cautious up till then; but God seemed to be urging us forward, filling us with badly needed confidence and assurance that, having called us to this ministry, he was with us.

We invited the girls to join us the next evening for a meeting in our home nearby, and several of the young women brought their boyfriends. It was a memorable and exciting night. The boys were skeptical, but they came with the girls from "the house of beautiful women," and many of them decided for Christ too.

The days that followed demonstrated again and again the fact that God's hand was upon us and upon our ministry. In meeting after meeting— in fraternities, sororities, dormitories and with student leaders—the phenomenal response appeared to be approximately the same as that at our first meeting. The men were even more responsive than the women. In the course of a few months more than 250 students at UCLA—including the student body president, the editor of the newspaper and a number of the top athletes—committed their lives to Christ. So great was their influence for Christ on the entire campus that the chimes began to play Christian hymns at noonday.

By this time the news of what God was doing at UCLA had spread to other campuses, and students, faculty, laymen, and pastors in various parts of the country were asking, "Will you help us? We would like to start Campus

✦ CHAPTER 10

The Religious
Revolution in
Post–World War II
America: The
Pivotal Role of
Southern California

Crusade for Christ at our school." At this point I had to make a very important decision. The vision that God had given to me originally embraced the whole world. If I were to stay at UCLA and devote all of my own personal energies to reach only one campus, I would be disobedient to that heavenly vision. I had fallen in love with the students and could have easily spent the rest of my life serving Christ on that one campus. Yet there was only one thing for me to do—recruit and train other people to help reach all of the collegians of the world with the good news of God's love and forgiveness in Christ.

In the fall of 1952, we saw the ministry established on additional campuses, including San Diego State, University of Southern California, University of California at Berkeley, Oregon State and Washington University.

PROMPT: HISTORY TEXTBOOK CONTROVERSY

In 1966, the California State Board of Education called for a new American history textbook for eighth graders in the state's public schools. Well-known historians John W. Caughey, John Hope Franklin, and Ernest R. May had authored such a book in 1965 and it was submitted for adoption. A storm of protest erupted, as conservatives attacked the volume as "very distasteful, slanted, and objectionable," stressing one-world government (the United Nations), quoting accused communists, slanted in the direction of civil rights, and advocating the "liberal line." Some charged that the history book was part of a communist conspiracy, parents and citizens' groups opposed it, and one parent risked legal action by refusing to permit his daughter to be in the same room with the textbook Land of the Free. *Still others charged that it was hostile to religious concepts, "overemphasized Negro participation in American history," and criticized capitalism and free enterprise. Ultimately the textbook was approved but protests continued and eventually another book was chosen.[21]*

JERRY FALWELL

Prompt: *Jerry Falwell (1933–2007) founded the Thomas Road Baptist Church in Lynchburg, Virginia, when he was twenty-two years old and built that congregation into a megachurch with an hour-long television program ("The Old Time Gospel Hour"), a private school, and in 1971 Liberty University. Since the 1960s, Falwell had been attempting to merge evangelical religion and conservative politics, at first to oppose racial desegregation. In the late 1970s some conservative business and religious leaders were thinking about forming such an organization. In 1978, Republican activist Morton Blackwell traveled to Lynchburg to see if*

21. See Nicholas J. Karolides, *Banned Books: Literature Suppressed on Political Grounds* (New York: Facts on File, rev. ed. 2006), pp. 295–304. See also John Hope Franklin, *Mirror to America: The Autobiography of John Hope Franklin* (New York: Farrar, Straus, and Giroux, 2005), pp. 227–231.

Falwell was interested in heading up such an organization. Falwell was receptive and traveled to California where he, young Tim LaHaye from San Diego, and others established an organization called the Moral Majority. The new alliance's first major goal was to aid in the election of former California governor Ronald Reagan to the presidency. According to Republican leader Michael Deaver, "There is no question that the Moral Majority helped elect Ronald Reagan in 1980."[22]

Source 10 from Jerry Falwell, ed., with Ed Dobson and Ed Hindson, *THE FUNDAMENTALIST PHENOMENON: THE RESURGENCE OF CONSERVATIVE CHRISTIANITY* (Garden City, NY: Doubleday and Co., 1981), pp. 186–188, 192–193

10. Jerry Falwell, "An Agenda for the Eighties."

These are the greatest days of the twentieth century. We have the opportunity to formulate a new beginning for America in this decade. For the first time in my lifetime we have the opportunity to see spiritual revival and political renewal in the United States. We now have a platform to express the concerns of the majority of moral Americans who still love those things for which this country stands. We have the opportunity to rebuild America to the greatness it once had as a leader among leaders in the world.

The 1980s are certainly a decade of destiny for America. The rising tide of secularism threatens to obliterate the Judeo-Christian influence on American society. In the realm of religion, liberal clergy have seduced the average American away from the Bible and the kind of simple faith on which this country was built. We need to call America back to God, back to the Bible, and back to moral sanity. . . .

As a pastor, I kept waiting for someone to come to the forefront of the American religious scene to lead the way out of the wilderness. Like thousands of other preachers, I kept waiting, but no real leader appeared. Finally I realized that we had to act ourselves. Something had to be done now. The government was encroaching upon the sovereignty of both the Church and the family. The Supreme Court had legalized abortion on demand. The Equal Rights Amendment, with its vague language, threatened to do further damage to the traditional family, as did the rising sentiment toward so-called homosexual rights. Most Americans were shocked, but kept hoping someone would do something about all this moral chaos. . . . We have been labeled by our critics as arrogant, irresponsible,

22. Hart and Strober, *Billy Graham*, p. 96: Dochuk, *Bible Belt to Sunbelt*, p. 385. Falwell himself believed he was a "kingmaker," although some politicos believed that the election numbers suggested otherwise. See Miller, *The Age of Evangelism*, pp. 63–64.

◆ CHAPTER 10

The Religious
Revolution in
Post–World War II
America: The
Pivotal Role of
Southern California

and simplistic. They accuse us of violating the separation of church and state. However, the National Council of Churches (NCC) has been heavily involved in politics for years, and virtually no one has complained. Since many moral problems, such as abortion, require solutions that are both legal and political, it is necessary for religious leaders to speak on these matters in order to be heard.

We appeal to you to reacknowledge your fundamentalist roots. Stop being intimidated by what others think. Stop worrying about academic credibility and social acceptability. If Evangelicals have one glaring weakness, it is that you are too concerned [about] what the world thinks about you. You are hesitant to speak up on vital issues for fear of what the intellectual elite may think. Let them think what they wish. They have been wrong before, and they will be wrong again! . . .

Evangelicals need to reaffirm the foundation. Come back to the fundamentals of the Christian faith and stand firm on that which is essential. Throw down the anchor of truth and stop drifting with every new wave of religious fad that comes along. Stop trying to accommodate the gospel to the pitiful philosophies of unregenerate humankind. You have the truth, and the truth shall set you free. . . .

We conservative Fundamentalists and Evangelicals can be used of God to bring about a great revival of true Christianity in America and the world in our lifetime.

Prompt: *Soon after President Reagan's election, Senate majority leader Howard Baker (R. Tenn.) "suggested that cultural issues would have to wait until the economic recovery, a conclusion the White House apparently accepted." Rumors circulated that one of President Reagan's advisers had "described abortion and school prayer as 'no-win issues'." Although it claimed over four million members at its peak, in 1989 the Moral Majority disbanded.*[23]

RONALD REAGAN

Prompt: *Ronald Reagan (1911–2004) grew up in small-town Illinois, graduated from Eureka College, became a radio announcer, and in 1937 went to Hollywood to pursue a career in motion pictures. He was elected president of the Screen Actors Guild, fought the communist-dominated Conference of Studio Unions, and in 1947 testified before the House Committee on Un-American Activities (HUAC) about communists in the film industry. While working in television, he served as a spokesman for General Electric and traveled throughout the country honing his pro-business anti-communist speech. His first major step into politics was his*

23. See J. Brooks Flippen, *Jimmy Carter, the Politics of Family, and the Rise of the Religious Right* (Athens: University of Georgia Press, 2011), pp. 321–323.

October 27, 1964, televised speech in support of Republican presidential candidate Senator Barry Goldwater. The public response to Reagan's speech was astounding: it raised approximately $8 million, about half of the Goldwater campaign's entire budget. And one North Carolinian who heard Reagan's speech on the radio exclaimed, "That's who we should be running for president."[24]

Source 11 from Ronald Reagan, "A Time for Choosing," October 27, 1964 in www .reagan.utexas.edu/archives/reference/timechoosing

11. Reagan, "A Time for Choosing."

I have spent most of my life as a Democrat. I recently have seen fit to follow another course. I believe that the issues confronting us cross party lines. Now, one side in this campaign has been telling us that the issues of this election are the maintenance of peace and prosperity. The line has been used, "We've never had it so good."

But I have an uncomfortable feeling that this prosperity isn't something on which we can base our hopes for the future. No nation in history has ever survived a tax burden that reached a third of its national income. Today, 37 cents out of every dollar earned in this country is the tax collector's share, and yet our government continues to spend 17 million dollars a day more than the government takes in. We haven't balanced our budget 28 out of the last 34 years. We've raised our debt limit three times in the last twelve months, and now our national debt is one and half times bigger than all the combined debts of all the nations of the world. We have 15 billion dollars in gold in our treasury; we don't own an ounce. Foreign dollar claims are 27.3 billion dollars. And we've just had announced that the dollar of 1939 will now purchase 45 cents in its total value.

As for the peace that we would preserve, I wonder who among us would like to approach the wife or mother whose husband or son has died in South Vietnam and ask them if they think this is a peace that should be maintained indefinitely. Do they mean peace, or do they mean we just want to be left in peace? There can be no real peace while one American is dying some place in the world for the rest of us. We're at war with the most dangerous enemy that has ever faced mankind in his long climb from the swamp to the stars, and it's been said if we lose that war, and in so doing lose this way of freedom

---

24. See House Committee on Un-American Activities, *Hearings Regarding the Communist Infiltration of the Motion Picture Industry, October 20–30, 1947* (Washington: Government Printing Office, 1947), pp. 103–104. For "The Speech" see James H. Broussard, *Ronald Reagan: Champion of Conservative America* (New York: Routledge, 2015), pp. 57–58.

◆ CHAPTER 10

The Religious
Revolution in
Post–World War II
America: The
Pivotal Role of
Southern California

of ours, history will record with the greatest astonishment that those who had the most to lose did the least to prevent its happening. Well I think it's time we ask ourselves if we still know the freedoms that were intended for us by the Founding Fathers. . . .

This is the issue of this election: Whether we believe in our capacity for self-government or whether we abandon the American revolution and confess that a little intellectual elite in a far-distant capitol can plan our lives for us better than we can plan them ourselves.

You and I are told increasingly we have to choose between a left or right. Well I'd like to suggest there is no such thing as a left or right. There's only an up or down—[up] man's [age-old] dream, the ultimate in individual freedom consistent with law and order, or down to the ant heap of totalitarianism. And regardless of their sincerity, their humanitarian motives, those who would trade our freedom for security have embarked on this downward course. . . .

[Reagan then attacked the government's agricultural program as dominated by a burgeoning bureaucracy that regulates a shrinking number of farmers. He then criticized the government's housing and antipoverty programs.]

But beyond that, "the full power of centralized government"—this was the very thing the founding Fathers sought to minimize. They knew that governments don't control things. A government can't control the economy without controlling people. And they know when a government sets out to do that, it must use force and coercion to achieve its purpose. They also knew, those Founding Fathers, that outside of its legitimate functions, government does nothing as well or as economically as the private sector of the economy. . . .

Yet anytime you and I question the schemes of the do-gooders, we're denounced as being against their humanitarian goals. They say we're always "against" things—we're never "for" anything.

Well, the trouble with our liberal friends is not that they're ignorant; it's just that they know so much that isn't so.

[At this point Reagan's target was the social security program. Along with Senator Goldwater, he called for privatizing the program. He then shifted to attacking the government's foreign policy.]

Admittedly, there's a risk in any course we follow other than this, but every lesson of history tells us that the greater risk lies in appeasement, and this is the specter our well-meaning liberal friends refuse to face—that their policy of accommodation is appeasement, and it gives no choice between peace and war, only between fight or surrender. If we continue to accommodate, continue to back and retreat, eventually we have to face the final demand—the ultimatum. And what then—when Nikita Khrushchev has told his people he knows what our answer will be? He has told them that we're retreating under the pressure of the Cold War, and someday when the time comes to deliver the final ultimatum, our surrender will be voluntary, because by that time we will have been weakened from within spiritually, morally, and economically. He believes this because from our side he's heard voices pleading for "peace at any price" or "better Red than dead," or as one commentator put it, he'd rather "live on his knees than die on his feet." And therein lies the road to war, because those voices don't speak for the rest of us.

You and I know and do not believe that life is so dear and peace so sweet as to be purchased at the price of chains and slavery. If nothing in life is worth dying for, when did this begin—just in the face of this enemy? Or should Moses have told the children of Israel to live in slavery under the pharaohs? Should Christ have refused the cross? Should the patriots at Concord Bridge have thrown down their guns and refused to fire the shot heard 'round the world'? The martyrs of history were not fools, and our honored dead who gave their lives to stop the advance of the Nazis didn't die in vain. Where, then, is the road to peace? Well it's a simple answer after all.

You and I have the courage to say to our enemies, "There is a price we will not pay." "There is a point beyond which they must not advance." And this—this is the meaning in the phrase of Barry Goldwater's "peace through strength." Winston Churchill said, "The destiny of man is not measured by material computations. When great forces are on the move in the world, we learn we're spirits—not animals." And he said, "There's something going on in time and space, and beyond time and space, which, whether we like it or not, spells duty."

You and I have a rendezvous with destiny.

We'll preserve for our children this, the last best hope of man on earth, or we'll sentence them to take the last step into a thousand years of darkness.

We will keep in mind and remember that Barry Goldwater has faith in us. He has faith that you and I have the ability and the dignity and the right to make our own decisions and determine our own destiny.

Prompt: *In late February 1965, a small group of wealthy conservative Southern California business leaders approached Reagan to attempt to interest him in running for governor in 1966. Money was plentiful, former Goldwater supporters regrouped in favor of Reagan, and California evangelicals who had "enlisted their*

◆ CHAPTER 10

The Religious
Revolution in
Post–World War II
America: The
Pivotal Role of
Southern California

churches, schools, associations, and ministries" for Goldwater were enthusiastic
about the possibilities of a Reagan victory. After taking some time to think it over,
Reagan accepted, professional political organizers and campaign "handlers" were
enlisted, and forty-two Southern California conservatives formed a committee to
raise money. The campaign's triumvirate consisted of former Union Oil president
A. C. "Cy" Rubel, oilman Henry Santori, and automobile dealer Holmes Tuttle.
Although he worked hard in Reagan's behalf, Santori had doubts about the former
actor. "We knew then as we know now," quipped Santori, "that he doesn't have
any depth. But boy was he good on his feet." Reagan won the governor's race and
reelection in 1970. In 1980 he was nominated as the Republican presidential
candidate to face incumbent Jimmy Carter, who had won much of the evangelical
vote in 1976.

Source 12 from *San Francisco Chronicle*, August 23, 1980, quoted in Dochuk, *From Bible Belt to Sunbelt*, p. 393.

12. Portion of Ronald Reagan's Remarks to the National Affairs Briefing (which drew thousands of evangelical pastors and church members).

I know you can't endorse me because this is a non-partisan crowd, but I . . . want you to know that I endorse you and what you are doing.

Source 13 from Republican National Convention, Presidential Nomination, Acceptance Address by Ronald Reagan, July 17, 1980, in *VITAL SPEECHES OF THE DAY* (Southold, NY: City News Publishing Co., 1980), vol. 46, 1976–1980, pp. 642–646.

13. Reagan's Acceptance Speech at the 1980 Republican National Convention, July 17, 1980.

Never before in our history have Americans been called upon to face three grave threats to our very existence, any one of which could destroy us. We face a disintegrating economy, a weakened defense and an energy policy based on the sharing of scarcity.

The major issue of this campaign is the direct political, personal, and moral responsibility of Democratic Party leadership—in the White House and in the Congress—for this unprecedented calamity which has befallen us. They tell us they've done the most that humanly could be done. They say that the United States has had its day in the sun, that our nation has passed its zenith. They expect you to tell your children that the American people no longer have the will to cope with their problems; that the future will be one of sacrifice and few opportunities.

My fellow citizens, I utterly reject that view. The American people, the most generous on earth, who created the highest standard of living, are not going to accept the notion that we can only make a better world for others by moving backward ourselves. And those who believe we can have no business leading this nation.

I will not stand by and watch this great country destroy itself under mediocre leadership that drifts from one crisis to the next, eroding our national will and purpose. We have come together here because the American people deserve better from those to whom they entrust our nation's highest offices, and we stand united in our resolve to do something about it.

We need a rebirth of the American tradition of leadership at every level of government and in private life as well. The United States of America is unique in world history because it has a genius for leaders—many leaders— on many levels....

[Here Reagan attacked President Carter for his failure of leadership, in economics and national defense.]

Isn't it once again time to renew our compact of freedom; to pledge to each other all that is best in our lives; all that gives meaning to them—for the sake of this, our beloved and blessed land?

Together, let us make this a new beginning. Let us make a commitment to care for the needy; to teach our children the virtues handed down to us by our families; to have the courage to defend those values and virtues and the willingness to sacrifice for them.

Let us pledge to restore, in our time, the American spirit of voluntary service, of cooperation, of private and community initiative; a spirit that flows like a deep and mighty river through the history of our nation.

As your nominee, I pledge to you to restore to the Federal Government the capacity to do the people's work without dominating their lives. I pledge to you a Government that will not only work well but wisely, its ability to act tempered by prudence, and its willingness to do good balanced by the knowledge that government is never more dangerous than when our desire to have it help us blinds us to its great power to harm us....

[Here the nominee pointed to Democrats' failure to make the government live within its means, levy high taxes, poor energy policy, too large federal government, a "sorry chapter" in foreign affairs, the sense of unease among our allies.]

[333]

✦ CHAPTER 10

The Religious
Revolution in
Post–World War II
America: The
Pivotal Role of
Southern California

It is impossible to capture in words the splendor of this vast continent which God has granted as our portion of His creation. There are no words to express the extraordinary strength and character of this breed of people we call Americans.

Everywhere we've met thousands of Democrats, Independents and Republicans from all economic conditions, walks of life bound together in that community of shared values of family, work, neighborhood, peace and freedom: They are concerned, yet, they're not frightened. They're disturbed, but not dismayed. They are the kind of men and women Tom Paine had in mind when he wrote, during the darkest days of the American Revolution, "We have it in our power to begin the world over again."

Nearly 150 years after Tom Paine wrote those words, an American President told the generation of the Great Depression that it had a "rendezvous with destiny." I believe this generation of Americans today also has a rendezvous with destiny. . . .

The time is now, my fellow Americans, to recapture our destiny, to take it into our own hands. And to do this it will take many of us, working together. I ask you tonight, all over this land, to volunteer your help in this cause so that we can carry our message throughout the land.

Isn't it time that we, the people, carry out these unkept promises? That we pledge to each other and to all America on this July day 48 years later, that now we intend to do just that.

I have thought of something that's not a part of my speech and worried over whether I should do it. Can we doubt that only a Divine Providence placed this land, this island of freedom, here as a refuge for all those people in the world who yearn to breathe free? Jews and Christians enduring persecution behind the Iron Curtain; the boat people of Southeast Asia, Cuba and of Haiti: the victims of drought and famine in Africa, the freedom fighters in Afghanistan, and our own countrymen held in savage captivity.

I'll confess that I've been a little afraid to suggest what I'm going to suggest. I'm more afraid not to. Can we begin our crusade joined together in a moment of silent prayer?

God bless America.

Thank you.

[Ronald Reagan won the presidential election of 1980 with 489 electoral votes to President Carter's 49 electoral votes—from 6 of the nation's 50 states. Reagan's coattails were strong, as Republicans won control of the Senate for the first time since 1954.]

Questions to Consider

Historians generally agree that no single event, trend, or movement takes place in a vacuum. Rather, that event, trend, or movement may be both *caused by* and *related to* other simultaneous events, trends, or movements. Understanding those important relationships assist historians in determining *why* an event, trend, or movement took place *when it did* and *how* an event, trend, or movement affected and was affected by other events, trends, and movements.

By rereading the Background section of this chapter and consulting your instructor, you will be able to understand *why* the post–World War II religious movement in America occurred *when* it did and *how* it "fit" with other simultaneous phenomena.

Once you have answered those "leading" questions, you should reexamine the Evidence section with a new understanding of how the so-called religious revolution in postwar America was an important part of the overall events and trends of the period. Your answer to this chapter's central question will have considerably more sophistication and depth.

Epilogue

By the beginning of the twenty-first century, it was evident that the so-called Age of Evangelism had reached its peak and was slowly ebbing. For one thing, many evangelical Christians had come to believe that their primary goal was not to become overly involved in America's often sordid political arena but rather to return to their original charge of "winning individuals to Christ." Also, in the 1980s evangelicals were disappointed in President Reagan, who praised them in his speeches but never really supported their programs. If they kept insisting that Reagan and his allies follow their words with actions, they would split the country's conservatives: Wall Street and libertarian conservatives versus the Religious Right.[25]

At the same time, American public opinion regarding social issues began to change, albeit gradually: more

25. Edwards, *The Conservative Revolution*, pp. 143–144, 154–160; Schuparra, *Triumph of the Right*, pp. 37–39, 172n; Dochuk *From Bible Belt to Sunbelt*, p. 246; Broussard, *Reagan*, pp. 61–62. On Salvatori's quip see Schuparra, *Triumph of the Right*, p. 150. The most significant fundraiser was Walter Knott, who remained in the background because he was so controversial.

◆ CHAPTER 10

The Religious
Revolution in
Post–World War II
America: The
Pivotal Role of
Southern California

accepting of divorce (Reagan himself had been divorced in 1948), of gays and same-sex marriage, and even of the bans of prayer in public schools. And the sudden death of Jerry Falwell in 2007 left the political leaders of many evangelicals comparatively rudderless.

Instead of stubbornly trying to hold their own against the evangelical upsurge, many "mainline" churches had begun to copy the evangelicals' methods. "Contemporary" services, complete with new music and even "Christian rock," sprouted throughout the country and many other programs aimed at young people attracted what the denominations hoped would be a new generation of "mainline" church members. It is too early to tell what these comparatively new ways would garner.[26]

On a worldwide scale, it is particularly interesting to note that in the latter part of the twentieth century each of the world's major faith traditions witnessed the rise of a strong conservative movement. Moreover, all of these movements (American evangelism, Islamic fundamentalism, Jewish conservatism, and Hindu fundamentalism) had in common certain ideas:

1. All of these conservative movements look back to sometime in the past that they believe was a "golden age." In the United States, that so-called golden age was one of universal Christianity and church membership (certainly a myth).

2. This "golden age" was destroyed by the forces of secularism or, in the cases of Islam and Hinduism, Western secular ideas brought by European colonizers.

3. That "golden age" must be recaptured by a return to the dominant religious tradition and to traditional social and political themes. In all, then, these major faith traditions do not accept the separation of church and state and believe that the moral and social teachings of the religious tradition must be protected and strengthened by the state.[27]

Lastly, a survey conducted in 2007 by the Pew Religious Forum showed the comparative strength of America's Christian traditions:[28]

26. See Sidney Blumenthal, "The Religious Right and Republicans," in Richard John Neuhaus and Michael Cromartie, eds., *Piety and Politics: Evangelicals and Fundamentalists Confront the World* (Washington, DC: Ethics and Public Policy Center, 1987), pp. 269–286; Richard V. Pierard, *The Unequal Yoke: Evangelical Christianity and Political Conservatism* (Philadelphia: J.B. Lippincott, 1970), p. 35.

27. See Merry E. Wiesner, William Bruce Wheeler, Franklin Doeringer, Kenneth Curtis, "Religious Fundamentalism in the Modern World: Faith, Identity, and Contemporary Politics," in *Discovering the Global Past: A Look at the Evidence* (Boston: Houghton Mifflin, 3rd ed. 2007), vol. 2, pp. 460–486.

28. Pew Research Forum on Religion and Public Life, at religion: pewresearch.org.

Christian Religious Tradition	Total Percentage (%)
Evangelical Protestant	26.3
Mainline Protestant	18.1
Roman Catholic	23.9
Historically Black Churches	6.9
Others	8.7
Unaffiliated	16.1

In the American West, including Southern California, the figures are somewhat different:

Christian Religious Tradition	Total Percentage (%)
Evangelical Protestant	17.0
Mainline Protestant	18.0
Roman Catholic	23.0
Historically Black Churches	8.0
Other	8.0
Unaffiliated	29.0

Clearly this important trend is one that is still in flux and probably will be a major movement in American intellectual, social, and political life.

CHAPTER

11

The War on Drugs and the Rise of the Prison State

◆

The Problem

On December 18, 1993, forty-year-old Jeff Mizanskey accompanied a friend, Atilano Quintana, to a Super 8 motel in the small town of Sedalia, Missouri, located about a hundred miles east of Kansas City. The two men bought around seven pounds of marijuana, not knowing the motel room was being monitored as part of an undercover sting operation. As soon as Quintana and Mizanskey left the motel, authorities arrested them for possession of marijuana with intent to distribute: a felony. Both men were convicted. Quintana, the actual target of the sting, served a ten-year sentence. Mizanskey, who insisted that he had no direct involvement in the drug deal and no prior knowledge of Quintana's intentions, received a far harsher punishment. By May 2015, he had served twenty-two years of a life sentence. During that time, he was incarcerated at the Jefferson County Correctional Center, alongside rapists and murderers, many of whom served out their sentences and were released, while Mizanskey remained behind bars.[1]

Why the stark discrepancy between the two men's sentences? Missouri has a "prior or persistent drug offender" law that metes out longer prison sentences to recidivist criminals. Many states passed similar legislation in the 1980s and 1990s, commonly known as "three-strikes" laws. The laws work just like they sound: three strikes and you're out. These laws were part of a nationwide effort to get tough on crime—contraband drug use and trafficking in particular. America's late twentieth-century "war on drugs" came about from federal initiatives operating in tandem with state statutes. At both the national and state levels, new laws promoted zero tolerance for drug offenses; funded aggressive enforcement of drugs laws; and imposed longer, mandatory sentences on offenders.

1. Journalist Ray Downs detailed the specifics of the Mizanskey case in an extended essay for the (St. Louis) *Riverfront Times*, on December 5, 2013.

In some states, "three-strikes" punishments—often life without the possibility of parole—are reserved for persistent violent criminals. But the war on drugs led other states, including Missouri, to take repeat nonviolent drug felonies every bit as seriously as violent crimes. Jeff Mizanskey's 1993 arrest was not his first run-in with the law. In 1984, he was charged with selling an ounce of marijuana and possessing over thirty-five grams; he pled guilty and served five years of probation. And again in 1991, he was charged with marijuana possession. Both offenses were felonies.

Jeff Mizanskey has never committed a violent crime, and none of his marijuana offenses involved weapons, minors, or any other aggravating circumstances—that is, factors that routinely result in harsher punishments. Had this been his first offense, or his second, he would have likely received a sentence closer to Quintana's. But because he was convicted of a third felony, the judge in his case sentenced him to life in prison without the possibility of parole.

The Mizanskey case has attracted growing national and international attention in the past few years, in part because several states have recently moved to decriminalize marijuana use. (There have been no such efforts within states to decriminalize other contraband drugs, such as heroin or cocaine.) The fact that Jeff Mizanskey's felonies were all based on marijuana makes his case unusual in some regards. In a larger context, however, his story is exceedingly common: as part of the war on drugs a user and low-level dealer received a felony conviction and long prison sentence.[2]

The United States has the highest rate of imprisonment in the world, fueling what scholars call the American carceral (or prison) state. The rate of incarceration in the United States is five times that of Great Britain, six times Canada, three and a half times Mexico, and over seven times France and South Korea. In 2010, the last year for which firm figures exist, the number of men and women supervised in the United States by adult correctional systems—that is, in prison and jail, on probation, or on parole, and *excluding* young people in the juvenile justice system—is staggering: 7,076,200 among a national population of just under 310 million.

Mass incarceration is also profoundly shaped by class, gender, and especially race. Arrests and prosecutions and convictions all disproportionately involve poor and minority communities. African American men in particular are far more likely to be detained by police, arrested after questioning, prosecuted, and convicted than any other demographic group. One third of all African American men and one in six Latinos will go to jail at some point in their lives, whereas one in seventeen white men will be

---

2. Even short jail or prison terms for felony drug convictions can have lifelong consequences. Felons can suffer tremendous difficulty getting jobs or professional licenses after release. Restrictions limit their access to federal student loans, public housing, and some welfare benefits. As the Evidence section in this chapter indicates, felony convictions also have serious, long-term civil rights consequences.

incarcerated. These figures indicate how racial disparities permeate the criminal justice system and drive mass incarceration.

In this chapter you will study federal and state laws, public policy debates, and statistics to investigate the origins and structure of the prison state. The evidence will allow you to thoughtfully investigate this central question: **What are the causes and consequences of the United States having the highest incarceration rate in the world?**

Background

States began passing laws prohibiting the use of drugs including opium and cocaine as far back as the nineteenth century. But the history behind the war on drugs and rise of the prison state begins in the 1960s, with the growing availability and use of illicit drugs such as marijuana, heroin, cocaine, and LSD. During the turbulent decade of the 1960s, drug use emerged as a symbol of youthful rebellion and political dissent—in effect becoming mainstream within the counterculture movement. Smoking marijuana and taking LSD became fashionable among white, middle-class college students, too. And soldiers returned home from Vietnam with marijuana and heroin habits. All these factors combined to cause contraband drug use to skyrocket in the 1960s.

In a way, the growing use of illicit drugs by young people was part of an increasing American enthusiasm for pharmacology. In the mid-twentieth century, new antibiotics and vaccines saved countless lives, enabling Americans to treat or avoid entirely formerly deadly illnesses. There were also path-breaking innovations in blood pressure and heart medications.

Lithium and valium were used in treating psychological disorders. (LSD was initially designed for this purpose.) A new oral contraception became so popular and transformative that it quickly became known simply as The Pill.[3] By the 1960s, then, Americans were taking far more drugs, far more often, for far more conditions than ever before.

From the point of view of many older Americans, however, contraband drugs were another matter entirely from medications prescribed by physicians. Violence deriving from illicit drug trafficking was very concerning. The cocaine businesses run out of Colombia were especially dangerous. Sociological studies charted spikes in crime alongside increased drug use. Medical researchers also exposed the psychiatric and physiological damage done by drug addiction. And Americans could see the toll drug addiction took in their families and neighborhoods—especially among the younger generation. As drug use and drug addiction escalated, then, so too did medical,

3. To learn more, read Elaine Tyler May, *America and the Pill: A History of Promise, Peril, and Liberation* (New York: Basic Books, 2010).

societal, and political responses. The more young people embraced illicit drug use, the more the older generation recoiled. Contradictory attitudes toward contraband drugs thus widened the already deep generational divide besetting 1960s America.

The year 1968 was one of the most tumultuous in all of U.S. history. In January, the Tet Offensive laid bare hard truths about the prospects of the U.S. war in Vietnam and added fuel to the antiwar movement. In April, Martin Luther King, Jr., was assassinated in Memphis, Tennessee. Riots erupted in cities across the country in the largest violent civil uprisings of the twentieth century. Early that summer, another assassin killed another Civil Rights advocate: Democratic presidential frontrunner Robert Kennedy. In August, the Democratic National Convention devolved into a violent collision between protesters and police. The country seemed to be falling apart, or at least spiraling out of control. That November, Richard Nixon won the presidency promising to restore "traditional" values and ensure law-and-order. A centerpiece of that agenda was combating drugs.

Soon after he took office in 1969, President Nixon, pointing to increases in illicit drug usage and consequent street crimes, called drug abuse a "serious national threat." By 1971, he escalated his concern and rhetoric. With illegal drug use—marijuana, amphetamines, opiates, and hallucinogens—and drug-related crimes continuing to grow, Nixon pronounced drugs "public enemy #1."

The federal government launched the first "war on drugs" under President Nixon, who, during his second term, created the Drug Enforcement Administration (DEA), to oversee drug interdiction—to stop international smuggling of illegal drugs—and to enforce federal drug laws. At the time he created the DEA, Nixon was already embroiled in the "Watergate" controversy that would ultimately expose the president's criminal activities and force his resignation. Indeed, the same month President Nixon issued the executive order creating the DEA—July 1973—his aide Alexander Butterfield revealed in testimony before Congress the existence of the president's secret system of taping conversations and phone calls in the White House. Those tapes ultimately spelled the undoing of Nixon.[4]

Jimmy Carter's presidency marked a temporary pivot, reflecting the nation's division over drug policy. Carter won the 1976 election running on a political platform that included decriminalizing marijuana at the federal level, and in the late 1970s eleven states moved to permit marijuana possession. Four years later, however, federal policy shifted again.

Republican Ronald Reagan, elected to the presidency in 1980 over the incumbent Democrat Jimmy Carter, made a revived war on drugs a centerpiece of his domestic policy. During Reagan's first term in office, FBI expenditures on drug enforcement rose from

4. Students interested in knowing more about Watergate should start with the book written by the *Washington Post* journalists who broke the story. Their reportage is often praised as the most significant in American political history. Bob Woodward and Carl Bernstein, *All the President's Men* (New York: Simon and Schuster, 1974).

$8 million to $95 million, and DEA spending escalated, too. International drug enforcement, especially targeting Colombia, proved very expensive. By the end of Reagan's presidency, the DEA was committing nearly a billion dollars a year to fight drug smuggling as well as domestic trafficking and possession.[5]

During the 1980s, illicit drug use was increasingly seen as a criminal enterprise in and of itself, rather than a public health concern or an underlying cause of crimes such as burglary. First Lady Nancy Reagan did lead a national campaign for drug education and prevention, known as "Just Say No." But funding for drug abuse prevention and addiction treatment was dramatically reduced at both the federal and state levels, as more and more Americans embraced a tough-on-crime sensibility that saw drug users as criminals.

This emphasis on the criminality of drug use was deepened by the spread of a new, cheaper from of cocaine known as "crack." Crack cocaine is highly addictive and the early trade was volatile and often violent. Crack hit the streets of American cities in 1985 and everywhere the drug market spread, law enforcement saw spikes in violent crimes: from addicts, between rival dealers, and among traffickers.

5. A widely read and important study of the war on drugs and rise of the prison state, which emphasizes the centrality of race to both, is Michelle Alexander, *The New Jim Crow: Mass Incarceration in the Age of Colorblindness* (New York: New Press, 2010). Alexander, a prominent civil right attorney and legal scholar, is a brilliant lecturer and has spoken often about her research. Students can view her public talks through YouTube.

Media reports sensationalized what was dubbed the "crack epidemic," too. The drug was more commonly used in poor African American neighborhoods, whereas middle-class and wealthy white drug users favored powder cocaine. Public perceptions of the respective dangers of the two forms of the essentially same chemical compound led to wildly divergent mandatory sentencing guidelines, as you will see in the Evidence section in this chapter. At the same time, drug addiction and drug-trafficking violence—including but certainly not limited to crack—posed serious public health risks; deeply damaged American cities by fueling crime, poverty, and out-migration; and robbed people of their health, wealth, and lives.

Interpreting policy approaches to contraband drugs in the 1970s and 1980s requires an appreciation of the larger context in which the war on drugs was pursued. First, drug interdiction and enforcement in this era reflected the expansion of federal government powers. The size and scope of the federal government grew from the 1930s, led by Franklin Roosevelt's New Deal programs, through the turn of the twenty-first century, regardless of which political party controlled Congress and the White House. The war on drugs was pursued through expanding federal powers: the creation of new agencies, starting with the DEA, and changes in the responsibilities of others. The U.S. Customs Service, for example, assumed more law enforcement duties, especially regarding drug smuggling. The DEA also began in the 1980s to enforce American laws abroad, particularly in Mexico—an extraterritorial and extralegal extension of criminal jurisdiction and a violation of national sovereignty.[6]

Political and legal opposition to drugs did not simply emanate from the federal government, however, so it is essential to understand the interplay of state and federal agencies during this era. States aggressively pursued new drug policies in the late twentieth century alongside the federal government. The same cultural tensions that fueled the national war on drugs shaped the passage of stricter state laws—the kind that resulted in Jeff Mizanskey receiving a life sentence. Federal agencies including the DEA, Customs, and the FBI often worked closely with state and local authorities to counter drug trafficking and smuggling in the 1980s and 1990s. In addition to stopping contraband drugs at the borders of the United States and enforcing federal drug laws, DEA and FBI agents sometimes became involved in what had previously been the exclusive responsibility of state and local police agencies, providing additional resources to those agencies while also blurring the lines between jurisdictions. Even when federal authorities took the lead in the war on drugs, most drug arrests were made under state laws and most cases adjudicated on the local level. (You will see the figures of state versus federal incarcerations in the charts included in this chapter's evidence.)

Many historians interpret the nationwide enthusiasm for the war on drugs

in the 1980s as part of a conservative backlash against the youth culture of the 1960s and 1970s. Young people's opposition to the Vietnam War and rejection of traditional attitudes about morality—to say nothing of their embrace of consciousness-raising and mind-expanding drugs—distressed middle-class and middle-age Americans. The countercultural call to "turn on, tune in, drop out" seemed to many a recipe for a national disaster: a harbinger of a complete moral collapse. The grassroots, youth-centered embrace of liberal attitudes toward sexuality, race and gender relations, and casual drug use was thus met by a conservative move to restore social order. Perceptions of recreational drug use (and abuse) became a defining feature of the fierce generational conflict dividing Americans. Republican leaders in particular saw stopping illicit drugs—including enacting harsh penalties for using and distributing contraband drugs—as vital to the country's identity and future. As President Ronald Reagan put it, "Drug abuse is a repudiation of everything America is."

Race, too, became a cornerstone of the war on drugs. The conservative movement in the 1970s and 1980s in general and the war on drugs in particular cannot be understood apart from racial politics in the post–Civil Rights era. What we now often call the "mainstream" Civil Rights Movement of the 1950s and 1960s was, in fact, decidedly radical. Like the mostly white-centered countercultural movement, the Civil Rights Movement—in its various manifestations—forced profound changes in American life. As you learned in Chapter 8, the NAACP

6. See Maria Celia Torro, "The Internationalization of Police: The DEA in Mexico," *Journal of American History* 86 (September 1999): 623–640.

legal defense team, the SCLC, and the African American student protest movement all directly challenged centuries-long patterns of legalized black disfranchisement and white power. By the mid-1960s, the Black Power movement was redefining civil rights activism again, with a new ideology that resonated especially with young people tired of remaining passive in the face of brutality and frustrated by the social and economic limitations of the legal changes brought about by the older generation of African American leaders.

Many white Americans feared and fought the legal innovations achieved during the Civil Rights Movement and the societal transformations promoted by Black Power advocates. Some directly defended segregation, while others urged a slower, "moderate" transformation, and others still pushed back against the philosophical underpinning of Civil Rights legislation. In 1964, Senator Barry Goldwater ran for president as the Republican nominee; he voted against the Civil Rights Act that same year. Goldwater's campaign courted the right wing of the Republican Party, especially white southerners, by focusing on states' rights and law-and-order. When Goldwater blasted "crime in the streets"—as he often did in his campaign—his opponents (and some of his supporters) intuited a not-so-subtle condemnation of African American activism. This appeal to white southerners disaffected with Lyndon Johnson's embrace of Civil Rights legislation was taken up in 1968 by Richard Nixon in what became known as his "southern strategy."

Both Goldwater and Nixon advocated stronger stands against crime and a rejection of young activists' social liberalism with a decidedly racial undertone.

The war on drugs under Presidents Nixon and Reagan—and under Democratic president Bill Clinton in the 1990s—disproportionately targeted African American communities. The general linking of crime and blackness has deep roots in American history, running as far back as the creation of racial slavery. As historian Khalil Gibran Muhammad revealed in his powerful 2010 study, *The Condemnation of Blackness: Race, Crime, and the Making of Modern Urban America*, social scientists and policy makers in the Progressive Era linked crime and race together in the urbanizing North in still persistent ways. By the mid-twentieth century, racist notions generated in the Progressive Era about African Americans—men in particular—as especially dangerous and inclined to criminality were firmly entrenched in popular imagination and public policy.[7]

The war on drugs reflected that history. Studies consistently show that zero-tolerance policies in schools and workplaces, arrests for drug possession, conviction rates, lengths of jail and prison terms, and enforcement of "three-strikes" legislation were—and

7. This stereotyping tended to be gendered: African American women were often depicted as exploiting public assistance—of being "welfare queens." See Martin Gilens, *Why Americans Hate Welfare: Race, Media, and the Politics of Antipoverty Policy* (Chicago: University of Chicago Press, 1994).

still are—all disproportionately applied to members of poor African American as well as Hispanic communities. These patterns are connected to the racialization of poverty in America. Crime is higher and law enforcement is stricter in poor neighborhoods. And in the United States, a disproportionate number of poor people are African American and Hispanic. The consequences of growing up in poor neighborhoods, including overburdened schools and limited job opportunities, all contribute to youthful drug use and to criminal activity. But the racial dimensions of the war on drugs cannot be explained by poverty alone, as indicated by the discrepancy between crack and powder cocaine sentences. Racist stereotypes and disproportionate enforcement matter, too.

However one interprets the complicated origins of the war on drugs, one thing is abundantly clear: it played a fundamental part in creating America's prison state. The following evidence will allow you to explore the political and legislative origins and the statistical bases of mass incarceration.

But some information will be useful at the outset. In less than thirty years after the inception of the war on drugs, the penal population in the United States went from around three hundred thousand to over two million. Drug offenses accounted for two-thirds of the increase in federal incarcerations and more than half the increase of state incarcerations during those decades. For the past ten years, driven in great measure by drug arrests and incarcerations, the number of Americans under the supervision of adult correctional authorities has stood at approximately one in every thirty-three adults. African Americans comprise 12 percent of the U.S. population but make up over 40 percent of the country's prison population. They are incarcerated at six times the rate of white Americans.

The consequences of America's war on drugs and prison state are myriad, resonant, and still unfolding. This chapter should therefore offer you and your classmates a thought-provoking and worthy conclusion to your work discovering the American past.

The Method

As you arrive near the end of your class, hopefully you will have learned some important analytical lessons that transcend the study of American history. The chapters in this book have aimed to reveal to you the complexity of the past, the necessity of reasoned consideration of a wide range of issues, and the intellectual value of open-minded inquiry. By now, you have practiced being an historian with a host of different sources and methodologies. As you have seen, the past gets a lot messier—and a lot more interesting—when you move beyond facts and dates. The skills you have cultivated in this course should give you richer insight into understanding contemporary debates. This chapter tests that skill set.

The evidence in this chapter includes some primary-source materials with which you are very familiar from your work in earlier chapters. You've practiced several times analyzing political speeches, laws and legislation, and newspaper reports, and you should be very confident in using those kinds of sources. This chapter also includes statistical data, complied into charts and graphs, similar to what you first encountered in Chapter 10. However, the statistical evidence here is more expansive and more complex.

The challenge in this chapter is twofold. First, answering the chapter's central question requires you to balance a greater diversity of sources than you've managed in prior chapters. Sorting out cause and effect will take time and diligence. The textual materials are generally presented in chronological order but the statistics trace change over time—but in different ways and for slightly different periods. You must pay close attention to exactly what the charts and graphs indicate. For example, three of the tables varyingly show changing patterns in state prison populations, federal prison populations, and the total number of men and women under all adult corrections supervision—that is, incarcerated in state and federal prisons as well as on parole and on probation. You will have to evaluate this vital part of the evidence alongside the legal and policy changes made

in the late twentieth century and the evolving political culture.

Secondly, you and your classmates may struggle to remain dispassionate as you discuss this subject. As with the material in Chapter 10, members of your class may hold personal convictions that make scholarly objectivity tricky. It is, of course, perfectly understandable for students to find inspiration (or infuriation) in a deeper knowledge of the past. We hope your study of history leaves you a better informed, more engaged citizen. But as you read the primary sources and discuss them with your classmates, remember that you are seeking historical understanding, not deciding public policy. The central question before you is not "Was the war on drugs a good idea?" or "Is the American prison system just?" Instead of reaching a moral or political judgment you are considering the evidence in order to comprehend recent history: **What are the causes and consequences of the United States having the highest incarceration rate in the world?** Answering that central question may lead you to present-day policy advocacy, but first be certain that you understand the history.

We decided not to provide subquestions or further advice about organizing the evidence in this last chapter. By now, you've earned the right—and the responsibility—to make your own choices about engaging historical evidence. You should trust your ability to put your skills into action.

The Evidence

Source 1 is drawn from Ronald and Nancy Reagan's address to the nation on September 14, 1986, Ronald Reagan Presidential Library and Museum website, maintained by the National Archives and Records Administration.

1. Excerpts from Ronald and Nancy Reagan Speech, September 14, 1986.

The president and first lady spoke at 8 p.m. from the Residence at the White House. The address was broadcast live on nationwide radio and television.

THE PRESIDENT: Good evening. Usually, I talk with you from my office in the West Wing of the White House. But tonight there's something special to talk about, and I've asked someone very special to join me. . . .

Nancy's joining me because the message this evening is not my message but ours. And we speak to you not simply as fellow citizens but as fellow parents and grandparents and as concerned neighbors. It's back-to-school time for America's children. And while drug and alcohol abuse cuts across all generations, it's especially damaging to the young people on whom our future depends. . . . Drugs are menacing our society. They're threatening our values and undercutting our institutions. They're killing our children. . . .

The president then described several of his administration's successes in countering drug use and trafficking.

. . . Despite our best efforts, illegal cocaine is coming into our country at alarming levels, and 4 to 5 million people regularly use it. Five hundred thousand Americans are hooked on heroin. One in twelve persons smokes marijuana regularly. Regular drug use is even higher among the age group 18 to 25—most likely just entering the workforce. Today there's a new epidemic: smokable cocaine, otherwise known as crack. It is an explosively destructive and often lethal substance which is crushing its users. It is an uncontrolled fire.

And drug abuse is not a so-called victimless crime. Everyone's safety is at stake when drugs and excessive alcohol are used by people on the highways or by those transporting our citizens or operating industrial equipment. Drug abuse costs you and your fellow Americans at least $60 billion a year.

From the early days of our administration, Nancy has been intensely involved in the effort to fight drug abuse. She has since traveled over 100,000 miles to 55 cities in 28 States and 6 foreign countries to fight school-age drug and alcohol abuse. She's given dozens of speeches and scores of interviews and has participated in 24 special radio and TV tapings to create greater awareness of this crisis. Her personal observations and efforts have given her such dramatic insights that I wanted her to share them with you this evening. Nancy.

MRS. REAGAN: Thank you. As a mother, I've always thought of September as a special month, a time when we bundled our children off to school, to the warmth of an environment in which they could fulfill the promise and hope in those restless minds. But so much has happened over these last years, so much to shake the foundations of all that we know and all that we believe in. Today there's a drug and alcohol abuse epidemic in this country, and no one is safe from it—not you, not me, and certainly not our children, because this epidemic has their names written on it. Many of you may be thinking: "Well, drugs don't concern me." But it does concern you. It concerns us all because of the way it tears at our lives and because it's aimed at destroying the brightness and life of the sons and daughters of the United States. . . .

Drugs steal away so much. They take and take, until finally every time a drug goes into a child, something else is forced out—like love and hope and trust and confidence. Drugs take away the dream from every child's heart and replace it with a nightmare, and it's time we in America stand up and replace those dreams. Each of us has to put our principles and consciences on the line, whether in social settings or in the workplace, to set forth solid standards and stick to them. There's no moral middle ground. Indifference is not an option. We want you to help us create an outspoken intolerance for drug use. For the sake of our children, I implore each of you to be unyielding and inflexible in your opposition to drugs.

Our young people are helping us lead the way. Not long ago, in Oakland, California, I was asked by a group of children what to do if they were offered drugs, and I answered, "Just say no." Soon after that, those children in Oakland formed a Just Say No club, and now there are over 10,000 such clubs all over the country.[8] Well, their participation and their

8. This was the effort that President Reagan mentioned above. The first lady's wide-ranging campaign included direct engagement on many popular network television shows, a PBS documentary, a partnership with the Girl Scouts of America, and appearances at and support of drug treatment centers, schools, and communities across the country. The movement went global with a conference Nancy Reagan hosted for first ladies from around the world and in an address she delivered before the United Nations.

courage in saying no needs our encouragement. We can help by using every opportunity to force the issue of not using drugs to the point of making others uncomfortable, even if it means making ourselves unpopular.

Our job is never easy because drug criminals are ingenious. They work every day to plot a new and better way to steal our children's lives, just as they've done by developing this new drug, crack. For every door that we close, they open a new door to death. They prosper on our unwillingness to act. So, we must be smarter and stronger and tougher than they are. It's up to us to change attitudes and just simply dry up their markets.

And finally, to young people watching or listening, I have a very personal message for you: There's a big, wonderful world out there for you. It belongs to you. It's exciting and stimulating and rewarding. Don't cheat yourselves out of this promise. Our country needs you, but it needs you to be clear-eyed and clear-minded.... So, open your eyes to life: to see it in the vivid colors that God gave us as a precious gift to His children, to enjoy life to the fullest, and to make it count. Say yes to your life. And when it comes to drugs and alcohol just say no.

THE PRESIDENT: I think you can see why Nancy has been such a positive influence on all that we're trying to do. The job ahead of us is very clear. Nancy's personal crusade, like that of so many other wonderful individuals, should become our national crusade. It must include a combination of government and private efforts which complement one another. Last month I announced six initiatives which we believe will do just that.

First, we seek a drug-free workplace at all levels of government and in the private sector. Second, we'll work toward drug-free schools. Third, we want to ensure that the public is protected and that treatment is available to substance abusers and the chemically dependent. Our fourth goal is to expand international cooperation while treating drug trafficking as a threat to our national security. In October I will be meeting with key U.S. Ambassadors to discuss what can be done to support our friends abroad. Fifth, we must move to strengthen law enforcement activities such as those initiated by Vice President Bush and Attorney General Meese. And finally, we seek to expand public awareness and prevention.

In order to further implement these six goals, I will announce tomorrow a series of new proposals for a drug-free America. Taken as a whole, these proposals will toughen our laws against drug criminals, encourage more research and treatment, and ensure that illegal drugs will not be tolerated in our schools or in our workplaces....

Your government will continue to act aggressively, but nothing would be more effective than for Americans simply to quit using illegal drugs. We seek to create a massive change in national attitudes which ultimately will separate the drugs from the customer, to take the user away from the supply. I believe, quite simply, that we can help them quit, and that's where you come in.

My generation will remember how America swung into action when we were attacked in World War II. The war was not just fought by the fellows flying the planes or driving the tanks. It was fought at home by a mobilized nation—men and women alike—building planes and ships, clothing sailors and soldiers, feeding marines and airmen; and it was fought by children planting victory gardens and collecting cans. Well, now we're in another war for our freedom, and it's time for all of us to pull together again. So, for example, if your friend or neighbor or a family member has a drug or alcohol problem, don't turn the other way. Go to his help or to hers. Get others involved with you—clubs, service groups, and community organizations— and provide support and strength. . . .

Those of you in union halls and workplaces everywhere: Please make this challenge a part of your job every day. Help us preserve the health and dignity of all workers. To businesses large and small: We need the creativity of your enterprise applied directly to this national problem. Help us. And those of you who are educators: Your wisdom and leadership are indispensable to this cause. From the pulpits of this spirit-filled land: We would welcome your reassuring message of redemption and forgiveness and of helping one another. On the athletic fields: You men and women are among the most beloved citizens of our country. A child's eyes fill with your heroic achievements. Few of us can give youngsters something as special and strong to look up to as you. Please don't let them down. . . .

The president then called on media outlets and U.S. allies around the world to do their part.

. . . In this crusade, let us not forget who we are. Drug abuse is a repudiation of everything America is. The destructiveness and human wreckage mock our heritage. Think for a moment how special it is to be an American. Can we doubt that only a divine providence placed this land, this island of freedom, here as a refuge for all those people on the world who yearn to breathe free?

The revolution out of which our liberty was conceived signaled an historical call to an entire world seeking hope. Each new arrival of immigrants rode the crest of that hope. They came, millions seeking a safe harbor from the oppression of cruel regimes. They came, to escape starvation and disease. They came, those surviving the Holocaust and the Soviet gulags. They came, the boat people, chancing death for even a glimmer of hope that they could have a new life. They all came to taste the air redolent and rich with the freedom that is ours. What an insult it will be to what we are and whence we came if we do not rise up together in defiance against this cancer of drugs. . . .

President Reagan continued to link the war on drugs to World War II, emphasizing the national obligation to honor that legacy of fighting for freedom.

. . . As we mobilize for this national crusade, I'm mindful that drugs are a constant temptation for millions. Please remember this when your courage is tested: You are Americans. You're the product of the freest society mankind has ever known. No one, ever, has the right to destroy your dreams and shatter your life. . . .

Source 2 provides excerpts of H.R. 5484, the Ninety-Ninth Congress, Anti-Drug Abuse Act of 1986, Summary. The full text of the legislation is available at https://www.congress.gov/bill/99th-congress/house-bill/5484

2. The U.S. Congress Anti-Drug Abuse Act of 1986.

H.R. 5484 sped through the U.S. Congress. It was first proposed in the House in early September 1986 and passed three days later by a vote of 392–16. The bill was slightly amended in the Senate and passed on September 30 by a vote of 97–2. Reconciliation between the House and Senate versions was completed on October 27, and President Reagan signed the bill into law that same day. As you read this summary of the larger bill, note the internationalization of drug enforcement and how many government agencies were involved in this phase of the war on drugs.

Anti-Drug Abuse Act of 1986—Title I: Anti-Drug Enforcement— Subtitle A: Narcotics Penalties and Enforcement Act of 1986—Narcotics Penalties and Enforcement Act of 1986—Amends the Controlled Substances Act to modify the threshold quantities and kinds of controlled substances which trigger revised enhanced penalties.

Grants Federal courts limited authority to impose a sentence below a statutory minimum.

Subtitle B: Drug Possession Penalty Act of 1986—Drug Possession Penalty Act of 1986—Establishes criminal penalties for simple possession of a controlled substance.

Subtitle C: Juvenile Drug Trafficking Act of 1986–Juvenile Drug Trafficking Act of 1986—Establishes increased criminal penalties for employing persons under 18 years of age in drug operations.

Establishes increased criminal penalties for the manufacture or distribution of a controlled substance in or near an elementary school, vocational school, secondary school, or college. . . .

Subtitle I: Armed Career Criminals—Career Criminals Amendment Act of 1986—Amends the Federal criminal code to provide increased criminal penalties for any person who transports firearms or ammunition in interstate or foreign commerce if such person has multiple convictions for serious drug offenses and/or violent felonies. . . .

Subtitle K: State and Local Narcotics Control Assistance—State and Local Law Enforcement Assistance Act of 1986—Amends the Omnibus Crime Control and Safe Streets Act of 1968 to authorize the Director of the Federal Bureau of Investigation (FBI) to make grants to State and local law enforcement agencies for narcotics assistance.

Subtitle L: Study on the Use of Existing Federal Buildings as Prisons—Requires the Secretary of Defense to provide the Attorney General with a list identifying Federal buildings under the jurisdiction of the Department of Defense which could be used as detention facilities. . . .

Subtitle O: Prohibition on the Interstate Sale and Transportation of Drug Paraphernalia—Mail Order Drug Paraphernalia Control Act—Makes it a Federal criminal offense for any person to: (1) use the U.S. Postal Service or any private parcel service as part of a scheme to sell drug paraphernalia; (2) offer for sale and transportation in interstate or foreign commerce drug paraphernalia; or (3) import or export drug paraphernalia. . . .

Subtitle R: Precursor and Essential Chemical Review—Directs the Attorney General to study and recommend methods to control the diversion of legitimate precursor and essential chemicals to the production of illegal drugs. Requires the Attorney General to report all findings to the Congress.

Subtitle S: White House Conference for a Drug Free America—White House Conference for a Drug Free America—Establishes the White House Conference for a Drug Free America. . . .

Subtitle V: Death Penalty for Certain Offenses—Amends the Controlled Substances Act to establish procedures for the imposition of the death penalty for certain continuing criminal enterprise drug offenses.

Title II: International Narcotics Control—International Narcotics Control Act of 1986—Amends the Foreign Assistance Act of 1961 to increase the FY 1987 authorization for assistance for international narcotics control. . . .

Imposes certain restrictions on the provision of U.S. assistance to illicit drug producing countries and drug-transit countries.

Earmarks a specified amount of the FY 1987 international narcotics control assistance for research, development, and testing of safe and effective herbicides for use in the aerial eradication of coca.

Requires the Comptroller General to investigate and report to the Congress on the effectiveness of the international narcotics control assistance program.

Requires the President's annual report to the Congress on the international strategy to prevent cultivation and trafficking in narcotics to include a discussion of the extent to which each source country has cooperated with U.S. narcotics control efforts through the extradition or prosecution of drug traffickers and a description of the state of negotiations on updated extradition treaties. . . .

Amends the International Security and Development Cooperation Act of 1985 to place conditions on assistance for Bolivia.

Requires the President to transmit biannual reports to the Congress on major illicit drug producing countries and major drug-transit countries. Requires restrictions on U.S. assistance to such countries.

Earmarks a specified amount of the FY 1987 administration of justice program authorization to be used to provide Colombia (and other countries in the region) assistance to protect officials who are targets of narcoterrorism attacks.

Expresses the sense of the Congress that a reward should be established for information leading to the arrest or conviction of Jorge Luis Ochoa Vasquez.[9]

Urges the Secretary of State to increase efforts to negotiate with relevant countries to facilitate the interdiction of vessels suspected of carrying illicit narcotics. Directs the President to take appropriate actions against countries

---

9. Jorge Luis Ochoa Vasquez was a cofounder of the Medellín Cartel, which controlled much of the international cocaine trade in the 1980s. He was briefly jailed in Colombia in the 1990s but, despite the best efforts of the U.S. government, he avoided extradition. He died of a heart attack in Medellín, Colombia, at age sixty-five in early 2013.

which refuse to negotiate. Requires the Secretary to submit semiannual reports to the Congress identifying such countries.

Requires the President to direct that an updated threat assessment of narcotics trafficking from Africa be prepared.

Requires the Secretary of the Treasury to promote the development and implementation of a drug eradication program through multinational development bank assistance.

Urges the President to explore the possibility of engaging security-oriented organizations (such as the North Atlantic Treaty Organization) in cooperative drug programs.

Declares congressional support for the United Nations General Assembly decision to convene an International Conference on Drug Abuse and Illicit Trafficking.

Calls for the conduct of a study of the effectiveness of the United Nations drug-related declarations, conventions, and entities. Requires the President to report any recommendations which result from such study to the Congress.

Urges the United Nations Commission on Narcotic Drugs to complete work on a new draft convention against illicit traffic in narcotic drugs and psychotropic substances.

Urges the President to direct the Secretary of State to enter into negotiations with Mexico to create the Mexico-United States Intergovernmental Commission on Narcotics and Psychotropic Drug Abuse and Control.

Urges Pakistan to adopt and implement a comprehensive narcotics control program. Requires the Secretary of State to report to the Congress with respect to the adoption and implementation of such program.

Urges the President to instruct the U.S. Ambassador to the United Nations to request that the problem of illicit drug production in Iran, Afghanistan, and Laos be raised at the International Conference on Drug Abuse and Illicit Drug Trafficking.

Increases FY 1987 authorization for drug education programs abroad. Requires the Director of the U.S. Information Agency and the Administrator of the Agency for International Development to include in their annual reports to the Congress a description of the drug education programs carried out by their respective agencies.

Urges the President to take certain actions regarding narcotics control in Mexico.

Title III: Interdiction—National Drug Interdiction Improvement Act of 1986—**Subtitle A: Department of Defense Drug Interdiction Assistance**—Defense Drug Interdiction Assistance Act—Requires the Secretary of Defense to use specified funds to acquire certain equipment and aircraft for drug interdiction assistance activities of the Department of Defense. Requires the Secretary of Defense to make such aircraft available to the U.S. Customs Service.

Directs the Secretary of Defense and the Secretary of Transportation to provide for the assignment of Coast Guard personnel to naval vessels for law enforcement purposes.

Authorizes appropriations for the installation of 360-degree radar on Coast Guard surveillance aircraft. . . .

Subtitle B: Customs Enforcement—Customs Enforcement Act of 1986—**Part 1: Amendments to the Tariff Act of 1930**—Amends the Tariff Act of 1930 to establish certain entry and reporting requirements for aircraft, vessels, and vehicles arriving in the United States and the Virgin Islands. Sets forth penalties for violations of such requirements. . . .

Allows the Secretary [of Transportation], when authorized by treaty or executive agreement, to station customs officers in foreign countries to examine persons or merchandise prior to their arrival in the United States. Provides that merchandise seized at a foreign station may be transported to the United States for customs proceedings. Permits the stationing of foreign customs officers in the United States (if similar privileges are extended to the United States). Establishes penalties for making fraudulent statements to such foreign officials. . . .

Part 4: Miscellaneous Customs Amendments—Subjects recreational vessels to applicable customs regulations.

Allows any customs officer needing assistance in making an arrest, search, or seizure, to demand such assistance from any person. Subjects any person who refuses such assistance to criminal penalties. . . .

Subtitle E: United States-Bahamas Drug Interdiction Task Force—Authorizes the establishment of a United States-Bahamas Drug Interdiction Task Force. Authorizes appropriations for such Task Force and for the construction of a Coast Guard-Bahamas drug interdiction docking facility. . . .

Sources 3 and 4 from *The New York Times*, "Poll Finds Public Favors Tougher Laws Against Drug Sales and Use," 15 August, 1989; "Reno Backs Strict Sentences for Sellers of Crack Cocaine," 16 April, 1995.

3. "Poll Finds Public Favors Tougher Laws Against Drug Sale and Use," *The New York Times*, August 15, 1989.

President George H. W. Bush continued Ronald Reagan's efforts after his election in 1988. In 1989, he created the Office of National Drug Control Policy, and he appointed William J. Bennett national drug "czar"—to lead legal, political, and cultural campaigns against contraband drugs.

Poll Finds Public Favors Tougher Laws Against Drug Sale and Use

By Michael Wines

WASHINGTON, Aug. 14—William J. Bennett, director of the Bush Administration's anti-drug effort, today sought to bolster his case for stepped-up law enforcement by releasing a public opinion poll showing that most Americans favor tougher sanctions against those who sell and use illegal narcotics.

The survey, by the new George H. Gallup International Foundation, found that nearly 8 in 10 Americans say tougher laws against users are a "very important" weapon in the drug war. The ratio jumped to 9 in 10 when the questions dealt with tougher sanctions against those who sell drugs.

The Gallup Foundation survey was based on telephone interviews with 1,005 adults and 500 teen-agers in June and July. It has a margin of sampling error of plus or minus four percentage points for adults and six percentage points for teen-agers. . . .

Mr. Bennett, who made the poll results public at a White House news conference, said that its results show that the American public is "ready to take action on all fronts, including their own back yard," against illegal drugs. He heads the Office of National Drug Control Policy, a newly created agency to help curb the use of illegal drugs.

He said at the news conference that he requested the survey after the Gallup Foundation, a nonprofit group, offered to help the anti-drug effort.

The poll was released as Mr. Bennett and top police executives met with President Bush to discuss Mr. Bennett's proposed new strategy for fighting drug abuse. The proposal has not yet been made public.

Mr. Bennett emphasized that he believes that the Gallup survey underscores public support for an all-out war on the drug problem, but he again stopped short of saying that he would favor an increase in taxes to finance it.

The Gallup Foundation survey found that 32 percent of all teen-agers and 27 percent of adults now rank narcotics abuse as the nation's leading problem, nearly triple the percentage among both groups that was found in a similar Gallup Poll two years ago.

The level of concern by adults is slightly above that expressed in similar polls by The New York Times and CBS News, in which drugs have ranked as the leading national concern in most of the polls taken since May 1988.

4. "Reno Backs Strict Sentences for Sellers of Crack Cocaine," *The New York Times*, April 16, 1995.

The 1993 transition to a Democratic president, Bill Clinton, did little to alter the war on drugs. While campaigning for president, Clinton famously responded to a question about whether he had ever smoked marijuana by saying that he tried it a time or two before adding, "I didn't inhale." After Clinton defeated the incumbent Bush, he appointed Janet Reno as U.S. attorney general.

Reno Backs Strict Sentences for Sellers of Crack Cocaine.

WASHINGTON, April 15 (AP) – Attorney General Janet Reno says she will ask Congress to reject a plan that would reduce sentences for sellers of crack cocaine.

In a statement issued by the Justice Department on Friday, Ms. Reno said she disagreed with a report of the United States Sentencing Commission that said crack sentences were too harsh when compared with those for similar crimes involving powder cocaine.

"I strongly oppose measures that fail to reflect the harsh and terrible impact of crack on communities across America," the Attorney General said.

On Monday the independent commission voted, 4 to 3, to make crack cocaine sentences equal to those for powder cocaine. The proposal will become law on Nov. 1 unless Congress takes action on it.

In a report in March, the commission said that crack cocaine crimes should be punished more severely than powder cocaine offenses, but that current Federal policy goes too far.

It recommended that Congress change rules requiring a first-time offender to serve five years in prison for selling more than five grams of crack cocaine. A first-time offender would have to sell 100 times as much powder cocaine to get the same sentence.

"While some aspects of drug use and distribution may justify a higher penalty for crack than for powder cocaine, the present 100-to-1 quantity ratio is too great," the report said. "The factors that suggest a difference between the two forms of cocaine do not approach the level of a 100-to-1 quantity ratio."

[357]

The Justice Department recognizes that the penalty structure may need changing, but "it has maintained that any such adjustment must reflect the greater dangers associated with crack as opposed to cocaine powder," Ms. Reno's statement said. . . .

Ms. Reno also opposed a commission decision to reduce sentences in money-laundering cases.

Sentences for Federal cocaine offenses are based on mandatory minimum penalties Congress passed in 1986. In writing the law, Congress drew a distinction between two forms of cocaine—crack and powder—and decided that offenses involving crack deserved longer punishment.

Two years later, Congress created a five-year mandatory minimum sentence for simple possession of more than five grams of crack cocaine.

According to the report, the mandatory minimums created unintended results, punishing lower-level retail crack cocaine dealers far more severely than upper-level suppliers of powder cocaine.

Source 5 excerpts part of the guidelines for prison sentences for drug felonies issued by the U.S. Sentencing Commission in 1995. The complete list is available at http://www.ussc.gov/guidelines-manual/1995/1995-ch2ptd

5. United States Sentencing Commission Guidelines Manual, 1995.

The following are three examples of 1995 federal sentencing guidelines for drug offenses. These federal guidelines imposed mandatory sentences for drug crimes based on the specific drug and weight (or quantity in the case of some pills). For example, all the drug weights listed as Level 38 received the same sentence. So, thirty kilograms of heroin resulted in the same prison term as thirty thousand kilograms of marijuana. The higher the level of offense, the harsher the prison sentence. As the following examples indicate, the discrepancy between powder cocaine and "crack" cocaine was stunning: 100-to-1. The guidelines also contained regulations for moving drug crimes up levels (and in some instances down levels) because of extenuating circumstances. These varied from the specific, such as using aircraft or submersible vessels for trafficking drugs, to the subjective, for example, "creating a substantial risk of harm to the life of a minor."

Level 38

30 KG or more of Heroin (or the equivalent amount of other Schedule I or II Opiates);

150 KG or more of Cocaine (or the equivalent amount of other Schedule I or II Stimulants);

1.5 KG or more of Cocaine Base[10];

30 KG or more of PCP, or 3 KG or more of PCP (actual);

30 KG or more of Methamphetamine, or 3 KG or more of Methamphetamine (actual), or 3 KG or more of "Ice"[11];

300 G or more of LSD (or the equivalent amount of other Schedule I or II Hallucinogens);

12 KG or more of Fentanyl;

3 KG or more of a Fentanyl Analogue;

30,000 KG or more of Marihuana;

6,000 KG or more of Hashish;

600 KG or more of Hashish Oil.

Level 24

At least 80 G but less than 100 G of Heroin (or the equivalent amount of other Schedule I or II Opiates);

At least 400 G but less than 500 G of Cocaine (or the equivalent amount of other Schedule I or II Stimulants);

At least 4 G but less than 5 G of Cocaine Base;

At least 80 G but less than 100 G of PCP, or at least 8 G but less than 10 G of PCP (actual);

At least 80 G but less than 100 G of Methamphetamine, or at least 8 G but less than 10 G of Methamphetamine (actual), or at least 8 G but less than 10 G of "Ice";

At least 800 MG but less than 1 G of LSD (or the equivalent amount of other Schedule I or II Hallucinogens);

At least 32 G but less than 40 G of Fentanyl;

At least 8 G but less than 10 G of a Fentanyl Analogue;

At least 80 KG but less than 100 KG of Marihuana;

At least 16 KG but less than 20 KG of Hashish;

At least 1.6 KG but less than 2 KG of Hashish Oil.

10. The guidelines contain the following explanations: "'Cocaine base,' for the purposes of this guideline, means 'crack.' 'Crack' is the street name for a form of cocaine base, usually prepared by processing cocaine hydrochloride and sodium bicarbonate, and usually appearing in a lumpy, rocklike form."

"Unless otherwise specified, the weight of a controlled substance set forth in the table refers to the entire weight of any mixture or substance containing a detectable amount of the controlled substance. If a mixture or substance contains more than one controlled substance, the weight of the entire mixture or substance is assigned to the controlled substance that results in the greater offense level."

11. The guidelines contain the following explanation: "'Ice,' for the purposes of this guideline, means a mixture or substance containing methamphetamine hydrochloride of at least 80 percent purity."

Level 14

At least 5 G but less than 10 G of Heroin (or the equivalent amount of other Schedule I or II Opiates);

At least 25 G but less than 50 G of Cocaine (or the equivalent amount of other Schedule I or II Stimulants);

At least 250 MG but less than 500 MG of Cocaine Base;

At least 5 G but less than 10 G of PCP, or at least 500 MG but less than 1 G of PCP (actual);

At least 5 G but less than 10 G of Methamphetamine, or at least 500 MG but less than 1 G of Methamphetamine (actual), or at least 500 MG but less than 1 G of "Ice";

At least 50 MG but less than 100 MG of LSD (or the equivalent amount of other Schedule I or II Hallucinogens);

At least 2 G but less than 4 G of Fentanyl;

At least 500 MG but less than 1 G of a Fentanyl Analogue;

At least 5 KG but less than 10 KG of Marihuana;

At least 1 KG but less than 2 KG of Hashish;

At least 100 G but less than 200 G of Hashish Oil;

At least 5,000 but less than 10,000 units of Schedule I or II Depressants or Schedule III substances.

Source 6, an editorial, appeared in *The New York Times* in 1995. Reprinted courtesy: *The New York Times*, 5 November 1995, Editorial, "Cocaine Sentencing, Still Unjust."

6. "Cocaine Sentencing, Still Unjust," *The New York Times*, November 5, 1995.

Even as the federal government and many states moved toward stricter, mandatory drug sentences, some Americans began to question the efficacy and validity of this approach. Keep in mind that, unlike the news reports presented earlier, this essay appeared as an editorial, reflecting the opinions of staff members of The New York Times.

Cocaine Sentencing, Still Unjust

A decade ago a Congress panicked by the latest drug epidemic decreed that crimes involving crack cocaine be punished 100 times as harshly as crimes involving powdered cocaine. That unjust disparity remains in force despite a recommendation from the United States Sentencing Commission that it be abandoned. A demagogic Congress passed legislation maintaining the disparity and last week a timid President Clinton signed it into law.

Crack, the cheaper, smokable form of cocaine is chemically nearly identical to the powder form, usually snorted. But selling five grams of crack brings a mandatory five-year minimum sentence while it takes a sale of 500 grams of powder to bring the same penalty. Crack is the only drug for which the penalty for simple possession is a mandatory five years. Possession of powder carries a one-year *maximum* and is often punished simply by probation and treatment.

If Congress did not realize at first that these disparities have racial consequences, it knows so now. Crack defendants are overwhelmingly black. Whites are more often convicted of powdered cocaine violations, which yield lesser sentences.

Congress ordered a study by the Sentencing Commission, a body created to correct disparities like these. The commission heartily condemned the 100-to-1 ratio but initially declined to recommend a cure, saying that further research might support "somewhat higher penalties" for crack than for powder cocaine. The commission cited crack's stronger association with violence and the quicker, more psychologically addictive high it produces.

Then last April the commission, again unanimously denouncing the current ratio, voted 4 to 3 to equalize the penalties by lowering crack sentences to the levels for powder. The three dissenters argued for imposing some disparity in sentences and charged that the majority never overcame its own feeling that crack, though hardly 100 times as dangerous, caused more harm than powder.

Although the Justice Department has a member on the commission, it offered no alternative to the current ratio. The department said feebly that to choose a ratio like 5 to 1 or even 10 to 1 would be futile because demagogues in Congress would only double it. More likely, Attorney General Janet Reno, who once took strong stands against automatic minimum sentences, and President Clinton simply were afraid to appear remotely soft on drugs.

When the commission proposal reached Congress, Ms. Reno opposed it, again offering no alternative. Congress had until Nov. 1 to reject the proposal or let it become law. Both houses voted to reject it after debate that made clear no Senator or representative defended current law.

That need not be the end. Senator Edward Kennedy inserted a provision in the bill calling on the commission to study the issue still further. The commission owes Congress and the public a new, practical proposal, more rigorously argued. It is shameful to maintain a disparity with no rational basis.

Source 7 is excerpted from the State of California Penal Code, which established the state's "three-strikes" law. The full text can be read at www.leginfo.ca.gov/cgi-bin/displaycode?section=pen&group=00001-01000&file=654-678

7. Excerpts from State of California, Section 667 of the Penal Code.

Any person convicted of a serious felony who previously has been convicted of a serious felony in this state or of any offense committed in another jurisdiction which includes all of the elements of any serious felony, shall receive, in addition to the sentence imposed by the court for the present offense, a five-year enhancement for each such prior conviction on charges brought and tried separately. The terms of the present offense and each enhancement shall run consecutively.

This subdivision shall not be applied when the punishment imposed under other provisions of law would result in a longer term of imprisonment. There is no requirement of prior incarceration or commitment for this subdivision to apply. . . .

It is the intent of the Legislature . . . to ensure longer prison sentences and greater punishment for those who commit a felony and have been previously convicted of one or more serious and/or violent felony offenses. . . .

None of the following dispositions shall affect the determination that a prior conviction is a prior felony:

(A) The suspension of imposition of judgment or sentence.

(B) The stay of execution of sentence.

(C) The commitment to the State Department of Health Services as a mentally disordered sex offender following a conviction of a felony.

(D) The commitment to the California Rehabilitation Center or any other facility whose function is rehabilitative diversion from the state prison. . . .

A prior juvenile adjudication shall constitute a prior felony conviction for purposes of sentencing enhancement if:

(A) The juvenile was 16 years of age or older at the time he or she committed the prior offense.

(B) The prior offense is . . . a serious and/or violent felony.

(C) The juvenile was found to be a fit and proper subject to be dealt with under the juvenile court law. . . .

If a defendant has one prior felony conviction that has been pled or proved, the determinate term or minimum term for an indeterminate term shall be twice the term otherwise provided as punishment for the current felony conviction.

If a defendant has two or more prior felony convictions ... that have been pled and proved, the term for the current felony conviction shall be an indeterminate term of life imprisonment with a minimum term of the indeterminate sentence calculated as the greatest of:

(i) Three times the term otherwise provided as punishment for each current felony conviction subsequent to the two or more prior serious and/or violent felony convictions.

(ii) Imprisonment in the state prison for 25 years. . . .

Source 8, a Voter Information Guide, issued by the California Secretary of State, can be accessed at http://www.voterguide.sos.ca.gov/past/2012/general/propositions/36/arguments-rebuttals.htm

8. California Proposition 36, 2012, Official Voter Guide.

California has a long history of propositions—of ballot initiatives proposed by citizens or the state legislature and directly voted on by the electorate. In 2012, Californians debated Proposition 36, which sought to repeal the state's "three-strikes" law. In another tradition, the state government published a voter information guide, which allowed advocates on both sides of the debate to offer arguments for their position and against their opponents. In November 2012, Californians passed Proposition 36, repealing their "three-strikes" law by a margin of 69 percent to 31 percent.

Prop 36. Three Strikes Law. Repeat Felony Offenders. Penalties. Initiative Statute.

ARGUMENT IN FAVOR OF PROPOSITION 36

The Three Strikes Reform Act, Proposition 36, is supported by a broad bipartisan coalition of law enforcement leaders, civil rights organizations and taxpayer advocates because it will:

- **MAKE THE PUNISHMENT FIT THE CRIME**
  Precious financial and law enforcement resources should not be improperly diverted to impose life sentences for some non-violent offenses. Prop. 36 will assure that violent repeat offenders are punished and not released early.

- **SAVE CALIFORNIA OVER $100 MILLION EVERY YEAR**
  Taxpayers could save over $100 million per year—money that can be used to fund schools, fight crime and reduce the state's deficit. The Three Strikes

law will continue to punish dangerous career criminals who commit serious violent crimes—keeping them off the streets for 25 years to life.

- **MAKE ROOM IN PRISON FOR DANGEROUS FELONS**
  Prop. 36 will help stop clogging overcrowded prisons with non-violent offenders, so we have room to keep violent felons off the streets.

- **LAW ENFORCEMENT SUPPORT**
  Prosecutors, judges and police officers support Prop. 36 because Prop. 36 helps ensure that prisons can keep dangerous criminals behind bars for life. Prop. 36 will keep dangerous criminals off the streets.

- **TAXPAYER SUPPORT**
  Prop. 36 could save $100 million every year. Grover Norquist, President of Americans for Tax Reform says, "The Three Strikes Reform Act is tough on crime without being tough on taxpayers. It will put a stop to needlessly wasting hundreds of millions in taxpayers' hard-earned money, while protecting people from violent crime." The California State Auditor projects that taxpayers will pay millions to house and pay health care costs for non-violent Three Strikes inmates if the law is not changed. Prop. 36 will save taxpayers' money.

- **TOUGH AND SMART ON CRIME**
  Criminal justice experts and law enforcement leaders carefully crafted Prop. 36 so that truly dangerous criminals will receive no benefits whatsoever from the reform. Repeat criminals will get life in prison for serious or violent third strike crimes. Repeat offenders of non-violent crimes will get more than double the ordinary sentence. Any defendant who has ever been convicted of an extremely violent crime—such as rape, murder, or child molestation—will receive a 25 to life sentence, no matter how minor their third strike offense.

- **JOIN US**
  With the passage of Prop. 36, California will retain the toughest recidivist Three Strikes law in the country but will be fairer by emphasizing proportionality in sentencing and will provide for more evenhanded application of this important law.
  Please join us by Voting Yes on Proposition 36.
  Learn more at www. FixThreeStrikes.org

STEVE COOLEY, District Attorney, Los Angeles County

GEORGE GASCON, District Attorney, San Francisco City and County

DAVID MILLS, Professor, Stanford Law School

REBUTTAL TO ARGUMENT AGAINST PROPOSITION 36

Don't believe the scare tactics used by opponents of Prop. 36.
  Here are the facts:

- Prop. 36 requires that murderers, rapists, child molesters, and other dangerous criminals *serve their full sentences.*
- Prop. 36 *saves taxpayers hundreds of millions of dollars.*
- Prop. 36 *still punishes repeat offenders* of nonviolent crimes by doubling their state prison sentences.

Today, dangerous criminals are being released early from prison because jails are overcrowded with nonviolent offenders who pose no risk to the public. Prop. 36 prevents dangerous criminals from being released early. People convicted of shoplifting a pair of socks, stealing bread or baby formula don't deserve life sentences.
  Prop. 36 is supported by law enforcement leaders, including:

- Steve Cooley, District Attorney of Los Angeles County
- Jeffrey Rosen, District Attorney of Santa Clara County
- George Gascon, District Attorney of San Francisco City and County
- Charlie Beck, Chief of Police of Los Angeles

They know that Prop. 36:

- *Requires:* Life sentences for dangerous criminals who commit serious and violent crimes.
- *Makes the Punishment Fit the Crime:* Stop wasting valuable police and prison resources on nonviolent offenders.
- *Saves Over $100 Million Every Year.*

STEVE COOLEY, District Attorney, Los Angeles County

JEFFREY F. ROSEN, District Attorney, Santa Clara County

CHARLIE BECK, Chief of Police of Los Angeles

ARGUMENT AGAINST PROPOSITION 36

In 1994 voters overwhelmingly passed the Three Strikes Law—a law that increased prison sentences for repeat felons. And it worked! Almost immediately, our state's crime rate plummeted and has remained low, even during the current recession. The reason is pretty simple. The same criminals were committing most of the crime—cycling through our courts and jails— over and over again. The voters said enough—Three Strikes and You're Out!
  In 2004, the ACLU and other opponents of tough criminal laws tried to change Three Strikes. The voters said NO. Now they are back again with Proposition 36. They couldn't fool us last time and they won't fool us this time.

Just like before, Proposition 36 allows dangerous criminals to get their prison sentence REDUCED and then RELEASED FROM PRISON! So who does Proposition 36 apply to?

- Criminals so dangerous to society that a District Attorney chose to charge them with a Three Strike offense;
- Criminals so dangerous that a Judge agreed with DA's decision to charge;
- Criminals so dangerous that a jury convicted them of that offense;
- Criminals so dangerous that a Judge imposed a 25-to-life prison sentence; and
- Criminals whose legal appeals were denied.

After all that, Proposition 36 would let those same criminals ask a DIFFERENT Judge to set them free. Worse yet, some of these criminals will be released from prison WITHOUT PAROLE OR ANY SUPERVISION!

Here's what the Independent Legislative Analyst says about the early release of some prisoners under Proposition 36: *"Some of them could be released from prison without community supervision."*

No wonder Proposition 36 is OPPOSED by California Police, Sheriff's and law enforcement groups, including:

California Police Chiefs Association
California State Sheriff's Association
California District Attorneys Association
Peace Officers Research Association of California
Los Angeles Police Protective League

What do you think these newly released hardened criminals will do once they get out of prison? We already know the answer to that: They will commit more crimes, harm or kill more innocent victims, and ultimately end up right where they are today—back in prison. All of this will cost taxpayers more than keeping them behind bars right where they belong.

No wonder Proposition 36 is opposed by victim rights groups, including:

Crime Victims United of California
Crime Victim Action Alliance
Citizens Against Homicide
Criminal Justice Legal Foundation

At the time Three Strikes was approved by the voters, some thought it might be too harsh or too costly. Voters rejected that view in 2004. But even if you believe that the Thee Strikes law should be reformed, Proposition 36 is not the answer. Any change to the sentencing laws should only apply to future crimes committed—it should not apply to criminals already behind

bars—cutting their sentences short. It is simply not fair to the victims of crime to have to relive the pain of resentencing and early release of these dangerous criminals. We kindly ask you to VOTE NO ON PROPOSITION 36.
www.save3strikes.com

SHERIFF KEITH ROYAL, President, California State Sheriff's Association
DISTRICT ATTORNEY CARL ADAMS, President, California District
Attorneys Association
HARRIET SALERNO, President, Crime Victims United of California

REBUTTAL TO ARGUMENT IN FAVOR OF PROPOSITION 36

HERE'S WHAT THE SUPPORTERS OF PROPOSITION 36 DON'T TELL YOU:

- A hidden provision in 36 will allow thousands of dangerous criminals to get their prison sentence REDUCED and then RELEASED FROM PRISON early. According to the Fresno Bee:

    "If Proposition 36 passes, about 3,000 convicted felons serving life terms under Three Strikes could petition for a reduced sentence..."

- Some of these dangerous criminals will be released WITHOUT STATE PAROLE OR ANY LAW ENFORCEMENT SUPERVISION. According to the Independent Legislative Analyst:

    "Third strikers who are resentenced under this measure would become eligible for county community supervision upon their release from prison, rather than state parole... some of them could be released from prison without community supervision."

- PROPOSITION 36 IS TOTALLY UNNECESSARY. Prosecutors and judges already have the power to implement Three Strikes fairly. Here's what the President of the District Attorneys Association says:

    "Judges and Prosecutors don't need Proposition 36. In fact, it reduces our ability to use Three Strikes to target dangerous repeat felons and get them off the streets once and for all."

- 36 IS OPPOSED BY EVERY MAJOR LAW ENFORCEMENT ORGANIZATION AND VICTIM RIGHTS GROUP, including those representing California police chiefs, sheriffs, prosecutors, and police officers. Note that the supporters of 36 can't name a single law enforcement organization on their side!

- 36 WON'T REDUCE TAXES. Government doesn't spend too much fighting crime. It spends too little. More crime costs taxpayers too!

We urge you to SAVE Three Strikes. Please Vote NO on 36.

CHIEF RICK BRAZIEL, President, California Peace Officers
Association

HENRY T. NICHOLAS, III, Ph.D., Author, California's Victims Bill of
Rights

CHRISTINE WARD, Executive Director, Crime Victims Action
Alliance

Sources 9 through 16 offer a sampling of the kind of statistical evidence available to
scholars and citizens interested in exploring the war on drugs and mass incarceration.

9. Crime Rate in the United States, 1960–2012.

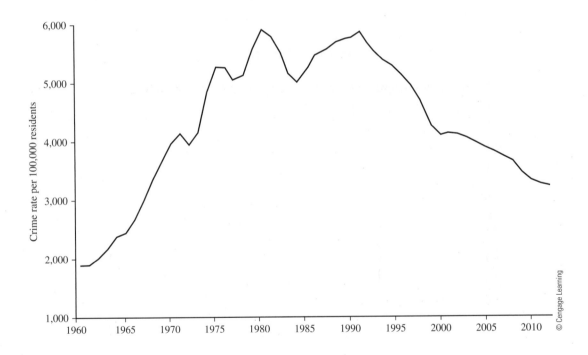

10. Incarceration Rate in the United States, 1960–2012.

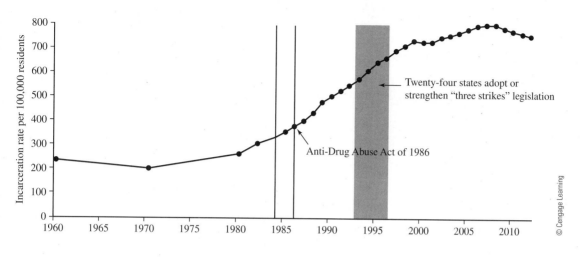

11. Incarceration Rates around the World.

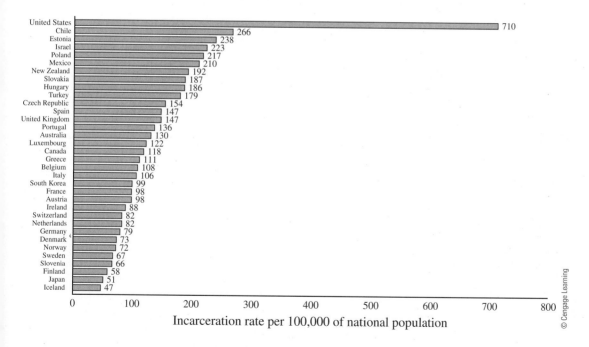

12. Adolescent Risk Behaviors by Family Income Level.

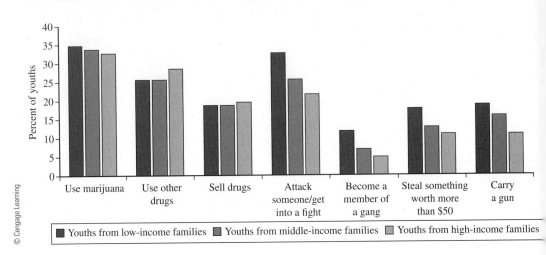

© Cengage Learning

13. U.S. Incarceration Rates per One Hundred Thousand Residents by Race and Gender.

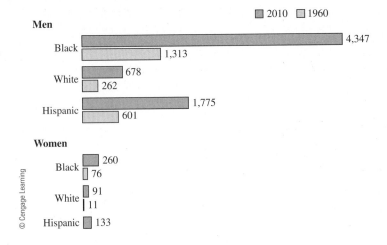

© Cengage Learning

14. Estimated Number of Sentenced Prisoners under State Jurisdiction, by Offense, Sex, Race, and Hispanic Origin, December 31, 2010.

Offense	All inmates	Male	Female	White[a]	Black[a]	Hispanic
Total	1,362,028	1,268,974	93,054	468,528	518,763	289,429
Violent	725,000	689,000	34,100	231,800	286,400	164,200
Murder[b]	166,700	157,000	9,400	47,200	70,100	38,900
Manslaughter	21,500	18,800	2,700	8,600	7,800	3,300
Rape	70,200	67,900	700	32,500	22,200	8,600
Other sexual assault	90,600	89,100	1,300	44,100	17,200	26,200
Robbery	185,800	178,000	8,300	40,400	96,600	38,000
Assault	146,800	137,700	8,500	44,300	57,200	38,500
Other violent	43,400	40,500	3,200	14,900	15,400	10,700
Property	249,500	223,100	26,900	110,800	76,300	41,900
Burglary	130,000	123,900	6,500	54,400	43,000	22,600
Larceny	45,900	38,500	7,900	20,500	14,600	6,700
Motor vehicle theft	15,000	13,600	1,000	6,000	3,100	5,700
Fraud	30,800	21,800	9,000	15,900	8,400	2,800
Other property	27,700	25,300	2,400	14,000	7,200	4,000
Drug[c]	237,000	215,600	23,400	69,500	105,600	47,800
Public-order[d]	142,500	134,100	7,800	53,100	47,800	34,400
Other/unspecified[e]	7,900	7,100	900	3,300	2,700	1,200

Note: Counts based on state prisoners with a sentence of more than 1 year. Detail may not add to total due to rounding and missing offense data.

[a]Excludes persons of Hispanic or Latino origin and persons of two or more races.

[b]Includes non-negligent manslaughter.

[c]Includes trafficking, possession, and other drug offenses.

[d]Includes weapons, drunk driving, court offenses, commercialized vice, morals and decency offenses, liquor law violations, and other public-order offenses.

[e]Includes juvenile offenses and other unspecified offense categories.

Sources: Based on US Department of Justice Prisoners in 2011 report.

15. Estimated Number of Sentenced Prisoners under Federal Jurisdiction, by Offense, December 31, 2000, 2010, and 2011.

Offense	2000	2010	2011	Percent change Average annual, 2000–2010	Percent change 2010–2011
Total	125,044	190,641	197,050	3.8%	3.4%
Violent	13,000	15,000	14,900	1.3	−0.7
Homicide[a]	1,300	2,900	2,800	7.3	−3.4
Robbery	9,200	8,300	8,100	−0.9	−2.4
Other violent	2,500	3,800	4,000	3.8	5.3
Property	9,600	10,300	10,700	0.6	3.9
Burglary	400	400	400	0.0	0.0
Fraud	7,100	7,500	7,700	0.5	2.7
Other property	2,100	2,400	2,500	1.2	4.2
Drug[b]	70,500	99,300	94,600	3.1	−4.7
Public-order	30,700	65,000	69,000	6.8	6.2
Immigration	13,000	20,200	22,100	4,0	9.4
Weapons	10,300	29,200	29,800	9,5	2.1
Other	7,400	15,600	17,100	6.8	9.6
Other/unspecified[c]	1,200	1,100	:	-0.8	:

Note: Counts are based on prisoners with a sentence of more than 1 year. Detail may not sum to total due to rounding.

[a]Includes murder, negligent, and non-negligent manslaughter.

[b]Includes trafficking, possession, and other drug offenses.

[c]Includes offenses not classified.

: Not calculated. 2011 data included individuals commiting drug and public-order crimes that could not be separated from valid unspecified records.

Sources: Based on US Department of Justice Prisoners in 2011 report.

16. Estimated Number of Persons Supervised by Adult Correctional Systems, by Correctional Status, 2000 and 2005–2010.

Year	Total correctional population[a]	Community supervision			Incarcerated[c]		
		Total[b]	Probation	Parole	Total	Jail[d]	Prison[e]
2000	6,460,000	4,565,100	3,839,532	725,527	1,937,500	621,149	1,316,333
2005	7,051,300	4,946,800	4,162,495	784,354	2,195,900	747,529	1,448,344
2006	7,202,100	5,035,200	4,237,023	798,202	2,258,800	765,819	1,492,973
2007	7,337,900	5,119,300	4,293,163	826,097	2,298,000	780,174	1,517,867
2008[f]	7,312,400	5,095,200	4,270,917	828,169	2,308,400	785,533	1,522,834
2009	7,232,800	5,018,900	4,203,967	819,308	2,291,900	767,434	1,524,478
2010	7,076,200	4,887,900	4,055,514	840,676	2,266,800	748,728	1,518,104

Note: Estimates rounded to the nearest 100. Data may not be comparable to previously published BJS reports because of updates and changes in reference dates. Community supervision, probation, parole, and prison custody counts are for December 31 within the reporting year; jail population counts are for June 30. The 2007 and 2008 totals include population counts estimated by BJS because some states were unable to provide data.

[a]Estimates were adjusted to account for some offenders with multiple correctional statuses. Details may not sum to total.

[b]Estimates include some offenders held in prison or jail but who remained under the authority of a probation or parole agency. The 2007 through 2010 estimates were adjusted to account for offenders with dual community supervision statuses. Details may not sum to total.

[c]Includes jail inmates and prisoners held in privately operated facilities.

[d]Estimates were revised to include all inmates confined in local jails, including inmates under the age of 18 who were tried or awaiting trial as an adult and the number held as juveniles. Totals for 2000 and 2006 through 2010 are estimates based on the Annual Survey of Jails. Total for 2005 is a complete enumeration based on the 2005 Census of Jail Inmates.

[e]Includes prisoners held in the custody of state or federal correctional facilities or privately operated facilities under state or federal authority. The custody prison population is not comparable to the jurisdiction prison population.

[f]Two jurisdictions changed their method of reporting probation data in 2008 resulting from changes in scope. The apparent decreases in the probation, community supervision, and total correctional populations between 2007 and 2008 were due to these changes in scope and do not reflect actual declines in the populations.

Sources: Based on US Department of Justice Prisoners in 2011 report.

Source 17 is excerpted from an October 1996 report by the Department of Justice. The full report can be accessed at https://www.ncjrs.gov/pdffiles1/pr/195110.pdf

17. Federal and State-Mandated Civil Disabilities of Convicted Felons, 1996.

In this October 1996 report, the Department of Justice compiled civil rights consequences of a felony conviction after the sentence is served.[12] *These collateral consequences can continue for years after release and in some cases remain permanently in place. Many of these post-sentence civil disabilities are enforced by the state in which the convicted felon resides, even when the crime was a federal offense. According to the report, as a result, in at least sixteen states, "federal offenders cannot avail themselves of the state procedure for restoring one or more of their civil rights, either because state law restores that right to state offenders only through a pardon and federal offenders are ineligible for a state pardon, or because a state procedure to restore rights to state offenders is unavailable to federal offenders."*

Alabama: a person convicted of certain enumerated offenses, of any crime punishable by imprisonment in the penitentiary, or of any infamous crime or crime involving moral turpitude, is disqualified from voting.[13] Civil rights lost as a result of a felony conviction may be regained only through a pardon from the State Board of Pardons and Paroles.

California: The right to vote is suspended while a person is imprisoned or on parole for the conviction of a felony.

Delaware: A person convicted of a felony forfeits the right to vote. Offenders convicted of certain election law violations are prohibited from voting for 10 years following completion of sentence. The power to pardon, except in cases of impeachment, is vested in the Governor but only upon the written recommendation of a majority of the Board of Pardons after a full hearing. According to the State's Attorney General, a pardon restores the right to serve on a jury and probably the right to vote, but does not restore the right to hold public office.

Georgia: A person convicted of a felony under the laws of any state or the United States loses the right to receive, possess, or transport a firearm (defined to include handguns, rifles, and shotguns).[14]

12. To learn most about post-release treatment, see Jeff Manza and Christopher Uggen, *Locked Out: Felon Disenfranchisement and American Democracy* (New York: Oxford University Press, 2006); and Devah Pager, *Marked: Race, Crime, and Finding Work in an Era of Mass Incarceration* (Chicago: University of Chicago Press, 2007).
13. In many states, only registered voters serve on juries and only registered voters are eligible to hold elective office, so voter disqualification often means denial of the right to serve on a jury or in public office, too.
14. Most states prohibit or at least restrict gun ownership for convicted felons.

Hawaii: A felon's right to vote is suspended during incarceration, but not during probation or parole. The right to serve on a jury is forfeited upon conviction of a felony in state or federal court. The right to vote is restored upon release from incarceration; the right to seek and hold public office is (except for treason) restored upon final discharge. Only a pardon restores the right to serve on a jury.

Nevada: A person convicted of a felony under federal law or the law of any state may not own, possess, or have in his custody or control any firearm.

New Hampshire: A person sentenced for a state or federal felony loses the right to seek or hold public office from the time of sentencing until final discharge, and loses the right to vote while actually incarcerated. The right to vote is automatically restored upon release from incarceration. The right to seek and hold public office is automatically restored upon final discharge

North Dakota: A person convicted anywhere for a felony involving violence or intimidation may not own, possess, or have under his control a firearm for 10 years from the date of conviction or release from incarceration or probation, whichever is later.

Ohio: A state or federal felon loses the rights to hold an office of honor, trust, or profit, and to serve on a jury. If a person who holds a professional or occupational license is convicted of certain drug offenses, his conviction must be reported to the licensing agency.

Oklahoma: It is unlawful for any person required to register as a sex offender to work with or provide services to children or to reside in a child care facility, and for any employer who offers or provides services to children to employ or continue to employ such a person.[15]

Pennsylvania: Employers may consider felony and misdemeanor convictions only to the extent they relate to the applicant's suitability for employment in that position. A professional or occupational license may be denied, suspended, or revoked because of conviction of a felony or misdemeanor related to the occupation.

Tennessee: A person convicted of a felony involving the use or attempted use of force, violence, or a deadly weapon, or a person convicted of a felony drug offense may not possess a handgun. No specific state procedure exists for restoring the rights lost as a result of this provision.

Texas: A person convicted of a felony or "crime involving moral turpitude" may not receive a Texas tuition assistance grant unless he has received a pardon or two years have passed since discharge or completion of probation. A convicted federal or state felon may not serve as the executor or administrator of an estate, unless he is pardoned or has had his civil rights restored.

---

15. Many states have special laws restricting where individuals convicted of sexually based offenses can live and work.

Vermont: Felons are permitted to vote by absentee ballot even during the period of incarceration. Vermont law does not prohibit felons from possessing firearm. **Wyoming:** An occupational or professional license may be denied, revoked, or suspended because of certain convictions. Licenses include barber school operator, insurance agent, outfitter, dental hygienist, radiologic technologist, title agent, and cosmetologist.

Source 18, a 2013 address by Attorney General Eric Holder, can be read in its entirety at cwww.justice.gov/opa/speech/attorney-general-eric-holder-delivers-remarks-annual-meeting-american-bar-associations

18. Excerpts of Attorney General Eric Holder's Speech before the American Bar Association, August 2013.

Appointed by President Barack Obama, Eric Holder served as the attorney general of the United States from 2009 to 2015. In 2013, he delivered this address before the policy-making House of Delegates at the opening of the annual American Bar Association meeting, laying out sweeping policy revisions.

. . . As a prosecutor; a judge; an attorney in private practice; and now, as our nation's Attorney General, I've seen the criminal justice system firsthand, from nearly every angle. While I have the utmost faith in—and dedication to—America's legal system, we must face the reality that, as it stands, our system is in too many respects broken. The course we are on is far from sustainable. And it is our time—and our duty—to identify those areas we can improve in order to better advance the cause of justice for all Americans.

Even as most crime rates decline, we need to examine new law enforcement strategies—and better allocate resources—to keep pace with today's continuing threats as violence spikes in some of our greatest cities. As studies show that six in ten American children are exposed to violence at some point in their lives—and nearly one in four college women experience some form of sexual assault by their senior year—we need fresh solutions for assisting victims and empowering survivors. As the so-called "war on drugs" enters its fifth decade, we need to ask whether it, and the approaches that comprise it, have been truly effective—and build on the Administration's efforts, led by the Office of National Drug Control Policy, to usher in a new approach. And with an outsized, unnecessarily large prison population, we need to ensure that incarceration is used to punish, deter, and rehabilitate—not merely to warehouse and forget.

Today, a vicious cycle of poverty, criminality, and incarceration traps too many Americans and weakens too many communities. And many aspects of our criminal justice system may actually exacerbate these problems, rather than alleviate them.

It's clear—as we come together today—that too many Americans go to too many prisons for far too long, and for no truly good law enforcement reason. It's clear, at a basic level, that 20th-century criminal justice solutions are not adequate to overcome our 21st-century challenges. And it is well past time to implement common sense changes that will foster safer communities from coast to coast. . . .

Attorney General Holder spoke at length about several new federal initiatives to partner with state and local governments on enhanced law enforcement to keep Americans safer. Then, in the second half of his address, he turned to mass incarceration.

. . . As we come together this morning, this same promise [of equal justice for all] must lead us all to acknowledge that—although incarceration has a significant role to play in our justice system—widespread incarceration at the federal, state, and local levels is both ineffective and unsustainable. It imposes a significant economic burden—totaling $80 billion in 2010 alone—and it comes with human and moral costs that are impossible to calculate.

As a nation, we are coldly efficient in our incarceration efforts. While the entire U.S. population has increased by about a third since 1980, the federal prison population has grown at an astonishing rate—by almost 800 percent. It's still growing—despite the fact that federal prisons are operating at nearly 40 percent above capacity. Even though this country comprises just 5 percent of the world's population, we incarcerate almost a quarter of the world's prisoners. More than 219,000 federal inmates are currently behind bars. Almost half of them are serving time for drug-related crimes, and many have substance use disorders. Nine to 10 million more people cycle through America's local jails each year. And roughly 40 percent of former federal prisoners—and more than 60 percent of former state prisoners—are rearrested or have their supervision revoked within three years after their release, at great cost to American taxpayers and often for technical or minor violations of the terms of their release.

As a society, we pay much too high a price whenever our system fails to deliver outcomes that deter and punish crime, keep us safe, and ensure that those who have paid their debts have the chance to become productive citizens. Right now, unwarranted disparities are far too common. As President Obama said last month, it's time to ask tough questions about how we can strengthen our communities, support young people, and address the fact that young black and Latino men are disproportionately likely to become involved in our criminal justice system—as victims as well as perpetrators.

We also must confront the reality that—once they're in that system—people of color often face harsher punishments than their peers. One deeply troubling report, released in February, indicates that—in recent years—black male offenders have received sentences nearly 20 percent longer than those imposed on white males convicted of similar crimes. This isn't just unacceptable—it is shameful. It's unworthy of our great country, and our great legal tradition. And in response, I have today directed a group of U.S. Attorneys to examine sentencing disparities, and to develop recommendations on how we can address them.

In this area and many others—in ways both large and small—we, as a country, must resolve to do better. The President and I agree that it's time to take a pragmatic approach. And that's why I am proud to announce today that the Justice Department will take a series of significant actions to recalibrate America's federal criminal justice system.

We will start by fundamentally rethinking the notion of mandatory minimum sentences for drug-related crimes. Some statutes that mandate inflexible sentences—regardless of the individual conduct at issue in a particular case—reduce the discretion available to prosecutors, judges, and juries. Because they oftentimes generate unfairly long sentences, they breed disrespect for the system. When applied indiscriminately, they do not serve public safety. They—and some of the enforcement priorities we have set—have had a destabilizing effect on particular communities, largely poor, and of color. And, applied inappropriately, they are ultimately counterproductive.

This is why I have today mandated a modification of the Justice Department's charging policies so that certain low-level, nonviolent drug offenders who have no ties to large-scale organizations, gangs, or cartels will no longer be charged with offenses that impose draconian mandatory minimum sentences. They now will be charged with offenses for which the accompanying sentences are better suited to their individual conduct, rather than excessive prison terms more appropriate for violent criminals or drug kingpins. By reserving the most severe penalties for serious, high-level, or violent drug traffickers, we can better promote public safety, deterrence, and rehabilitation—while making our expenditures smarter and more productive. We've seen that this approach has bipartisan support in Congress—where a number of leaders, including Senators Dick Durbin, Patrick Leahy, Mike Lee, and Rand Paul have introduced what I think is promising legislation aimed at giving federal judges more discretion in applying mandatory minimums to certain drug offenders.[16] Such legislation will ultimately save our

16. All four men served in the U.S. Senate in 2012, representing a diversity of regions and both major political parties. Durbin is a Democrat from Illinois, Lee a Utah Republican, Leahy a Vermont Democrat, and Paul a Republican from Kentucky.

country billions of dollars while keeping us safe. And the President and I look forward to working with members of both parties to refine and advance these proposals.

Secondly, the Department has now updated its framework for considering compassionate release for inmates facing extraordinary or compelling circumstances—and who pose no threat to the public. In late April, the Bureau of Prisons expanded the criteria which will be considered for inmates seeking compassionate release for medical reasons. Today, I can announce additional expansions to our policy—including revised criteria for elderly inmates who did not commit violent crimes and who have served significant portions of their sentences. Of course, as our primary responsibility, we must ensure that the American public is protected from anyone who may pose a danger to the community. But considering the applications of nonviolent offenders—through a careful review process that ultimately allows judges to consider whether release is warranted—is the fair thing to do. And it is the smart thing to do as well, because it will enable us to use our limited resources to house those who pose the greatest threat.

Finally, my colleagues and I are taking steps to identify and share best practices for enhancing the use of diversion programs—such as drug treatment and community service initiatives – that can serve as effective alternatives to incarceration.

Our U.S. Attorneys are leading the way in this regard—working alongside the judiciary to meet safety imperatives while avoiding incarceration in certain cases. In South Dakota, a joint federal-tribal program has helped to prevent at-risk young people from getting involved in the federal prison system—thereby improving lives, saving taxpayer resources, and keeping communities safer. This is exactly the kind of proven innovation that federal policymakers, and state and tribal leaders, should emulate. And it's why the Justice Department is working—through a program called the Justice Reinvestment Initiative—to bring state leaders, local stakeholders, private partners, and federal officials together to comprehensively reform corrections and criminal justice practices.

In recent years, no fewer than 17 states—supported by the Department, and led by governors and legislators of both parties—have directed funding away from prison construction and toward evidence-based programs and services, like treatment and supervision, that are designed to reduce recidivism. In Kentucky, for example, new legislation has reserved prison beds for the most serious offenders and refocused resources on community supervision and evidence-based alternative programs. As a result, the state is projected to reduce its prison population by more than 3,000 over the next 10 years—saving more than $400 million.

In Texas, investments in drug treatment for nonviolent offenders and changes to parole policies brought about a reduction in the prison population of more than 5,000 inmates last year alone. The same year, similar efforts helped Arkansas reduce its prison population by more than 1,400. From Georgia, North Carolina, and Ohio, to Pennsylvania, Hawaii, and far beyond—reinvestment and serious reform are improving public safety and saving precious resources. Let me be clear: these measures have not compromised public safety. In fact, many states have seen drops in recidivism rates at the same time their prison populations were declining. The policy changes that have led to these welcome results must be studied and emulated. While our federal prison system has continued to slowly expand, significant state-level reductions have led to three consecutive years of decline in America's overall prison population—including, in 2012, the largest drop ever experienced in a single year.

Clearly, these strategies can work. They've attracted overwhelming, bipartisan support in "red states" as well as "blue states." And it's past time for others to take notice.

I am also announcing today that I have directed every U.S. Attorney to designate a Prevention and Reentry Coordinator in his or her district— to ensure that this work is, and will remain, a top priority throughout the country. And my colleagues and I will keep working closely with state leaders, agency partners, including members of the Federal Interagency Reentry Council—and groups like the American Bar Association—to extend these efforts.

In recent years, with the Department's support, the ABA has catalogued tens of thousands of statutes and regulations that impose unwise and counterproductive collateral consequences—with regard to housing or employment, for example—on people who have been convicted of crimes. I have asked state attorneys general and a variety of federal leaders to review their own agencies' regulations. And today I can announce that I've directed all Department of Justice components, going forward, to consider whether any proposed regulation or guidance may impose unnecessary collateral consequences on those seeking to rejoin their communities.

The bottom line is that, while the aggressive enforcement of federal criminal statutes remains necessary, we cannot simply prosecute or incarcerate our way to becoming a safer nation. To be effective, federal efforts must also focus on prevention and reentry. We must never stop being tough on crime. But we must also be smart and efficient when battling crime and the conditions and the individual choices that breed it.

Ultimately, this is about much more than fairness for those who are released from prison. It's a matter of public safety and public good. It makes plain economic sense. It's about who we are as a people. And it has the potential to positively impact the lives of every man, woman, and child—in every neighborhood and city—in the United States. . . .

◆

Questions to Consider

You may find it useful to begin your class conversation talking about process before turning to specific responses to the evidence. What sub-questions did you ask yourself as you tried to **reach conclusions about the causes and consequences of America's incarceration rate**? Were you able to settle on a satisfactory answer in your own mind? How did your process and your answer compare to that of your classmates?

Is there any consensus within your class on the most important factors leading to the United States having the highest rate of incarceration in the world? What about the consequences? Where did members of your class most sharply divide?

Now, test yourself even further. Though you have considered many different sources in this chapter and looked at the rise of the prison state from several perspectives, it is always important to think about what you *don't* know. What evidence is missing that might change your perceptions of the causes and consequences of America's incarceration rate? For example, how might firsthand accounts (similar to what you read in Chapters 2 and 9) from victims of drug-related crime, nonviolent drug offenders held in maximum-security prisons, recreational drug users, law enforcement officers, drug addicts, or recently released felons alter your opinions?

While your class will doubtlessly include history majors, other students will probably be studying finance, criminal justice, public health, philosophy, or social work. Together, consider how the insights of your respective disciplines might be brought to bear in developing a fuller understanding of the war on drugs and mass incarceration. For example, from public health officials we can understand the links between intravenous drug addiction and the spread of contagious diseases, whereas social workers teach us the effects of parental drug felonies on the well-being of minor children. Use the diversity of perspectives and disciplinary training within your class to push the conversation beyond the evidence in this chapter.

Finally, practice a bit of self-reflection. How would you characterize the tone of your class discussion? Did your classmates with differing experiences and opinions approach the conversation with open minds? Did you and they listen to be persuaded? Were you able to separate out your present-day political convictions and personal experiences from your exploration of the recent past? What have you learned from this exercise?

◆

Epilogue

As the 2013 address of Attorney General Eric Holder indicated, federal policy toward the war of drugs seems to be turning. The 2014 elections suggested that public opinion is shifting, too, particularly around the use of marijuana, and state legislatures are responding.[17] A relatively commonly used drug that during the 1980s and 1990s could, because of three-strikes laws, put men like Jeff Mizanskey in prison for decades is now undergoing major reevaluation in terms of its criminality and impact on users. In the last decade, twenty-three states and the District of Columbia have approved marijuana for some medical purposes. Many states and municipalities have quietly decriminalized the possession of small amounts of marijuana. And voters in four states, Alaska, Oregon, Colorado, and Washington, approved the sale and use of marijuana for adults over age twenty-one. However, using marijuana remains an offense under federal law, and state laws vary wildly.

Much of the controversy about marijuana revolves around contradictory views about the danger of abuse and its medical benefits. Increasingly, physicians and medical researchers believe marijuana (or cannabis) does not merit listing as a Schedule I drug—which is reserved for drugs with a high potential for abuse. Some researchers conclude that teens who are daily users of marijuana are less likely to graduate high school and more likely to move on to other illegal drugs in the future. Other studies discount these results, noting that other factors are likely to be at play in these projected outcomes. A growing number of medical research studies indicate that there are discernible health benefits from medical applications of marijuana, especially in the area of pain relief and the control of epileptic seizures and other neurological disorders.

All of these factors have prompted politicians from both major national parties to weigh the politics and the economics of implementing new drug laws—at least regarding marijuana. In March 2015, President Barack Obama observed that "our criminal justice system generally is so heavily skewed towards cracking down on non-violent drug offenders that it has not just had a terrible effect on many communities—particularly communities of color . . . . It costs a huge amount of money to states and a lot of states are figuring that out." What might the future hold? We will have to wait and see.

A change has already come for Jeff Mizanskey. In late May 2015, under mounting public pressure and after years of sustained effort on the part of Mizanskey's family, Missouri governor Jay Nixon commuted Jeff Mizanskey's sentence. In September 2015, he was granted parole. After more than two decades behind bars, Jeff Mizanskey is once again a free man.

17. Additional information about federal policies toward drug use and abuse can be found at the websites of the Office of National Drug Control Policy (https://www.whitehouse.gov/ondcp/) and the various agencies of the Department of Justice (http://www.justice.gov/agencies).

CHAPTER
12

History Skills in Action: Designing Your Own History Project

✦

The Problem

By now ("at last," you might say), you have come to the end of *Discovering the American Past*. As you worked your way through the individual chapters, we are confident that you have learned a great deal about how historians work: how they choose the various subjects to investigate; how they form central questions that will guide their research; how they find, examine, and analyze their sources; and how they present their findings in cogent and readable prose.

Indeed, at this point not a few of you have shown interest in doing research and writing on an historical topic of your own. You may think that all the historical subjects already have been investigated, but actually there are countless topics that have not been researched and written, and some that have been in need of further examination and analysis. Years ago a college president asked the chair of a history department how many history books there were in the college library. "Mr. President," the historian replied, "*all* the books in our library are history

books." The president understood the point his department chair made.

So let us begin to flesh out the bones that you already have learned. First, however, we should offer a *definition* of history.

Many intelligent individuals use the following three words interchangeably, as if they are all the same thing, but in fact they are not:

1. **Past:** that which actually happened in a time before this time, something that is irretrievable, since no primary source can tell the entire story from every one of the historical actors' points of view.

2. **Memory:** that which is remembered about a time before this time, something that is flawed by changing and/or eroding memories and by the lack of memories by all the historical actors.

3. **History:** the attempt to ***find meaning*** about a time before this time. This is why historians' works are called ***interpretations*** (presentations,

opinions, and renditions such as "a feminist's interpretation of American society").

Now you can see why there are so many books on certain historical events. For example, a book written on the Boston Massacre of 1770 that was written in the 1840s or 1850s would be comparatively harsh to the British, whereas a book on the same subject written in 1917 or 1944, when Britain and the United States were allies, would be less critical of Great Britain. Therefore, as the *present* changes, so also does the *interpretation* of a historical person, event, or movement.

✦

Background: Choosing a Topic

Many people who want to write about the past often choose something near to them: a town, something that happened in that town, a person, a business, a family, and so on. We have read many good histories of local churches, of groups of veterans, of an exciting event (a bank robbery by Jesse James or Bonnie and Clyde), of a natural disaster (flood, hurricane, tornado, and so on), and so forth.

But going farther afield can be stimulating as well. Some students have investigated and written histories of their own major fields (the history of medicine, law, architecture, psychology, chemistry, nursing, journalism, engineering, agriculture, and so forth) or their colleges (most institutions have kept very good records). Military history is one of the most popular fields for professional historians and nonacademic historians alike, and the study of warfare has changed radically in the past decades.[1]

Another way to choose a topic is to be attracted to the sources themselves.

For example, for a person interested in statistics, a study such as Roger Ransom's and Richard Sutch's *One Kind of Freedom: The Economic Consequences of Emancipation* (Cambridge UK: Cambridge University Press, 2nd ed., 2001) examines and analyzes the lives of former slaves through statistics on incomes, educations, and so on. A statistical analysis of an election (to understand why a particular candidate won, or lost) would be very exciting.

Remember that *all things* created by humans (buildings, statues, paintings, gardens, monuments, and so on) have histories. For example, the monument honoring the Fifty-Fourth Massachusetts Infantry Regiment of the Civil War (depicted in the film "Glory") itself has a fascinating history, as does the Jefferson Memorial in Washington, the statue of a soldier on a courthouse lawn, or other things humans made. Music, poetry, art, literature, cartoons, films, television shows, and sports, *all have histories*. So a *type* of evidence might well attract you to a particular historical topic.

1. Jeremy Black, *War: A Short History* (London, UK: Continuum, 2009), pp. 2–11.

The Method: Formulating Your Questions

Your questions are extremely important for three reasons:

1. A central question or questions will clarify what you want to know about your topic. No book in your school's library will tell you *everything* about a topic. One of our former students, a nutrition major, wanted to know how well or poorly Americans ate during the Great Depression of the 1930s. Her interest helped her narrow, clarify, and define her research and writing about the Depression. Another student wanted to research and write about the desegregation of the U.S. Army following World War II. Once again, the student's central question had defined the topic.

2. A central question or questions will serve to guide you to important sources, and tell you what sources you *do not have to use* and, therefore, can avoid. This will set students on the right road.

3. A central question or questions will tell you almost immediately whether the topic you have chosen is either too broad (so you must narrow the topic and the question to make the project "doable"), OR too narrow, or is lacking in sources. It is very disappointing to spend time looking for sources that may not exist or may be lost—in a fire, flood, hurricane, or just over time. One premedical student wanted to research and write about medical practices in the time of the American War for Independence. Some sources do exist, but others are either nonexistent or too difficult to locate. Most people who own things that might be good sources simply *do not think about future historians when they decide whether to keep or discard potentially important sources.*

Faculty members look forward to talking with students or former students who are interested in history. These men and women can offer immeasurable help in choosing a topic, asking questions, and searching for sources. They may be former instructor or person whose general specialty is in your area of interest. They don't want to research and write *your* project, but they will be very helpful in *getting you started.* Remember that *only you* can know if a project is personally interesting. Independent research, unlike weekly readings or taking class notes, requires a high level of self-motivation. So be *genuinely interested* in the topic before you begin.

For example, some time ago a first-year student researched and wrote a paper on an epidemic in an American city in 1800 (the city was Baltimore, in 1800 the nation's third-largest city) The paper was good—very good, so good that the student was encouraged to do more research and undertake some rewriting. One year later, he submitted his revised paper to a historical journal, and it was accepted and published. When he interviewed for admission to graduate school (*not* in history), the faculty committee was impressed with the quality of his published undergraduate paper *and* his first-rate work ethic. After he was admitted, one of his professors told him that it was *that research paper* that earned him his place in the entering class. Research and writing are by no means easy, but the rewards (including seeing your name in print) will be significant.

The Evidence

Evidence can be divided into two categories: primary evidence and secondary evidence. Primary evidence is sources that are created during the period you are studying: newspapers, diaries, government documents, photographs and contemporary works of art, statistics, trial records, music, architecture, advertisements, speeches, laws, cartoons, and so forth. Secondary sources are those that have been created by historians who have examined the primary sources and then used them to write an account of something that happened in the past. Remember, therefore, that a secondary source is an *interpretation* of that period or event and *not* the period or event itself. A secondary source is an *historian's opinion*, not an objective recounting. See the earlier definition of history.

Secondary sources can be very helpful. If you can locate two or three secondary sources, you will have more than one opinion. At the end of your research, then *you* will be asked to state *your* opinion, or your interpretation. Some people like to find out two things about a secondary source they will read: (1) some biographical information about the author, to see if he or she has any biases, and (2) the date the book was written. *When* the book or article was written will give you some clues as to the *climate of opinion* that was prevalent when the author(s) were researching and writing. In spite of what some students think, history instructors do not live in the library and only do research and writing. Most have friends, families, hobbies, and favorite TV programs or music, and *are affected by the climate of opinion* in which they live and work.

Primary sources are more valuable, since no one has researched and written about the *meaning* of an event, trend, movement, and so on. But primary sources must be read or examined carefully. A newspaper written in 1776, for instance, will be slanted, as will every other primary source. So take care and examine a primary source with some skepticism. The more primary sources you find and examine will make your own work more objective than just using one source.

Because of the digital revolution, never before has conducting historical research been so accessible. Online resources like ancestry.com have made exploring individual family history much quicker and more rewarding. Digital history projects managed by the Library of Congress and National Archives allow Americans free and immediate access to some of the nation's most meaningful and rich historical records.[2] At their websites you can listen to early sound recordings, study photographs and artifacts, and read everything from personal letters to international treaties. Universities also fund digital humanities projects that make studying the past more democratically available than ever before. The Avalon Project of the Yale University Law School, for example, the Rotunda collections through the University of Virginia Press,

---

2. www.loc.gov and www.archives.gov.

and the National Historical Geographic Information System at the University of Minnesota are marvelous examples of digital humanities projects that inspire greater curiosity and understanding of American history.[3]

Digital projects are great, but don't forget the rich opportunities available through published primary sources in your library. Published primary sources are often annotated. That is, historians who have transcribed the primary sources for print also may have included footnotes identifying individuals and events, clarifying the meanings of words or ideas, and offering invaluable context to the primary source. This is especially useful for apprentice historians like you and your classmates. Immediate access on your computer to primary sources is not nearly so beneficial if you don't understand the larger context of those materials. Outstanding models of published primary sources include documentary editorial projects funded by major universities and the National Historical Publications and Records Commission (NHPRC). These projects include the papers of Thomas Jefferson, Frederick Douglass, Lucretia Mott, Harriet Jacobs, and Andrew Jackson and are of the highest scholarly standard. NHPRC publications represent an ideal place for beginning historians to research primary sources.[4]

Many students have come to rely on Internet sources, such as Google.com. These sources must be used with great care. When you select a book or a historical journal (like *The Journal of American History*, for example, or *The William and Mary Quarterly* for early America), those books or journals have been reviewed by experts who make suggestions, correct errors, and criticize unsupported statements. Most of the sources on the Internet have no such referees or reviewers. Some of the pieces are very slanted, poorly researched, and contain important omissions and errors. You may read these sources, but extremely carefully.

◆

Questions to Consider

Finally, as you seek out sources to answer your question, the evidence you discover may actually lead you to refine your central question or consider a new question. For example, you might start out wanting to learn more about the presidency of Thomas Jefferson and stumble across the letters President Jefferson wrote to his grandchildren. Or, you might be curious about protests against the Stamp Act and, in reading the press coverage of events, decide to explore newspaper publishing in colonial America. Be open to changes in ideas driven by evidence and your own curiosity.

3. The Avalon project at www.avalon.law.yale.edu contains a remarkable number and range of documents in law, history, and diplomacy. The American Founding Era collection at Rotunda (www.upress.virginia.edu/rotunda) offers access to the decades-long magisterial documentary edition projects of leading members of the founding generation, as well as new "born digital" projects. Through the Minnesota NHGIS website (www.nhgis.org) users can access, explore, and create their own research using U.S. census materials.
4. For NHPRC-funded projects, visit http://www.archives.gov/nhprc/.

Citations

Most historical works contain footnotes or endnotes, to inform readers as to what sources were used, where quotations came from, the author(s) of a statement, and so forth. Some historians add things in citations that assist readers with a statement, a historical character, or event. These are called "content footnotes," and, as you can see, we used them to help our readers or add interesting information.

Writing and Citing

There are many guidebooks for developing clear historical writing as well as reference books for the mechanics of historical research: how to take notes, organize citations, and structure arguments. Your professor or history department may also provide you with style manuals, such as *The Chicago Manual of Style*, which explain how to cite primary and secondary sources. But the starting point for historical research and writing begins with a question you want to answer, a topic you want to explore. This chapter builds on the historical detective skills you've developed so far using *Discovering the American Past* to help you imagine your own research project.

◆

Epilogue

History is a discipline that can remain a lifelong passion and pursuit even if your vocation turns out to be in business, for example, or a medical field or the arts. You likely know people in your family or community who read history for pleasure or research history as a hobby. History enthusiasts also volunteer at historical sites, join reenactor groups, build their own artifact collections, and write stories and books based on their personal explorations of the past. Even if you don't spark to history at quite that level, you will surely find the skills of historical research invaluable to your intellectual and career pursuits. Weighing all relevant sources, critically evaluating evidence, and developing thoughtful interpretations of complex issues are life skills that you learn through history class. We sincerely hope that we have been some help.

As this book went to press, we came across a new book that can be used as an example of many of the points in this chapter. The book is Cynthia Barnett's *Rain: A Natural and Cultural History* (New York: Crown Publishers, 2015), a bold and exciting volume about a nearly everyday event that has been important in shaping human societies, religion, language, economics, the environment, and so forth. The volume has a very clearly stated central question, has used a wide variety of primary sources, and has offered new interpretations (meanings) of past events. In many ways, this book is a model of how history can be researched and written.

WBW
LG